TRANSACTIONS
of the
American Philosophical Society
Held at Philadelphia for Promoting Useful Knowledge

VOLUME 78, Part 6

The Right of Spoil of the Popes of Avignon 1316–1415

DANIEL WILLIMAN

Department of Classical and Near Eastern Studies
State University of New York, Binghamton

THE AMERICAN PHILOSOPHICAL SOCIETY
Independence Square, Philadelphia
1988

Copyright © 1988 by The American Philosophical Society

Library of Congress Catalog
Card Number 87-72870
International Standard Book Number 0–87169–786–6
US ISSN 0065–9746

CONTENTS

Preface v

Abbreviated Citations vi

I. The Papal Right of Spoil, 1316-1417
   1. Introductory Definitions...1
   2. The Law of Succession to Clerics' Property 3
   3. The Pope as Protector of Clerical Property
       and the Testamentary License...9
   4. *Jus spolii* and *plenitudo potestatis*..13
   5. The Administration and Documentation of Spoils 19
   6. The Extent and Incidence of the Right of Spoil 23
   7. Curbing the Right of Spoil..29

Appendix A: A Typical Testamentary License, 1327 38
Appendix B: A Typical Commission for Spoils, 1346 39
Appendix C: A *consilium* for Spoils (1368?) 40
Appendix D: Negotiations between the French Royal Council
       and the Camera Apostolica, after 1385 43

II. Repertory of Cases of the Papal Right of Spoil 46

Bibliography 251

Indices
Index to the Introduction...254
Annual Index of Spoils Cases...256
Index of Territorial Incidence 260
Indices by Groups...268

PREFACE

Earlier versions of the study of papal spoils which introduces this volume appeared in unpublished dissertations for the Licentiate in Mediaeval Studies in the Pontifical Institute of Mediaeval Studies (1969) and for the Ph.D. in the University of Toronto (1973). The present version was largely finished at the Institute for Advanced Study, Princeton, during spring term 1985, supported by a grant in aid from the American Philosophical Society. The original records of the individual spoils processes, preserved in the Vatican Archives, were indexed in my *Records of the Papal Right of Spoil, 1316–1412* (Institut de recherche et d'histoire des textes: Bibliographies-colloques-travaux préparatoires; Paris: CNRS, 1974). A revised and expanded edition of that repertory, outfitted with fuller and more accurate indices, completes this volume.

Among the reviewers of *Records* when it first appeared, the one who offered the most valuable suggestions for its improvement was the late dean of French medieval historians, Charles Samaran, writing in the *Journal des Savants* (1976) and looking back three quarters of a century to his own first major contribution on the subject. This study is dedicated to his memory.

ABBREVIATED CITATIONS

Series of the Archivio Segreto Vaticano:
  Arm. = Armadio
  Coll. = Collectoriae
  DC = Diversa cameralia
  IE = Introitus et Exitus
  IM = Instrumenta miscellanea
  OS = Obligationes et Solutiones
  RA = Registra Avinionensia
  RV = Registra Vaticana

Publications:
  AFH = *Archivum franciscanum historicum*
  DDC = *Dictionnaire de droit canonique*
  EFR = Bibliothèques des Ecoles Françaises d'Athènes et de Rome, troisième série: *Registres et lettres des Papes du XIVe siècle* :

EFR J1 = *Jean XXII. Lettres communes ...*, ed. G. Mollat
EFR J2 = *Lettres secrètes et curiales du pape Jean XXII relatives à la France*, ed. A. Coulon and S. Clémencet

EFR B1 = *Benoît XII. Lettres communes ...*, ed. J.-M. Vidal
EFR B2 = *Lettres closes, patentes et curiales se rapportant à la France*, ed. G. Daumet
EFR B3 = *Lettres closes et patentes intéressant les pays autres que la France*, ed. J.-M. Vidal and G. Mollat

EFR C1 = *Clément VI. Lettres closes, patentes et curiales se rapportant à la France*, ed. E. Déprez, J. Glénisson and G. Mollat
EFR C2 = *Lettres closes, patentes et curiales intéressant les pays autres que la France*, ed. E. Déprez and G. Mollat

EFR I1 = *Innocent VI. Lettres secrètes et curiales*, ed. P. Gasnault and M.-H. Laurent

EFR U1 = *Les registres d'Urbain V ...*, ed. M. Dubrulle
EFR U2 = *Lettres secrètes et curiales se rapportant à la France*, ed. P. Lacacheux and G. Mollat
EFR U3 = *Lettres communes ...*, ed. M.-H. Laurent, P. Gasnault, M. Hayez et al.

EFR G1 = *Grégoire XI. Lettres secrètes et curiales relatives à la France*, ed. L. Mirot, H. Jassemin, J. Vieillard et al.

EFR G2 = *Lettres secrètes et curiales intéressant les pays autres que la France*, ed. G. Mollat

Gall. Christ. = *Gallia Christiana* ... (vols. 1-13 in 2d ed., 1870-1874; vols. 14-16 in 1st ed., 1856-1865)
RHE = *Revue d'histoire ecclésiastique*
VQ = *Vatikanische Quellen zur Geschichte der päpstliche Hof- und Finanzverwaltung (1316-1378)* ... (Paderborn)
VQ 1 = Emil Göller, *Die Einnahmen der apostolischen Kammer unter Johann XXII* (1910)
VQ 4 = Emil Göller, *Die Einnahmen ... unter Benedikt XII* (1920)
VQ 5 = Ludwig Mohler, *Die Einnahmen ... unter Klemens VI* (1931)
VQ 6 = K. H. Schäfer, *Die Ausgaben ... unter den Päpsten Urban V. und Gregor XI* (1937)
VQ 7 = Hermann Hoberg, *Die Einnahmen ... unter Innocenz VI* (1953)

Legal citations:
X = *Decretales Gregorii IX*
VI = *Liber Sextus Bonifatii VIII*
C. q. c. = Causa, questio and canon of the *Decretum*
D. c. = Distinctio and canon of the *Decretum*
D = *Digestum*
C = *Codex*

References to manuscript records and to some early printed books use the superscripts *r* for the recto and *v* for the verso of a folio, *a* and *b* for columns.

In transcriptions from manuscript, the diagonals \ / enclose text that was added to the original writing marginally or between the lines. [--] indicates text that was stroked out of the original writing, but is still legible.

Two dates joined by a dash, as "1354-1362," represent the ends of a duration, e.g. one bishop's time in office. If one of the dates is unknown, it is simply left out. Two dates joined by x, as "1360 x 1363" are points between which, at some unknown time, some event took place.

Monetary Reckoning:

For a complete understanding of the moneys, accountry, and exchange techniques mentioned in these records, see Peter Spufford, Wendy Wilkinson and Sarah Tolley, *Handbook of Medieval Exchange* (London, 1986). Moneys of account appear in the records without commas. Libri, solidi, denarii are shown on the model £120.18.10; florins, solidi, denarii have the form 150 fl. 7 s. 10 d.; uncie, tari, grani appear as 20 unc. 25 tari 15 grani. When real coins are being counted, the coins are listed, the different currencies separated by commas. The following moneys of account and coinages appear:
   agnus = mouton, gold coin of France
   Alamannia, fl. = Rheingulden (Spufford, 240)

Avin. = silver of Avignon (Spufford, 122)
Barc. = silver of Barcelona (Spufford, 139)
Cam., fl. = Cameral florin (Spufford, 123)
car. = carlino of Naples, silver coin valued at 1/2 tari (Spufford, 62)
cathedra = chaise, q.v.
chaise = chaise à l'écu, gold coin of France (Spufford, 189)
coron. = silver royal coronat, a penny of Marseille (Spufford, 117)
curr. = current or Cameral florins valued at 24 s. Avin. (Spufford, 125)
cygnus = a type of franc
ducat = gold of Venice (Spufford, 81)
dupla = gold of France, about twice the value of a florin
écu = chaise à l'écu (Spufford, 189)
Fl., fl. = florin of Florence (Spufford, 1)
Fr., fl. = florin of France (Spufford, 172)
fr. = franc (Spufford, 191)
Gen. = silver of Genoa (Spufford, 106)
georgius = a gold coin, worth more than a florin
gr. = grossi or gros
lb. = one pound Troyes weight of gold or silver
leopardus = a short-lived gold coin of Bordeaux, worth about 1.1 florin
m. = mark, as a count of silver pennies or as a weight, ca. 225 grams, of bullion or worked silver
maravedi = account money of Castile, 10 d. (Spufford, 157)
massa = bullion
muton = agnus or mouton, gold coin of France
noble = English double florin (Spufford, 198)
pabalhi = denarii auri ad papilionem
Paris. = silver of Paris (Spufford, 167), or a gold double florin
parv. = parva moneta (i.e., not grossi)
Pied. = (florins) of Piedmont (Spufford, 131)
Port. = silver of Portugal (Spufford, 162)
Prov. = denarii refortiati of Provence (Spufford, 117)
real = base silver penny of Mallorca (Spufford, 162)
regalis = silver royal coronat of Marseille (Spufford, 117)
s. = solidus, sou, count of 12 d.
sent. = (floreni) sententie, count of 24 s. Avin. (Spufford, 125)
tari = tari of Naples, count of 20 grani of gold or 2 silver carlini
Tur. = tournois, silver of Tours (Spufford, 172)
unc. = uncia of Naples, count of 60 carlini (Spufford, 62); or an ounce Troyes weight of gold or silver

I. The Papal Right of Spoil, 1316 – 1417

1. Introductory Definitions

The popes of Avignon, beginning with the election of John XXII in 1316 and ending with the deposition of Benedict XIII by the Council of Constance in 1415, laid claim to the movable property of some twelve hundred ecclesiastical persons, exercising a power that has subsequently been named *jus spolii*, the "right of spoil." The term *jus spolii* to designate the right of the pope to collect the goods of deceased clerics for his own use seems to appear for the first time at the end of the fifteenth century, although such goods themselves were frequently called *spolia* in the fourteenth-century records.[1]

The concrete ancient meaning of the Latin *spolium* is "the skin, hide, fleece, etc. (of an animal, as stripped off from the body)."[2] Its transferred meanings, usually in the plural, are "plundered armor," "plunder," "portable belongings, especially clothing." The corresponding verb *spoliare* means "to strip," (commonly used reflexively, like the Italian *spogliarsi* and the French *se dépouiller*) or "to rob or plunder." The meaning of plunder or robbery is the one picked out by the Roman civil law's *actio spolii*, a process to recover damages; and this is the meaning usually found in the English derivatives "to despoil" and "spoils." In the usage *jus spolii / droit de dépouille / Spolienrecht*, the *spolia* are the movable goods (and the papal records refer many times to *spolia siue bona mobilia*) of which a person has been divested by death; and it is interesting to recall that the French *dépouille mortelle* means, like the English "mortal remains," a corpse. The *jus spolii*, then, is a right, title, or claim to succeed in possession of the movable goods of a deceased person. Now, the Middle Ages knew several kinds of customary rights, besides the right of the natural heir to inherit, which could have been called *jura spolii*, although as far as I know they were not so designated. After the execution of a capital sentence, for example, the felon's goods became the property of the court; in the English *heriot* a dead man's weapons reverted to the lord who had granted them, and later the name was applied to a customary burden on servile, not military, tenements: the landlord would claim by this title a deceased tenant's best animal.

The possessions of clerics in particular were subject at various times to

---

[1] F. de Saint-Palais d'Aussac, *Le droit de dépouille (jus spolii)* (Strasbourg-Paris, 1930), 19.
[2] *Oxford Latin Dictionary* (1982).

a number of claims which could reasonably be called "rights of spoil."[3] After the Gregorian Reform the principle was securely planted in the law that an ecclesiastical person could have no legitimate heir of his body, only an heir instituted by testament; and because it was further presumed that clerics derived their wealth from their ecclesiastical benefices, they had only vague and tenuous rights to devise goods by testament. Consequently, the death of a wealthy prelate could easily become the occasion of a legal clash. The churchman's possession lapsed with his death, and many claimants might be in rivalry to take it up, none of them with a right so clear and strong that the others could not contest it: a designated heir, such as a nephew; the widowed church or orphaned monastery, in the corporate person of its chapter or conventual community; the successor to the title, once he was elected or provided; a secular or ecclesiastical patron, who might by custom claim the fruits of the vacant office, and could argue that the spoils of the last incumbent were precisely the first fruits of the vacancy; finally, the executor of the testament, if there was one, acting for its beneficiaries. It was in the context of such a confusion of legal and customary rights of succession that the popes of Avignon began to exercise a power of reservation over the goods left behind by certain clerics and prelates, and this power has been denominated the *jus spolii*.

But what was the nature of the papal right of spoil, and what was its foundation? Was it customary, did it rest on a papal decretal or a conciliar constitution, or did it lie implicit in the canonical tradition until the Camera Apostolica, the financial office of the papal government, gave it administrative expression?

---

[3]For a survey of earlier rights of spoil over clerics' goods, see Saint-Palais d'Aussac, *Le droit de dépouille*; Fritz Prochnow, *Das Spolienrecht und die Testierfähigkeit der Geistlichen im Abendland bis zum 13. Jahrhundert* (Historische Studien 136; Berlin, 1919, repr. Vaduz, 1965); Louis Thomassin, *Ancienne et nouvelle discipline de l'Eglise* (2d ed. revised by M. André; 7 vols.; Bar-le-Duc, 1864-1867) 7:179-182; and Guillaume Mollat, "Dépouille," *Dictionnaire de droit canonique* 4:1160-1165. Robert Caillemer, *Confiscations et administration des successions par les pouvoirs publiques au moyen âge* (Lyon, 1901) sets the *jus spolii* aside as a quite distinct category, and refrains from exploring it.

2. The Law of Succession to Clerics' Property

The Judeo-Christian and the Roman conceptions of dedicated property, or *sacra*, were sufficiently harmonious to blend together in an imperial law against the alienation of church property. Theodosian Code 5.3.1, repeated in the Code of Justinian 1.3.20,[1] further set up the right of a church or of a monastery to succeed to the personal property of a priest, deacon, deaconess, subdeacon, or hermit who died intestate and without relatives capable of inheriting. A rather severe rule for the deathbed dispositions of bishops and other administrators of ecclesiastical corporations, the foundation of medieval law on the subject, is *Novellae* 131.13:[2]

> We forbid bishops to transfer any goods, movable or immovable or self-moving, which may come to them in any way after consecration, to their own relatives or to any other persons. But they have license to spend from such goods for the redemption of captives, feeding the hungry, or other pious causes. 1. Whatever of such goods remains in their possession after death, we order it to go into the property of the churches where they held their priestly offices. We give them license to alienate, or to leave to whomever they please, only in respect of those things which they are proven to have held before consecration; but after consecration, those things which came to them from their families. And in case of intestacy, those may inherit who are within the fourth degree. 2. But all that we have said regarding the goods which come to the holy bishops after consecration we also intend to apply to the reverend orphaners, almoners, nurses of the sick and of the aged, guest-masters and other rectors of venerable houses, in regard to those things which come to them in the aforesaid way during the period of their administration. 3. But if any bishop or cleric or minister of whatever ecclesiastical rank, or deaconess of the church should die without a testament or legitimate successor, the succession belongs to the church in which they were established.

The law of the middle ages on the subject never departed far from these well-considered provisions.

The *Decretum* of Gratian marshals an array of laws against the alienation of church property by its administrators in Causa 12, questions 1 and 2, although the right of a bishop to pass his own goods to heirs is mentioned in C.12 q.1 c.19. Question 5 takes up the problem of the succession *post mortem* to bishops' goods. The first three canons of question 5, all excerpted from letters of Gregory the Great, declare that bishops may alienate freely anything which they had possessed before

---
[1] Ed. Krueger 2:20 b.
[2] Ed. Schoell-Kroll, 661–662.

consecration, but that a bishop's testament should be prevented from diminishing the wealth of his church in any way. A canon from a Council of Paris in 829 (C.12 q.5 c.4) allows a bishop the free disposition of his own goods, even if these came to him, by inheritance, after his consecration. Canon 7, fathered upon a fictitious "Council of Tribur," is a summary of the *Novellae* rule above, stating that the church succeeds a bishop *ab intestato*; the ordinary gloss later commented at this point that a bishop's church is his closest heir.

The decretal collections of the early thirteenth century dealt with this matter in the titles *De peculio clericorum* and *De testamentis et ultimis voluntatibus*. The *Summa decretalium* of Bernard of Pavia tried to settle the question by defining and distinguishing different types of *peculium*, disposable property, without treating bishops differently from other clerics:[3]

What is called *peculium* here is what is possessed by any cleric as his own. Usually, however, the term is used with regard to sons or slaves: it means what a father allows to a son or a master to his slave.... There are two types of *peculium* of clerics, one coming from the church, which can be called *profectitium*, the other coming from any other source, which can be called *adventitium*, for instance what comes to a cleric from his own craft, or from any acquisition intended for his own person.[4] All clerics are allowed to have *peculium* who, like secular canons, have not renounced ownership; but not canons regular, monks and nuns. ... Let us see now what power clerics have over their *peculium*. They can certainly have and hold their *profectitium peculium* while they are living in the church, and they can make moderate donations from it; but when they move out of the church or die, they ought to leave it to that church, as below in the canon *Cum in officiis*. That the fruits of a church are to be held in common by its clerics does not prevent individual *peculium*, because this rule applies only before each one's portion is assigned to him. But a cleric has power over his *peculium adventitium*, even the power of conferring it *inter vivos* or *causa mortis*, upon anyone he pleases, even King Arthur.

The canon *Cum in officiis*, mentioned by Bernard of Pavia in the passage just quoted, was a constitution of the Third Lateran Council (1179), published in the *Compilatio prima* and then as 3.26.7 in the *Decretales* of Gregory IX (1234).[5] It simply confirmed the traditional law against alienation of church goods by clerics' testaments:[6]

In the duty of charity we are under obligation first of all to those from whom we are conscious of having received a favor. Some clerics, however, when they have received a great deal of property from their churches, presume to transfer

---

[3]Ed. T. Laspeyres (Ratisbon, 1860), 92-94.
[4]Guillelmus Durandus, *Speculum juris* 4.3 "De peculio clericorum" (ed. Venice, 1576, 2:375-376) cites Roffredus of Benevento for a third category from the Civil Law, a *peculium quasi castrense*, "which comes from a public sort of work, such as defending clients in ecclesiastical cases, especially in the Roman Curia, according to him [Roffredus]."
[5]Ed. Friedberg, 2:540.
[6]Translation by H. J. Schroeder, *Disciplinary Decrees of the General Councils: Text, Translation, and Commentary* (St. Louis, 1937), 226-227.

property thus acquired to other uses. As this is prohibited by the ancient canons, we also prohibit it. With a desire, therefore, to protect the churches against loss, we command that such goods remain in the possession of the churches, whether their incumbents died intestate or expressed a wish that these goods be transferred to others.

The foremost canonist of the fourteenth century, Giovanni d'Andrea, performed a thorough review of the law relating to the property of clerics and attached it as a gloss to the word *remanere* toward the end of the passage just quoted.[7] His *Novella commentaria*, published in 1338, can be taken as an authoritative statement of the applicable law in the Avignon period: the Camera made use of this particular gloss to justify certain testamentary provisions in a spoils case of 1375 (Repertory, n. 582). Here is the gloss in my translation. The legal citations are given in the customary modern form, with the texts cited, in the footnotes.

No one, prelate, cleric, nor layman, can bequeath the goods, even the movables, of the church, as it says here and in the following canon, although they can, even from the deathbed, allot some things, for the sake of alms[8] and in repayment for services rendered to them by their relatives as well as by others.[9]

The same prohibition applies to the goods which they have purchased from their ecclesiastical incomes,[10] unless the recipients should give to the church as much in compensation as they receive,[11] or unless, as some say, the practice obtains by custom.[12] But if a cleric has goods of his own, he can bequeath them.[13]

---

[7]Joannes Andreae, *Novella commentaria in Decretales* (ed. Venice, 1581; reprint Turin, 1963), 3:107vb-108ra.

[8]X 3.26.8, a letter of Alexander III: "Viventes tamen et sui compotes moderate valent aliqua de bonis ipsis non ratione testamenti, sed eleemosynae intuitu in aegritudine etiam constituti."

[9]X 3.26.12, also of Alexander III: "Consuetudinis tamen est non improbandae, ut de his pauperibus, et religiosis locis, et illis, qui uiuenti seruierant, siue consanguinei sint siue alii, aliqua juxta seruitii meritum conferantur."

[10]C.12 q.2 c.34, from the Council of Agde (an. 506); C.12 q.3 c.1, from the Third Council of Cartagena (an. 397); C.12 q.5 c.4, from the Council of Paris (an. 829): "Postquam autem episcopus factus est, quascumque res de facultatibus ecclesiae ... conparauerit, decreuimus, ut non in propinquiorum suorum, sed ecclesiae, cui preest, iura deueniant." X 3.25.4: "Inquirendum est, si quis presbyterorum de reditibus ecclesiae, uel oblationibus, uel uotis fidelium alieno nomine res comparauit."

[11]C.12 q.5 c.5, from the Council of Agde (an. 506): "nisi tantum de propriis iuris facultate suppleuerit"; and C.12 q.2 c.56, from the same council: "Si quis qualibet conditione de rebus ecclesiae aliquid alienare presumpserit, si de suo proprio tantum ecclesiae contulerit, quantum uisus est abstulisse, tunc demum istud stare licebit."

[12]E.g. Huguccio of Pisa, *Summa super decretis*, on C.12 q.5 c.5. The force of custom is approved by X 3.24.3: "Illius terrae consuetudo, quae tamen sacris canonibus manifeste non obiet, est diligentius attendanda"; and X 3.26.12, the reference to *consuetudo* quoted above, note 9.

[13]C.12 q.5 c.1 and c.2, from Gregory I; the texts assure the validity of bishops' testaments if the goods bequeathed were their own property. The Gregorian rule is that goods acquired before consecration are the bishop's property; after, the church's. C.12 q.1 c.20 and c.21 also distinguish the two kinds of property, without giving any guidelines for separating them in practice. Also *Novellae* 123, 19: "Presbyteros autem et diaconos et subdiaconos et lectores et cantores, quos omnes clericos appellamus, res quolibet modo ad eorum dominium uenientes habere sub sua potestate praecipimus ad similitudinem castrense peculiorum, et donare secundum leges et in his testare, licet sub parentum sint

But in case of intestacy, those things go to the instituted heirs which the cleric had before he became a cleric, or even those things which came to him afterward from gifts, hereditary succession, a craft, or teaching.[14]

Regarding the goods which he acquired after becoming a cleric, it is to be presumed *prima facie* that he acquired them as gifts to the church or from church income.[15] This is the presumption in the case of any cleric, but it is most strongly to be presumed in the case of prelates;[16] I should say that such is the status of this presumption that the sentence must be in favor of the church unless the opposite is proven or there is a contrary presumption.[17] But some say, perhaps not wrongly, that in the case of non-prelates an acquisition is assumed to be intended for the person, not for the church, when he has no office by which to acquire it in the name of the church; and so he seems to have acquired in his own name if he has goods from other sources than the church, and hence his legitimate heir will licitly take those things after his death.[18]

But since in these matters it would be difficult, almost impossible, to prove by witnesses or documents just what or how much he purchased from the income of the church and how much from his own property, on that account a judge proceeds in this matter largely on the basis of presumptions; and since it sometimes happens that one presumption confuses another,[19] the judge will be arbiter of how much is the cleric's patrimony and just what things are from church income, and likewise whether anything is profit from a craft or teaching, and so on.[20]

But in making his computation, the judge should always first deduct the cleric's expenditures for food and clothing from the church's account, for he who serves

---

potestate, sic tamen ut horum filii aut his non extantibus parentes eorum legitimam partem ferant."

[14]X 3.26.9 and 12, both from Alexander III; c.9: "Clerici de his, quae paternae successionis uel cognationis intuitu aut de artificio suo sunt adepti, seu dono consanguineorum aut amicorum suorum, non habitu respectu ad ecclesiam, peruenerunt ad ipsos, libere disponere ualeant." And c.12: "Ceterum, quae ex hereditate, uel artificio aut doctrina proueniunt, distribuantur pro arbitrio decedentis."

[15]X 3.26.1, from Gregory I: "quicquid ipsum [episcopum defunctum] habuisse patuerit, a qualibet persona detineri nullatenus patiaris, nisi hoc solum, quod eum ante episcopatus ordinem proprium habuisse constiterit." C.12 q.3 c.1, from the Third Council of Cartagena: a bishop who had nothing at the time of his consecration must have acquired everything afterward.

[16]C.12 q.3 c.2 and q.4 c.1, both from the Ninth Council of Toledo, and c.3, from the Council of Agde: the private nature of a prelate's purchases must be proven by contemporary documents.

[17]*Novellae* 131.13.

[18]X 3.26.15, from Innocent III: "Illud autem est generaliter obseruandum circa eam, qui potest proprium possidere, praelationem uel administrationes ecclesiae non habentem, quod si ei aliquid specialiter relinquatur, non solum a propinquo, uerum etiam ab extraneo, intelligitur esse relictum non intuitu ecclesiae, sed personae, nisi probatio in contrarium appareret."

[19]X 2.23.10: "Efficacior probatio requiritur ab eo, qui probare uult illud, quod non est uerisimile." Ibid., c.11: "Per cohabitationem diutinam et famam de matrimonio et contractibus matrimonialibus ac alia adminicula probantur matrimonia." Ibid., c.14: "Propter praesumptionem etiam uehementem non debet quis de graui crimine condempnari."

[20]Citations as for note 16 above.

the altar ought to live by the altar.[21] Likewise, since a prelate ought to segregate his goods from those of the church,[22] and ought to do everything always with the counsel of his clergy,[23] there is a strong presumption against him if he does not, and often through his own fault his oath to the church can be held against him,[24] especially where an extensive and obvious fault of the prelate is discovered.[25] Likewise the judge should first deduct all vain and indulgent expenses from the cleric's goods; he will approve only those expenses out of the church's wealth which were made toward its own support and that of the poor, for the redemption of captives, and for hospitality or other pious causes.[26]

We do not believe that either party, the church or the heir, is in a better position for proof, in this case, by being in possession, as if the burden of proof thus fell upon the other; for the presumption is always in favor of the church, unless the heir of the deceased cleric shall have proven that the deceased owned a particular thing before he became a cleric, or that it came to him for his private use.[27] The judge arrives at proof "by truth or by presumption,"[28] and in this case he acts according to what is said of a wife: what she acquires during the marriage she is presumed to have acquired from the goods of her husband.[29] The similarity, however, is not always complete; what a wife acquires by her own work, her husband acquires, but a cleric, even a prelate, acquires for himself, not for the church.[30]

But if a cleric has many churches, his goods are to be divided among those churches by an equitable distribution.[31] And if a cleric has no heir within the seventh degree, his church succeeds.[32]

The question has been asked, "Who succeeds to the goods of one who dies

---

[21]C.12 q.1 c.22: "Lex enim Dei precepit, ut qui altario deseruiunt pascantur ex ipso"; cf. I Cor. 9; C.12 q.1 c.23 quotes I Tim. 6.8 on restricting expenses to food and clothing. C.12 q.2 c.45, a letter of Gregory I: those who make the inventory after the death of a bishop are not to be paid out of the goods of the church. For contrary arguments, see C.1 q.2 c.7, from *De contemplativa vita* of Julianus Pomerius: the church should not support those who can support themselves. And X 3.5.4, of Alexander III in the Third Lateran Council (1179): a bishop must support anyone whom he ordains without a title until he shall acquire one, unless he can support himself from his patrimony.

[22]C.12 q.1 c.21, cited above, n. 13.

[23]C.12 q.1 c.23.

[24]C.2 q.1 c.7, from Gregory I.

[25]X 1.40.7; *Codex* 2.58.1 and 2: rules of evidence.

[26]C.12 q.2 c.70, from Ambrose, *De officiis*; and ibid., c.71, a letter of Jerome giving these as justifiable alienations of *res sacrae*. D.44 c.1, a letter of Augustine against immoderate feasts in honor of the martyrs; X 1.10.2, that monks and canons should not use the fruits of the benefices of which they have the presentation to the detriment of the pious works for which such benefices are liable.

[27]*Novellae* 131.13.

[28]X 3.26.15: rules for the presumptions in the case of a legacy which was disputed between a bishop and the clergy of his church.

[29]*Codex* 5.16.6; *Digest* 24.1.51.

[30]X 3.26.9 and 12, quoted above, n. 18.

[31]X 3.26.12: "Quia uero nonnulli in diuersis ecclesiis beneficia possidunt, ita distinguimus, ut diuidantur quae habuerant per aestimationem congruam inter ipsos."

[32]C.12 q.5 c.6 and c.7, both from the Council of Tarragona (an. 516); and *Novellae* 131.13; but the former texts do not directly address this question, and the latter does not specify the permissible degree of kindred for an heir.

intestate?" I answer in accordance with what has already been said, that in the goods of the church, he has no heir but his successor, and so the church will take possession of them. The heir will take possession of other things which certainly belonged to the testator. And the church will take possession of the things that are doubtful, because the presumption is in favor of the church.

3. The Pope as Protector of Clerical Property and the Testamentary License

The general tendency of canon law in the classical period, as we find it expounded by Giovanni d'Andrea, was to protect the orderly succession, by the church and by the heirs, each according to their rights, to the various goods left by beneficed clerics when they died. The law recognized no other normal right of succession. To reinforce the earlier law in its defense of those rights against unjust usurpations, Boniface VIII and Clement V issued decretals against spoliation, *Praesenti* and *Frequens* respectively. Another aid to the law of orderly succession to goods was the papal privilege embodied in the testamentary license.

The decretal *Praesenti* (1298) of Boniface VIII[1] was concerned with spoliations that so impoverished a benefice that it could not support its pastoral function. This decretal is of paramount importance among the legal circumstances of later papal spoliations; it notes and condemns (in lesser patrons) the extension of a right of presentation to a benefice into a presumptive right of spoil on the goods of its deceased incumbent. When John XXII first began reserving to himself the spoils of his own beneficiaries, he evidently had *Praesenti* in mind, although his bulls of reservation did not mention it by name. When Innocent VI found it necessary to moderate the activity of his collectors of spoils, he did so with rules suggested by *Praesenti*. And when the Council of Constance in 1417 forbade the popes to collect spoils, *Praesenti* was the authority explicitly cited. Here is the text in translation.

By the present edict we forbid bishops and their superiors,[2] abbots, and all other prelates regular and secular and all ecclesiastical persons to dare to reserve,[3]

---

[1] *VI* 1.16.9, ed. Friedberg (1879) 2:989; my translation follows.

[2] The ordinary gloss by Giovanni d'Andrea (1301) specified arch-bishops and patriarchs.

[3] Gl. ord.: "Et nota quod dicit reseruari, per hoc enim uidetur quod de illis non possunt decedentes testari. ... Et distinguebat ... inter clericum habentem administrationem et non habentem, nam clericus habens administrationem, quandiu uiuit et sanus est, dare potest, moderate tamen; ... comparatur enim usufructuario, quia eius morte finitur, sicut usufructuarii. ... Potest ergo dum uiuit uoluntatem suam facere, dummodo moderate donet. Cum incipit infirmari, comparatur usuario, et ita nihil habet nisi usum tantum; eleemosynam tamen facere potest. Si uero sit clericus non habens administrationem, sed personaliter et simpliciter beneficiatus, et in morte comparatur usufructuario quantum ad faciendum fructus suos, et de ipsis potest testari; ecclesia tamen succedit ei in istis si decedat ab intestato ... et consuetudo generalis quasi ubique eam [distinctionem] approbat." The distinction, between administrators who cannot make gifts from their ecclesiastical incomes by testament or *in articulo mortis* and simple clerics who may do so, anticipates the glossator's own *Novellae*.

occupy, or convert to their own uses in any way the goods of deceased rectors or ministers, which are found in their deaneries, parsonages, priories, or churches, when these are vacant, or which are collected during the vacancy, even though such deaneries [etc.] may be subject to them or belong to their collation, ordination, presentation, or custody. Such goods ought to be spent in ways useful to the churches, or faithfully preserved for the successors, unless it is determined that this right belongs to them by special privilege or by custom already legitimately prescribed, or for another reasonable cause.[4] ... Furthermore, where anyone asserts that these goods belong to them by privilege or custom or other reasonable cause, only this part of the goods may be understood: the things which are found to remain after the debts, if any, are paid and those things duly set aside which will be necessary to support the servants and ministers and other burdens until the next payment of dues.

Clement V in the Council of Vienne (1311) used the constitution *Frequens*[5] to list and make provisions against thirty *gravamina* of which various religious interests had complained. Like *Praesenti*, this decretal is directed at "bishops and their superiors," and is concerned with the wasting of beneficial properties during vacancies. The twenty-second and twenty-third *gravamina* are of particular interest here; they are also strikingly similar to the protests against papal collections of spoils late in the fourteenth century:

Sometimes also, under pretext of privilege which they claim to possess for a certain time, they collect from vacant benefices the revenues of the first year, and thus unjustly deprive abbots, priors and others of revenues belonging to them. Not content with this, they unlawfully seize the horses, cattle, treasure and other properties of monasteries and vacant benefices, all of which should be reserved to their successors.[6]

The law embodied in *Praesenti* and *Frequens* continued valid in the fourteenth century, though not as a restriction on the pope's collections. Following a petition by the Dominican proctor general in 1369, the camerarius ordered the Hospitalers of Rhodes to surrender the spoils of the late Catalan Dominican Joannes Bernardi, which they had illegally collected.[7]

The general canon law left the distribution of a deceased cleric's spoils still problematic. In order to apply the rules for *peculium*, it was necessary to determine whether the particular goods at issue had come from the income of church property or from elsewhere; but in the nature of the case, this question only arose when the best witness of fact, the owner, was dead. Giovanni d'Andrea in his *Novella commentaria* was compelled, as we have seen, to balance the presumptions which a judge would have to use in lieu of good testimony or documents. One way to

---

[4] "Alia causa rationabili" was the justification for spoils later adduced in the papal commissions: below, chapter 4.
[5] Promulgated by John XXII in 1317: *Clem.* 5.6, ed. Friedberg, 2:1185-1186.
[6] Translation by Schroeder, *Disciplinary Decrees*, 432.
[7] Coll. 353, 160^v-161^v, not citing either canon explicitly.

prevent the problem from arising *post mortem* was to allow the cleric to make a testament of his goods under a special papal privilege, laying on his own conscience the duty of dividing his ecclesiastical from his patrimonial and other "peculiar" wealth. In this way, the cleric's personal knowledge of the facts and his own equitable skill would be combined with the authority of the Apostolic See to defend his dispositions after his death, and it could be hoped that the legitimate interests would be served without litigation. This privilege, the *licentia testandi* or *facultas testandi*, was used with increasing frequency beginning with the pontificate of Innocent III, if not earlier.[8]

The flow of testamentary licenses, moderate through the thirteenth century, became a flood in the pontificate of John XXII (1316-1334). There are about 320 licenses in the papal registers that have been published in the calendars of Potthast, the Ecole Française de Rome, and the Benedictines of Montecassino for the century between 1209 and 1314; John XXII, in the eighteen years of his pontificate, issued at least 400.

The Chancery used a few different formulary letters for the testamentary license, but all granted substantially the same privilege with the same guidelines for its use. In 1367 Urban V directed his cardinal vice-chancellor Pierre de Monteruc to issue the license routinely from the Chancery to any prelate who requested it, without the formalities of a petition to the pope.[9] Appendix A is a typical testamentary license as drafted in the Avignon period. It begins with an *arenga* on the instability of human life, then goes on to concede to the cleric (usually a bishop or higher) "full and free faculty" to dispose of his own goods for alms and his funeral expenses, and to remunerate "moderately" those who had served him, after he had divided his own wealth from that of the church. Finally, the letter of license counseled the testator to be generous to the churches from which he had acquired his wealth.[10]

Because it was under John XXII that testamentary licenses became commonplace and spoils began to be reserved and brought in to the Apostolic Camera, one critical contemporary observer, the political philosopher Marsiglio of Padua, linked the two exercises of papal power in a single condemnation:[11]

And here is another bud from the same root of *plenitudo potestatis*. The Roman Bishop has forbidden the holders of ecclesiastical benefices anywhere to make wills without his license; and he has decreed that the goods of intestates

---

[8]There is a history of the testamentary license, informative in general if inaccurate in many details, by Richard Mather, "The Codicil of Cardinal Comes of Casate," *Traditio* 20 (1964): 319-322.

[9]Von Ottenthal, 14-25, n. 35 at 22.

[10]It is clear from actual testaments that the plural "churches" refers to a testator's earlier benefices, not to the several dependencies of his last church, as Mollat inferred in *Revue d'histoire ecclésiastique* 29 (1933): 333.

[11]*Defensor pacis* 2.24.14, ed. C. W. Previté-Orton (1928), 376; my translation.

(whether really intestate or merely unlicensed) devolve directly to his own See and should be brought there.

As we will see, *plenitudo potestatis* is perhaps the best legal principle from which the papal "right of spoil" can be derived; but for the rest, Marsiglio was imperfectly informed. Papal spoliation was not decreed, nor was it universally imposed. On the other hand, where it was active, it struck intestate and testate clerics, whether licensed or not. What can have been Marsiglio's actual experience of the papal collection of spoils? Thirty cases had begun with deaths before the publication of *Defensor pacis* on 24 June 1324.[12] Sixteen of these lay in Languedoc and five more in Iberia, all outside Marsiglio's sphere of activity, though rumors may well have reached him. Four cases in northern France included the bishop of Arras who died in 1320 and was said to have exceeded his *licentia testandi* (Repertory, n. 177), and the Franciscan bishop of Tréguier (n. 707) who died in 1323, also possessed of a license. I know of no testamentary license in any of the five Italian cases, and the earlier four of these may well have been known to Marsiglio: the bishops of Florence and Spoleto (Repertory, nn. 57 and 968), the archbishop of Naples (n. 567) and, especially to the point, the Franciscan archbishop of Cosenza, Pietro Boccaplanola, who died in 1319 (Repertory, n. 887). The first document in Boccaplanola's spoils case, a papal letter of 4 June 1320, could almost be cited as authority for Marsiglio's strictures on spoils; it ordered the rector of Benevento to inquire whether the late archbishop had a license to make a will, and if not, to take his movable goods from the executors. The archbishop's books were taken as spoils, and the Franciscan Order's resentment at losing these may have carried the news to Marsiglio.

The testamentary license did not afford protection from the reservation and collection of spoils. Rather the contrary. The pope was the sole judge of his own privileges, and the gatherers of spoils held commissions to probate the wills as papal judge-executors. They decided on the validity of testamentary bequests, and collected the residues for the Apostolic Camera.

---

[12]Ibid., Introduction, x-xi.

4. *Jus spolii* and *plenitudo potestatis*

The alert and possibly impatient reader will have observed that the foregoing exposition of the law on clerical property does not explain or justify any papal right of spoil, much less the massive reservations and collections made by the popes of Avignon. In fact, canon law does not sanction the papal reservation of spoils, nor even refer to it. Consequently, the historical explanations which have been devised for the papal *jus spolii* have almost unanimously accounted for it in terms of some supralegal principle such as eminent domain.

Late in the sixteenth century, in the wake of the Council of Trent, the Roman apologist Guglielmo Rodano undertook to justify in legal theory the papal right of spoil, by then much attenuated. Rodano could find no canonical text that explicitly warranted it, but only the principle, implied by law and long practice, that the pope is the supreme dispensator and administrator of the whole church's goods.[1] If this were not so, he argued, the pope could not grant the first fruits of vacancies, nor reserve them to himself, nor grant testamentary licenses. For the pope's right to give such licenses, Rodano was compelled to cite Thomas Aquinas, and that theologian had a more severely restrictive notion of a bishop's relation to church property than the law supported:[2]

> Bishops absolutely cannot have property. [If they claim a patrimony] they claim it not as their own, but as due to the church. The canon[3] says, "After a bishop is ordained he should restore to the altar at which he is anointed whatever he has been able to acquire." He absolutely cannot make a testament, because only the administration of ecclesiastical things is committed to him, and that ends with death, when a testament's validity begins, as the Apostle says.[4] But if, by the pope's concession, he makes a testament, he is not to be understood as making a testament by his own right; rather, his administration should be understood as extended by apostolic authority, so that it might have validity after his death.

Rodano also mentioned testamentary licenses as a custom going back

---

[1] *Tractatus de spoliis ecclesiasticis* (Rome, 1585), 6-8. The tract had an earlier and a later edition, 1569 and 1619. Rodano, bishop of Nebbio (d. 1574), was also author of a successful study of alienation of ecclesiastical property in canon law.
[2] *Summa theologiae* 2a 2ae, 185, 8 ad 3; my translation.
[3] C.18 q.1 c.1.
[4] Hebr. 9, 16, referring to the new covenant and the death of Christ as bringing it into force.

to Innocent III, and he cited the canonist Henry of Susa to the effect that cardinals could not make valid testaments without such licenses.⁵

Louis Thomassin,⁶ writing early in the eighteenth century, without recourse to the Vatican Archives, and finding no canonical justification for papal spoliation, had to rely on the evidence of the chronicles. These led him to believe that the practice, a violation of Gallican liberties, only began when the church was split by the Great Western Schism and France weakened by the minority of Charles VI. He quoted the decretals *Praesenti* and *Frequens* against spoils, and wondered "comment tant de constitutions canoniques et tant de décrétales auraient-elles pu autoriser un usage simoniaque?" The question remains for us to answer.

Franz Ehrle in his monumental history of the papal library at Avignon, a library which benefited grandly from the spoils of prelates, apologetically offered one of the best legal and administrative explanations for the practice: the reservation of benefices to papal collation, so greatly extended by John XXII, implicitly reserved the fruits of the vacancy, including the spoils of the last incumbent.⁷

It is most regrettable that the rationale of "spoils," especially those which were reserved to the Apostolic Camera, has been treated so far by writers on canon law only lightly and meagerly. Not wishing to harvest someone else's field, I will just sketch a few points that seem to me probable and necessary to my treatment. I should think that the custom of reserving to the Apostolic Camera the spoils of those who died in the curia either originated or expanded along with the reservation of the benefices of those same prelates.

Charles Samaran seems at first to have interpreted the collection of spoils as a sort of profitable penalty for prelates' irregularities: intestacy, non-pious or excessive bequests, or their deaths in the curia or at least away from their sees or monasteries.⁸ In his study of the Camera at Avignon with Guillaume Mollat, spoils are seen to be linked with the increase in papal reservation of benefices.⁹ In his later studies, Mollat rested content with a theory of implicit eminent domain, and the argument that the pope had the better right to the clerics' goods in cases where laymen could usurp their spoils.¹⁰ Saint-Palais d'Aussac added

---

⁵Two licenses from Innocent III, both to cardinals, are calendared in Potthast, *Regesta pontificum romanorum* (2 vols.; Berlin, 1874-1875), nn. 1703 and 2736, edited in PL 214:1033C-1034A and PL 215:843D-844A. Henry of Susa, *Summa aurea*, lib. 5, c. 16, *Cui cardinales* (ed. Venice, 1570), 416ᵛ: "[Cardinales] confiteri debent papae sine cuius licentia non possunt testamentum condere, nec etiam mutationem facere secundum consuetudinem Romanae ecclesiae."

⁶*Ancienne et nouvelle discipline*, 7:179-182 on lesser and earlier rights of spoil, and 7:183-190 on the papal practice.

⁷*Historia bibliothecae romanorum pontificum* 1 (Rome, 1890): 185-186; my translation.

⁸"La jurisprudence pontificale en matière du droit de dépouille (jus spolii) dans la seconde moitié du XIVe siècle," *Mélanges d'archéologie et d'histoire* 22 (1902): 141.

⁹*La fiscalité pontificale en France au XIVe siècle* (Rome, 1905), 47-55.

¹⁰"Dépouille," DDC 4:1160-1165; and "A propos du droit de dépouille," RHE 29 (1933): 316-347.

nothing to this interpretation of the right.[11] William Lunt assumed that the deceased whose spoils were reserved to the Camera were papal beneficiaries,[12] and this was in fact usually the case.

Further exploration could be done into the legal and political theory which surrounded the papal reservation of spoils in the fourteenth century, but the most satisfying explanation seems to be that the Avignonese popes' right of spoil stood legally upon a local custom of the papal court, longstanding and unopposed, which was vastly expanded in the fourteenth century by the administrative power of the Camera Apostolica in response to its own needs and opportunities.

Tracing backward the practice of spoliation for the benefit of the papal treasure, we come, not to a general canonical warrant, but to a narrowly confined usage: in 1262, Urban IV was able to claim that "the goods of clerics who die intestate at the Apostolic See devolve by approved custom to the Roman Church."[13] The custom would have had certain easily perceived equitable justifications: that the curia deserved some recompense for the costs of such a cleric's burial, and that if he had a curial post, his possessions came from that source of income.[14] As the financial burdens of the papacy became heavier, there were pressures toward an extension of the custom of spoils outside the curia. According to Matthew Paris, Innocent IV laid claim in 1246 to the spoils of all clerics who died intestate in England, and commanded the mendicant orders to collect them. This "unheard-of statute" was prompted by recent events. Three English archdeacons had died, very rich but intestate, and great wealth had been transferred from their churches to the royal treasure by regalian right. Henry III, says the chronicler, forbade the novel collections.[15]

A new crusade was in the air on the eve of the Council of Vienne (1311–1312), and at least two of its programmatists, Pierre Dubois and Ramon Lull, suggested that the anticipated expenses of the expedition should be met by despoiling the higher clergy, whose wealth they regarded as scandalously great. Pierre Dubois recommended to Edward II of England that one half of the goods of all cardinals and prelates, and the whole property of clerics who died intestate, should be collected as a subsidy for the duration of the crusade.[16] The Catalan philosopher

---

[11]*Le droit de dépouille* (Strasbourg-Paris, 1930).

[12]*Papal Revenues in the Middle Ages* (2 vols.: New York, 1934), 105-106.

[13]Guiraud, *Registres d'Urbain IV,* n. 20 (18 March 1262), quoted by Mollat in RHE 29 (1933): 316 n. 3.

[14]This seems to have been the rationale of Urban V in his viva voce edict (Montefiascone, August 1368) forbidding all the curial notaries from making testaments at all: VQ 6, 35.

[15]Matthew Paris, *Chronica maiora* (Rolls Series 57), 4:552-553. This and the reference to Ramon Lull below were cited by Noel Valois, *La France et le Grand Schisme d'Occident*, 2:351.

[16]*De recuperatione terrae sanctae*, ch. 42, ed. Charles-Victor Langlois (Paris, 1891), 31-32: "Statuuntur et quod medietas bonorum omnium cardinalium et quorumcumque praelatorum tam maiorum quam minorum decedentium, subsidio terrae sanctae quousque integraliter recuperata munitaque fuerit, applicetur, una cum omnibus bonis

Ramon Lull, in his seventies, offered some crotchety proposals to the Council of Vienne: the resources of the churches should be mobilized for the crusade by a confiscatory tax on pluralities, by allowing bishops to raise small armed companies at their own expense, and by collecting the plate, jewelry, and clothing of prelates when they died.[17]

In fact, within five years after the Council of Vienne, John XXII did begin reserving to himself the spoils of bishops who died, even at home in their sees, even with testaments licensed and duly drawn up. Thus he was invading the proprietary interests which canon law had been at pains to protect. He was acting above the law, by what is called *plenitudo potestatis*, the fullness of power. It might fairly be objected that such a principle, since it could explain any fiscal outrage, explains nothing. But J. A. Watt has illuminated the mode of operation of the *plenitudo potestatis*, and his description sheds light on the *jus spolii* as one instance of it. Watt was especially concerned with the manner in which papal collations interfered with canonical elections, but his explanation holds equally good for the papal invasion of canonical property rights.[18]

For if the function of the pope was to provide for the "communibus utilitatibus," it was necessary to postulate for him an unfettered discretionary power to decide how such provision should best be made. "Plenitudo potestatis omnia supplet." Papal letters illustrate this process in action in a number of ecclesiastical matters as a routine feature of thirteenth-century papal government. When the language in which such exercises of the discretionary power [were expressed] was already established in the formulae of the papal chancery, canonists took note of it to clarify their understanding of the terminology. Hostiensis distinguished between the papal *plenitudo officii* and the papal *plenitudo potestatis*. The former applied when the pope exercised his authority in ways which canon law already prescribed for him, namely, in all circumstances canonists listed as "maiores causae" reserved to the pope alone. The latter applied when the pope, by exercising his absolute power, acted outside the normal course of the law — either *supra ius* because he had decided to set existing law aside (dispensation was the best example of this) or because existing law was inadequate for the particular circumstances in question. "Plenitudo potestatis" thus stood for a theory of prerogative, in that sense of the word which sees its essence as an indefinite power to act out of the ordinary course of the law.

Let us see how Watt's model applies to the reservation of spoils,

---

quorumcumque clericorum quos decedere contigerit intestatos."

[17] BN lat. 15450 [543vb] "Petitio Raymundi in concilio generali ad acquirendum terram sanctam ... [544ra] De quarta ordinatione ... dico quod multi clerici habent multas prebendas, et ideo bonum magnum et pium esset quod dominus papa et reuerendi domini cardinales ordinarent quod nullus clericus haberet nisi unicam prebendam, et prebende quas haberet preter unam darentur ad passagium dum uiueret. Et etiam quod prelatus habeat certos scutiferos et equitaturas, licet temperate ad euitandum uanam gloriam et etiam malum exemplum. [544rb] Et quod prelato mortuo uasa eius argentea et etiam omnia jocalia, uestes et alia darentur ad passagium." Cited in Samaran-Mollat, 48 and Viollet 2: 350-352.

[18] "The Theory of Papal Monarchy in the Thirteenth Century: the Contributions of the Canonists," *Traditio* 20 (1964): 277-278.

considered as an exercise of papal prerogative. The decretal *Praesenti*[19] forbids the collection of clerics' spoils except where this is justified by approved custom, *seu alia de causa rationabili*, and this is the key phrase by which the development of *jus spolii* beyond the law can be traced. The Chancery of Boniface VIII was using the unspecified "reasonable cause" in place of a canonical justification as early as 3 February 1296.[20] A bull of that date erected the diocese of Pamiers in the territory of Toulouse; such a division of a diocese was a *maior causa*, reserved to the pope alone, and the letter began *Dudum nobis rationabili causa*. This is the first example I have discovered of an *arenga* that uses the phrase.[21] It occurs later in the pontificate of Boniface VIII, in a letter appointing a bishop to the administration of his see before consecration, a papal dispensation;[22] and in three letters which ordered the confiscation of goods from the adherents of the Colonna cardinals, condemned as schismatics.[23] Benedict XI, on 3 May 1304, reserved the provision of the metropolitan see of Aix with a bull beginning *Ex certis causis et rationabilibus*.[24] The phrase occurs in the registers of Clement V, in letters restoring bishops to the administration of their churches and ordering a cardinal legate to select and induct a bishop for the reserved see of Florence, translating a bishop from elsewhere if necessary.[25]

The centralization of the beneficial system undertaken by John XXII rested canonically on his decretals *Ex debito* (1316) and *Execrabilis* (1317). The former reserved a large class of benefices to papal collation, and the other called for the holders of plural benefices to surrender all but one of them into that reserved class. Long practice, defined in legislation by Boniface VIII and Clement V, allowed the pope to reserve to himself the collation of benefices that fell vacant by the death of the incumbent in the Roman curia. *Ex debito*, adducing these precedents and the good of the church, *ex causis rationabilibus*, reserved them to John XXII for his lifetime, and vastly extended the meaning of *vacans apud apostolicam sedem*. It now applied to all benefices, major (episcopal and abbatial) and minor, which fell vacant by any act in the Roman curia, not only by the death of the incumbent there, since the beginning of the pontificate of Clement V; and all benefices held by cardinals and curial officials, wherever these might happen to die.[26]

---

[19]Quoted above in chapter 3.
[20]Digard et al., *Registres* n. 891.
[21]It has a long history in decretal language in general: III Lateran (1179), e.g., allowed rectors to absent themselves from their parishes "prout causa rationabili expedierit." For the rhetorical character of the *arenga*, Heinrich Fichtenau, *Arenga: Spätantike und Mittelalter im Spiegel von Urkundenformeln* (Graz, 1957).
[22]Digard et al., *Registres*, nn. 4261, 4402.
[23]Ibid., n. 2881.
[24]Grandjean, *Registre*, n. 1226.
[25]*Regestum*, nn. 2372-2373 and 5076-5077.
[26]Carolus Lux, *Constitutionum ... collectio et interpretatio* (Breslau, 1904), 24-32 for interpretation, 51-54 for the text: *Extravagantes communes* 1.3.4, also ed. Friedberg, 2:1240-1242.

On 19 November 1317, when *Ex debito* had been in force for about a year, the bull *Execrabilis* required those clerics who held plural benefices to surrender all but one of them into the pope's hands. Those surrendered benefices, becoming *vacantes apud apostolicam sedem*, would be reserved to papal collation under the terms of *Ex debito*.[27] The measure is reminiscent of Ramon Lull's suggestion of six years earlier. No variant of the phrase *certis ex causis rationabilibus* occurs anywhere in the decretal, and yet the glossator, Jesselinus de Cassanis, took note of the Chancery's language, as Watt leads us to expect that he should, and in his gloss to the word *reservamus* he brings up *plenitudo potestatis* and "reasonable cause":

> According to the *plenitudo potestatis*, no one can say to the pope, "Lord, why are you doing this?" ... But if you ask *me* what could be the "reasonable cause" why he holds the collation of such benefices, I can answer that the burdensome care of the papal office requires many ministers, that while the harvest is great the laborers are few, and that he is required to remunerate those whom he must call to his aid, and also those who served his predecessors, ... and to his seat needy clerics flow from everywhere, whom he is obliged to provide for with fatherly foresight lest the shame of mendicancy fall upon the clergy. ... And he has to show his favor to many great men of the world, especially to those who have endowed the church of God with many gifts, or whose ancestors have done so, and who are devoted to the church of God ... by conferring benefices at their instance, so that they can the more readily be induced to come to the church's aid when necessary, and not hold themselves aloof. ... It was necessary to find a just and equitable way by which the pope could provide to many benefices, so that a just distribution could be made of them by him, ... especially since there is said to be in him an immeasurable quantity of giving.

The letters of commission to collect spoils almost invariably justify the reservation by *certis causis rationabilibus* or *causis legitimis*, thus grounding the pope's claim to the spoils upon his *plenitudo potestatis* and evading *Praesenti*'s prohibition against spoliation by an appeal to the exception allowed within that very decretal.

---

[27]*Extravagantes Joannis XXII* title 3, ed. Friedberg 2:1209 at n. 39; ed. Jacqueline Tarrant (1983) pp. 190-198.

5. The Administration and Documentation of Spoils

A regular pattern for the reservation and collection of spoils was established before the pontificate of Clement VI.[1] Each case began with a reservation of spoils by the pope. This reservation was an act of his will, communicated orally to his camerarius or implicitly assumed by the latter. There was usually no "bull of reservation," strictly speaking. The first written form of the reservation was a close or secret letter of commission, by which a judge-executor was deputed to investigate and collect the spoils. An example, in the case of Arnaldus Cescomes, archbishop of Tarragona, is edited below as Appendix B.

From the pontificate of Clement VI onward, the commissioner for spoils was usually the regional collector, whose duties and powers were extended to spoils by a particular letter of commission in each case. When the spoils of the clergy had been reserved in general, regionally or universally, the ordinary collectors were given general commissions to investigate and gather them. General reservations were made by Benedict XII for Corsica and Sardinia,[2] and by Clement VI for the kingdom of Naples;[3] the latter reservation was repeated by Innocent VI.[4] Under the universal reservation of clerical spoils by Urban V (see below, chapter 7), commissions were granted to collect them in Castile, Leon, Navarre, and Portugal by Urban V himself,[5] and by Gregory XI in the provinces of Bordeaux and Auch, Tarragona, Zaragoza and Mallorca, and in both Sicilies and Sardinia.[6] Such blanket reservations and commissions seem to have been intended to prevent the delays incidental to long-distance correspondence, delays during which goods could disappear if the collector were not ready to secure them immediately after the owner died.

---

[1] For studies of individual cases of spoils, see Guillaume Mollat, "L'application du droit de dépouille sous Jean XXII," *Revue des sciences religieuses* 19 (1939): 50-57; idem, "A propos du droit de dépouille," RHE 29 (1933): 325-329; Jean Glénisson, "Un agent de la Chambre apostolique au XIVe siècle: les missions de Bertrand de Mazel (1364-1378)," *Mélanges d'archéologie et d'histoire* 59 (1947): 89-119; M.-H. Laurent, "Guillaume des Rosières et la bibliothèque pontificale l'époque de Clément VI," *Mélanges Auguste Pelzer* (Louvain, 1947), 579-603.
[2] EFR *Benoît XII closes, autres* n. 3157.
[3] EFR *Clément VI closes, France* n. 3047.
[4] EFR *Innocent VI secrètes* nn. 229, 314.
[5] EFR *Urbain V secrètes, France* n. 2639.
[6] EFR *Grégoire XI secrètes, autres* nn. 463, 1234, 1273; Coll. 358, 7^{rv}.

The letters of commission and subsequent letters of instruction sometimes specified precisely what spoils should be collected. Almost always, as in the letter edited in Appendix B, they made the commissioner a judge-executor with full papal jurisdiction for the case in hand, to be exercised summarily and without respect of persons, and to stand without appeal. It is no wonder that the right of spoil, driven as it was with such extraordinary powers, focused the displeasure of the conciliarist reformers.

The collector or special commissioner would begin his work by publishing his letters, often by having them read in the chapter of the cathedral, monastery, or collegiate church concerned. He would cite witnesses to appear before him with information about the movables owned by the late cleric and debts owed to him, and would seal his house or houses. He would then make an inventory of the goods, room by room and item by item, frequently employing a notary to record his search and local experts such as stationers and silversmiths to estimate the value of precious pieces. He would hear and record depositions from servants and relatives, and gather the written records of the property: wills and codicils, inventories, and the documents which had to do with loans in and out or with the purchase, sale, donation, and pawn of goods. Sometimes these records were carried back to the Camera in the original or in notarial copies, and are to be found among the *Instrumenta miscellanea* of the Vatican Archives. Often they would be copied into the collectors' regular account books which survive in the Archives as *Collectoriae* volumes.

The commissioner then would sequester the cash, goods, and valuable paper such as notes receivable. Frequently he would offer the goods for sale, trying to get the estimated value from the general public or from persons close to the household. When the local market for precious commodities such as books, worked gold and silver, rings, gems and vestments was depressed or uncertain, these had to be shipped to the Camera rather than sold.[7] The grain, wine, livestock, and domestic furniture, when these were considered spoils, were usually left to the heirs, executors, or successors, or were shared among them, in return for a cash composition or a note of promise (*obligatio*) to pay a composition; such a settlement had to be approved by the Camera. All these acts, with their gross proceeds, would be entered under *recepta* in the commissioner's account book. He would pay for the funeral and its incidental alms and the servants' wages, and allot to the executors of the testament the bequests in cash or kind which were considered legitimate. All these items, with the commissioner's expenses for the whole process — travel and lodging for himself and his servants and mounts, fees to the special masters, and freight for the remaining goods to Avignon — were entered and summed up as *expensa*. Under the heading

---

[7] Tihon, *Lettres de Grégoire XI* n. 2272, of 23 August 1373.

assignationes, the collector recorded his payments to the treasury or, at the order of the camerarius, to others.

Returning to the papal court, the commissioner would turn over the goods and cash which he had received to the treasury, securing a receipt or *quittancia*, sometimes in great detail. The quittances would sometimes also be registered as *solutiones* in the registers of the thesaurarius, now gathered in the Vatican Archives series *Obligationes et Solutiones*. If the collector had taken a note for a composition, this would be registered as an *obligatio*. Now the collector was ready to sort his papers, finish his formal account book, and submit it to the Cameral council (the camerarius, treasurer, auditor and clerks) for audit. One of the clerks would examine the accounts and write a brief summary for the rapid perusal of the camerarius, who would note his approval of the sums and balances with the siglum *APP[robatum]*, or his concern about irregularities with a curt *doce*: "explain." When the collector had appeared in person before the council and answered for his activity, his explanations, supported by documents, would be noted with a *docuit*. The collectors' account books are the major and eponymous part of the series *Collectoriae*.[8]

The treasurer submitted monthly reports of his receipts, and these were cumulated semiannually as *introitus* in the *Introitus et Exitus* series. The *introitus* reports occasionally included detailed lists of spoils received. The spoils of clerics who died in the curia, collected by the sealbearer of the auditor of the Camera, would be reported here.[9]

After about 1360, when the right of spoil had acquired the legal force and administrative facility of an old custom, it could be managed by executive orders that originated with the camerarius and under his seal, rather than by papal letters. By that time, too, the camerarius possessed and could delegate the supreme legal authority for the summary processes of spoils.[10] The letters of the camerarii began to be registered in 1361.[11]

At the same period, the pontificate of Urban V (1362-1370) and the administration of camerarius Arnaud Aubert (1361-1371), we find spoils being bought, along with the fruits of the vacant benefice, without any

---

[8]For an introduction to the use of the *Fondo Camerale* in the Vatican Archives, see Yves Renouard, "Intérêt et importance des Archives vaticanes pour l'histoire économique du Moyen Age, spécialement du XIVe siècle," *Miscellanea Angelo Mercati* (Studi e Testi 165; Vatican City, 1952), 21-41; and Joseph de Loye, *Les archives de la Chambre apostolique au XIVe siècle I: Inventaire* (Paris, 1889). Pietro Guidi composed the typescript *Indice* 1036 to the *fondo*, including many Cameral records which had strayed into the *Registra Avenionensia*. For the whole Archives, see Leonard E. Boyle, *A Survey of the Vatican Archives and of Its Medieval Holdings* (Toronto, 1972).

[9]E.g. VQ 4:192-193; VQ 7:371.

[10]See my "Summary Justice in the Avignonese Camera," (1985), 444.

[11]My "Letters of Etienne Cambarou, Camerarius Apostolicus (1347-1361)," *Archivum Historiae Pontificiae* 15 (1977): 195-215 provides a conspectus of the registers of the Camerarii and a calendar of the first fragmentary register. A calendar of the letters of Cambarou's successor, Arnaud Aubert (1361-1371), is ready for the press.

question of the Camera's right to sell them, in a series of legal *Allegationes* drafted by the former collector of Portugal, Bertrand du Mazel, on behalf of Raymond de Canilhac, the cardinal bishop of Praeneste (1361–1373).[12] Apparently intervening in litigation in the Auditio Camerae, Mazel argued that the movable goods of the late provost of Mainz, Wilhelm Pinchon, as well as the fruits of the vacancy, should not have gone to the executors of his testament but rather to the cardinal, because the pope had reserved the dignity to his own provision and then provided it to the cardinal. The movables considered accessory to the benefice had thus been reserved to the Camera, and the cardinal had bought them from the Camera for a fixed composition. Mazel cited canon- and civil-law sources and the commentators Guido de Baysio, Innocent IV, and Giovanni d'Andrea (on *Praesenti*) against the executors' claim. He assumed the pope's right to reserve and sell the spoils, and summed up, "saving the better advice of the experts," in favor of the cardinal. This diffident *consilium* shows how completely the papal prerogative, as administered at Avignon, had perverted the original intention of the law. A pluralist absentee, a cardinal in favor in the curia (he was the general supervisor of the gabelles and defensive works of Avignon while the curia was in Italy)[13] could claim the benefice by papal collation, and the fruits of the vacancy and the last incumbent's spoils by purchase, all without regard to the needs of the church of Mainz, to serve which the benefice originally existed.

---

[12]The original document, now IM 6427, is edited in Appendix C.
[13]A.-M. Hayez, "Les gabelles d'Avignon d'Innocent à VI Grégoire XI," *Etudes sur la fiscalité au moyen âge* 1 (Paris, 1979): 184–185.

6. The Extent and Incidence of the Right of Spoil

On 16 August 1316, only nine days after the election of John XXII, and twenty days before his coronation, Bertrand de Malsang, abbot of Montmajour, died. His nephews plundered the monastery's treasure and granaries, and other neighbors followed suit. The Camera intervened vigorously to protect the papal reservation of the abbacy and spoils against such a scandalous abuse.[1] On 5 December of the same year Arnaldus de Puyana, bishop of Pamplona, died at Toulouse. The records do not indicate whether or not he had made a will, but he had a license to do so from Clement V.[2] Papal letters of 11 March 1317 and 5 September 1318 called for the surrender of his goods to the safekeeping of the Franciscan convent of Toulouse.[3] These were the first two cases of spoils outside the curia reserved to papal disposition. I have found 1191 cases under the papal *jus spolii* in the following century, and these are documented in the Repertory which follows. The cases are found to be distributed on a roughly bell-shaped secular curve, illustrated by the table on the following page and by the Index on pp. 256–9. There was an irregular increase in frequency during 1316–1342, the pontificates of John XXII and Benedict XII, as the Camera improved its methods and extended its reach.[4] The right of spoil was in its fullest vigor during the pontificates of Clement VI and his three successors, 1342–1376, partly because their camerarii were able to take advantage of the plague mortalities of 1348, 1361, and 1375. Two hundred and sixty-seven cases, or almost a quarter of the total, belong to the time of Clement VI (1342–1352). The frequency of cases declined sharply from 1376 to 1409, as the Great Western Schism, and then the Subtraction of Obedience by France, reduced the area under tribute and the complaisance of the local clergy. Spoils were probably collected in the Avignonese obedience after 1409, but only within the shrinking court of Benedict XIII at Peñiscola, and I have been able to find record of only one case, that of the bishop of Oviedo (Repertory, n. 466) in 1412.

About a hundred of the despoiled were clerics who died in the curia, with no note of any benefice that they held outside it. These were mostly lower-level curial officials, typified by the famous visionary scrivener of

---
[1] Mollat in RHE 29 (1933): 324-325.
[2] *Regestum*, n. 5922, of 6 September 1310.
[3] EFR *Jean XXII communes* nn. 5478, 8109.
[4] Mollat, in RHE 29 (1933): 319, estimated 57 cases under John XXII and 30 under Benedict XII; I find 107 and 65 respectively.

THE INCIDENCE OF SPOILS

In this table, each case of spoils is counted below the name of the pope reigning when the case began, and opposite the territory in which the despoiled person held his last principal benefice. When the deceased held a title in the Orient along with the administration of a western see, the latter is counted as his benefice. Collectors and nuncios, and the rectors and treasurers of papal states, are counted with the territories where they had their fiscal responsibilities, rather than the locations of their benefices. The "undistributed" cases are those of persons whose benefices are not known; almost all of these held curial offices or died in the curia.

	John XXII 1316–1334	Benedict XII 1334–1342	Clement VI 1342–1352	Innocent VI 1352–1362	Urban V 1362–1370	Gregory XI 1370–1378	Clement VII 1378–1394	Benedict XIII 1394–1424	Total	% Share
I. A. Languedoc	35	20	50	50	29	45	47	16	292	24.6
B. Northern France	9	6	27	24	14	19	27	1	127	10.7
II. A. Provence	17	7	14	11	7	1	5	4	66	5.5
B. Naples	11	7	40	38	6	4	2		108	9.0
III. A. Comtat-Venaissin	3	2	3	5	5		2	2	22	
B. Patrimonio	1		5	2	5	2			15	
C. Campagna-Marittima	1	5	8	7	1	3			25	
D. Ducato di Spoleto	1		4	3	3	1	1		13	
E. Marca di Ancona			3		5	6			14	
F. Emilia-Romagna			2	2	1	3			8	8.1
IV. Northern Italy	2	5	18	16	11	8	4		64	5.4
V. Portugal	8		6	7	8	2	2		33	2.8
VI. Castile & Leon	6	3	4	8	4	9	6	2	42	3.5
VII. A. Aragon	2	3	17	19	13	12	7	9	82	
B. Sicily			1	4	3	5			13	
C. Sardinia		1	3	2	1			2	9	8.7
VIII. Empire	5		5	15	8	11	8	2	54	4.5
IX. A. England		3	4		5			12		
B. English France	3		6	14	16	9			48	5.0
X. Other: Europe	2		6	2	6	5			21	1.8
XI. Orient	3		3	3	6	1	1	2	19	1.6
Undistributed		8	36	41	4	8	5		102	8.6
Total	109	67	264	277	156	159	117	40	1189	100%
Cases per year	5.9	9.1	24.7	28.4	18.9	21.9	7.3	22.2	12.3	

the Penitentiary, Opicino de Canistris (no. 833), who probably derived most or all their property from their salaries and other curial opportunities. Some were proctors, that is, lawyers who practiced in the courts and offices of the curia on behalf of outsiders. Seventy or so were or had been fiscal agents of the Camera, collectors, subcollectors, or provincial rectors or treasurers, and their spoils were usually presumed to include goods and money which they had collected in the course of their Cameral service, although they usually had benefices as well, sometimes major ones. For the most part, it was the landed wealth of ecclesiastical benefices that bore the burden of the right of spoil. More than a quarter of the cases touched benefices in Languedoc, some 200 of them bishoprics or abbeys and a third as many minor benefices. The prerogative of the pope in this matter was potentially in conflict with the regalian rights of other sovereigns. Those who were most cooperative with the papal collectors were the kings of France (where four hundred of the cases occurred) and Aragon (a hundred cases), the king and then the queen of Naples (175 cases), and of course the pope himself, as secular prince in central Italy and in the Comtat Venaissin (80 cases). Other princes resisted. England was exempt from spoliation, except in six cases of English beneficiaries who died in the curia, and English France nearly so (45 cases). Only about fifty cases occurred in the Empire.

The popes of Avignon and their chief ministers, the camerarii apostolici,[5] confronted a radical choice. Without the centralization of the beneficial system and a hardheaded fiscal policy to extract the maximum profit from it, even at the risk of weakening the hierarchical constitution of the church, their control of the papal states in Italy stood in danger of complete collapse. The reversal of losses there required the militant legations of the cardinals Bertrand du Pouget (1319–1334) and Gil Albornoz (1353–1367), backed to the limit of papal resources. The large building programs at Avignon, to satisfy Benedict XII's defensive requirements and Clement VI's desire "to live like a pope" also drank money, and until the Italian patrimony was recovered, a fiscal substitute had to be established by prerogative. The consequences were clear even at the beginning to Marsiglio of Padua: he saw *plenitudo potestatis* in the time of John XXII creating a monster, an ecclesiastical body in which all the organs were directly attached to the head rather than arranged in their proper hierarchical constitution; concretely, he pointed to fiscal, beneficial, and disciplinary connections, created by spoils and annates, papal collations and immunities.[6] But the papal prerogative marched on, guided by the camerarius Gasbert de Laval. Before John XXII died, the Apostolic See was thriving on an income derived from a fiscal

---

[5]The office is described, and the successive camerarii at Avignon listed, in my "Letters of Etienne Cambarou," *Archivum Historiae Pontificiae* 15 (1977): 195-198.

[6]*Defensor pacis*, tr. Alan Gewirth (New York, 1967), 321-331; cf. above, pp. 11–12.

system centered in Languedoc rather than its old patrimonial base in central Italy. By means of services, annates, charitable subsidies, tenths, and Chancery taxes for the collation of benefices,[7] the Roman Church at Avignon tapped the landed wealth of churches and monasteries of all grades, through their living incumbents. The reservation to the Camera of spoils and vacancies did the same, after the incumbents died.

The fiscal system operated with a high level of cooperation from the clergy affected, who were increasingly dependent upon papal collations for their advancement.[8] Protests, even against such a novelty as spoliation, were few and isolated until the conciliarist movement for reform grew strong late in the fourteenth century. Prerogative, therefore, seldom had to explain itself. When a legal justification for spoils did exist in a particular case, for example when the spoliand died in the curia, or intestate, or in debt to the Camera, or without having rendered final account of some fiscal responsibility, this circumstance would be mentioned in the documents of the case, but not as a necessary condition for the reservation of the spoils. Having, as a prerogative function, neither conditions nor explicit legal warrant, papal spoils in the Avignon period also had no firm limits, and if we are to define the institution we must infer a definition from its individual instances. In this study, a broad definition has been applied: spoils are the movable goods of any cleric or religious person reserved to the Camera Apostolica for any reason. It has been suggested that some cases belong not to the *jus spolii* but to a seigneurial or other fiscal right.[9] This may be true, but the procedure that appears from the documents is that of spoils, and I can construct no abstract legal definition of the *jus spolii* to supersede the functional or descriptive one in such a way as to exclude them.

In at least seven cases, bishops were despoiled on the occasion, not of their deaths but of their translations to other sees. Gasbert de Laval, camerarius apostolicus, was despoiled a first time (Repertory, n. 335) on his transfer from Arles to Narbonne in 1341; and Peytavin de Montesquieu when he advanced from Montauban to Albi in 1339 (n. 994). The goods of Angelo dei Ricasoli, bishop of Sora, were reserved

---

[7]The various imposts are explained in William E. Lunt, *Papal Revenues in the Middle Ages* (New York, 1934), 1:57-136; Yves Renouard, *La papauté à Avignon* (Paris, 1962), 101-103; and Guillaume Mollat, *Les papes d'Avignon* (10th ed.; Paris, 1965), 530-543.

[8]For the law on papal provisions, see Carolus Lux, *Constitutionum ... collectio*; for practice, Guillaume Mollat, *La collation des bénéfices ecclésiastiques à l'époque des papes d'Avignon* (Paris, 1921); Bernard Guillemain, *La politique bénéficiale de Benoît XII* (Paris, 1952); and Geoffrey Barraclough, *Papal Provisions* (Oxford, 1935). Barraclough concentrated on the local effect of papal provisions in the 13th century, and rather neglected Languedoc, where papal government and its beneficial-fiscal system operated most intensely in the fourteenth century.

[9]Michel Hayez in his perspicuous review of my *Records of the Papal Right of Spoil* in *Bibliothèque de l'Ecole des Chartes* 134 (1976): 210-212, specifying *Records*, nn. 232, 356, 630, 657 and 1041, which are nn. 234, 362, 650, 681, and 1080 in the Repertory below.

when he was translated to Aversa in 1357 (n. 50). Jacques Fournier, translated from Pamiers to Mirepoix in 1326 (n. 591), had his goods reserved on that occasion. Some of the items in this account were only paid ten years later, when he received them himself as Pope Benedict XII! These prelates, like Marino del Giudice (n. 776), Angel de Lordado (n. 76) and Roger d'Armagnac (n. 1091) no doubt stood deep in debt to the Camera for their past common services, and the Camera was securing the debts by way of spoils rather than by litigating obligations of debt, quite likely with the consent of the debtors. The procedure resembles a modern business receivership in bankruptcy. Similarly, in 1372,[10] Gregory XI reserved the movable goods of Lambert de Born, bishop of Strassburg and papal collector of Germany (n. 745), and commissioned special agents to collect them, probably because of accounts improperly rendered. Five years earlier, Urban V reserved the movable goods of Androin de la Roche, the cardinal of Cluny, whom he had recently removed as legate in Italy, legally incapacitating him from alienating them during his life.[11] I have seen no indication, however, that his spoils were gathered after his death, which occurred in the plague at Viterbo in 1369. Where large sums, especially large debts to the Camera, were involved, the collectors were sometimes commissioned in anticipation of death, as in nn. 427, 442, 449 and 450.

Under John XXII, we find spoils confiscated after the condemnation of one Eudes, prior of S. Martin, Chartres, for heresy (n. 832) and in the magic and murder case of Hugues Géraud, bishop of Cahors (n. 553). The defendant in a Cameral action for 16,000 ducats, Demetrios de Matafaris, bishop of Knin in Dalmatia, broke his arrest at Rome in 1368. A Cameral warrant for his capture, addressed to the Doge and officials of the Veneto in January, seems to have been fruitless, and the few books and liturgical items that he had left behind at Rome were seized by the Camera in December.[12]

Six cardinals, as far as I know, had their movable goods reserved and collected *post mortem*. The earliest, Andrea Ghini Malpigli (*Records* n. 40), who died in 1343, was treated like any other subject of spoils, and it is conceivable that his colleagues, anxious for their privileges, prevented Clement VI and his successors from touching their college again in this way. The other five were exceptional cases. Arnaud Bernard du Pouget (n. 67) and Fortanerio Vassalli (n. 289) were not fully cardinals, the former having died three weeks before his creation, the other before entering the curia to receive his red hat and title. Only those goods of Guillaume de la Jugie (n. 476) which he had left in the collectory of

---

[10] Tihon, *Lettres de Grégoire XI*, 2 (Analecta Vaticano-Belgica 20), n. 1565.
[11] In a viva-voce order to the Camerarius in the presence of Cardinal Guillaume de la Jugie and the collector of the Veneto: VQ 6:33.
[12] Coll. 353, 97^v-98^r and 133^v-134^v.

Hungary were reserved for papal collection, and he may have been, like Pedro Gomez Albornoz (n. 919), the object of papal solicitude for his testament rather than spoliation. Finally, the spoils of Pierre d'Estaing (n. 960) were collected against his enormous debts to the Camera for his administration of the Papal States in Italy.

7. Curbing the Right of Spoil

The law which guaranteed the rights of the legitimate heirs and successors of despoiled clerics, outlined in chapter 2, seems to have guided the practice of the papal collectors of spoils without being explicitly enjoined upon them during the first half of the century.[1] The bereaved churches and relatives, and the officials of various regalian rights, nevertheless resisted the collections, passively or actively. The collectors sometimes abused their large powers. Thus, for example, clerics of Cahors brought charges against the collector Jean des Paumes:[2]

That when [Jean Desprez] the bishop of Castres of good memory had ended his days [1348], and the said lord Jean [des Paumes] had received the spoils of the said lord bishop, among which was a certain precious vestment from the said lord bishop's body, who was nephew of my lord [Pierre Desprez, cardinal-bishop] of Palestrina; and the proctor of my lord of Palestrina requested the said vestment from the said lord Jean, the same lord Jean swore by God's holy Gospels that he had lost the said vestment, which was not true but the contrary, and the said vestment was in his possession and still is. And the same lord Jean settled with the said proctor for forty florins.

During the twenty-six years from the death of Clement VI to the Schism, the right of spoil, by then a custom in the strict canonical sense — a practice of forty years' prescription — became more commonplace, more a regular function of the regional collectors. Accustomed to using their extraordinary powers to intervene in the disposition of prelates' goods, they became high-handed, aroused resentment, and required regulation. The popes of this period, Innocent VI, Urban V, and Gregory XI, extended the general reservation of spoils, but restrained the operations of their fiscal officers so as not to violate the spirit of canon law, which protected the right of a dying man to make pious donations for his soul's good, of an ecclesiastical successor to receive the

---

[1] IM 1667, a letter moderating the claims of the Camera, was formerly indexed among documents of 1345, but its true date is 1382. It bears the short pontifical date 16 May, 4 Clement. Samaran-Mollat, 207-209; Saint-Palais, 127; Lunt 1:106; and Mollat in DDC 4:1163; in RHE 29 (1933): 335-336 and 343; and in *Les papes d'Avignon*, 511; and Favier, *Les finances pontificales* (Paris, 1966), 251, all took the date to mean 4 Clement VI, that is, 1345. Déprez in EFR *Clément VI closes, France*, n. 2486, put the letter in 1346, using the election-anniversary of Clement VI instead of his coronation-anniversary. But from internal and external evidence, it is a letter of Clement VII, issued 16 May 1382, simply repeating the *moderatio* established by Innocent VI. The Vatican Archives' chronological index to the *Instrumenta miscellanea* now places the letter in 1382.
[2] Samaran-Mollat, 218-219, my translation.

land and buildings of the benefice in working condition and furnished with the necessary equipment, and of the heirs to recover the patrimonial goods.

Innocent VI, who continued his predecessor's general reservation of spoils in the kingdom of Naples, was compelled by the protests of the clergy there to impose limitations on the collectors in 1356. The cause of the local reaction was a major sweep of spoils, carried out between October 1351 and December 1354 by Pierre Dupin, nuncio in the kingdom of Naples and archbishop of Benevento. His summary accounts of the campaign are found in *Collectoriae* 169, 45^v–52^v. Instead of attending each process in person, the prelate-collector mobilized eight subcommissioners including his brother Jean Dupin, and gathered the spoils of three archbishops,[3] eight bishops,[4] and six abbots.[5] The reported net proceeds were more than 6300 florins, a large sum, considering that the region was just recovering its productivity after the Black Death, and that there had already been an energetic harvest of spoils in 1343–1349, directed by Guillaume des Rosières.[6] The actual collections may have been even harsher. The Cameral records do not show what orders the subcommissioners were given, nor how they carried out their tasks. According to the complaints, however, they had been stripping the churches of the necessities of worship, and the landed properties of their tools and weapons of defense. The pope responded with a general restraining order, *Quamvis in cunctis*.[7] This papal *moderatio* was open to interpretation according to the various interests in the kingdom. Some said that it prohibited the collection of goods belonging to the church for worship, including whatever the late incumbent had left to it by his testament, up to a quarter of his goods; some held that there was no limit to the pious bequests of prelates, and that these should all be respected by the collectors. A third opinion, which Innocent III himself approved in his determination of the debate, *Quamquam fabricam*, said that the *moderatio* forbade the seizure of those goods which had been given to the service of the land or altar before the last illness of the owner, and moderate pious bequests "to which the collectors show themselves favorable."[8] The collectors, of course, remained the judges of their own activities; they were to be guided by the rules of *Quamquam fabricam*, but because their decisions were still not subject to appeal, the *moderatio* did not provide the Neapolitan clergy any defense at law against spoliation.

---

[3]*Repertory*, nn. 300, 304, and 749.
[4]*Repertory*, nn. 112, 236, 305, 528, 747, 802, 805 and 847.
[5]*Repertory*, nn. 113, 416, 540, 1095, 1153 and 1161.
[6]*Collectoriae* 168, 37^r-91^r.
[7]Dated 30 April 1356, according to the interpretive letter of 1358.
[8]*Quamquam fabricam militantis*, 9 June 1358, ed. Samaran in *Mélanges* 22 (1902): 149-152 from a handbook of Cameral administrative orders, Coll. 359A, 13^v-15^r. The letter was expedited, patent, on 23 June 1358 to Petrus, archbishop of Benevento, by hand of the papal *domicellus* Raymond d'Aubefeuille: Coll. 352, 119^v.

The general reservation of clerics' spoils was made universal by Urban V in 1362, but not in a published decree and not intended for unlimited application. In his viva voce instructions to his camerarius Arnaud Aubert, three months after his coronation,[9]

our lord Pope Urban V reserved during his lifetime, when, if, and however much he should please, the use of all the movable goods and debts of all patriarchs, archbishops, bishops, abbots, deans, provosts, priors, rectors, and any other ecclesiastical persons,[10] secular and regular of any order (even if they be of the Cistercian or another order who have only common property) who die anywhere, in the Roman curia or elsewhere. But note that our lord does not wish us to use this against those who have no private property, except at his word.[11]

But the same our lord wished that from the said reserved goods should be paid the dead man's debts contracted for the sake of the church in which he presided; likewise that the expenses of burial should be paid according to the dignity and status of the person; also the salaries of the servants; also the debts, if in fact they be bound to any. Likewise, he wished that from the said goods should be removed the books and other things which the deceased had acquired from his patrimony or by the work of his own hands or otherwise than from the church or benefice in which he presided, *if* he has a legitimate heir, not otherwise. Likewise our lord the pope wished that the said reservation should not extend to the books, chalices, crosses, vestments and other ornaments anciently reserved to the use of the church, either before the time of the dead man or by him during his lifetime, without fraud. He desired the same regarding the oxen and other animals and things likewise anciently reserved for agriculture or other uses of the benefice.

But the same lord pope wished us not to use this reservation in regard to the Gallican and Anglican churches. Done in the presence of myself, Arnaldus, camerarius, and of the lord archbishop of Vienne on 11 December in the first year of his pontificate.[12]

The camerarii who served Gregory XI and Clement VII noted their masters' confirmations of this general reservation, and it was mentioned, with its *moderatio*, in papal instructions to collectors.[13] The

---

[9]Ed. Samaran in *Mélanges* 22 (1902): 152-153, and Samaran-Mollat, 233-234, from Coll. 359A, 16ᵛ-17ᵛ; my translation.

[10]On 1 November 1364, the camerarius ordered the collector of Poland to restrict his spoils collections to prelates: Coll. 353, 20ʳ.

[11]On 25 January 1365, Urban V ordered the camerarius not to interfere with the collection of the spoils of dependent priors by Benedictine abbots, where this was customary: Samaran-Mollat, 234-235.

[12]Jean Desprez, commissioner for spoils in Sicily, wrote within a year a censorious account, preserved in IM 5344, of the opportunities which the local collectors had lost there by misfeasance.

[13]E.g. Gregory XI to Jean Maubert, collector of Reims and Siger von Neustein, collector of Cologne, 23 August 1373, ed. Tihon, *Lettres de Grégoire XI*, nn. 2273-2275; Clement VII to Jean François, collector of Bourges, 16 May 1382 (see the dating critique in the first note to this chapter), ed. Samaran-Mollat, 207-209; and 18 June 1390, ed. Samaran in *Mélanges* 22 (1902): 154-156.

moderatio is in general the same as Innocent VI's for Naples, and no novelty. It simply recognizes certain canonical rights which the reservation of spoils could not but affect adversely, while it tacitly buries others. The right of clerics to make pious bequests to their own churches was not mentioned in the *moderatio*, and a few years later Urban V explicitly closed that loophole, permitting the camerarius to collect spoils even when prelates had so devised their goods.[14] On the other hand, the hereditary and testamentary rights of the decedent over his patrimonial goods and *peculium*, and the profit derived from his own work and skill, were secured by the *moderatio* and observed in practice. For example, the collector was ordered to release to the heir of Jean de Lieux, bishop of Poitiers (n. 669), some spoils which were "bona aliqua patrimonialia uel de patrimonio ... prouenientia aut ex ipsius episcopi labore et industria antequam esset ad dictum episcopatum assumptus uel beneficia obtineret ecclesiastica acquisita."[15] Similarly, the heritage of Guillaume Caprarii, cantor of Tours (n. 450), was allowed to stand against the reservation of spoils because "erat magnus aduocatus et multas habebat pensiones a multis nobilibus partium illorum pro aduocatione sua."[16] A similar claim was allowed for Pierre de Montrebel, bishop of Lectoure (n. 938), and for Jacopo Muto, bishop of Spoleto (n. 595), "homo magne scientie, magni consilii et etiam magne industrie."

The general reservation was liable to arouse the same resentment and resistance as had met the individual reservations of the early period. Resentment could be even sharper, now that the collectors were acting on their own initiative, without a particular warrant in each case. Opposition became clamorous during the Great Western Schism. The chorus of protest convinced Louis Thomassin that the *jus spolii* was a new exercise by Clement VII, taking advantage of new opportunities in France:[17]

And so it was only the Schism of the church, the minority of Charles VI, and the self-serving conduct of the Prince Regent that allowed the entry of this novelty into France. Into France, I say, because it was apparently here that the spoliations by the popes began, because it was closest and most subject to the popes of Avignon.

It is true enough that the burden on France was more keenly felt during the Schism. Clement VII and Benedict XIII were dependent on a restricted base for their fiscal income, chiefly France and Spain, where the right of spoil had operated so vigorously for sixty-two years before the Schism. The popes of the Avignon sect in the Schism could not so well afford to restrain their collectors as could their uncontested prede-

---

[14] 17 June 1366: Samaran-Mollat, 233.
[15] 13 February 1365: Coll. 353, 29^v.
[16] 24 January 1367: Coll. 353, 78^v-79^r.
[17] Thomassin, 7:185, my translation; cf. Saint-Palais, 131-137.

cessors, and the rapacity of the collectors, accustomed for almost a generation to act on their own discretion, was allowed to grow. At the same time, the consensus of the French church was shifting, not toward the Roman obedience, but toward a conciliar solution of the Schism. The clergy were not inclined to cooperate with papal pretensions, especially not with those of a pope whose ability to reward their loyalty was diminishing. Stories about the extortionate collectors were retailed by Jean Petit:[18]

As for the spoliation of the dead, they say that if any churchman dies, prelate or otherwise, the pope will succeed to his goods and take away everything that is not attached to stone, wood, or iron. There is a story about a papal collector who took a door, which a prelate recently deceased had had made to put on his house, and because it was not yet hung, ordered it brought to him. Another one ordered that a dead priest be stripped who lay in the church for his funeral, clad in a chasuble; he said the chasuble was pretty, and took it away. Nothing like this was ever seen in France.

That door does not appear in any collector's accounts that I have seen, but the chasuble might be a souvenir of the scandalous collector Jean des Paumes, with whose rapacity in the year of the Black Death this chapter began.

Such scandalous gossip does not tell the whole story of the impact of spoils on the French churches, as Jean Favier, the major explorer of Schism finances, has warned. Favier considered the stories exaggerated, and he indicated examples where generous, even luxurious, allowances were made by the collectors for the funerals of the despoiled. Furthermore, he argued, the spoils that were collected actually represented debts which the deceased prelates owed for their services and other taxes, and consequently the pope's Camera was only using a confiscatory receivership to recover what was due to him.[19] But legitimate or not, spoils were a burden that the French church was ready to shed, with royal help if necessary. The chronicler Jean Juvenal des Ursins summarized the protests that came to the royal courts:[20]

When a bishop died, you could see nothing on the landscape but collectors and subcollectors of the Apostolic Camera coming to take whatever the bishop had acquired in the way of movables, even though these things should really have belonged to the heirs, or at least to the testamentary executors; it was not even permitted to use these things for the most necessary repairs to their houses. Furthermore, they seized the temporalities of monasteries after the deaths of abbots, and their successors could not undertake the subsistence of their

---

[18]Ed. Noel Valois, *La France et le Grand Schisme d'Occident*, (4 vols.: Paris, 1896-1902), 3:436, n. 2, quoted in Samaran-Mollat, 53; my translation here; also quoted by Jean Favier, "Temporels ecclésiastiques et taxation fiscal: le poids de la fiscalité pontificale au XIVe siècle," *Journal des Savants* (1964): 116-117.

[19]"Temporels ecclésiastiques," *Journal des Savants* (1964): 116-117.

[20]*Histoire de Charles VI*, quoted in Thomassin, 7:185 and in Samaran-Mollat, 53, my translation.

religious communities from the little that remained, and they had to sell or pawn the ornaments and silverware of their churches for a little money to keep themselves from beggary.

Charles VI consequently protested the levy of spoils in a letter patent of 6 October 1385, whose argument was implicitly grounded on the canons and the *moderatio:*[21]

> Now, when it befalls a bishop in our kingdom to migrate from the light, the collectors and subcollectors of the supreme pontiff, in the provinces subject to them, by the authority of the same supreme pontiff, seize the movable and immovable goods of such bishops, left behind at their death, even those things which they had acquired by their own industry, which things, furthermore, do not belong to those bishops and are not considered to belong to them, but rather to their heirs or executors; turning none of these things to the repair or rebuilding of the structures and other patrimonial properties of the said episcopal establishments in such a case, and also with no payment or satisfaction to the creditors of the said bishops being made by the collectors or subcollectors, but totally removing the said goods from the heirs of bishops so dying (even though, the richer they are, the more honorably they may and should serve us in our wars and elsewhere, according to their state), and disinheriting them against law and custom, they give us no small prejudice and trouble after the death of bishops in the said churches.

The king prohibited such fiscal abuses, but it remained unclear whether his ordinance applied only in the Gallican Church, i.e. in the north, or also in Languedoc; and whether it went beyond spoils to other operations of the papal fisc. The Camera sought by direct negotiation to get a clarification of the ordinance favorable to its interests. It was Pierre Gérard, bishop of Le Puy (1385–1390) who sat as the pope's proctor in the negotiations, and a memorandum, now *Instrumenta miscellanea* 4283, was made of the two positions; it is edited as Appendix D below. In a rather shocking reversal of traditional roles, the king was standing for the good of the churches, which were falling into ruin for want of the most elementary repairs, while the necessary funds were being carried off as the spoils of bishop after bishop. Furthermore, the noble houses to which the bishops belonged, and in which their patrimonies were needed to support military and other services to the crown, were being disinherited by spoils. The royal proctors could see no justification at all for collecting the spoils of abbots who owned no private property, and yet the monastic property which they administered was being plundered twice with each succession, in spoils and then in services due from the new abbot. In reply, Le Puy argued custom, and asked the king to rectify the damage done by his ordinance in its encouragement of disobedience by French prelates, not only in the matter of spoils but in other dues as well. The king's counsel offered to procure royal letters

---

[21]*Preuves des libertés de l'église gallicane* 22, no. 8, quoted in Thomassin, 7:186, my translation.

declaring that common services, both current and in arrears, and other customary dues, were not forbidden by the ordinance. The bishop then asked for recognition of the custom of spoils in Languedoc, where it had operated ever since the curia came to Avignon, and the royal reply was that the ordinance of prohibition would not be executed in the south as long as the *modificatio* of spoils was also observed as a custom.

The conciliar reformers of the early fifteenth century were strongly opposed to papal spoliation as one of the most blatant invasions of episcopal and national rights. The Pisan pope, Alexander V, renounced them, as an unreasonable burden on the churches, on 27 July 1409, immediately after his election by the Council of Pisa:[22]

Our lord notified all, through the mouth of the archishop of Pisa, that he did not intend in future to reserve the goods or spoils of prelates as in the past.

The acts of the Council of Pisa bear witness to the concerns and intentions of the reformers, but they had no lasting effect; when John XXIII succeeded Alexander V, he collected spoils.

The chorus of reforming voices against spoliation continued to swell, and it came to include Dietrich of Niem, clerk in the chanceries of eight successive popes,[23] whose *avisamenta* to the Council of Constance make a telling contrast to the *petitio* of Ramon Lull one century earlier (above, chapter 4). Lull had looked at the luxurious lives of his contemporary prelates and proposed collecting their spoils as part of a program of crusading discipline; Dietrich saw the enemy within the church and the luxury at the very top, while the papal collectors served their own interests with the unlimited powers vested in them by three simultaneous popes. He proposed eradicating the practice of spoils.[24]

When the bishop of a cathedral church or the abbot of any monastery dies, in Italy and certain other places, immediately the collectors of first-fruits of the Apostolic Camera receive the moneys, clothing, books, jewels, houses, utensils, horses, cows, oxen and other animals, the grain: in short, all the movables and moving creatures; and also all the credits and rights and legal actions whatsoever, which had belonged to the deceased when he was alive, which they call spoils, they grab and extort to the bottom, and apply them to their own and the Camera's uses, although these things should in reason remain to the same churches and monasteries, or at least be reserved for the successors. On this account, these churches and monasteries are greatly destroyed, and divine worship and regular observance in the monasteries is neglected, nor can the required works of charity be done in them. And on top of this, before provisions

---

[22]Mansi, 26 (1784): 1154E-1156B; my translation. The entry in Du Cange s.v. *spolium* is, consequently, just confusing: "Charta an. 1409 ex Tabul. S. Victoris Massil.: 'Ludovicus II rex Jerusalem et Siciliae et comes Provinciae jubet praelatos solvere Camerae Apostolicae omnia arreragia, debita etiam spoliorum defunctorum Praelatorum secundum [decretum] Alexandri PP III [sic] in Concilio Pisis habito.' "

[23]See E. F. Jacob, "Dietrich of Niem," *Essays in the Conciliar Epoch* (Manchester, 1953), 24-41.

[24]Ed. Finke, *Acta concilii constanciensis*, 4:625-626, my translation.

can be made to the said vacant churches and monasteries, it is necessary for the candidates to strike a bargain with the said officials of the Camera or their deputies for new large sums of money, and that they really pay these, even though on that account the churches and monasteries be nearly destroyed; and so what the worm does not eat, the locust consumes. The churches and monasteries are perceptibly declining in this way to a worse condition. Although this is an old observance, perhaps based on the apostolic *plenitudo potestatis*, still, because it is intolerably damaging to these churches and monasteries, it should definitely be abolished.

The topics of the argument against spoils had become commonplace by the time an anonymous French commentator (whose language and point of view remind me strongly of Honoré Bonet, prior of Salon, who died about 1410),[25] wryly offered fifty-eight theses for debate in the forthcoming Council. Here is one of them concerning spoils, accompanied by five more, for flavor:[26]

Should one of the cardinals be elected [pope]? They all belong to the three partisan factions, and each can be expected to be more worthless than his former master and a user of that master's methods, for to all the world is manifest their justice, charity, truth, benignity, generosity, and cupidity ...

Should the pope not be compelled to retain an almoner to visit hospitals, leprosaria and such, just as he has collectors to gather, *cubicularii* to serve him, secretaries to do evil, armed squires to help them, pedlars to sell benefices? ...

Should not the pope be compelled to provide for one holy man to visit the islands of the infidels and the lands of the schismatics, to comfort the hearts of the faithful of God who are captives and slaves there, just as they maintain collectors there to gather spoils? ...

Should the pope receive the spoils of prelates and others who do not die in the curia? In many places, out of these spoils, books could be copied, chalices, missals, vestments, and clothing for the poor could be bought and distributed, and churches repaired and roofed, all of which things are needed. Worse yet, the collectors do not pay off the servants of the deceased, but carry the spoils to their relatives, sons and daughters; and the pope has sometimes the smaller share in his purse and the greater load on his conscience.[27] Alexander V of happy memory made at Pisa a very good and laudable provision on this matter which his successor refused to follow. Testimony should be heard from the men of Languedoc in France, those of Lodève in Provence, and many places.[28]

Is it fitting that the pope have more than four protonotaries? There were only

---

[25]The anonymous author was also, like Bonet, well acquainted with the practice of the Camera at Avignon; see Alfred Coville, *La vie intellectuelle* ... (Paris, 1935), 214-318.

[26]Ed. Finke, *Acta concilii constanciensis*, 2:547-548, 580-592, my translation.

[27]There is an echo here of Innocent III, *De miseria humanae conditionis* 2.5.

[28]The meaning seems to be that in France, Languedoc was especially afflicted, and in Provence, Lodève. The latter may have been chosen as an outstanding case because of its experience of five despoiled bishops, 1331-1375; but Lodève is not in Provence strictly speaking, but in central southern Languedoc.

four evangelists. It seems to me that nothing is increased by the multiplication but expense. ...

Would it not be more fitting to fix the number of lord cardinals at twelve than to multiply them? Many do not have wherewith to live according to their taste, or rather their arrogance. This was partly the cause of the division of the church, or at least of the present extension of the schism, for anyone can see, since the time of Gregory XI, whether the cardinals have supported their masters on account of the miracles they worked, or the benefices they conferred! Incidentally, the more there are of them, the bigger the war they wage.

The reforming party had its day. The agenda of the University of Paris[29] were accepted by the national conciliar commissions and then adopted by the Council of Constance in plenary session on 9 October 1417:[30]

Because the reservation, exaction, and reception by the pope of the procurations owed to ordinaries and lesser prelates by reason of visitation, and of the spoils of deceased prelates and other clerics cause grave detriment to churches, monasteries and other benefices, and to ecclesiastical persons, we declare by the present edict that it is according to reason and helpful to the common good that such reservations by the pope and exactions or receipts by collectors and others deputed by apostolic authority, are absolutely not to be done or attempted henceforth; that instead these procurations of any prelates whatsoever, even cardinals, and the spoils or goods of the pope's own familiars, officials, or of any clerics at all, who die within the Roman curia or outside, at any time and anywhere, belong freely to, and should be received by, those to whom otherwise, the aforesaid reservations, mandates and exactions being ended, they belong and should pertain. And we forbid also the exaction of spoils by lesser prelates and others, as being beyond and against the form of the common law, the constitution of Boniface VIII which begins *Praesenti*, issued in this matter especially, which is to remain in full force.

---

[29]Finke, 1:145 and 4:581.
[30]Finke, 2:622-624, my translation.

Appendices

Appendix A

A Typical Testamentary License, 1327

This privilege was issued in 1327 by John XXII to Arnaldus Cescomes, bishop of Lerida, who died as archbishop of Tarragona in 1346. It was registered with the common letters when it was issued (EFR *Jean XXII communes*, n. 30352). Upon the archbishop's death, the papal commissioner, Guillelmus de Platulis, copied the original license into his accounts of the spoils, *Collectoriae* 473, 2^{rv}, from which the following transcription was taken.

Joannes episcopus seruus seruorum Dei uenerabili fratri Arnaldo episcopo Ilerdensi, salutem et apostolicam benedictionem.

Quia presentis uite conditio statum habet instabilem, et ea que uisibilem habent essentiam tendunt uisibiliter ad non esse, tu hoc salubri meditatione meditans diem tue peregrinationis extremum dispositione testamentaria desideres preuenire, nos itaque tuis supplicationibus inclinati, ut de bonis tuis undecunque tibi, non per ecclesiam seu ecclesias tibi commissas, alias tamen licite acquisitis, que ad te pertinere dinascuntur [sic] libere testari ualeas, ac de bonis mobilibus ecclesiasticis tue dispositioni seu administrationi commissis, que tamen non fuerunt altaris seu altarium ecclesiarum tibi commissarum in misterio seu alicui speciali earundem ecclesiarum diuino cultui seu usui deputata, necnon et quibuscumque bonis mobilibus a te per ecclesiam seu ecclesias licite acquisitis, pro decentibus et honestis expensis tui funeris, et pro remuneratione illorum qui tibi uiuenti seruiuerunt siue sint consanguinei siue alii iuxta seruitii meritum modice tamen disponere et erogare possis et alias prius earundem ecclesiarum ere alieno deducto ut eedem ecclesie non remaneant debitis obligate de illis in pios usus conuertendis, plenam et liberam[1] fraternitati tue auctoritate presentium concedimus facultatem. Volumus autem ut in earundem ecclesiarum dispositione bonorum, iuxta quantitatem residui erga ecclesias a quibus eadem percepisti te liberalem exhibeas prout conscientia tibi dictauerit et anime tue saluti uideris expedire.

Datum Auinione 3 idus Nouembris pontificatus nostri anno 12° [11 November 1327].

---

[1] In a viva voce order to his Chancery on 24 October 1363, Urban V declared that the inclusion or omission of the word *liberam* did not affect the value of a license: von Ottenthal, *Regulae Cancellariae Apostolicae* (1888), 14.

Appendix B

A Typical Commission for Spoils, 1346

Notwithstanding the testamentary license edited in Appendix A, the spoils of Arnaldus Cescomes were reserved and the following joint commission granted to investigate and collect them. It is edited from the final accounts in Coll. 473, 1ʳ-2ʳ.

Clemens episcopus seruus seruorum Dei, dilectis filiis [Guillelmo de Platulis] archidiacono Villeficte Terraconensis, et Almeracio de Cabrespino canonico Ilerdensis ecclesiarum, salutem et apostolicam benedictionem.

Cum bone memorie Arnaldus archiepiscopus Terraconensis in diuersis pecuniarum summis ex diuersis causis legitimis, necnon rationes reddere de diuersis bonis et prouentibus ad Cameram nostram spectantibus per eum perceptis hactenus eidem Camere dum adhuc uiueret teneretur adstrictus, nos, uolentes eiusdem Camere prouidere ut tenemur indempnitatibus in hac parte hiis et aliis rationabilibus causis suadentibus, pridem cum adhuc idem archiepiscopus in humanis ageret, bonorum mobilium ipsius archiepiscopi ac eorum que ad ipsum spectabant et poterant quomodolibet pertinere dispositionem ut inde ualeret prefate Camere de premissis rationabiliter satisfieri, et alias quod nobis uideretur expediens ordinari, nobis duximus specialiter reseruandam.

Cupientes igitur de bonis predictis certiores effici, et ea pro predictis complendis fideliter custodiri discretioni uestre per apostolica scripta comitimus et mandamus, quatinus per uos uel alium seu alios de bonis et debitis eisdem simpliciter et de plano sine strepitu et figura iudicii uos informantes ea in quibuscumque rebus consistant et per quascumque detineantur uel debeantur personas nomine nostra petere, exigere, recipere ac fideliter et integraliter conseruare curetis, contradictores quoslibet et rebelles cuiuscumque status, ordinis, dignitatis uel conditionis existant, etiam si pontificali uel quauis alia prefulgeant dignitate per censuram ecclesiasticam appelatione postposita compescendum, non obstante si eis uel eorum aliquibus communiter uel diuisim a sede apostolica sit indultum quod interdici, suspendi uel excommunicari non possint per litteras apostolicas non facientes plenam et expressam et de uerbo ad uerbum de indulto huiusmodi mentionem, et qualibet alia dicte sedis indulgentia generali uel speciali cuiuscumque tenoris existat, per quam presentibus non expressam uel totaliter non insertam effectus presentium impediri posset quomodolibet uel differi. Volumus autem quod eos qui nobis assignanda, restituenda uel soluenda duxerint dicta bona, possitis absoluere pleniusque quitare de hiis que inde ab ipsis recipere uos contigeret, facienda super singulis assignationibus, restitutionibus uel solutionibus huiusmodi duo confici publica instrumenta, quorum uno penes assignantes ipsis [sic] dimisso, et reliqum ad eandem mittere Cameram procuretis cum certificaturis de premissis nichilominus clare, particulariter et distincte.

Porro nostre intentionis existit quod redditis predictis rationibus et satisfactio[ne facta] prefate Camere de hiis in quibus idem archiepiscopus dum uiueret tenebatur eidem debita bona et legalia memorati archiepiscopi et legata pia pro remuneratione seruitorum, decenti et alia qua rationabilia fuerit de bonis predictis prout sufficienter paruerint persoluentur, et alias per nos ordinetur quod rationi et honestati uidebimus conuenire.

Datum Auinione 18 kalendas Octobris pontificatus nostri [Clementis VI] anno quinto [14 September 1346].

Appendix C

A *Consilium* for Spoils (1368?)

Instrumenta miscellanea n. 6427, written on two paper sheets sewn end to end: a legal assessment by Bertrand de Mazel in favor of the right of Cardinal Raymond de Canilhac to the movable goods of Wilhelm Pinchon, late provost of Mainz. The original legal citations have been placed in the notes, augmented with the modern forms.

Allegationes

Ad ostendendum quod bona, que erant domini G. Pinchon, predecessoris domini mei R[aymundi] Penestrensis episcopi cardinalis nunc prepositi Mog[untini], recondita et recollecta tempore mortis ipsius et que obuenerunt tempore uacationis et post fuit dicto domino meo cardinali reseruanda assignanda et restituenda, ostenditur rationibus que sequuntur.

Primo debent ad dictum dominum meum peruenire quia dignitas prepositure Mog[untine] ante mortem predecessoris domini mei erat Sedi Apostolice specialiter reseruata, ita quod nullus de ea disponere ordinare nec prouidere poterat nisi solus papa, qui de ea prouidit dicto domino meo cardinali.

Item ex quo dignitas predicta erat per papam reseruata et omnia bona [−Came] dicti predecessoris \censentur reseruata et sic/ Camere Apostolice debentur et non alii, quia accessorium sequitur principali,[2] et sic clause sunt manus et ligate super bonis predictis executoribus dicti domini G. et quibuscunque aliis Camera Apostolica excepta.

Item quod bona predicta debeant peruenire ad successorem probatur tam iure quam ratione, nam dictus dominus meus emit omnia bona a Camera Apostolica sui predecessoris et sub certa pecunie quantitate

---

[2]De regulis iuris: VI.5.13.42, "Accessorium naturam sequi congruit principalis," cum similibus.

prout Camera [−ue] sibi uendere poterat ratione predicta, quod non emisset nisi dicta bona essent reseruata ut predixi.

Preterea ostenditur quod de iure communi ad dictum dominum \ meum/ ut ad successorem bona omnia debent peruenire non solum bona mobilia ymmo et immobilia quia nomine bonorum bona mobilia et immobilia continentur,[3] nam breuius conscriptum siue inuentarium debet fieri scilicet de utensilibus et omni supellectili, ita quod omnia sunt restituenda, unde si aliqua fuerunt retenta, talis ut conuictus pro furtu debet condempnari.

Item secundum quod bona episcopi defuncti sunt futuro successori reseruanda et restituenda,[4] et si contrarium factum fuerit tales occupatores ut sacrilegi debent puniri, anatematis mucrone feriri, peregrina commune eis debet denegari et qualescumque fuerint excommunicationis sententie debet mandari. Sic et bona prepositi seu archidyaconi successori reseruantur.[5] Distinguendo tamen, quia si bona prepositure sei archidyaconatus distincta sunt [−et ordinata] a rebus canonicorum, ut in casu nostro, tunc successori bona [−de] sunt reseruanda et restituenda.[6] Si uero bona \ omnia/ archidyaconatus seu prepositure et canonicorum sunt communia, tunc ad capitulum bona deuoluntur.[7] Unde per hoc apparet quod ex quo bona reseruantur seu debent reseruari futuro successori quod de talibus bonis nullus testari potest.[8]

Preterea de dictis bonis predecessor ordinare, testari nec disponere poterat que fuerunt intuitu ecclesie et non persone acquisita nec aliqua legare, cum ipsius proprietas non fuerit sua sed ecclesie, sed si est consuetudo potest de dictis bonis aliqua dare et erogare pauperibus et religiosis locis et illis qui defuncto seruierant, siue sint consanguinei siue alii, iuxta seruitii meritum ipsorum; que tamen ex hereditate peruenerant distribuantur pro arbitrio decedentis prout hec habentur et leguntur.[9]

Item prelatus habens administrationem quandiu uiuit et sanus est potest [−dare] donare, moderate tamen, comparatur usufructuario cum nichil habeat nisi usum tantum, nam eius ius morte finitur sicut ius usufructuarii.[10] Clericus uero simpliciter beneficiatus administrationem non habens et in uita et in morte comparatur usufructuario quantum ad

---

[3] De verborum significatione, c. Bonorum: D 50.16.49 and 208; X 3.26.12; nota Archidiaconus in c. Presenti, Extra [sic] VI 1.16.9, super uerbo bona: "et dicit bona, scilicet a minimo usque ad maximum" ut C.12 q.5 c. Sicubi defunctus (6) et C.12 q.2 c. Caritatem (45).

[4] C.12 q.2 c. Hec huius placiti (38) et c. De laycis (46) et c. Illud (47).

[5] Prout notauit in gloza ordinaria in c. Relatum iam allegato, X 3.26.12.

[6] Archidiaconus in X 1.3.21.

[7] Archidiaconus in C.12 q.2 c.29 et X 3.30.30 et D 8 c.2.

[8] Prout notauit Archidiaconus in Extra [sic] De rescriptis, Statutum, VI 1.3.11, para.5 Assessorem, super uerbo *proprie*.

[9] X 3.26 c. Relatum (12) et c. Ad hec (8) et c. Quia nos (9).

[10] X 3.25 c. Si quis sane (5).

faciendum fructus suos; nam tales clerici de perceptis fructibus et [−recon] horreo reconditis testari possunt.[11]

Preterea nullus episcopus, archiepiscopus aut patriarcha aut alius superior seu abbas uel alius inferior potest nec debet occupare bona predecessoris nisi ex priuilegio speciali uel consuetudine iam prescripta licite \ vel alia causa rationabili/ quod si fecerint episcopi et superiores sunt suspensi ab ingressu ecclesie, alii inferiores ab [−ben] officio et beneficio quousque restitutionem fecerint receptori.[12]

Item si dicatur quod de consuetudine bona predicta peruenerint et peruenire debuerint ad executorem seu manufideles et non ad successorem, requirit antequam talis consuetudo preiudicium successori et iuri communi, cum de iure communi bona debeant peruenire ad successorem, quod consuetudo suffragetur rationi et ueritati cum semper ius preiudicet consuetudini, et consuetudo iuri et rationi sit postponenda.

Item requiritur quod consuetudo sit rationabilis et licite prescripta salti [sic] spatio XL annorum;[13] item quod fuit obtenta in contradictorio iudicio populi;[14] item quod cum animo fiat ut credatur se ius habere ut imposterum illud intendant facere, alioquin talis usus non dicitur usus sed abusus;[15] item quod res illa sit prescriptabilis;[16] item quod sit antiqua et approbata;[17] item debet continere uirtualem equitatem;[18] item quod sit de certa conscientia principis inducta, non tantum de tollerantia;[19] item quod non sit inducta per errorem sed ex certa scientia;[20] item quod maior pars consueuit illa consuetudine uti, quia sicut minor pars populi non possit inducere legem [−siue consue] sic nec consuetudinem. Unde dico quod nunquam ex sola consuetudine, licet esset prescripta, ius aliquod sit quesitum, nisi forte esset tanta [?] cuius memorie non esset.[21] Item sole uices non inducunt consuetudinem quia non exemplis sed legibus iudicandum est [−Item].[22] Item minor prescriptio quam centenaria non currit contra Romanam Ecclesiam.[23]

Item ubi in rebus ecclesiasticis aliquis allegat prescriptionem requiritur bona fides et iustus tytulus quando allegans non potest de iure communia talia possidere. Cum ergo dicti executores non possint bona

---

[11]Prout hec notantur per Johannem Andree in *VI* 1.16 c. Presenti (9).
[12]Ut in capitulo Presenti, *VI* 1.16.9.
[13] *X* 2.12 c. Cum ecclesia (3).
[14]Ut *X* 5.40 c. Abbate.
[15]*D* 43.19.1, para. Iulianus.
[16]D.90 c. Illud [sic].
[17] *X* 1.5 in II circa medium [sic].
[18]*X* 1.4 c. Ex parte (10).
[19]*X* 2.26 c. Causam (7) iamdudum [sic].
[20]D.8 c.Consuetudo (8).
[21]*D* 43.20 Hoc iure (3).
[22]*C* 7.45 l. Nemo (13), prout hec omnia leguntur et notantur *D* 8.7; C.18 q.2 Seruitium (31); et *X* 1.4 Cum tanto (11).
[23]*X* 2.26 Si diligenti (17) in fine; et *VI* 2.13.2.

predecessoris possidere de iure communi, cum ius commune eis resistat, necessario habent probare bonam fidem et iustum tytulum.

Item quando est presumptio contra possidentem non procedit prescriptio sine tytulo,[24] sed contra illos qui dicunt quod bona predecessoris non peruenerunt ad successorem est presumptio iuris, ergo bona fides illis non sufficit, sed est necessarius tytulus qui possessori tamen tribuat prescribendi.[25]

Item ubi petitor fundat intentionem suam de iure communi tunc prescribens habet necessarie probare tytulum nec sufficit probare prescriptum esse in tali ecclesia loco seu personis nisi probetur specificitate locum prescriptorem habuisse et prescripsisse in loco seu persona de quibus proprie agitur.[26] Cum ergo ius commune resistat executoribus cum ex tali iure bona predecessoris debent peruenire ad successorem, dicti executores habent probare consuetudinem et prescriptionem in ecclesia kathedrali Mog[untina] locum sibi diutius uendicasse. Ex predictis omnibus concluditur quod tam ex reseruatione quam de iure communi et ex consuetudine, bona predecessoris non debent peruenire ad executores sed ad dominum meum cardinalem antedictum.

Hec ego Bertrandus de Macello predixi et allegaui saluo meliori consilio peritorum.

Appendix D

Negotiations between the French Royal Council and the Camera Apostolica, after 1385

ASV Instrumenta Miscellanea 4283 is a file of four large paper sheets, formerly sewn as a roll, containing minutes of the pleading by Pierre Gerard, bishop of Le Puy (1385-1390) for the revocation of the royal ordinance against spoils (6 October 1385), and the replies of the royal council.

. . . Sequuntur articuli super quibus est prouisio seu ordinatio facta per regem super quibus queritur de remedio:

Primo quia papa uult habere bona episcoporum post mortem ipsorum, ipsa tollenda heredibus qui debent per consuetudinem succedere aut executoribus testamentorum suorum, unde sequitur quod edifficia et habitationes dictorum episcopatuum deueniunt in ruinam in desertum in maximum dampnum regis et sui dominii, preiudicium ecclesiarum et deformitatem regni, quia collectores nolunt pati sibi aliquas reparationes ad quas fuissent astricti heredes ipsorum episcoporum aut executores si bona ipsorum habuissent. Et una cum

---

[24]Prout notauit Innocentius ad X 2.30 in c. Cum dilecta (4), in glosa *nam si*.
[25]*VI* 2.13 c. Episcopum (1).
[26]Prout notauit Innocentius ad X 2.22.15.

hoc subditi regis quibus huiusmodi bona peruenire seu pertinere debuissent sunt exhereditati de hoc quod eis pertinebat, et propter hec non possunt seruire regi in suis guerris, nec aliter, ita bene seu conuenienter sicut si haberent illa bona.

Item quod peius est post mortem abbatum collectores recipiunt bona mobilia sub umbra quod per dominum nostrum papam sunt reseruata, quamuis abbates non habent bona propria, et propter hoc successores abbates non habent de quo substinere possint ediffica dictarum abbatiarum, unde deueniunt in ruinam, et eis opportet soluere seruitium curie Romane et administrare uictualia religiosis, propter quod eis opportet uendere libros, ornamenta et alia iocalia suarum ecclesiarum, et sepissime uendere redditus ad uitam, unde dicte ecclesie sunt et morantur destructe, et opportet diminuere numerum religiosorum et seruitium diuinum. ...

Sequuntur requisitiones facte per dictum dominum Aniciensem gentibus regis super reuocationem et emendationem ordinationum predictarum, et responsiones per consilium regis, eidem super hoc facte:

Super infrascriptis in quibus est certa ordinatio facta per regem, petitur quod placeat regi de remedio opportuno prouidere, nam propter dictam ordinationem iura Camere Apostolice sunt ex toto uel quasi adnichilata, ymo quod est de[te]stabile, illi qui tenentur Camere Apostolice quantumcumque sint potentes ad soluendum sunt omnino inobedientes, nec curant de sententiis latis, nec de processibus apostolicis, ymo uulgariter dicunt quod ex parte regis inhibitum est eis, ut de nullo satisfaciant gentibus dicti domini nostri pape.

(Responsio per regem) Per ordinationem regis iura domini nostri pape de quibus fit mentio in articulo precedente non impediuntur in aliquo, et nichilominus dominus noster rex dabit litteras declaratorias quod non fuit sue intentionis quod per ordinationem nouiter factum iura antiqua domini nostri pape seu eius Camere Apostolice, uidelicet in seruitiis communibus et arreragiis temporis preteriti, et aliis deneriis que Camera Apostolica ab antiquo de et super beneficiis regni accipere consueuit, in aliquo impediantur, mandabitur quia omnibus etc., quod de iuribus et deneriis predictis collectores domini nostri pape uti et gaudere permittatur. ...

Item cum predecessores domini nostri pape a tempore quo curia fuit citra montes et a tempore de quo non extat memoria de contrario reseruauerunt bona prelatorum decedentium in lingua occitana cum certa tamen modificatione rationabili, et ea post decessum dictorum prelatorum habuerunt sine contradictione quacumque, et per ordinationem nunc per regem factam generaliter sit mandatum quod bona prelatorum qualitercumque decedentium in regno pertineant ad heredes et ipsa habeant in magnum preiudicium dicti domini nostri pape et sue Camere, placeat regi super hoc de remedio opportuno prouidere et Cameram antiquam [sic] in suis libertatibus antiquis tueri, et ipsarum possessione et saisina teneri.

(Responsio per regem) Predicta ordinatio de presenti non mandabor executari in lingua occitana, attentis actis modificationibus per dictum dominum episcopum Aniciensem, traditis et declaratis quas ut asserit dominus noster papa uult inuiolabiliter obseruari, uidelicet quod quando Camera Apostolica capit bona prelatorum decedentium in lingua occitana predicta, primo fit super dictis bonis sepultura deffuncti condecedenter, secundo remunerantur seruitores ipsius, et soluantur debita hinc contracta, item utensilia necessaria ad hospitium ecclesie et animalia necessaria ad agriculturas numquam consueuit Camera recipere, prouidet etiam dicta Camera nouo successori usque ad nouos fructus, bona etiam mobilia que dictus deffunctus per industriam acquisierat, uel ex successione parentum eidem obuenerant, heredibus ipsius deffuncti aut executoribus sui testamenti, si quod fecerit, tradentur et deliberabuntur. ...

II. REPERTORY OF CASES OF THE PAPAL RIGHT OF SPOIL

1] Ademarus Amelii, papal treasurer, bishop of Marseille, died in curia 23 Dec 1333. Formerly canon and succentor of Albi, bishop from 1323.

10 Jul 1329 (EFR J2, 3902) licentia testandi.
20 Jul 1329 (Coll. 143, 289ʳ-293ᵛ) testament witnessed in Camera.
15 Dec 1333 (IM 5325) codicil; see *Gall. Christ.* 1:656E-657B.
23 Dec 1333 (IE 133, 1ʳ) commission to Pontius de Pereto and Raymundus de Marrolha.
2 Jan 1334 (IE 133, 8ʳ-58ᵛ) commissioners' accounts.
7 Apr 1335 (EFR B3, 148) quittance to camerarius Gasbertus de Valle and treasurer Guido Radolphi.
20 Jan - 16 Feb 1337 (EFR B2, 5211) accounts of the execution of the testament.
5 Sep 1337 (EFR B2, 361) camerarius is ordered to release goods for the payment of pious legacies.
13 Jan 1338 (IM 1340) payments of legacies by nephew-executor Bernardus Amelii.
5 Mar 1339 (VQ 4, 140) commissioners pay 2322 fl., etc.
25 Mar 1339 (EFR B1, 7424; B2, 583; B3, 2289) quittance to the nephew-executor.

2] Ademarus Froterii OCSA, provost of S. Salvy, Albi.

28 Nov 1330 (OS 12, 136ʳ) commissioner Raymundus de Cameraco pays 8 fl. Pied.
1335 (Coll. 29, 199ᵛ) accounts of commissioner Arnaldus de Verdala.

3] Ademarus Roberti, archbishop of Sens, died 25 Jan 1385. LL.D., formerly provost of Furnes, diocese of Thérouanne; bishop of Lisieux from 1359; of Arras from 1368; of Thérouanne from 1371; archbishop of Sens from 1376.

1 Feb 1385 (Coll. 360, 208ʳ-209ʳ) camerarius Franciscus de Conzia orders the nuncio Petrus Gerardi, bishop of Lodève, and Armandus Jusserandi, collector of Sens and Rouen, to take the spoils in order to pay overdue services.

4] Ademarus de Volta, bishop of Viviers, died 1365. Formerly provost of Apt; bishop of Viviers from 1326; of Valence-Die from 1331; of Viviers again from 1337.

27 Sep 1365 (IM 2378, 26; IE 303, 30ᵛ-31ʳ) executor Joannes de Chaylerio pays a composition of 750 fl.

27 Sep 1365 (Coll. 353, 49ᵛ-50ʳ) list of goods by Geraldus Mercaderii includes 1000 fl., 211 m. of silverware, 20 books, etc.

before 1370 (Coll. 19, 165ʳ) accounts of Geraldus Mercaderii.

5] Aegidius de Bellamera, bishop of Avignon, died before 29 Mar 1407. J.U.Prof., formerly auditor litterarum contradictarum; bishop of Lavaur from 1383; of Le Puy from 1390; of Avignon from 1392. See *Gall. Christ.* 1:826C-827A.

1 Apr 1407 (RA 51, 57ʳ; RA 54, 95ʳ) reservation of spoils.

6] Aegidius Blasii Boni de Cortonio OESA, bishop of Vicenza, died in curia before Jun 1361.

17 Sep 1361 (VQ 7, 357) Eblo de Mederio, clerk of the Camera, collects 1000 fl. composition.

15 Sep 1362 (Coll. 231, 142ʳ) commissioner Raymundus de Salgis, archbishop of Embrun, pays 300 fl.

16 Sep 1362 (ibid., 142ᵛ) commissioner pays 289 fl.

7] Aegidius de Viana, bishop of Idanha, died before 26 May 1363. Formerly dean of Idanha; bishop from 1358.

ca.1370 (Arm.XXXIII, to.18, 176ʳ-180ʳ) spoils accounts of Bertrandus de Macello: £2050.1.4 received for the last three bishops of Idanha.

8] Agapitus de Columna, bishop of Lisbon (Urbanist) deposed in 1378 by Clement VII and his goods confiscated. Lic.Decr., formerly papal chaplain and archdeacon of Bologna; bishop of Ascoli Piceno from 1363; of Brescia from 1369; of Lisbon from 1371.

1378 (RA 91, 302ᵛ-315ᵛ) inventory of confiscated goods, in Portuguese.

9] Aimon de Cossonay, bishop of Lausanne, died 4 Mar 1375. Formerly treasurer of Lausanne; bishop from 1355.

11 Apr 1375 (Coll. 356, 13ʳ-14ʳ) commissions and instructions by camerarius Petrus de Croso to Guillelmus de Lacu.

1 Jun 1375 (Coll. 479A, 1ʳ-17ᵛ) commissioner's accounts.

29 Sep 1375 (Coll. 356, 64ʳ) commission to Joannes de Cabrespino.

26 Jan 1379 (OS 42, 143ʳ) successor Guido de Prangins pays 200 fl. de Alamannia (Rheingulden), a composition settled with Guillelmus de Lacu.

10] Aimon de Villersexel, archbishop of Besançon, died 10 Dec 1370. Formerly archdeacon of Besançon; archbishop from 1363.

20 Jan 1371 (EFR G1, 18) commission to Petrus Ebrardi, abbot of S. Vincent, Besançon, and Aubricus Radolphi.
The collection of spoils caused a civic riot in which the abbot commissioner was killed: *Gall. Christ.* 15:191A-D.
8 Jul 1375 (EFR G1, 2604) orders Guillelmus de Vergy, archbishop of Besançon, to excommunicate the murderers of the abbot.
19 Apr 1384 (Coll. 360) Guillelmus de Vergy is granted a delay in his payment of 200 fr. for the sale of a mitre and crozier.

11] Alamandus de S. Gorio, bishop of Geneva, died before 10 Apr 1366. Bishop from 1342.

Jul 1366 (IM 2435, 13) commissioner Gerladus de Calma, administrator of the Pinhota, pays 598 fl., 40 fr., £28.6.6 Avin.
27 Feb 1368 (EFR U2, 2712) sentence against the nephew Petrus de S. Gorio, knight, for holding money, silverware, clothing, horses and cattle.
16 Mar 1372 (Coll. 358, 30^r) the subcollector of Geneva is ordered to collect the bishop's debts.

12] Alanus, bishop of Quimper, died before 3 Oct 1352. Bishop from 1336.

15 Oct 1352 (EFR C1, 5427) commission.
18 Apr 1358 (Coll. 255, 127^r) 500 écus collected.
15 Jun 1361 (VQ 7, 340) successor Goffridus de Coetmoisan, now bishop of Dol, pays 332 fl. Cam. 16s. of his composition.
14 Aug 1362 (Coll 231, 137^v) successor Goffridus pays 332 fl.

13] Alanus, auditor sacri palatii.

13 Aug 1348 (VQ 5, 410) executor pays 52 fl. of a composition for 100 fl.; (OS 23A, 96^v) the balance was still outstanding temp. Urban V.

14] Albertus Lordati, bishop of Mende, died 1361. Formerly archdeacon of Flavigny, diocese of Autun, papal chaplain; bishop from 1331.

4 Jul 1332 (EFR J1, 57691) licentia testandi.
2 May 1362 (Coll. 497, 78^r) successor Guillelmus obligated to a composition of 3000 fl.
20 May 1362 (VQ 7, 404) successor pays 1300 fl.
18 Jun 1362 (ibid., 409) successor pays 200 fl.
22 Jun 1364 (Coll. 353, 12^{r}v) composition payment delayed to next Easter.
20 Dec 1365 (IE 303, 32^v) successor pays 347 fl. Fr. 16s.
Jul 1366 (IM 2435, 14) successor pays 226 fl.

15] **Alelmus Boestel, archbishop of Tours. Formerly provost of S. Dié, diocese of Tulle, LL.Lic.; archbishop from 20 Jun 1380.**

Sep 1381 (Coll. 359, 86ᵛ-87ᵛ) successor Guido de Roya permitted to use the funds from spoils necessary for repairs to houses, mills and granaries.

16] **Alfonsus, bishop of Palencia, died before 29 Oct 1382. Bishop from 16 Sep 1381.**

9 Jan 1383 (Coll. 360, 32ʳᵛ) commission to Seguinus, patriarch of Antioch and administrator of Nîmes, nuncio in Spain, and to Fulco Pererii, to collect a debt of 500 fl. for services from the spoils.

17] **Alfonsus Annes, bishop of Silves, died before 31 Jul 1331. Formerly canon of Braga; bishop of Silves from 1313.**

26 Jun 1332 (VQ 1, 565) payments from spoils by successor Petrus.

18] **Alfonsus Dionysii, bishop of Evora, died before 3 Oct 1352. M.Theol.; formerly bishop of Idanha from 1346; of Evora from 1347.**

15 Oct 1352 (EFR C2, 2697) commission.

19] **Alfonsus Petri, bishop of Porto. Formerly canon of Porto; bishop from 1355.**

9 Dec 1372 (Coll. 504, 8 fols.) inventory by subcollector Dominicus, canon of Porto.

20] **Alvarus Petri de Biedma, bishop of Orense. Former archdeacon of Basconcillos, diocese of Orense; bishop of Mondoñedo from 1329; of Orense from 1343.**

6 Jun 1351 (EFR C2, 2443) commission.
13 Jan 1354 (EFR I1, 716) commission to Gometius Manrique, archbishop of Compostela, and Joannes de Cardalhaco, bishop of Orense, to cite the dean and chapter of Orense, who are holding the spoils and the income of the vacancy.

21] **Amalricus Augerii OCSA, prior of Espira, diocese of Elne, and collector of Narbonne, died in curia.**

1359 (RA 140, 17ʳ) rubric: licentia testandi.
13 Dec 1364 (Coll. 353, 23ʳ) commission to Joannes Garrigie.
Dec 1365 (IM 2339, 38) Joannes Manchini of the Barruchi company of Florence pays 76 fr. for spoils.
1368 (Coll. 156, 130ᵛ) £12 received for silver in spoils.
31 Mar 1373 (EFR G1, 1183) commission to Bertrandus Raffini.

23 Jul 1378 (OS 42, 127^v) quittance to Durandus Bartonis, officialis of Carpentras, for a *Rosarium*.

22] Amalvinus de Roquelaure OSB, abbot of S. Victor de Marseille, died in curia shortly after 8 Sep 1348. Abbot from 1340: *Gall. Christ.* 1:692D.

5 Aug 1342 (Coll. 143, 182^r) licentia testandi.
8 Sep 1348 (ibid., 182^r-187^r) testament.
8 Sep 1348 (EFR C1, 3949) commission to Joannes de Nabayrone, scriptor Papae.
12 Sep 1348 (EFR C1, 3953) same commission.
16 Dec 1348 (VQ 5, 415) executor Guillelmus de Leschemel, abbot of S. Guillem du Desert, diocese of Lodève, pays composition of 1500 fl. for goods in Avignon.
19 Jun 1350 (ibid., 437) commissioner Pontius de Hermaldis pays 97 fl.
16 Oct 1350 (ibid., 441) he pays 120 fl.
15 Nov 1350 (ibid.) successor Stephanus de Planteriis pays 174 fl. 13 s.
23 Jan 1352 (ibid., 451) Guillelmus Lufansant pays 100 fl.

23] Amanevus de Apta de Mota, archbishop of Bordeaux, died 27 Jun 1360. Formerly canon of Bordeaux; archbishop from 1351.

23 Feb 1361 (Coll. 497, 73^v) Petrus and Gallardus de Mota, knights, obligated to a composition of 1100 fl., to be paid to the collector of Bordeaux.
18 May 1362 (VQ 7, 403) they pay 228 fl. sent. 18 s.
1363 (IM 2281, 3^v) accounts of spoils, following the records of Elias Magnan, abbot of S. Salvator de Blaye, diocese of Bordeaux, collector.
10 Sep 1364 (EFR U2, 1221) commission to Sancius Vaquerii to collect from Petrus and Galhardus de Mota 1900 fl., owed for spoils and a debt for the thirtieth subsidy.

24] Amanevus de Arminiaco, archbishop of Auch, died 11 Sep 1318. Formerly canon of Toulouse; archbishop of Auch from 1262.

25 Oct 1316 (EFR J1, 1619) licentia testandi.
For this unusually long and complicated process, see the following published sources: EFR J2, 2724, 3292-3293, 3563-3564.
        B1, 6239.
        B2, 59-60, 153-154, 171-174, 205.
        C1, 565, 2693$^{bis.}$
        VQ 4, 116, 118, 123, 125, 126, 157.
        VQ 5, 131, 476.
        and ms. sources: OS 12, 98^r.
        RA 42, 397^r-405^r = RA 47, 232^r-254^v, 257^v.

RA 42, 408ʳ-409ᵛ.
Coll. 29, 68ʳ-73ᵛ.

25] Amanevus de Casis, archbishop of Bordeaux, died before 17 Sep 1348. Formerly canon of Bayeux, LL.D., papal chaplain and familiar; bishop from 1347.

9 Jan 1349 (EFR C1, 4024) commission.
1 Jun 1349 (ibid., 4181) commission.
9 Jul 1349 (Coll. 497, 41ᵛ) successor Bernardus de Casis obligated to compositions of 3000 écus and 1000 fl. for the spoils of his two immediate predecessors.
16 Sep 1351 (EFR C1, 5066) commission.

26] Amanevus de Fargis, bishop of Agen, died before 12 Jun 1357. Bishop from 1314.

30 Oct 1357 (VQ 7, 183-184) successor Deodatus Rotbaldo pays 250 fl. of a composition of 500 fl.
20 Jun 1358 (ibid., 221) he pays the remaining 250 fl.

27] Amelius, abbot of S. Michel de Cuxá OSB, diocese of Elne, died before 31 Jan 1357.

4 Feb 1357 (Coll. 352, 86ᵛ) commission expedited to Fulco Pererii, dated 31 Jan 1357.

28] Amelius Cabirolli, preceptor of the Hospital of S. André d'Albignac, diocese of Albi.

Nov 1375 (IM 2877, 9) successor Bertrandus Folcoadi pays composition of 107 fl. 4 s.

29] Amelius de Lautrico OCSA, bishop of Castres, died 3 Dec 1337. Formerly provost of Belmont d'Aveyron, diocese of Rodez; archdeacon of Lezat, diocese of Toulouse; abbot of S. Sernin, Toulouse, and rector of the March of Ancona; bishop of Castres from 1326.

1 Aug 1317 (EFR J1, 5419) licentia testandi.
2 Sep 1330 (EFR J2, 4276; IM 7190, 2ʳ) licentia testandi.
14 Oct 1337 (IM 7190, 2ʳ-7ʳ) testament and codicils.
22 Nov 1337 (EFR B2, 383) commission to Pontius de Pereto and Raymundus de Chameraco.
1337-1343 (IM 7190, 84 fols.) commissioners' accounts.
1 Dec 1338 (VQ 4, 150) commissioners pay £142.11.6.
23 Dec 1338 (ibid., 136) Pontius de Pereto pays £400 Tur. parv.
14 Jul 1340 (ibid., 161) commissioners assign 6 rings and gems to Camera.
27 Nov 1340 (ibid., 166) they pay £171.1.11 Tur. parv.

29 Dec 1340 (ibid., 167-168) payments by Raymundus de Chameraco for these and other spoils.

after 1340 (IM 5246) a memorandum that the spoils were sold to successor Joannes de Pratis, except 395 fr., vestments and books assigned directly to the Camera.

27 Nov 1343 (VQ 5, 340) assignment.

ca. 1344 (Coll. 73, 105^r) small collections by Petrus Hugonis.

30] Ancelmus de Glandava OCSA, bishop of Glandèves, died before 24 Feb 1328. Formerly canon of Pignans, diocese of Fréjus; bishop of Glandèves from 1309.

1 Apr 1328 (EFR J2, 3537) commission to Elias Magnan, abbot of S. Salvator de Blaye, diocese of Bordeaux.

20 May 1328 (VQ 1, 537) commissioner pays 217 fl.

10 Oct 1328 (ibid.) successor Jacobus de Monasteriis pays half of a composition for 600 fl.

18 Apr 1329 (ibid.) Raymundus de Glandava, preceptor of the Hospital of Claret, pays £300 for grain received from spoils.

31 Jan 1330 (ibid.) successor pays balance of composition.

31] Ancelmus de Miolans de Urteriis, abbot of S. Rambert OClun, diocese of Lyon, died 22 Jun 1361: *Gall. Christ.* 4:256D.

4 Jan 1362 (IM 2245) notarial instrument of the spoils inquest by Joannes Rosseti, canon of Chalon-sur-Saône; brief inventory.

32] Andreas, bishop of Arezzo.

22 Dec 1367 (Coll. 248, 49^r) Nicolaus Lippi pays collector Lucius, bishop of Cesena, 27 fl. for spoils.

6 May 1371 (ibid.) collector received pawned books worth 43 fl. for their pawned price of 15 fl.

33] Andreas OP, bishop of Beograd, died before 1330. Bishop from 1322.

15 May 1336 (VQ 4, 108) Andreas de Verulis, scriptor papae, pays 91 fl. for spoils deposited with Petrus de Verulis and Petrus de S. Laurentio.

34] Andreas, bishop of Schwerin, died in curia in Jan 1357. Formerly provost of Poznan; bishop of Poznan from 1347; of Schwerin from 1348.

31 Jan 1357 (VQ 7, 170) Balduinus Riccardi, sigillifer auditoris Camerae, pays 104 fl. from spoils.

16 Jan 1358 (ibid., 215) he pays 62 fl. 1 s. 1 d.

35] Andreas, bishop of Sora, died before 23 Dec 1364. Formerly archpriest of Aversa; bishop of Sora from 1358.

4 Nov 1368 (IE 325, 24ᵛ) Camera receives 29 fl. from spoils.

36] Andreas, abbot of Pomposa, diocese of Ravenna.

29 May 1360 (Coll. 130, 151ᵛ) the marquis of Ferrara pays 1100 ducats for spoils.

37] Andreas Advocati, bishop of Como, died in curia. Formerly prior of the secular church of SS. Joannes & Riparata, diocese of Lucca; bishop of Como from 1357.

17 Sep 1361 (VQ 7, 357) Eblo de Mederio, clericus Camerae, collects a composition of 400 fl.
27 Jun 1362 (OS 31, 154ᵛ-155ʳ) commission to Stephanus de Gattis, bishop of Como.

38] Andreas Dotto, patriarch of Grado. Formerly bishop of Chioggia from 1322; patriarch from 1337.

1 Mar 1351 (EFR C2, 2396) commission.
22 Feb 1352 (Coll. 130, 33ᵛ) the procurators of S. Marco pay a composition of 250 fl. for the goods which they hold to Raymundus de Treve, abbot of S. Nicola (Lido di Venezia), collector.

39] Andreas Fredoli, abbot of S. Afrodise OSB, diocese of Béziers. Abbot from 1317.

Note that Andreas was executor of the testament of cardinal Berengarius Fredoli, and died in possession of some of the latter's goods: EFR C1, 1083, 1088, 1779, 2303, 2509.
8 Apr 1334 (EFR J1, 62987) licentia testandi.
10 May 1348 (EFR C1, 3860) commission.
19 May 1348 (ibid., 3872) commission.
30 Sep 1348 (VQ 5, 411) commissioner Eustachio Piscis pays large sums to the Camera.
1348 (RA 101, 26ʳ-36ᵛ) inventory of goods at Narbonne.
28 Oct 1357 (Coll. 497, 63ʳ) Franciscus Baroni obligated to a composition of £270.
1357-1359 (Coll. 154, 210ʳ-211ʳ) accounts of spoils by Guillelmus Guilaberti.
8 Jan 1360 (VQ 7, 291) Guillelmus Albaronis pays the last 50 fl. of his composition.

40] Andreas Ghini Malpigli, cardinal priest of the title of S. Susanna, died at Perpignan, 2 Jun 1343. Formerly bishop of Arras from 1329; of Tournai from 1334; cardinal from 1342.

23 May 1343 (EFR C1, 188) the cardinal is ordered to return to the curia.
12 Sep 1343 (ibid., 400) his goods at Tournai are reserved.
20 Oct 1343 (VQ 5,340) Lucas de Abbatibus pays 119 fl. for six books.
23 Dec 1343 (ibid., 342) executors pay 300 fl. sent., 900 fl. Pied.
10 May 1344 (Coll. 497, 24^r) Angelus Galega, papal sergeant at arms, is obligated to pay 83 fl. for his purchase from the spoils.
17 Jul 1344 (VQ 5, 350) 112 fl. paid to Camera from the executors' sale of goods.
19 Aug 1344 (EFR C1, 1035) commission to Bertrandus Cariti to recover the goods held by Joannes Fava, merchant of Florence.
27 Sep 1345 (VQ 5, 361) Guillelmus de Bos pays 100 fl. for the sale of books.
21 Oct 1345 (EFR C1, 2058) further commission to Bertrandus Cariti.
7 Jul 1346 (VQ 5, 374-375) cardinal Stephanus Alberti pays 790 fl. for grain purchased from the executors.

41] Andreas de Langusello, provost of Nîmes, died 25 Nov 1341.

late 1341 (Coll. 30, 120^r) receipts from Raymundus de Cameraco.

42] Andreas Petri Navarro, bishop of Córdoba, died 14 Sep 1372. Formerly dean of Córdoba; bishop from 1363.

27 Nov 1372 (EFR G2, 1220) commission to Antonius Martini, dean of Córdoba and subcollector.

43] Andreas de Perusio OFM, bishop of Gravina, died before 3 Mar 1346. M.Theol.; bishop from 1343. See AFH 67 (1974): 585.

2 Apr 1346 (Coll. 168, 54^{rv}) chapter pays 15 unc. to Guillelmus de Roseriis for the spoils.

44] Angelus de Porta Sola OP, bishop of Grosseto, died 22 Feb 1334. Formerly bishop of Sulcis from 1325; of Grosseto from 1330.

2 Oct 1334 (EFR J1, 64098) commission.
1335-1337 (IE 145, 29^{rv}) accounts of the commissioner Pontius Stephani.

45] Andreas Seri Sari, archbishop of Sorrento. Formerly canon of Sorrento; bishop from 1341.

10 Jun 1348 - 9 Feb 1349 (Coll. 168, 73^{rv}) Guillelmus de Roseriis collects goods worth 6 unc. 11 car.

46] Angelus, abbot of S. Crispano, diocese of Taranto.

6 May 1346 (Coll. 168, 56^v) the prior Leo pays to Guillelmus de Roseriis 6 unc. for spoils.

47] Angelus, abbot of S. M. de Gripta OSBasil, diocese of Toscania.

31 Aug 1368 (IE 325, 23ᵛ) successor Jacobus pays 500 fl. of a composition of 1000 fl.

48] Angelus Acciajoli OP, bishop of Montecassino, died 4 Oct 1357. Formerly bishop of Aquila from 1328; of Florence from 1342; of Montecassino from 1355.

19 Nov 1349 (EFR C2, 2106) spoils reserved in advance.
29 Dec 1357 (Coll. 352, 118ᵛ) expedition, by hand of Reginaldus de Lupchaco, cantor of Auxerre, of the commission, dated 14 Dec 1357, addressed to the bearer himself and to Petrus, archbishop of Benevento.
23 Jun 1358 (ibid., 119ᵛ) expedition, by hand of Raymundus de Albofolio, domicellus papae, of letters of instruction to the commissioners, imposing the *moderatio* on their collection of spoils.

49] Angelus Acciajoli, archbishop of Patrai, died before 20 Oct 1367. Former archdeacon of Reggio; bishop of Ventimiglia from 1348; of Tricarico from 1350; archbishop of Patrai from 1365.

24-26 May 1372 (Coll. 358, 52ʳ-53ʳ) the nuncio Golferius is ordered to collect more than 1000 fl. owed by Jews of Patrai and to pay to the count of Nola, executor, the 417 fl. required for pious legacies, even using other funds if the collected debts are not enough.
n.d. (BN lat. 4191, n. 15) inventory of spoils.

50] Angelus de Ricasolis, bishop of Sora, despoiled on his translation to Aversa, 6 Mar 1357. Formerly canon of Cambrai; bishop of Sora from 1355; of Aversa; later bishop of Florence from 1370; of Faenza (by Urban V) from 1387; of Arezzo from 1391 to his death in 1403.

28 Dec 1357 (Coll. 352, 118ᵛ) expedition, by hand of Reginaldus de Lupchaco, cantor of Auxerre, of the commission dated 14 Dec 1357 to the bearer himself and to Petrus, archbishop of Benevento.

51] Antonius, OCist, bishop of Lombez. Formerly abbot of Fontfroide, diocese of Narbonne; bishop of Lombez from 1341.

23 Aug 1348 (EFR C1, 3939) commission to Petrus Hugonis for these and other spoils.
24 Jun 1350 (IM 1863) appeal by Petrus Boneti against the collector Arnaldus de Polhenis.
1 May 1351 (EFR C1, 4955) commission.
n.d. (Coll. 30, 282ᵛ) accounts of the collector Raymundus Rogerii.
n.d. (RA 101, 72ʳ-74ᵛ) executors' inventory and list of bequests.

after 1353 (Coll. 31, 190^v, 191^v, 192^r) collections by Martinus de Girardo and arrears.

before 1355 (Coll. 114, 67^v-68^r) Martinus de Girardo reports receipts of 577 écus, 29 fl., etc.

ca. 1360 (Coll. 235, 58^r-60^r) arrears of debts collected by Bertrandus de Castanherio.

1 Oct 1373 (Coll. 236, 147^r, 155^v, 251^{rv}, 253^r) Aymericus Pelicerii reports receipts and uncollectable arrears.

52] Antonius OFM, bishop of Malta, died at Genoa 1370. Formerly archbishop of Saloniki; bishop of Malta from 19 Aug 1370. See AFH 47 (1954): 224.

1 Sep 1371 (EFR G2, 279) commission to Raphael de Turre, collector of Genoa.

25 Feb 1372 (ibid., 563) the same commission.

1376 (Coll. 125, 59^r, 60^r) commissioner reports holding four books from spoils.

53] Antonius, abbot of S. Spirito, diocese of Palermo.

ca. 1375 (Coll. 222, 203^r) report of a debt owed by the nun Nastasia of the monastery of S. Maria de Castellano, diocese of Palermo.

54] Antonius de Collel, bishop of Mallorca. Formerly archdeacon of Barcelona; bishop of Mallorca from 1349.

Nov 1361 - Mar 1363 (Coll. 120, 157 fols.) accounts of the major-domo Petrus de Turicella, received and used by the commissioner Jacobus de Sirano.

27 Feb 1363 (Coll. 140, 1^r-42^v) accounts of the collectors Fulco Pererii and Jacobus de Sirano. Ed. J. N. Hillgarth (1953–60).

29 Sep 1363 (OS 31, 199^r-200^r) the bishop's legacy to Bernardus de Lamo is reduced by the amount of a fine levied on the latter for trading with Alexandria.

2 Oct 1363 (ibid., 202^{rv}) books ordered to be delivered to Bernardus de Olivis.

24 Dec 1363 (IM 2279, 22; IE 303, 16^v) Jacobus de Sirano assigns 500 Mallorcan reals from spoils and the income of the vacancy.

12 Jan 1364 (Coll. 353, 4^r-5^r) registered quittance to Jacobus de Sirano for silverware and books assigned to the Camera on 30 Dec 1363.

2 Jan 1365 - (Coll. 116, 128^v-129^r) commissioner's further accounts.

15 Jan 1368 (Coll. 353, 82^v-83^r) registered quittance to Jacobus de Sirano.

55] Antonius Draconis de Valencia, cleric of Pavia, scriptor Papae.

2 Aug 1329 (EFR J1, 45886) licentia testandi.

27 Mar 1349 (EFR C2, 1963) commission.

56] Antonius de Laurentia, secular abbot of the church of S. Simeon de Carrilano, diocese of Aversa, died in curia.

12 Feb 1375 (EFR G2, 3154) quittance to Florentine merchants for 418 fl. from spoils.

13 Jun 1375 (OS 42, 19^r) note that 100 fl. of a composition of 170 fl. should be paid to the Camera before 29 Sep by Ludovicus Laurentii de Adversa.

57] Antonius Orso, bishop of Florence, died July 1322. Formerly bishop of Fiesole; of Florence from 1310. See Boccaccio, *Decamerone* 6.3.

18 Feb 1323 (Coll. 414, 7^{rv},m 23^r, 26^v-27^r, 30^v) inventory.

23 Sep 1332 (IM 1222) original commission to Pontius Stephani to collect the spoils against the bishop's debt of 5000 fl. for the sexennial tenth of Clement V.

3 Feb 1333 (Coll. 414, 2^r-3^r) the same commission.

58] Archambaldus, bishop of Tulle, died 26 Feb 1361. Former abbot of Tournus, diocese of Chalon-sur-Saône; bishop of Tulle from 1348.

ca. 1361 (Coll. 78, 148^r-180^r, 187^r) accounts of the collector Joannes de Cavanhaco; receipts and arrears.

1361 - 1361 (Coll. 75, 244^r-245^r) collector's further accounts.

26 Jan 1362 (VQ 7, 387) the heirs' proctor pays a composition to the Camera.

22 Jun 1362 (IM 2279, 16) the camerarius orders Joannes de Cavanhaco to assign 300 fl. in cash and kind to the chapter of Tulle.

Sep 1363 (IM 2279, 16) Joannes Palaysini collects part of the executors' composition.

59] Armandus de Mirmanda, prior of S. Gemma OSB, diocese of Saintes.

9 Aug 1343 (EFR C1, 344) commission.

15 Dec 1343 (ibid., 569) spoils dedicated to the foundation of the abbey of Chaise-Dieu by Clement VI.

60] Armandus de Narcesio, archbishop of Aix, died 21 Jul 1348. Formerly dean of Chartres, papal chaplain, auditor sacri palatii, dean of Gaya, diocese of Troyes; archbishop from 1329.

13 Sep 1331 (EFR J1, 55938) licentia testandi.

19 Sep 1339 (RA 52, 443^r-450^r; EFR B1, 6513) testament.

1 Mar 1348 (EFR C1, 3764) the archbishop is ordered to the curia to answer the complaints of some nobles and commons of Provence.

29 Oct 1348 (VQ 5, 414) commissioner Joannes de Nabayro pays 1000 gold agni.

61] Arnaldus, bishop of Troia, died before 27 Jun 1332. Bishop from 1322.

20 Jan 1332 (EFR J1, 58253) commission.
29 Jul, 17 Aug 1334 (VQ 1, 383) commissioner Raymundus de Salgis pays 6000 fl. for this and other commissions.

62] Arnaldus, abbot of S. Maria de Bouillas OCist, diocese of Auch.

28 Jan 1347 (EFR C1, 3082) commission.

63] Arnaldus, abbot of S. Maria de Noyers OSB, diocese of Tours.

6 Jun 1352 (EFR C1, 5320) commission.

64] Arnaldus Alberti, archbishop of Auch and camerarius. Nephew of Innocent VI, LL.Lic. Formerly elect of Agde 1354; bishop of Carcassonne from 14 Nov 1354; archbishop of Auch from 1357.

24 Feb 1354 (RA 128, 598^r) licentia testandi.
11 Jun 1371 (EFR G1, 259) commission to Petrus de Vernolis, treasurer.
22 Jun 1371 (ibid., 274, 276) commission and instructions to Petrus de Croso, camerarius.
11 May 1372 (ibid., 773) commission to Joannes Alamandi, subcollector of Auch.
1 Aug 1372 (Coll. 358, 72^v-73^v) Bertrandus Raffini, collector of Narbonne and commissioner in Auch, is ordered to pay 3000 fl. from the spoils in order to build a chapel of S. Martial as provided in the testament.
21 Jan 1374 (VQ 7, 501) the Camera paid to the successor Joannes Rogerii 500 fl. from the spoils toward building the tower of Bassoues as provided in the testament.
5 Jan 1385 (Coll. 360, 199^v) camerarius Franciscus de Conzia orders Sicardus de Brugarosio to collect the arrears of spoils left by the collectors Sancius Vaquerii and Arnaldus de Peyraco.
The accounts of the building projects, found in Coll. 32, were edited by Charles Samaran and A. Branet, "Le château et les deux tours de Bassoues d'après les comptes de construction inédits (1370-1371)," *Bulletin de la Société archéologique du Gers* 3 (1903): 197-221.

65] Arnaldus Andreae, provost of Agde and collector of Narbonne, died before 25 Aug 1386.

10 Sep 1386 - (Coll. 152, 189^r-204^r, 205^r-225^v, 227^r-238^v) three copies of an inventory of his goods at Narbonne.
14 Sep 1386 - (ibid., 175^r-188^r) inventory of goods at Agde and Narbonne.
4 Nov 1386 (Coll. 362, 6^{rv}) commission to Raymundus de Verduno.

66] Arnaldus Barbazano OCSA, bishop of Pamplona. Formerly canon of Pamiers; bishop of Pamplona from 1318.

17 Nov 1355 (Coll. 352, 85ʳ) expedition, by hand of Petrus Magister, cursor-mercator, of a commission to Fulco Pererii, collector of Aragon.
1358 (Coll. 114, 12ᵛ, 161ʳ-162ᵛ) collector's accounts.

67] Arnaldus Bernardi de Pogeto, patriarch of Alexandria and administrator of Montauban, died 1 Sep 1368. Nephew of cardinal Bertrandus de Pogeto and executor of his testament; J.U.Prof., papal chaplain. Formerly dean in the diocese of Montauban; archbishop of Aix from 1348; patriarch, with administration of Montauban, from 1361. Erroneously created cardinal posthumously, 22 Sep 1368. See *Gall. Christ.* **13:237B-238B.**

Sep 1363 (OS 31, 192ʳ) erroneous premature commission to collect spoils from the patriarch's chaplain Lucianus de Senis.
20 Feb 1369 (Coll. 353, 174ᵛ-175ʳ) the camerarius Arnaldus Alberti orders the collector Aymericus Pelicerii to pay a legacy to the patriarch's cubicularius.
14 Apr 1369 (ibid., 214ʳ-215ʳ) camerarius orders collector to send to the Claretians of S. Marcel de Pouget, diocese of Cahors, the goods left to them by cardinal Bertrandus de Pogeto, found in the possession of the late patriarch his executor.
n.d. (Coll. 235, 170ʳ-179ᵛ, 138ʳ-139ᵛ) accounts of the collector 14 Jan 1371 (Coll. 358, 23ᵛ) camerarius orders collector to pay a legacy to the patriarch's chaplain Guillelmus Engilberti.
11 Oct 1373 (Coll. 236, 148ʳ, 156ᵛ) report of collections and arrears.

68] Arnaldus de Brusaco OSB, archbishop of Benevento, died at Maguelonne 20 Jan 1344. Formerly abbot of S. Sophia, Benevento; archbishop from 1332.

7 May 1344 (EFR C2, 496) commission.
7 Feb - (IE 230, 246 fols.) accounts of the commissioners Guillelmus de Roseriis, bishop of Trani, and Arnulphus Marcellini.
18-27 Apr 1346 (Coll. 168, 55ᵛ-56ʳ) Guillelmus de Brusaco, nephew of the archbishop, pays to Guillelmus de Roseriis 1900 fl. of a composition for 2000 fl.

69] Arnaldus de Caucina, collector of Hungary and Poland, died 28 Oct 1371.

1371-1373 (Coll. 182, 1ʳ-11ʳ) testament, inventory and dispositions of goods at Crakow.
28 Apr 1372 (EFR G2, 697) orders Florianus Mokrski, bishop of Crakow,

to turn over the goods held by him to Elias de Vodronio, nuncio in Germany, Bohemia, Hungary and Poland.

14 Jul 1373 (ibid., 1990) commission to Petrus Stephani, collector of Hungary and Poland.

70] Arnaldus Cescomes, archbishop of Tarragona, died 9 Sep 1346. Formerly archdeacon in the diocese of Barcelona; bishop of Lerida from 1327; archbishop of Tarragona from 1334.

11 Nov 1327 (EFR J1, 30352) licentia testandi.
17 Jun 1345 (EFR C2, 687) commission.
2 Dec 1345 (ibid., 832) instructions.
14 Sep 1346 (Coll. 113, 88^{rv}; EFR C2, 1207) commission.
17 Oct 1346 (EFR C2, 1241) instructions.
26 Nov 1346 (Coll. 473, 1^r-19^r) accounts of commissioner Guillelmus de Platulis.
12 Jan 1347 (EFR C2, 1295-1297) instructions.
15 Mar 1347 (ibid., 1326-1327) instructions.

71] Arnaldus de Falgario, abbot of Gaillac OSB, diocese of Albi.

10 Sep 1361 (OS 31, 246^v) commission to Joannes de Cavanhaco, collector.
1 Apr 1362 (OS 31, 146^v-147^r; Coll. 497, 78^r) successor Guillelmus obligated to a composition of 500 fl.

72] Arnaldus Fredeti OP, bishop of Couserans, died 31 May 1329. Bishop from 1309; chaplain and confessor to Clement V: See *Gall. Christ.* 1:1134C-1135A.

16 Jun 1329 (EFR J2, 3881) commission to Arnaldus de Verdala.
25 Jun 1329 (ibid., 3892) commissioner ordered to apply legal pressures against the holders of the spoils.
12 Jul 1329 (IE 83, 53^r-59^v) commissioner's inventory and accounts.
10 Sep 1329 (VQ 1, 558) Elias de Ferreriis OP, provincial of Toulouse, pays 1465 fl. for goods deposited with him.
2 Dec 1329 (EFR J2, 4036) commissioner ordered to allow a delay of payment to the holders of spoils if they pay one half of their debt.
20 Feb 1330 (OS 12, 120^v) quittance to Guillelmus Fabri, Vitalis Fredeti and others for moneys paid.
29 Mar 1330 (ibid., 124^r) quittance to Arnaldus de Verdala for 94 marks of silverware, etc.
1 May 1330 (EFR J2, 4185) commissioner allowed to settle for two thirds of the value of goods held by the bishop's servants.
1330-1333 (IE 83, 158^r-160^r) further commissioner's accounts.
27 Dec 1331 (VQ 1, 371) quittance to Arnaldus de Verdala.
1333-1335 (IE 83, 186^v) accounts of arrears by commissioner.

3 Feb 1334 (VQ 1, 371) commissioner pays £83 Tur. parv., etc.
30 Nov 1335 (EFR B2, 122) general quittance to Arnaldus de Verdala.

73] Arnaldus Guillelmi, abbot of Foix OCSA, diocese of Pamiers, died 1375.

11 Aug 1375 (Coll. 356, 49^r; IM 2877, 5; OS 42, 28^r) quittance to Arnaldus de Laro, governor of the royal citadel of Montpellier, for his composition of 2000 fl. Fr., paid in 1714 fl. Cam., 8 s. Tur.
15 Aug 1375 (Coll. 356, 47^{rv}) letters of the camerarius Pierre de Cros empowering Arnaldus de Laro, domicellus and secretary of the king of France, to collect the spoils in consideration of the composition which he has paid, and ordering the clergy of Narbonne to surrender the goods to him.

74] Arnaldus Guillelmi de Barta OCSA, bishop of Albi. Formerly canon of Auch; bishop of Lectoure from 1346; of Albi from 1350.

26 Jun 1332 (EFR J1, 57586) licentia testandi.
23 Nov 1354 (EFR I1, 1214) commission to Joannes de Baro, Joannes de Palmis and Bartholomeus Cadorcii.
8 Apr 1355 (Coll. 73, 230^r) Joannes de Palmis received 1000 fl.

75] Arnaldus de Lavardenchis, provost of S. Justin, diocese of Auch, died in curia.

26 Sep 1327 (EFR J2, 3359) commission.
Oct 1328 - 27 Dec 1330 (Coll. 29, 76^{rv}, 80^r) accounts of the commissioner Arnaldus de Verdala.
10 Nov 1335 (EFR B2, 117) quittance to the commissioner.

76] Arnaldus de Lordato, bishop of Urgel, despoiled on his translation to Tortosa 3 Oct 1341. Formerly sacristan of Urgel; bishop of Urgel from 1326. See also the next article (77).

16 Oct 1341 (EFR B3, 3217) commission to collect the goods at Urgel as spoils.
1341 (Coll. 229, 101^r-106^v) accounts of collector Almeracius de Cabrespina.
1343 (ibid., 169^v) further accounts of the collector.

77] Arnaldus de Lordato, bishop of Tortosa, died 3 May 1346. Bishop since 1341: see also the preceding article (76).

10 May 1346 (EFR C2, 984; C1, 2482) commission.

78] Arnaldus de Moleriis, papal secretary and officialis of the curia.

22 Oct 1361 (VQ 7, 366) Joannes de Lacmolio assigns to the Camera a bag containing various moneys.

12 Jan 1362 (ibid., 384; OS 23A, 110^r) the executor Raymundus de Valle pays a composition of 300 fl.

79] Arnaldus de Monredondo, bishop of Gerona, died 21 Nov 1348. Bishop since 1335.

21 Jan 1349 (VQ 5, 416-417) executors pay 500 fl. of a composition of 2000 fl.
22 Jan 1349 (EFR C2, 1910) commission.
1 Oct 1349 (VQ 5, 429) executors pay 1000 fl. of their composition.
30 Sep 1350 (ibid., 440) executors pay 500 fl.

80] Arnaldus de Puyana OCSA, bishop of Pamplona, died at Toulouse 15 Dec 1316. Formerly prior of S-Avit-Sénieur, diocese of Périgueux; bishop of Pamplona from 1310.

6 Sep 1310 (*Regesta Clementis V* n. 5922) licentia testandi.
11 Mar 1317 (IM 600) instrument of publication, in the Franciscan convent of Toulouse, of letters patent (dated 28 Feb 1317) of Jacobus de Via, cardinal and nephew of John XXII, forbidding the friars to deliver the bishop's goods to his successor Guillelmus or to anyone else.
5 Sep 1318 (EFR J1, 8109) orders the friars to hold the spoils.

81] Arnaldus de Quimballo, bishop of Lombez, died at Toulouse 2 Apr 1382. Formerly bishop of Famagusta; of Lombez from 1379.

n.d. (RA 54, 460^r-464^r) inventory by Geraldus de Portali.
n.d. (Coll. 235, 145^v, 200^r-211^r) collector's accounts.
18 Jul 1382 (Coll. 359, 131^r) collector Aymericus Pelicerii is ordered to restore the wine, grain and books to the bishop's brother Guillelmus de Quimballo.

82] Arnaldus de Roseto, bishop of Asti. Formerly canon of Asti; bishop from 1327.

4 Jan 1331 (EFR J1, 52174) licentia testandi.
6 May 1348 (EFR C1, 3844) commission.

83] Arnaldus Sterela, scriptor Poenitentiariae, died in curia.

26 Nov 1354 (VQ 7, 60) Balduinus Riccardi, sigillifer auditoris Camerae, pays 12 fl. from spoils.

84] Arnaldus Tisonis, dean of Angoulême.

9 Nov 1372 (EFR G1, 976) commission to Arnaldus Garini.

85] Arnaldus de Tremolia, bishop of Mirepoix, died 24 Oct 1393. D.Decr., former prior of S. Giovanni nei Monti OCSA, diocese of Bologna; bishop of Mirepoix from 1377. See *Gall. Christ.* 13:271C-D.

18 Jan 1394 (Coll. 366, 135^r-136^v) quittance for books to Petrus de Tarascone, collector of Toulouse and Auch.

86] Arnaldus de Verdala, bishop of Maguelonne, died 23 Dec 1352. Formerly dean in the diocese of Alet, papal chaplain; bishop of Maguelonne from 1339.

26 Nov 1352 (EFR C1, 5469) commission.

87] Arnaldus de Villanova, scriptor Papae, died in curia.

31 Mar 1361 (VQ 7, 366) executor pays composition of 50 fl. to commissioner Bertrandus, bishop of Comminges.

88] Arnaldus de Villari, bishop of Alet. Formerly secular abbot of S. Paul, Narbonne; bishop of Mirepoix from 1361; of Alet from 1363.

31 Dec 1384 (Coll. 360, 198^v) collector Arnaldus Andreae ordered to pay the Camera's debt of 400 fl. to Joannes de Tornemira.
Jan 1385 (IM 3203, 3) collector pays 250 fr. to Camera from spoils.
1403 x 1406 (Coll. 159, 94^r) collector Joannes Martini receives debts to a total of £131.5.

89] Arnulphus Marcellini, canon of Embrun, rector of Benevento, died before 21 Jan 1345. Formerly treasurer of Campagna.

23 Jan 1345 (Coll. 168, 79^r-88^v) goods collected by Guillelmus de Roseriis.
8 Feb 1345 (EFR C1, 1479) commission.

90] Astorgius, abbot of S. Michel de Cuxá OSB, diocese of Elne.

21 Sep 1379 (Coll. 359, 159^r) collector ordered to give one half of the spoils to Aaron de Cayraco, knight.

91] Audebertus de Gorsis, canon of Bourges, collector of Bourges and Limoges.

3 Apr 1364 (EFR U2, 875) commission to Petrus Bori.
29 Oct 1371 (EFR G1, 443) commission to Guillelmus Thebardi, archdeacon of Bourbon, diocese of Bourges.
21 Aug 1373 (ibid., 1319) a grange, claimed as spoils because the movables did not satisfy the canon's debts to the Camera, is granted to the dean and chapter of Bourges.

92] Augustinus, abbot of S. Salvatore, diocese of Telese.

26 Apr 1361 (Coll. 169, 128^v) spoils yield 9 unc. 18 tari 4 grani.

93] Augustinus Tinacii de Florentia OESA, bishop of Narni. Bishop since 1343.

15 Feb 1367 - (Coll. 477, 1^r-27^r) accounts of the collector Guillelmus de Lordato and his lieutenant Mattheus Salvi.

94] Austencius de S. Columba OFM, bishop of Sarlat, died before 2 Oct 1370. M.Theol.; bishop since 1361.

20 Mar 1371 (RA 182, 234^{rv}) camerarius releases 5500 fl. worth of goods to the executor Sancius Arnaldi de Behasquen for a composition of 2500 fl.

95] Aymericus, abbot of Aurillac OSB, diocese of S. Flour. Not found in *Gall. Christ.* 2:445D.

28 Apr 1362 (Coll. 497, 79^v) successor Petrus is obligated to a composition of 100 fl. for spoils and fruits of the vacancy.
7 Jul 1375 (Coll. 356, 29^v-30^r) successor is empowered as a judge executor to collect the debts.

96] Aymericus, prior of Aspucino OESA, diocese of Elne, died in curia.

5 Dec 1364 (IE 303, 25^v) Joannes Manchini de Ramechinis pays 76 fr.

97] Aymericus Chatti de Jussaco, bishop of Limoges, died 10 Nov 1390. Formerly cantor of S. Martin, Tours, elect of Volterra in 1358; bishop of Bologna from 1361; of Limoges from 1371.

1363 or 1364 (RA 157, 47^r) rubric: licentia testandi.
ca. 1391 (*Gall. Christ.* 2:533D-E; Samaran in *Mélanges* 22 [1902]: 148 and note) the collection of spoils was opposed by a royal action for regalia.
ca. 1391 (Coll. 485, 40 fols.) report by Geraldus de Coumersio, subcollector of Limoges, citing a licentia testandi from Gregory XI.

98] Aymericus Guenaudi, archbishop of Rouen, died before 31 Jan 1343. Formerly bishop of Auxerre from 1332; archbishop of Rouen from 1339.

28 May 1344 (EFR C1, 870) commission to Bertrandus Cariti.
6 Sep 1345 (VQ 5, 507) commissioner assigns £63.15 Tur. to Camera.

99] Aymericus Hugonis, bishop of Lodève, died 24 Apr 1370. Formerly prior "de Vastino," diocese of Bourges; J.U.Prof., auditor sacri palatii; bishop of Lodève from 1361.

1370 x 1377 (Coll. 157, 185^r) collector Arnaldus Andreae reports no receipts because the nephew-executors made a composition in the Camera.

4 Apr 1372 (Coll. 358, 34^r-35^r) a note that the executors paid the composition but have not acted in the execution of the testament; this has been transferred to Joannes, archdeacon of Vic in the diocese of Auch and Petrus, prior "de Suregio" OESA, diocese of Maguelonne, both canonists of Montpellier.

2 Mar 1375 (Coll. 356, 5^v-6^r) camerarius Petrus de Croso orders the subcollector of Maguelonne to compel the holders of the spoils to pay the heirs of the nephew and executor Hugo de Chassanh.

100] Aymericus de Mercato, archdeacon of S. Antoine, diocese of Rodez, D.Decr., died after 5 Jan 1405.

5 Jan 1405 (Coll. 488, 12 fols.) testament.

1405 x 1407 (Coll. 91, 337^v) a note that the hand of the Camera was removed from the spoils by the influence of powerful men.

101] Aymericus de Murato, abbot of Brantosme, diocese of Périgueux, died 17 Oct 1352. See *Gall. Christ.* 2:1492-1493.

27 Oct 1352 (VQ 5, 459) executors pay a composition of 80 fl.

102] Aymericus Pelicerii, canon of Albi, former collector of Toulouse, died in curia early in 1389.

Apr 1389 (IM 3337, 49) Bertrandus de Coviarengis, dean of S. Pierre, Avignon, pays a composition of 107 fl.

103] Aymericus de Peyraco, abbot of Moissac, diocese of Cahors, died before 11 Jan 1407. See *Gall. Christ.* 1:170B-C: "scripsit vitam quartam Urbani Papae V."

1404 x 1407 (Coll. 91, 338^r) collector Petrus Berengas made an inventory, but took no further action out of fear of royal officials.

104] Aymericus de Quarto, bishop of Aosta, died before 24 Jul 1372. Formerly archdeacon of Aosta; bishop since 1361. See *Gall. Christ.* 12:816B.

12 Jun 1387 (Coll. 362, 48^v-49^r) camerarius Franciscus de Conzia directs Antonius, patriarch of Jerusalem and legate, to collect the debts.

105] Aymericus de Rochefort, abbot of Sorèze OSB, diocese of Lavaur, died 14 Jan 1327: *Gall. Christ.* 13:364.

after Easter 1330 (IE 83, 147^{rv}) successor pays a composition of £300 Tur. to Arnaldus de Verdala.

3 Feb 1334 (VQ 1, 371) Arnaldus de Verdala pays £300 Tur. to the Camera.
30 Nov 1335 (EFR B2, 122) general quittance to Arnaldus de Verdala.

106] Ayquelinus de Blavia, bishop of Angoulême, died before 25 Feb 1363. Formerly archdeacon of Angoulême; bishop from 1328.

27 Jul 1363 (OS 23A, 94^v) Ayquelinus Tabarias, canon of Angoulême, is obligated to a composition of 150 fl.
15 Nov 1363 (OS 31, 206^{rv}) collector Vitalis Vassali is ordered to restore liturgical goods to the church.
4 Jan 1365 (Coll. 353, 26^r-27^v) the heir of Vitalis Vassali pays the money which he had collected before his death.

107] Ayquelinus de Malavoltis, bishop of Siena, died 1 Jan 1371. Formerly canon of Siena; bishop from 1351.

18 Apr 1371 (Coll. 248, 42^r) the relatives pay a composition of 65 fl. to the collector Lucius, bishop of Cesena.
1 Jul 1371 (ibid.) a list of goods still held by the collector.

108] Balduinus, bishop of Famagusta, Cyprus. Bishop no earlier than 1306.

14 Oct 1328 (EFR J1, 43119) commission.

109] Balduinus de Lützelburgo, archbishop of Trier, died 21 Jan 1354. Archbishop from 1308.

26 Aug 1343 (EFR C2, 264-265) reservation of spoils.
16 Jun 1345 (ibid., 688-689) reservation of spoils.
7 Feb 1354 (EFR I1, 752) asks the favor of Charles, king of the Romans, to Henricus de Tremonia, commissioned to collect the spoils in order to pay the tenth of Clement VI.
8 Feb 1354 (ibid., 754) the same, to Guillelmus, archbishop of Cologne.
8 Feb 1354 (ibid., 755) the same, for Boemundus de Saraponte, archdeacon of Trier.
8 Feb 1354 (ibid., 756) the same, for Fulco Bertrandi, primicerius of Metz.
13 Feb 1354 (ibid., 772) commission to Boemundus de Saraponte, Henricus de Tremonia, and Fulco Bertrandi.
May 1354 (Coll. 497, 52^r) successor Boemundus de Saraponte is obligated to a composition of 40,000 fl. to be paid by 1 Nov; a marginal note: "solvit ut dicitur."
17 May 1354 (EFR I1, 949) orders the goods released to the successor Boemundus.
30 Oct 1354 (VQ 7, 59) successor pays 11,200 fl. of the composition.
27 Sep 1356 (ibid., 135) successor pays 3000 fl. of composition.

110] Barnabas Malaspina, archbishop of Pisa, died 7 Nov 1380. Formerly bishop of Luni from 1363; of Penne and Atri from 1374; archbishop of Pisa from 1380.

12 Feb 1390 (DC 1, 160^{rv}) books from the spoils assigned to the Camera at Rome.

111] Bartholomeus, bishop of Alet, died 30 May 1333. Formerly abbot of S. M. d'Alet; bishop from 1318.

28 May 1324 (EFR J1, 19642) licentia testandi.
29 Sep 1329 (EFR J2, 3976) reservation of spoils.
13 Jun 1330 (ibid., 4220) reservation of spoils.
9 Jun - 30 Jul 1333 (IE 83, 187^v) successor Guillelmus makes a composition with Arnaldus de Verdala for £7000 Tur.
17 May 1335 (VQ 4, 99) successor pays £2800.
23 Nov 1335 (ibid., 104) he pays £1012.14.1.
24 May 1336 (ibid., 108) he pays £516.4.2.
25 Nov 1336 (ibid., 114) he pays £508.18.
3 Feb 1338 (ibid., 125) he pays £300.
28 Jul 1338 (ibid., 132) he pays £200.
6 Oct 1338 (ibid., 146) he pays 100 pabalhi of gold.
28 Feb 1340 (ibid., 156) he pays 166 pabalhi.
4 Nov 1340 (ibid., 165) he pays 134 duple of gold.
25 Oct 1341 (ibid., 183-184) he pays 59 duple, 10 agni.
21 Nov 1344 (EFR C1, 1271).
10 Apr 1346 (VQ 5, 367-368) successor pays 418 écus, 200 fl.
7 Sep 1351 (VQ 5, 448) successor pays 477 fl.

112] Bartholomeus, bishop of Termoli.

4 Dec 1352 (Coll. 169, 47^r-48^r) Dominicus de Fulgineo, subcommissioner of Petrus, archbishop of Benevento, pays 10 fl., 32 unc. 19 car. and 8 lb. 6 unc. of silver from the sale of the spoils.
12 Oct 1353 (ibid., 49^v) vessels sold for 54 unc. 7 d. by subcommissioner Thomasius de Limosano.

113] Bartholomeus, abbot of S. Pietro della Canonica, diocese of Amalfi.

3 Jul 1354 (Coll. 169, 52^r) spoils yield 1 unc. 12 car.

114] Bartholomeus, abbot of S. Giorgio OSB, Venice, diocese of Castello, died before 16 Nov 1357.

21 Nov 1357 (Coll. 352, 114^r) commission (dated 16 Nov) to Geraldus, abbot of S. Nicola in Lido, expedited by hand of Johanotus Venetiarum.

7 Feb 1359 (Coll. 497, 67ʳ) collector Geraldus succeeds the late abbot, under obligation to a composition of 2500 fl., "in magnum dampnum mei et monasterii" (Coll. 130, 149ᵛ-150ʳ).

115] Bartholomeus de Boscario, capellanus commensalis, auditor sacri palatii.

30 Oct 1361 (OS 31, 253ᵛ) spoils released to nephew Peyronetus.
13 Nov 1361 (VQ 7, 370) executors pay a composition of 150 fl.

116] Bartholomeus de Cuino, abbot of Aisnay OSB, diocese of Lyon, died 1361; D.Decr.: *Gall. Christ.* 4:239.

13 Apr 1354 (RA 128, 598ᵛ) licentia testandi.
12 Nov 1363 (OS 23A, 118ʳ) successor Guillelmus de Onciato is obligated to a composition of 400 fl.
n.d. (Coll. 66, 99ʳ) successor pays his composition to the collector Aubricus Radolphi, partly in books.
15 Dec 1364 (Coll. 353, 23ᵛ-24ʳ) Cameral quittance to the collector for books.

117] Bartholomeus Galmari, archbishop of Torrès, Sardinia, died 7 Sep 1352. Formerly canon of Torrès, nuncio in Sardinia and Corsica; archbishop from 1349.

7 Sep 1352 (Coll. 211, 47ʳ-62ᵛ) inventory in Spanish by the canons of Torrès.
6 Apr 1353 (EFR I1, 219) commission to Dominicus de Turribus, canon of Cagliari.
8 Apr 1353 (ibid., 220) the same.
8 Apr 1354 (ibid., 875) commission to Raymundus, bishop of Sulcis.
7 Nov 1354 (ibid., 1185) the commissioner is directed to order Didacus, elect of Torrès, to restore the spoils and fruits of the vacancy.

118] Bartholomeus Grassi, bishop of Fréjus, died 5 Mar 1340. Bishop since 1318. See André Vernet in *Revue de l'histoire de l'Eglise en France* 34 (1948): 92, n. 209.

31 Aug 1330 (EFR J1, 50680) licentia testandi.
1338-1343 (Coll. 105, 341 fols.) testament, codicil, accounts of Raymundus Naulonis to 4 Dec 1340, then of Arnaldus Costolani and Berengarius Blasini.
7 Mar 1340 (EFR B2, 702; B3, 2707) commission to Raymundus Naulonis, referring to a reservation of 18 Nov 1339.
15 Feb 1341 (VQ 4, 170) commissioner assigns money, plate and books to Camera.
15 Feb 1341 (EFR B2, 813; B3, 3004) quittance to commissioner.
2 Mar 1341 (VQ 4, 171) Guillelmus Lombardi pays 6 fl.

26 Mar 1341 (ibid., 175) Raymundus de Eremo, executor, assigns rings and books.

28 Mar 1341 (ibid., 176) Petrus de Tornavia, a familiar of the late bishop, restores four books.

14 Apr 1341 (ibid.) Bartholomeus Galhardi, executor, assigns 28 fl. 21 s. 6 d. Tur. parv.

25 Jun 1341 (ibid., 178-179) Bartholomeus Blanqueti, the late bishop's viceclavarius, pays £52.8.2 Prov.

16 Jul 1341 (EFR B2, 858-861; B3, 3127) commission to Arnaldus Costolani and Berengarius Blasini.

14 Aug 1341 (VQ 4, 181) two horses sold for 44 fl.

20 Sep 1341 (EFR B2, 887; B3, 3193) 1000 fl. released for a pious legacy of dowries.

10 Jan 1342 (VQ 4, 188) commissioners pay 1736 fl. etc.

1 Feb 1342 (ibid., 189) 12 fl. for sale of a ring.

23 Feb 1342 (ibid.) debt of 200 fl. paid to Camera.

14 May 1342 (VQ 5, 325) Paulus and Bernardus de Caunalhor pay their debt of 100 fl.

Jun 1343 (Coll. 289, 40^r, ed. Hoberg, *Inventare* p. 73) the bishop's goods in an inventory of the papal treasure.

27 Nov 1343 (VQ 5, 341) payments on this and other accounts.

1 Jun 1344 (VQ 5, 349) commissioner Raymundus de Eremo pays 320 fl. from debts and condemnations.

22 Sep - Oct 1344 (Coll. 106, 1^r-13^v) inquest by commissioner Arnaldus Costolani.

26 Dec 1344 (EFR C1, 1363) the papal treasurers Stephanus Cambaruti and Guillelmus de Albusacco are ordered to prosecute the Camera's claim to a house.

2 Mar 1345 (ibid., 1511) commission to Bartholomeus Galhardi and Raymundus de Eremo.

Mar 1345 (Coll. 106, 14^r-69^r) spoils case before the auditor of the Camera.

2 Jun 1345 (VQ 5, 358) Raymundus de Eremo pays 240 fl.

11 Apr 1346 (Coll. 497, 26^v) the goods taken by Guillelmus Lombardi will be restored by his heir, as promised by his proctor.

15 Jan 1347 - 7 May 1347 (Coll. 106, 70^r-89^v) spoils case before the auditor of the Camera.

119] Bartholomeus Peyroni OCarm, bishop of Elne. M.Theol.; bishop from 1384.

10 Sep 1408 (RA 331, 52^r-54^v) quittance to Guillelmus Fabri, banker of Perpignan.

120] Bartholomeus Sancii, archdeacon "de Mecinacolini."

27 Feb 1375 (OS 42, 5^v-6^r) the executor of fr. Antonius de Ispania paid to the Camera 68 fl. Cam. 16 s. Avin. for goods in the archdeacon's spoils.

121] Bartholomeus de Sauceto OFM, bishop of Forli, died before 14 Jul 1372. Bishop from 1351.

22 Jul 1372 (Coll. 129, 237^r) spoils and vacancy yield 212 ducats 6 s.

122] Bartholomeus de Virgilio OFM, bishop of Jerusalem, died 28 Oct 1397. See AFH 47 (1954): 224.

25 Nov 1400 (Coll. 123, 35^r) Joannes de Marello, subcollector of Tarragona, delivers five books to Berengarius Ribalta.

123] Bartolus Bardi OESA, bishop of Spoleto. Bishop from 1320.

13 Sep 1348 (EFR C2, 1707) commission to Berengarius Blasini, treasurer of the Patrimony of S. Peter in Tuscany.
13 Sep 1348 - (Coll. 232, 174^v-219^v) commissioner's accounts.
4 May 1349 (EFR C1, 4157) instructions to the commissioner.
10 May 1349 (EFR C1, 4159) instructions.
14 May 1349 (ibid., 4165; IM 6216) directions for the disposition of moneys.
29 May 1349 (EFR C1, 4180; C2, 1999-2001) orders the treasurer to compel payment, by Joannucius de Montefalcone and Angelicus Raynerii OESA, of 8000 fl.
7 Jul 1349 (EFR C1, 4208) orders the treasurer to receive 6000 fl. from Joannes Scafredi, rector of the Duchy of Spoleto.
16 Mar 1350 (VQ 5, 439) the treasurer of the Patrimony pays 3800 fl.
21 May 1350 (VQ 5, 536) Antonius Malabayla, merchant of Asti, pays to the Camera 600 fl. of 8000 fl. sent by the commissioner.
26 Aug 1350 (IM 1838) commissioner pays 3800 fl.
11 Sep 1350 (VQ 5, 439) last payment received by the Camera.
26 Sep 1350 (EFR C2, 2309) revokes the excommunication of the Augustinian friars.

124] Baudetus Renaudini de Quercu, canon of Reims, secretarius Papae, scriptor litterarum apostolicarum, abbreviator, died between 14 Jul and 26 Aug 1383.

14 Jul 1383 (IM 3145) testament.
26 Aug 1383 (IM 3149) Joannes Rosseti, collector of Lyon, pays from spoils at Chalon-sur-Saône 100 fr. to the creditor Andreas de Grolia.
26 Sep 1383 (IM 3155) collector pays 70 fr. to Petrus Brossarii, merchant of Pisa.
16 Aug 1384 (Coll. 360, 164^r-165^v) quittance to collector.

125] Belinus de Chanilipto, physician to Petrus Bertrandi, cardinal of S. Susanna, died in curia 1348.

29 Oct 1348 (VQ 5, 414) executors pay a composition of 500 fl.

126] **Beltraminus Paravicini, bishop of Bologna. Formerly advocatus Romanae curiae; bishop of Chieti in 1336; of Como from 1339; of Bologna from 1340.** See Francesco Fossati, "Il vescovo Beltramino Parravicino e il suo testamento," *Periodica della Società storica per la provincia e antica diocesi di Como* 6 (1888): 41-67.

1 May 1324 (EFR J1, 19476) licentia testandi.
15 Nov 1340 (EFR B1, 7936) licentia testandi.
20 Aug 1350 (VQ 5, 438; IM 6640) Henricus de Sossa, J.U.Prof., pays a composition of 1000 fl. for goods in curia.

127] **Benedictus, bishop of Guardialfiera.**

13 Apr - 8 Nov 1346 (Coll. 168, 54^{rv}) accounts of the commissioner Guillelmus de Roseriis.

128] **Benedictus OP, bishop of Pola, died before 17 Apr 1360. Formerly bishop of Sora from 1344; of Chioggia from 1348; of Pola from 1353.**

18 May 1360 (Coll. 130, 150^v) the syndic of the chapter pays a composition of 50 ducats.

129] **Benedictus, archbishop of Salerno, died before 23 May 1347. Formerly archdeacon of Capua; archbishop of Salerno from 1334.**

15 Oct 1347 (EFR C1, 3518) commission.

130] **Benedictus, rector of S. Maria di Castro Vedi, diocese of Rimini.**

1370 x 1377 (Coll. 129, 234^r) 86 ducats paid for spoils.

131] **Benedictus de Asnago OP, bishop of Como, died 9 Oct 1339. M.Theol.; bishop from 1328.**

25 Oct 1339 (EFR B3, 2577) commission.
7 Jan 1340 (ibid., 2635) instructions for the disposition of books among the spoils.
25 May 1340 (VQ 4, 158; OS 18, 158) commissioner Bernardus de Lacu assigns a silver cup and books to the Camera.

132] **Benedictus de Facifeis, scriptor Poenitentiariae.**

14 Jul 1375 (Coll. 356, 38^v-39^r) spoils released to the executor Jacobus Textoris, who paid a composition.

133] **Benedictus de Solerio, rector "de Gandesia," diocese of Valencia, capellanus honoris, died at Tortosa before 1402.**

before 1402 (Coll. 123, 47ʳ) a Bible from the spoils was sold at Valencia for 60 fl. Aragonese 3 s. (= £32.12.6).

134] Berengarius, bishop of Couserans, died 17 Oct 1362. Former archdeacon of Lodève; bishop from 1361.

1 Nov 1375 (Coll. 34, 51ʳ-53ʳ) accounts of collector Arnaldus de Payraco.
19 Nov 1379 (Coll. 359, 100ᵛ) Raymundus de Ruppe asks Cameral ratification of his purchase from the collector of the remains of spoils, both of Berengarius and of his successor Pontius de Villemur (q.v.) for 300 fl.
Jan 1382 (ibid., 104ʳ) confirmation that the buyer is free to collect the goods.

135] Berengarius, bishop of Lucca, died between 10 Jan and 9 Feb 1368. Formerly rector "de Cerviano," diocese of Béziers; bishop from 1349.

9 Feb - 2 May 1368 (Coll. 248, 11ᵛ-13ᵛ) accounts of Lucius, bishop of Cesena and collector of Tuscany: 1641 fl. 6 gr. and other sums received.

136] Berengarius Batle, bishop of Mallorca, died 1 Nov 1349. Formerly bishop of Elne from 1320; of Mallorca from 1332.

1 Aug 1321 (EFR J1, 13938) licentia testandi.
12 Nov 1349 (EFR C2, 2098) commission.
3 Aug 1350 (Coll. 497, 44ʳ) successor Antonius de Collel (q.v.) is obligated to a composition of 350 fl.

137] Berengarius de Cruillas, bishop of Gerona, died 25 Jul 1362. Formerly precentor of Gerona; bishop from 1348.

1362 (Coll. 116, 20ᵛ-21ʳ) accounts of collector Fulco Pererii, with mention of a licentia testandi.
1 Jul 1363 (IE 303, 12ᵛ) collector pays 3808 fl. recovered from the king of Aragon.
29 Jan 1369 (Coll. 353, 156ʳᵛ) Bernardus, abbot of S. M. Amariensis OSB, diocese of Gerona, claims 100 fl. as a debt from the deceased; the collector is ordered to investigate.

138] Berengarius Galhardi, frater, almoner of the Pinhota, died in curia.

11 May 1341 (VQ IV, 177) Petrus Natalis, paneterius, pays money from goods and silver.

139] Berengarius Maynardi OCist, bullator litterarum.

18-19 Apr 1341 (RA 55, 485^r-490^r; EFR B1, 9247) donation inter vivos and spoils inventory.

140] Berengarius de Olargiis, canon of Narbonne, auditor sacri palatii since 1313 (Guillemain, *Cour*, 348 f., 354).

2 Jul 1331 (OS 12, 143^v; VQ 1, 524) heir pays a composition of 1000 fl.

141] Berengarius de Prats, bishop of Tortosa, died 19 Feb 1340. Bishop from 1310.

16 Oct 1341 (EFR B3, 3218) commission.
1341 (Coll 229, 107^r-116^r) accounts of collector Almeracius de Cabrespino.

142] Bernardus, archbishop of Cagliari, died at Barcelona 5 Aug 1399. Formerly archdeacon of Mazzara, collector of Sardinia and Corsica; bishop of Ploaghe from 1361; archbishop of Torres from 1368; of Cagliari from 1369.

n.d. (Coll. 486, 20^r-28^v) inventory.

143] Bernardus, bishop of Rapolla, died before 21 Aug 1330. Formerly archdeacon of Venosa; bishop from 1316.

16 Jan 1331 (IM 6072) inquest by Petrus Regis for the nuncio Geraldus de Valle.
1330 x 1332 (Coll. 221, 152^r) the nuncio collects 30 unc. 5 car.
n.d. (IM 7188) report by Petrus Regis on inventories.
29 Jul - 17 Aug 1334 (VQ 1, 383) commissioner Raymundus de Salgis pays 6000 fl. for this and other commissions.

144] Bernardus, abbot of S. Chaffre, diocese of Le Puy. See Gall. Christ. 2:768A-B.

6 Apr 1357 (IM 6227) minute of the commission to Petrus Gervasii, canon of Clermont.
6 Feb 1358 (VQ 7, 216) successor Amblardus pays 125 fl. of a composition of 250 fl.
23 Jun 1358 (ibid., 222) he pays the rest (cf. OS 23A, 108^v).

145] Bernardus de Agrifolio OClun, bishop of Viviers, died before 11 Aug 1382. Former prior of S. Martin des Champs, Paris, B.Decr.; bishop from 1376.

11 Sep 1382 (Coll. 360, 18^{rv}) the subcollector is permitted to make a composition with the successor.

146] Bernardus de Altsiaco, provost of Pezilla de la Rivière, diocese of Elne, capellanus honoris.

1393 x 1405 (Coll. 160, 123^{rv}) Joannes de Ripis Altis, collector of Elne, receives £39.11 for grain.

147] Bernardus de Barbarano, prior of Tortosa.

12 Apr 1329 (OS 12, 105^v) bishop Berengarius de Prats was issued a quittance for 80 fl. worth of spoils.
10 Sep 1330 (VQ 1, 356) he pays 8 fl. 10 d. Tur. gr.
17 Sep 1335 (EFR B3, 569) commission to Pontius Textoris, archdeacon in the church of Liège.
6 Oct 1335 (ibid., 603) permits him to compound for spoils.

148] Bernardus Bruni, bishop of Auxerre, died 29 Oct 1349. Formerly dean of Le Puy; bishop of Le Puy from 1327; of Noyon from 1342; of Auxerre from 1347 (*Gall.Christ.* 12:319B-D and 2:724C-725B).

23 Jul 1334 (EFR J1, 63608) licentia testandi.
1 Oct 1349 (IM 1811) testament, copied 15 Dec 1349.
17 - 21 Oct 1349 (IM 1814) codicil and donations inter vivos.
17 Oct - 1 Nov 1349 (IM 1813) inventory for the executor, Guido, bishop of Autun.
n.d. (IM 1816) list of claimants to goods.
12 Nov 1349 (RV 143, 100^v; EFR C1, 4299) commission to Stephanus Chautardi.
14 Nov 1349 (ibid., 4302) instructions to commissioner.
20 Jul 1350 (RV 144, 48^v; EFR C1, 4607) successor Petrus Ayme (q.v.) is ordered to collect the spoils and render accounts.
26 Jul 1350 (Coll. 497, 48^v) successor is obligated to a composition of 5000 fl. for spoils; Petrus de Agrifolio, bishop of Clermont, obligated to a composition of 500 fl. for a loan-debt.
29 Aug 1350 (RV 144, 96^{rv}; EFR C1, 4681) executors are declared accountable to the successor and the collector.
7 Sep 1350 (IE 261, 32^r; VQ 5, 439) executors pay a composition of 5000 fl.
10 Sep 1350 (Coll. 497, 45^r) executors undertake to render full accounts.
30 May 1352 (IE 265, 19^r; VQ 5, 455) Archambaldus, bishop of Tulle, pays 100 fr. chaises of a debt owed by his predecessor Petrus to Bernardus.
23 Jan 1355 (VQ 7, 95) Petrus de Agrifolio, bishop of Clermont, pays 200 fl.

149] Bernardus Bruni, grossator, died in curia.

16 May 1348 (VQ 5, 406) composition of 10 fl. and a debt of 40 fl. paid by his executors.

150] Bernardus Cariti, bishop of Evreux, died Aug 1383. Formerly collector of Sens and Rouen; archdeacon in the diocese of Rouen; bishop of Evreux from 1376.

12 Jan 1384 (Coll. 359, 194^v-195^r) commission to Sicardus de Brugayrosio, collector of Toulouse, and also to the collector of Cahors.

151] Bernardus de Casis, archbishop of Bordeaux. Formerly canon of Bordeaux, LL.B.; archbishop from 1348.

16 Sep 1351 (EFR C1, 5066) commission.
5 Nov 1353 (IM 1954) successor Amanevus de Apta (q.v.) is confirmed in his use of the goods.
25 Feb 1354 (VQ 7, 47) successor Amanevus pays 200 fl. composition for the spoils of three predecessors: Petrus de Luca, Amanevis de Casis, Bernardus de Casis.
5 Nov 1354 (EFR I1, 1179) successor granted power to collect the remaining spoils of his predecessors.

152] Bernardus de Castelnau, bishop of S. Papoul, died 12 May 1375. Formerly abbot of Aniane OSB, diocese of Maguelonne; bishop from 1370.

n.d. (Coll. 235, 145^v) 503 fl. received from spoils.
n.d. (Coll. 236, 323^v-324^r) collector Aymericus Pelicerii reports collections and remains of spoils.
12 Jul 1380 (Coll. 359, 45^{rv}) a legacy of 100 fr. is granted to the prior of Villanova, Béziers.

153] Bernardus de Caulasone, archdeacon of Elne, capellanus Papae, auditor sacri palatii, died intestate in curia.

9 Apr 1354 (VQ 7, 50) Guillelmus de Gemallo and Fr. Stephanus de Marlhaco pay a composition of 150 fl.
25 Aug 1355 (Coll. 497, 55^v) Bertrandus de Requenhio is obligated to a composition of 80 fl.
28 Aug 1355 (VQ 7, 97) Brunus de Requenhio has been excommunicated for holding goods without right; his brother Bertrandus pays 2 fl. 14 s. for execution of letters releasing him in consideration of an obligation to a composition of 80 fl.

154] Bernardus de Champeriis, camerarius of the monastery of Grasse OSB, diocese of Carcassonne.

22 May 1371 (EFR G1, 240) commission to Bertrandus Raffini and Petrus Viguerii.

155] Bernardus Fabri, prior of S. M. Daurade, Toulouse. Formerly prior of S. Martin des Champs, Paris (Coll. 236, 254ʳ).

8 Nov 1387 (Coll. 359, 148ʳᵛ) report of spoils by Petrus de Tarascone, collector of Toulouse and Auch.

156] Bernardus de Fargis, archbishop of Narbonne, died Jul 1341. Nephew of Clement V; bishop of Agen from 1306; archbishop of Rouen from 1306; of Narbonne from 1311; see *Gall. Christ.* 6:87D-90B.

1337-1340 (Coll. 146, 257 fols.) accounts of the episcopal mensa before the death of the archbishop.
1337-1341 (Coll. 148, 1ʳ-45ᵛ) process of the succession by Martinus Curte, the archbishop's treasurer.
3 May 1341 (EFR B2, 834; B3, 3076-3077) commission.
7 Dec 1341 (VQ 4, 187-188) silver vessels received by the Camera from cardinal Raymundus Guillelmi de Fargis.
6 Sep 1342 (IM 1611) instrument of the inquest by commissioner Morerius de Moreriis into the debts owed to the archbishop.
10 Jan 1343 (Coll. 289, 39ʳ) inventory of spoils in the papal treasure.
9 Jun 1343 (EFR C1, 216) imprisonment of the archbishop's treasurer Martinus Curte.
11 Sep 1343 (ibid., 399) the king of France is asked not to interfere in the spoils process.
20 Sep 1343 (ibid., 419).
8 Dec 1343 (ibid., 1309).
27 Nov 1344 (VQ 5, 352) chaplains pay 100 fl. of a debt of 300 fl.
17 Mar 1345 (ibid., 354) Jacobus de Placentia, papal chaplain, pays 38 fl.
24 Jan 1346 (Coll. 497, 26ʳ) Guillelmus Borserii, administrator of a castle for the archbishop, is obligated to pay £207.8.9 and shares of grain.
n.d. (Coll. 30, 128ᵛ) Raymundus de Chameraco assigns to the Camera £4546.16.9 Tur., 585 m. 4 unc. of silver.
1341-1347 (Coll. 148, 46ʳ-221ᵛ) accounts of Morerius de Moreriis.
1347-1348 (Coll. 150) process by Bernardus de Abbate to collect the spoils left deposited by Morerius de Moreriis.
16 Sep 1355 (VQ 7, 97-98) the archbishop's treasurer pays 120 fl. of a composition for 170 fl. for the cash and grain which he had kept.
n.d. (Coll. 114, 80ᵛ) Bernardus de Abbate reports receipts of 37 écus.

157] Bernardus Folcaudi, bishop of Pamplona, died 7 Jun 1377. Formerly archdeacon in the diocese of Huesca, capellanus Papae, auditor sacri palatii; bishop of Huesca from 1362; of Pamplona from 1364.

14 Mar 1383 (Coll. 360, 39ʳ-40ʳ) the camerarius directs the successor Martinus to collect his composition from the holders of the spoils.

158] Bernardus Gaucelmi, emptor coquinae papae, died in curia between 29 Dec 1357 and 6 Feb 1359.

6 Feb 1359 (VQ 7, 260) his brother Aymericus pays 100 fl. composition (cf. OS 23A, 105^r).

159] Bernardus de Grumigen, priest of the diocese of Kammin in Pomerania, died in curia.

19 Jan 1361 (VQ 7, 332-333) Balduinus Riccardi, sigillifer auditoris camerae, pays 20 fl.

160] Bernardus Guidonis OP, bishop of Lodève, died 30 Dec 1331. Bishop of Tuy from 1323; of Lodève from 1324.

30 Jul 1329 (EFR J1, 45848) licentia testandi.
1332 (IE 83, 156^r) commissioner Arnaldus de Verdala makes a composition with the executors for £200 Tur.
3 Feb 1334 (VQ 1, 371) commissioner pays £200 to Camera.
30 Nov 1335 (EFR B2, 122) general quittance to Arnaldus de Verdala.

161] Bernardus Hugonis Furnerii de S. Arthemia OCSA, bishop of Elne, died between 5 Jun 1347 and 20 Jul 1348. D.Decr.; formerly prior "de Saboneriis" OCSA, diocese of Lombez; bishop of Elne from 1346.

20 Jul 1348 (EFR C1, 3923) commission.
18 Jun 1351 (VQ 5, 608) the bishop's brother Guillelmus Fornerii pays 200 fl. composition to Bernardus de Abbate, collector of Narbonne.
1357 (Coll. 114, 81^r) collector reports the income of the vacancy.
1357-1359 (Coll. 154, 213^r) accounts of Guillelmus Guilaberti.

162] Bernardus Joannis, notarius sacri palatii, died in curia.

17 Jan 1361 (Coll. 231, 119^r; VQ 7, 332) Geraldus de Podio Fulconis, elect of Benevento, pays a composition of 20 fl.

163] Bernardus de Lacu, bishop of Viterbo, rector of the Patrimony. Former archdeacon of Elne, canon of Rodez, LL.D.

7 Feb 1336 (EFR B1, 3376; B3, 762) licentia testandi.
16 Sep 1346 (EFR C2, 1211) commission.
23 Jul 1347 (VQ 5, 392) commissioner Petrus Chautardi's composition of 300 fl. is paid by the executors.
27 Jul 1347 (EFR C1, 3396) commission to Berengarius Blasini.
28 Aug 1347 (ibid., 3423) quittance to Raymundus de Albofolio for 2000 fl.
19 Sep 1347 (EFR C2, 1484) orders Raymundus, bishop of Orvieto and

Petrus de Pinu to pay 4000 fl. into the treasury of the Duchy of Spoleto.

19 Sep 1347 (EFR C1, 3464) orders Berengarius Blasini, treasurer of the Duchy of Spoleto, to pay the two commissioners 4000 fl. [there is a direct contradiction between these two letters, as abstracted in the calendars].

27 Jul 1347 - (Coll. 232, 126^r-141^v) accounts of Berengarius Blasini.

164] Bernardus de Lipasse, bishop of Dax. Formerly archdeacon in the diocese of Saintes, capellanus Papae; bishop from 1327.

16 Nov 1350 (VQ 5, 441) nephew Guinbaldus de Conpona pays 6 écus.

30 Oct 1353 (EFR I1, 613) commission to Martinus de Girardo, canon of Agen.

165] Bernardus Marchesii, vestiarius of Nîmes.

1403 x 1406 (Coll. 159, 352^r-355^v) Joannes Martini, collector of Narbonne, receives £539.7.4 from debts.

166] Bernardus Martini, abbot of Foix OCSA, diocese of Pamiers, died Aug 1371. Not in *Gall. Christ.* 13:182.

n.d. (Coll. 235, 139^v-140^v) successor Arnaldus Guillelmi is obligated to a composition of 2283 fl.

20 Mar 1372 (Coll. 358, 31^v-32^v) collector Aymericus Pelicerii is informed of the composition for 3000 fr. made by the successor.

8 Apr 1372 (ibid., 46^r) the officialis and subcollector of Pamiers are instructed to collect for the Camera all goods not listed in the inventory, and to assign one-third of their net value, after expenses, to the successor.

14 Aug 1372 (ibid., 75^r) successor is to be compelled to pay a debt of his predecessor to Raymundus Gavarta, LL.Lic.

n.d. (Coll. 18, 290^v) collector receives 2500 fl. of the composition.

1 Oct 1373 (Coll. 236, 148^r, 157^r) collector reports receipt of 2500 fl.; 1250 fl. is still owed of 3000 fl.

16 Jul 1377 (OS 42, 107^r) quittance to Raymundus Ripperie, priest of Foix, for 70 fl. and £3 of his debt of 300 fl.

167] Bernardus Maynardi a Stephanotio, abbot of Caunes OSB, diocese of Narbonne, died before 13 Mar 1355. See *Gall. Christ.* 6:173D-E.

10 Oct 1355 (Coll. 497, 56^r) executor Matheus Constantini is obligated to a composition of 100 fl.

5 Mar 1356 (VQ 7, 130) Guillelmus Borserii, archdeacon in the diocese of Alet, pays 50 fl.

168] Bernardus Michaelis, died in curia.

17 Sep 1361 (VQ 7, 357) Eblo de Mederio, clerk of the Camera, pays 200 fl. from the spoils.

169] Bernardus de Mornaco, bishop of Tarbes, died before 6 Nov 1374. M.Theol.; abbot of Fontfroid OCist, diocese of Narbonne; bishop of Aire from 1354; of Tarbes from 1361.

16 Jul 1375 (OS 42, 26^r) Arnaldus de Peyraco, collector of Auch, pays 290 fl. Cam. 4 s. 1 d. for vessels, some of which were among the goods of Hugo de Bonovillari, bishop of Lectoure.

5 Mar 1380 (Coll. 359, 126^v) the collector is ordered to pay the bishop's debt of 45 fl. to Vitalis de Boulaco, canon of Tarbes.

after 1385 (Coll. 35, 217^r-222^r) remains of spoils collected by Sicardus de Brugayrosio.

170] Bernardus de Nexonio, archdeacon of Antwerp, diocese of Cambrai, clerk of the Camera from 1348, died in curia.

27 Aug 1361 (OS 31, 147^{rv}) quittance to executors for a composition of 500 fl. paid to Eblo de Mederio.

17 Sep 1361 (VQ 7, 357) Eblo de Mederio, clerk of the Camera, pays 500 fl. from goods.

171] Bernardus de Novodampno, administrator of Tarentaise, auditor sacri palatii. Former canon of Beauvais, papal chaplain, Lic.Decr.; treasurer of Tours in 1340; administrator of Tarentaise from 1341.

22 Jul 1341 (EFR B1, 8769; B3, 3141) licentia testandi.
2 May 1347 (RA 91, 607^{rv}, 616^{rv}) inventory.
n.d. (RA 122, 220^r) inventory.
28 Dec 1352 (VQ 5, 460) moneys paid to Camera.

172] Bernardus Oliveri OESA, M.Theol., bishop of Tortosa, died 14 Jul 1348. Formerly bishop of Huesca from 1337; of Barcelona from 1345; of Tortosa from 1346.

2 Oct 1349 (VQ 5, 579) Bernardus Alanyani, collector of Zaragoza and Tarragona, makes payment to the Camera.

173] Bernardus de Quitania, camerarius to cardinal Raymundus de Fargis.

2 Jul 1349 (VQ 5, 427) executor Joannes de Capella pays 50 fl. composition.

174] Bernardus Raffata, priest of Tarragona.

10 Nov 1375 (IM 2877, 9; OS 42, 42^r) Joannes Baroncelli, papal sergeant

at arms and banker (Guillemain, *Cour*, 428 n.), his executor, pays 407 fl. Cam. 22 s. 9 d. for goods left in his care.

175] Bernardus Rebolli, prior of SS. Antonius and Andreas, Rome.

7 Nov 1368 (Coll. 353, 111ʳ) camerarius orders the restoration of the spoils to the abbot of S. Antonius, Vienne.
16 Jan 1369 (ibid., 137ʳ) to the same effect.

176] Bernardus de Rodes, archbishop of Naples, auditor of the Camera, died before 14 Nov 1377. LL.Lic., former archdeacon in the diocese of Cahors; auditor from 1366; archbishop from 1368.

22 Jul 1379 (Coll. 143, 303ʳ) commission under the general reservation of spoils in Provence, to Vitalis Guillelmi and Bartoletus de Cassarmis de Placentia, to collect the spoils of the bishop, who died near Marseille while traveling to the curia.

177] Bernardus Rouiardi, auditor litterarum contradictarum, bishop of Arras, died in curia before 29 Oct 1320. Former archdeacon of Saintes; bishop from 1316.

1 Feb 1320 (EFR J1, 12904) licentia testandi.
28 Nov 1322 (VQ 1, 309) the bishop exceeded his licentia testandi; his brother Arnaldus, bishop of Salerno, pays 500 fl. (see Mollat in RHE 29 [1933]: 320).

178] Bernardus Sabaterii, perpetual vicar of S. M. de Mari, Barcelona.

9 Jul 1375 (Coll. 356, 29ʳ) executors pay a composition of 300 fl.

179] Bernardus de S. Stephano, bishop of Uzés. Former archdeacon of Béziers, notarius apostolicus, papal familiar; bishop from 1371. In his presence, at Montefiascone in Aug 1368, Urban V forbade the papal notaries to make testaments: VQ 6, 35.

12 Jul 1374 (EFR G1, 1634) papal warning to the holders of spoils.

180] Bernardus de Sault, bishop of Saintes, died before 1 Mar 1381. Former cantor of Compostela; bishop from 1362.

4 Sep 1381 (Coll. 359, 80ʳ-81ʳ) commission to Elias de Serra, Lic.Decr., canon of Agen, noting that the *moderatio* should be observed.
2 - 3 Oct 1381 (ibid., 90ʳ-92ᵛ) further directions to the commissioner: he is to collect the successor's composition of 200 fl. and give him the goods listed in the inventory and half of any further goods.

181] Bernardus de Scossaco, registrator litterarum apostolicarum.

28 Jun 1357 (VQ 7, 177) executors pay a composition of 1000 fl.

182] Bernardus de Serrer, prior "de Sigoterio," diocese of Gap.

29 Mar 1375 (Coll. 356, 10^r) camerarius Petrus de Croso orders the officialis of Gap to make an inventory and to hold the spoils until further orders.

183] Bernardus de Sistre, archdeacon of Canterbury, nuncio in England, died 1343. Formerly canon of S. Hilaire, Poitiers.

23 Mar 1336 (EFR B1, 3378; B3, 798) licentia testandi.
20 Jan 1344 (VQ 5, 353) executors pay a legacy of 50 fl. to the Apostolic See.
19 Apr 1344 (EFR C1, 788) the nuncio's spoils are sequestered, pending the verification of his final accounts.
10 Dec 1344 (ibid., 1310) quittance.
4 Feb 1345 (VQ 5, 354) executors pay 897 fl. to clear accounts.

184] Bernardus Stephani, notarius Papae, died in curia.

n.d. 1361 (OS 31, 249^r-250^r) quittance to the nephew executor Joannes Stephani for a legacy of 200 fl. and a composition of 100 fl.
17 Sep 1361 (VQ 7, 357) Eblo de Mederio, clerk of the Camera, pays 300 fl. from spoils.

185] Bernardus Tardivi, dean of S. Paul de Fenouillet, diocese of Alet, died 1334 or earlier.

20 Sep 1337 (EFR B1, 5099; B2, 364) commission, referring to a reservation by John XXII.
16 Jun 1341 (Coll. 30, 133) Raymundus de Chameraco reports collections from the vacancy.

186] Bernardus de Turre OSB, bishop of S. Papoul, died 27 Dec 1317. Former abbot of S. Papoul OSB; bishop from 1317.

31 Mar 1319 (VQ 1, 453) commissioner Petrus Bodeti, precentor of Lavaur, pays £5000 Tur. parv.
17 Mar 1320 (ibid.) he pays £1000 Tur. parv.
20 May 1320 (ibid., 454) he pays £900.18 Tur. parv.
14 Apr - 1 May 1324 (EFR J2, 3567).
31 Dec 1324 (ibid., 2346-2347).
12 Apr 1326 (VQ 1, 454) Michael Bodeti, brother of Petrus deceased, pays £100 Tur. parv.
21 Apr 1327 (ibid., 527) Raymundus Gasconis pays £50.11.8 Tur. parv.
7 Apr 1328 (OS 12, 87^r-88^r) quittance to commissioner Raymundus Gasconis.

15 Jan 1331 (VQ 1, 454) quittance to commissioner Michael Bodeti for 83 fl. etc.
27 Dec 1331 (OS 12, 137^r-138^r) quittance to Arnaldus de Verdala.
20 Nov 1335 (EFR B2, 122) general quittance to Arnaldus de Verdala.

187] Bernardus la Vernha, canon of Auxerre, subcollector.

5 Mar 1375 (EFR G1, 1821) commission to Jacobus Militis, new subcollector of Auxerre.
8 Mar 1375 (Coll. 356, 7^{rv}) camerarius Petrus de Croso orders the subcollector to discover and collect the spoils, including money and gold and silver vessels, from unnamed holders.
8 Mar 1375 (ibid., 7^v) the camerarius asks his "dear friend" Nicolaus de Archeis, bishop of Auxerre, as the major holder of the goods, to answer the commissioners fully.
28 May 1375 (ibid., 19^v) the commissioners need not cite the bishop to appear in their inquest.
23 Jun 1375 (ibid., 32^{rv}) Laurentius Marcelli and his wife are released from excommunication.
21 Jul 1375 (ibid., 51^r-52^r) the goods are released to the executor in consequence of an agreement between him and the fiscal procurator.
28 Sep 1375 (OS 42, 37^r) Nicolaus, bishop of Auxerre, executor, pays 214 fl. Cam. of a composition for 2000 fl.
Apr 1376 (IM 2924, 3) Joannes, abbot of S. Maur, diocese of Châlons-sur-Marne, pays 535 fl. Cam. of a composition of 2000 fl.
9 Apr 1376 (OS 42, 63^r) executor Joannes de Sergiis, D.Decr. pays 625 fl. curr. of a composition for 2000 fl.
30 Jul 1376 (ibid., 76^v-77^r) he pays 875 fl. through Bernardus Cariti.

188] Bertrandus, bishop of Alife, died before 10 Nov 1361. Bishop from 1348.

Feb 1362 (Coll. 169, 132^r) inventory of spoils collected.

189] Bertrandus OP, archbishop of Brindisi, died before 6 Dec 1333. Archbishop from 1319.

1324 x 1332 (Coll. 221, 152^r) Geraldus de Valle collects 209 unc. 11 car. from the spoils and vacancy.

190] Bertrandus, bishop of Dax. Not in Eubel; in Gams, bishop from 1351.

9 Oct 1358 (IM 4594, 10^v, 12^r) the spoils of the bishop, who died in the Sinai desert, were collected and sold by nuncio Goffredus Spanzo, archdeacon of Famagosta, for £3200.

191] Bertrandus, bishop of Sénez. Formerly provost of Sénez; bishop from 1317.

31 Dec 1345 (EFR C1, 2244) commission to Raymundus Naulonis.
20 Feb 1348 (ibid., 3752) orders Raimbaudus Flote to hold goods, because Raymundus Naulonis cannot pursue the process.
16 Feb 1354 (Coll. 497, -) Stephanus Marronis, LL.D., judge of the temporal court of Avignon, and Ludovicus de Marronis, canon of Sénez, obligate themselves to a composition of 200 fl.
12 Sep 1358 (Coll. 497, 65^r; VQ 7, 224) the successor Bertrandus pays a composition of 60 fl.

192] Bertrandus, abbot of S. Gilles OSB, diocese of Nîmes, died before 25 Jul 1348. Not in *Gall. Christ.* 6.

late 1348 (RA 101, 52^r-55^r) inventory by commissioner Raymundus de Salerio.
25 Oct 1348 (Coll. 497, 39^v; OS 23, 27^v) successor obligated to a composition of 800 fl.
31 Jan 1349 (VQ 5, 417) successor Raymundus pays 100 fl. of his composition.
n.d. (Coll. 149, 165^r-167^r; Coll. 155, 237^r-238^r) Guillelmus Guilaberti accounts for receipts of 398 fl. 14 s. 3 d.; remains of 1053 fl. 22 s.

193] Bertrandus de Bariolis, operarius of Arles.

16 Apr 1334 (VQ 1, 374-375) Durandus Mercatoris assigns various moneys and books to the Camera through Rostagnus Alziaci, archdeacon of Arles.

194] Bertrandus de Barreyra, abbot of Conques, diocese of Rodez, died Mar 1368. See *Gall. Christ.* 1:248B.

3 Apr 1368 (Coll. 81, 139^r-151^r) inventory and accounts by the collector Guillelmus Amarinti.
1368 (Coll. 80, 135^r) collector notes his receipts and sales, 1210 fl. 10 1/4 gr.
1 Oct 1371 (Coll. 81, 131^r-132^r) collector receives 309 fl. and books.
3 Apr 1374 (IM 2833) books delivered to successor Raymundus by order of the camerarius.
1386 (Coll. 84, 90^r-92^r) arrears of spoils in accounts of the collector Raymundus de Senancio.
1396 x 1398 (Coll. 90, 139^v) Guillelmus Amarinti pays £11 Tur., 20 fl. from sales to Bernardus Benguerii, subcollector.

195] Bertrandus de Baucio, prior "de Bolena," diocese of S. Paul-Trois-Châteaux, died 1344.

13 Feb 1344 (EFR C1, 667).

11 Jul 1346 (VQ 5, 375) Petrus de Artisio, treasurer of the Comtat-Venaissin, pays 247 fl. Piedmont.

16 Mar 1375 (Coll. 356, 3ʳ) mentions the murder of Dondinus de Pistoriis, in the Comtat, by Bertrandus de Baucio and accomplices.

196] Bertrandus Berengarii OSB, bishop of Sarlat. Formerly abbot of S. Tiberius, diocese of Agde; bishop from 1324.

13 Jan 1330 (EFR J1, 48103) licentia testandi.

15 Apr 1330 (EFR J2, 4165) commission.

30 Sep 1330 (IE 105, 36ʳ-45ᵛ) accounts of Guillelmus Cabiroli, commissioner, delivered on 3 Nov by the messenger Petrus Raymundi de Verfolio.

3 Nov 1330 (ibid., 39ʳ) a bull protecting the licensed testament.

27 Mar 1332 (VQ 1, 555) Guillelmus Cabiroli pays 300 fl. from the goods "ratione subsidii promissi pape dum episcopus viveret" (ibid., 565) he pays 700 fl., 43 d. Paris.

197] Bertrandus Besauduni, archbishop of Genoa, died before 2 Jul 1358. Former canon of Toulon; archbishop from 1349.

26 Nov 1359 (VQ 7, 268) successor Guido Scettem (q.v.) pays 20 fl. of a composition for 120 fl.

24 Apr 1360 (Coll. 231, 81ᵛ-82ʳ) he pays 100 fl.

9 Mar 1363 (OS 31, 170ᵛ-171ʳ) those payments of 120 fl. are accepted as fruits of the vacancy, and Guido Scettem is still liable for the spoils.

198] Bertrandus de Bitteris, prior "de Cassiano" OCSA, diocese of Béziers, died 1329.

1 Dec 1329 (EFR J2, 4032) commission.

23 Apr 1330 (OS 12, 125ᵛ; VQ 1, 557) successor Bernardus de Bossiacis pays 500 fl. of a composition for 1000 fl.

23 Nov 1330 (ibid., 132ᵛ) he pays 500 fl.

8 Mar 1331 (ibid., 139ʳ) he pays 250 fl.

199] Bertrandus de Campinhaco, canon of Périgueux.

18 Dec 1384 (Coll. 37, 10ᵛ-11ʳ) commission to Petrus de Moreriis.

n.d. (Coll. 37, 1ᵛ) mutilated inventory on parchment, used as a register-cover.

n.d. (ibid., 21ʳ) expenses in the process of collecting the spoils.

5 Oct 1387 (Coll. 359, 241ᵛ-242ʳ) camerarius Franciscus de Conzia directs Petrus de Campinhaco to pay his debt to his late brother, 40 fr., as a stipend to the bearer, Joannes de Mauriaco.

REPERTORY OF CASES

200] Bertrandus de Cardilhaco, bishop of Cahors, died before 15 Feb 1366. Formerly bishop of Rieux from 1321; of Cahors from 1324.

15 Mar 1367 (Coll. 80, 135^r) his nephew, the marquis de Cardilhaco, pays 898 fl. of a composition for 1000 fl. to the collector Guillelmus Amarinti.

Apr 1367 (OS 23A, 92^v) nephew's obligation of 1000 fl. noted paid.

Oct 1371 (Coll. 81, 131^r) the collector notes that 106 fl. are still due on the composition.

201] Bertrandus de Cardilhaco, bishop of Montauban, died before 16 Jun 1361. Bishop since 1357.

10 Oct 1360 (VQ 7, 300) the executor Petrus de Calezio, as commissioner, pays 768 fl. sent. 18 s. 11 d.

7 Apr 1361 (ibid., 335) executors pay 2835 fl. of a composition for 4000 fl. (cf. OS 23A, 110^v; Coll. 116, 141^r).

and see G. Mollat, "Jean de Cardaillac," RHE 48 (1953): 85 n. 4. The late bishop's nephew Joannes de Cardilhaco, bishop of Orense, made a composition for 3000 fl., of which he paid 2800 fl. (Arm.35, t.23, 82^r).

202] Bertrandus de Castronovo, bishop of Viviers. Formerly elect of Taranto, 1348; archbishop of Salerno from 1349; of Embrun from 1364; bishop of Viviers from 1365.

23 Mar 1372 (EFR G1, 723) commission to Petrus de Vernolis, papal treasurer.

203] Bertrandus de Deux, bishop of Nîmes, died Jul 1348. Formerly prior "de Sumena" OCSA, diocese of Nîmes; bishop from 1342.

23 Aug 1348 (EFR C1, 3939) orders Petrus Hugonis to collect these and other spoils.

31 Jan 1349 (VQ 5, 417) executors pay 1000 fl. of a composition for 2000 fl.

1 Oct 1349 (ibid., 428) they pay 1000 fl.

16 Mar 1350 (Coll. 497, 43^r) Gaucelmus de Deux, abbot of Psalmody, obligated to a composition of 250 fl.

5 Nov 1354 (VQ 7, 59) Antonius de Fontenaco, papal courier, pays 100 fl. of his debt of 250 fl.

204] Bertrandus Eraclii, prior of "S. Evimia," diocese of Mende.

31 Jul 1333 (VQ 1, 484) Bernardus, abbot of S. Chaffre, diocese of Le Puy, pays 448 fl. Flor., 153 fl. Piedmont, 9 d. Tur. gr.

205] Bertrandus Gasqui, provost of Pignans OCSA, diocese of Fréjus.

3 Aug 1345 (EFR C1, 1862) commission to Joannes Regis and Raymundus Naulonis.
9 Sep 1345 (ibid., 1954) commission to Petrus Chautardi and Joannes Regis.
26 May 1346 (VQ 5, 370) Joannes Regis, commissioner, pays 90 fl. Flor., 8 fl. Piedmont.
17 Jun 1346 (ibid., 372) successor Guigo pays 200 fl. of a composition for 1000 fl.
31 Oct 1346 (ibid., 377-378) he pays 350 fl.
22 Dec 1346 (ibid., 379) he pays 275 fl.
19 Jul 1347 (EFR C1, 3377) Imbertus Raynouardi, who stole goods, is freed from prison by the influence of relatives at Avignon.
4 Aug 1347 (VQ 5, 393) Ambertus Raymundi, camerarius of Pignans, pays 250 fl. of a composition for 1000 fl. for stolen goods.
31 Oct 1347 (ibid., 396) successor pays 275 fl. of a composition.

206] Bertrandus la Lana, priest of Bordeaux, died in curia.

6 Feb 1375 (Coll. 356, 2^v-3^r) Raymundus, abbot of Sauve-Majeure, executor, obligated to a composition for 500 fl., and promises to observe the *moderatio*.
Aug 1375 (IM 2877, 5) Raymundus pays 18 fl. of his composition.
Oct 1375 (IM 2877, 8) he pays 18 fl.
30 Oct 1375 (OS 42, 40^r) he pays the composition in full.

207] Bertrandus de Langusello, bishop of Nîmes, died 8 Jan 1323. Bishop from 1280.

30 Aug 1324 (VQ 1, 487) the executor of the successor Armandus de Vernovo pays 1000 fl.

208] Bertrandus Malisanguinis, abbot of Montmajour OSB, diocese of Arles, died 16 Aug 1316. See *Gall. Christ.* 1:612.

14 Jul 1318 (EFR J1, 7763-7766) judgements against nephews and holders of goods.
13 Mar 1329 (EFR J2, 3801).
15 Oct 1329 (ibid., 3996).
(VQ 1, 538).
and see Mollat in RHE 29 (1933) 324 n. 4 - 325 n. 1.

209] Bertrandus de Malomonte, bishop of Poitiers, died 12 Aug 1385. Formerly secular abbot "de Dauraco," diocese of Limoges, papal chaplain and familiar; bishop of Tulle from 1371; of Poitiers from 1376.

6 Mar 1388 (IM 3344) collector Joannes Francisci returns a missal to the nephew Bertrandus de Malomonte, prothonotary apostolic.

210] Bertrandus de Maso, bishop of Lodève, died 21 Jul 1348. Bishop since 1322.

19 Jul 1348 (EFR C1, 3921) commission to Bernardus Andreae.
25 Jul 1348 (Coll. 474, 2^r-16^r) inventory by commissioner Bernardus Andreae.
22 Sep 1348 (VQ 5, 411) payments by commissioner.
27 Apr 1349 (ibid., 425) he pays 600 écus, 30 fl.
19 Oct 1349 (ibid., 430) he pays 300 fl. for animals sold.
11 Feb 1350 (ibid., 433) he pays 67 fl. Pied., 82 s. Tur.
4 Dec 1350 (ibid., 442) Berengarius Guillelmi, lord of Clermont, pays 30 fl. which he had owed to the bishop.
11 Feb 1351 (ibid., 443) commissioner pays 100 écus.
2 Aug 1351 (ibid., 447-448) he pays 70 écus, 24 fl. Pied.
5 Apr 1354 (VQ 7, 49-50) vicar Pontius de Onsseria pays 1 gold georgius for a debt of conscience received by him.
5 Apr 1354 (ibid., 50) Raymundus Andreae pays a composition of 200 fl. (cf. OS 23A, 102^v).
25 Apr 1354 (Coll. 474, 17^r-54^v) commissioner's accounts.

211] Bertrandus de Massello, collector of Aragon. See Jean Glénisson, "Un agent de la Chambre apostolique au XIVe siècle: les missions de Bertrand du Mazel (1364-1378)," *Mélanges* 59 (1947): 89-119.

2 Apr 1384 (Coll. 360, 105^v-106^r) camerarius Franciscus de Conzia accepts the obligation of the nephew Guillelmus Passabas to a composition of 400 fr.

212] Bertrandus de Pebraco, bishop of Vabres. Formerly prior of S. Martin des Champs OClun, diocese of Paris; bishop of Vabres from 1352.

13 May 1359 (IM 2162) minute of the commission to Joannes Garrigie, collector of Portugal.
1357 x 1359 (Coll. 154, 213^v-214^r) accounts of Guillelmus Guilaberti, collector general in Spain.
n.d. (Coll. 149, 168^v) Guillelmus Guilaberti accounts for net receipts of 323 fl. 4 s.
Nov 1359 - Mar 1362 (Coll. 75, 233^r-236^v) Joannes de Cavanhaco, collector of Rodez, gathered 378 fl. after the departure of Guillelmus Guilaberti. Note on 236^v-237^v of the spoils of benefices belonging to the episcopal mensa, collected as fruits of the vacancy.

5 Mar 1361 (Coll. 231, 127ʳ) cardinal Guillelmus de Agrifolio of Zaragoza pays 300 fl. for a mitre (cf. VQ 7, 334).

31 May 1361 (VQ 7, 338) collector Joannes de Cavanhaco pays 310 fl. 15 s. from the sale of a cross, mitre, etc.

1361 (Coll. 78, 141ʳ-146ᵛ) remains, including the subspoils mentioned above, in the accounts of Joannes de Cavanhaco.

1363-1366 (Coll. 80, 124ʳ-126ᵛ, copy 265ʳ-267ᵛ) collector Guillelmus Amarinti reports the remains of all spoils as 177 fl. 2 gr. and £13.6.8.

1386 (Coll. 84, 260ʳ-262ʳ) remains reported by Raymundus de Senancio.

213] Bertrandus de Podio, bishop of Montauban. Formerly abbot of Montauban OSB; bishop from 1317.

11 Nov 1316 (EFR J1, 1802) licentia testandi.

21 Aug 1317 (ibid., 4812) commission.

214] Bertrandus Raffini, bishop of Rodez, died in curia. Formerly archdeacon in the diocese of Lerida, Lic.Decr., papal chaplain, clerk of the Camera.

13 May 1385 (Coll. 361, 6ʳᵛ) the camerarius orders Raymundus de Senancio and Joannes de Securo to make an inventory and to hold the spoils, subject to the *moderatio*.

22 May 1385 (IM 3203, 6) Ginnotus Bonasos, domicellus, pays 74 fl. Cam. 16 s. toward his composition.

1386 (Coll. 84, 93ʳ) accounts of collector Raymundus de Senancio.

215] Bertrandus Retranni, provost of Pignans OCSA, diocese of Fréjus.

21 Sep 1326 (VQ 1, 517) commissioners Ludovicus de Petragrossa and Guillelmus Lemozini pay the Camera 1060 fl. 49 s. 7 d. Tur. gr., 10 agni, and precious vessels.

4 Dec 1326 (ibid.) successor Rostagnus de Minulis (q.v.) pays 500 fl. of a composition for 1000 fl.

19 May 1327 (ibid.) he pays 500 fl.

216] Bertrandus de Ruppe, scriptor Papae, died in curia.

8 Jun 1375 (Coll. 356, 26ʳ) executors pay composition.

28 Jun 1375 (ibid., 28ʳ) executor Pontius de Gardia is permitted to collect spoils with the powers of a papal collector.

217] Bertrandus de Sabrano, prior of S. Genès "de Martico," diocese of Arles.

13 Dec 1329 (VQ 1, 561) Petrus Gervasii pays 380 agni and 41 m. 3 1/4 unc. of silver.

ca. May 1330 (OS 12, 128ʳ) Arnaldus de Villanova, knight, pays 100 agni of 400 agni which he had owed to the prior.
13 Dec 1330 (ibid., 129ᵛ) Petrus Gervasii pays 2300 agni.
17 Aug 1331 (ibid., 144ᵛ) Arnaldus de Villanova pays the balance of his debt.
9 Mar 1334 (VQ 1, 371) Pontius de Pereto pays 34 fl. owed by Bertrandus for the goods of his predecessor.

218] Bertrandus de S. Genesio, patriarch of Aquileia, died 6 Jun 1350. J.U.D.; former dean of Angoulême, papal chaplain and familiar, nuncio in Rome (see letters in IE 140, 54ʳᵛ); patriarch from 1334.

28 Aug 1333 (EFR J1, 61107) licentia testandi.
28 Jun 1350 (EFR C2, 2236) commission.

219] Bertrandus de S. Martiali, bishop of S. Papoul, died 9 Aug 1361. Formerly prior of Portus Dei OSB, diocese of Limoges; bishop of Tulle from 1344; of S. Papoul from 1347.

5 Jan 1362 (OS 31, 215ᵛ-216ᵛ) composition by executor Petrus de S. Martiali, bishop of Rieux, 2500 fl. for spoils and vacancy.
22 Aug 1362 (VQ 7, 419) executor pays 300 fl.
Sep - Oct 1362 (ibid., 422) he pays 460 fl.
1362 (OS 23A, 105ʳ) the full composition was paid.

220] Bertrandus Senherii, sacristan of Lombez, former treasurer of the March of Ancona.

24 Oct 1343 (EFR C1, 483).
5 Feb 1345 (VQ 5, 354) Joannes, rector of the March of Ancona, pays 38 fl. 13 s. 4 d. from spoils.

221] Bertrandus de Turre, bishop of Le Puy, died before 30 May 1382. Lic.J.Civ., former secular abbot of S. Genès, diocese of Clermont; bishop of Tulle from 1353; of Le Puy from 1361.

4 Jun 1382 (Coll. 359, 121ʳᵛ) the camerarius Petrus de Croso orders the collector Pontius de Croso to take the overdue services from the spoils, to observe the *moderatio*, and to give the family property to the successor and heir.
12 Jun 1382 (ibid., 123ᵛ) the collector is ordered to pay a debt of 120 fr. to Aysilia, the lady of Godet.
20 Jun 1382 (Coll. 85, 108ʳ-109ᵛ) spoils received by the collector Pontius de Croso from his predecessor Vitalis de Boscomedio: a net profit of £469.1.8.

222] Bisantius, bishop of Troia.

17 Aug 1340 (EFR B3, 2852) advance reservation.
23 Sep 1340 (EFR B1, 8325) commission.

223] Blasius O Cist, bishop of Chiusi, died before 21 Aug 1357. Formerly abbot of SS. Vito and Salcio, diocese of Chieti; bishop from 1353.

28 Dec 1357 (Coll. 352, 118^v) commission, dated 14 Dec, expedited by Reginaldus de Lupchaco, cantor of Auxerre, to Petrus, archbishop of Benevento, and himself.

224] Blasius, bishop of Jubail, Syria, died before 14 Apr 1334 at the monastery of Monteoliveti, diocese of Arezzo.

1334 (IE 145, 27^v-28^v) account by commissioner Pontius Stephani.

225] Blasius Fernandi, archbishop of Toledo, died 7 Mar 1362. Formerly dean of Toledo; bishop of Palencia from 1343; archbishop of Toledo from 1353.

30 Apr 1354 (RA 128, 599^r) licentia testandi.
9 Sep 1354 (EFR I1, 1117) commission to Petrus Cariti and Angerius de Osserano and Martinus Gundisalvi to collect the spoils in the event of the death of the archbishop, "magna corporis infirmitate gravati."

226] Bonabius de Rocaforte, bishop of Nantes. Bishop since 1338.

7 Jan 1340 (EFR B2, 673-674) commission.
9 Feb 1345 (EFR C1, 1481) instructions to the commissioner.

227] Bonasassius, prior of Daurade OSB, diocese of Toulouse, died 11 Sep 1361 x 1363 (see *Gall. Christ.* 13:107C-108A); prior from 1309.

9 Jan 1364 (EFR U2, 760) Pontius de Andorta, procurator to the prior, suspect of theft; commissioners Bertrandus de Castanherio and Guillelmus Dominici cited him and he did not appear; they are to cite him to appear before the camerarius within 20 days.
1364 (Coll. 235, 122^{rv}) commissioners' accounts.
1371 (Coll. 18, 215^r-216^r) commissioners' accounts; total collections 89 fl. 5 gr.
1 Oct 1373 (Coll. 236, 147^v, 156^r) Aymericus Pelicerii reports 88 fl. 16 gr. collected, 247 fl. 9 gr. and 21 m. silver remaining.

228] Bonifatius, bishop of Como, died 1351. D.Decr., former canon of Vicenza; bishop of Modena from 1336; of Como from 1340.

1 Sep 1352 (EFR C2, 2681) commission to Raymundus, abbot of S. Nicola in Lido, Venice.
8 Nov 1352 (ibid., 2700) orders him to recover goods from holders who claim them as gifts, etc.

229] Bonjoannes, elect of Patrai, died before 21 Jul 1363. Former bishop of Diacovar, Hungary from 1348; of Fermo from 1349; elect of Patrai, 5 Apr 1363.

24 Aug 1363 (EFR U2, 570) commission to Geraldus de Portali, treasurer of Romagnola.

230] Bonuspar Lordati, prior "de Chiraco," diocese of Mende.

16 Apr 1334 (VQ 1, 373) Ratherius, abbot of S. Victor, Marseille, pays 150 fl. through Durandus Mercatoris.

231] Bonuspar Virgili, bishop of Mende. Formerly provost of Mende, LL.D., papal subdeacon and familiar; bishop of Uzés from 1366; of Mende from 1371.

3 Oct 1375 (Coll. 356, 66^r-67^r) letters accepting the composition by the executor Blancus Duriane and ordering the collector Petrus de Monteaurosa to release the spoils to him.
Nov 1375 (IM 2877, 9) executor pays his composition of 2000 fl. Cam. with 1969 fl. and two mules.
15 Nov 1375 (OS 42, 42^v-43^r) composition received: 1838 fr. 12 s. and five mules for 161 fr. 9 gr.

232] Canhardus, bishop of Couserans, died before 28 Nov 1358. Bishop from 1348.

16 Apr 1359 (VQ 7, 261-262) executors and successor Joannes de Rochechouart pay a composition of 1200 fl. (cf. OS 23A, 105^r).

233] Capulus, abbot of S. Pietro, Perugia.

4 Nov 1363 (OS 23A, 94^v) successor Philippus obligated to a composition of 200 fl.

234] Catherina de Bullene de Avinione.

2 Mar 1358 (VQ 7, 218) Raymundus Mercerii, procurator animarum, and Bernardus de Colonis, physician, pay 100 fl. of 400 fl. "de bonis reservatis."

235] Centellus de Astariaco, provost of Toulouse, died 21 Aug 1361. See *Gall. Christ.* 13:80D-E.

Nov 1361 - (Coll. 235, 73^r-77^v) accounts of the collector Bertrandus de Castanherio.
1364 (ibid., 117^r-118^v) further receipts.
1371 (Coll. 18, 209^v-212^v) remains of debts collected by Bertrandus de Castanherio and Aymericus Pelicerii: 383 fl. 10 gr.

1 Oct 1373 (Coll. 236, 147ʳ, 155ᵛ) Aymericus Pelicerii reports 383 fl. 10 gr. 9 Barc. collected; 376 fl. 4 gr. 9 Barc. remaining, and grain as well.

236] Christoforus de Tramonto, bishop of Bisignano. Formerly canon of Nola; bishop of Umbriatico from 1333; of Bisignano from 1347.

16 Mar 1354 (Coll. 169, 51ʳ) subcommissioner Arnaldus de Gretuilla pays for spoils.

237] Conradus, treasurer of the church of Coimbra.

30 Apr 1355 (VQ 7, 91) Balduinus Riccardi, sigillifer auditoris Camerae, pays 35 fl. 30 gr. Tur. and 38 s. Avin.

238] Cyprianus, abbot of S. Sophia, Benevento, died 18 Oct 1344.

19 Oct 1344 - 17 Feb 1345 (Coll. 168, 43ᵛ-45ʳ) Guillelmus de Roseriis collects goods worth 70 unc. 33 car. 20 grani, and books.

239] Dalmacius de Podio, prior "de Campo," diocese of Elne, died 15 May 1395.

before 1405 (Coll. 160, 122ᵛ) collector Joannes de Ripis of Elne receives £6.7.3 for goods.

240] Dalphinus, bishop of Aire. Former provost of Rieux; bishop of Aire from 1349.

30 Jan 1356 (Coll. 497, 57ʳ) Bernardus de Bellomonte, lord of "Trapa," diocese of Rieux, as heir, obligated to a composition of 800 fl.
30 May 1356 (VQ 7, 133) heir pays 197 fl. of his composition.

241] Demetrius de Matafaris, bishop of Knin in Dalmatia. Formerly bishop of Pedena in Istria from 1345; of Knin from 1354.

20 Jan 1368 (Coll. 353, 97ᵛ) a letter of the camerarius to the doge and officials of the Veneto asks help in capturing the bishop, fugitive from arrest in Rome.
9 Dec 1368 (Coll. 353, 133ᵛ-134ᵛ) quittance to Bertrandus Ebrardi, who assigned the goods to the Camera in Rome.

242] Deodatus OClun, bishop of Castres, died before 20 Nov 1388. Formerly prior of S. Sernin du Port, diocese of Uzés, Lic.Decr.; bishop of Castres from 1385.

30 Nov 1388 (IM 3417) collector Raymundus de Senancio sends an inventory of spoils (lost), and asks whether he should sell the grain at the current favorable prices, or wait until the next payment of fruits to the successor.

16 Dec 1388 - (IM 3367) camerarius Franciscus de Conzia's actions: the reservation of spoils is limited by the *moderatio*; the goods have been redeemed by the successor Joannes for a composition of 3000 fl. curr., except the books of all faculties and the silver.

Dec 1388 (IM 3337, 26) Raymundus de Senancio pays 424 fl. Cam. 7 s. 3 d. from the spoils.

Feb 1389 (ibid., 33) Catalonus de Rocha, banker, buys the silver vessels for 297 fl. Cam. 25 s. 5 d.

n.d. (IM 5246) informal note of the disposition of money and goods.

243] Deodatus, abbot "de Novacula" OSB, diocese of Novara.

1 Oct 1356 (Coll. 497, 60^v) Bertrandus de Villato, prior of S. Maria Maggiore, promises to surrender the spoils.

244] Deodatus Boffias, subcollector of Narbonne, died 5 Apr 1375.

1375 (Coll. 157, 22^r-23^r) inventory of silverware.

245] Deodatus de Canillaco OSB, bishop of Maguelonne, died 15 Aug 1364. Formerly prior "de Cessenone" OSB, diocese of S. Pons de Thomières; bishop of S. Flour from 1347; of Maguelonne from 1361. See *Gall. Christ.* 6:790B-791C.

1363 - 1364 (IM 5216) record of emoluments of the episcopal mensa of Maguelonne.

1 - 15 Aug 1364 (IM 5140, 3^r-27^v) income of the house at Montpellier during the last month of the bishop's life.

1365 (Coll. 137, 1^r-2^r; RA 157, 48^{rv}) accounts of the collector Joannes Garrigie.

1365 (RA 305, 537^r = 542^r) summary of the collector's accounts.

246] Deodatus de Nogareto, prior "de Ispanico," diocese of Mende.

20 May 1375 (Coll. 356, 17^v) orders the collector Petrus de Monteaurosa to collect the spoils from the prior's superior, the abbot of S. Victor, Marseille, or others.

247] Deodatus Rotbaldo, bishop of Agen. Formerly canon of Agen; bishop from 1357.

4 Jan 1364 (EFR U2, 743) registered commission to Sancius Vaquerii and Guillelmus Dominici.

5 Jan 1364 (IM 2335) original commission, readdressed to Bertrandus de Castanherio.

9 Feb 1364 (Coll. 353, 1^{rv}) Bertrandus de Castanherio ordered to release the spoils to the successor Raymundus in consideration of a composition.

1371 (Coll. 18, 216^v-226^r) accounts of Aymericus Pelicerii: 304 fl. received, 185 fl. remaining.
n.d. (Coll. 235, 123^r-125^r) accounts, showing 185 fl. remaining.
1 Oct 1373 (Coll. 236, 147^v, 156^r) Aymericus Pelicerii reports 3093 fl. 11 gr., 16 Barc. collected; 185 fl., 1 gr., 9 Barc. remaining.

248] Didacus de Navasquez OCarm, elect of Torres, Sardinia, died about Jun 1355.

ca. Jun 1355 (Coll. 211, 103^r-110^v, 133^r-152^v) spoils process with original letters.

249] Didacus Ramirez Guzman, bishop of Leon, died before 15 Jan 1354. Bishop from 1344.

29 Jun 1354 (EFR I1, 1003) Pedro, king of Castile and Leon, is asked not to interfere in the spoils process conducted by the abbot of S. Facundus OSB, diocese of Leon.
before 1357 (Coll. 114, 39^r) collector Augerius de Offerano reports receipts of 6638 marks of silver, 208 fl., 9 écus.
25 Jun 1360 (Coll. 497, 72^r) chapter obligated to a composition of 400 fl.
5 Apr 1361 (Coll. 231, 129^v; VQ 7, 335) Martinus Alfonsi, portionarius of Leon, pays 200 fl. of the composition.
15 Jun 1361 (VQ 7, 340) he pays the other 200 fl. (cf. OS 23A, 98^v).

250] Dinus de Radicofano, archbishop of Pisa. Formerly provost of Genoa, D.Decr., papal chaplain; patriarch of Grado from 1332; archbishop of Genoa from 1337; of Pisa from 1342.

5 Oct 1340 (EFR B1, 7934) licentia testandi.
14 Oct 1348 (EFR C2, 1728) commission.
31 Mar 1349 - Jan 1350 (Coll. 245, 127^v-131^v) receipts of spoils by collector Andreas de Tuderto.
6 Jul, 8 Sep 1352 (Coll. 246, 91^v-92^v) sales of books.
5 Dec 1364 (Coll. 231, 13^r-16^r) Raynerius, subcollector and commissioner, is directed to pay for this and other commissions.

251] Dominicus d'Augays, abbot of Case-Dieu OPraem, diocese of Auch, died 27 Oct 1360. See *Gall. Christ.* **1:1033.**

21 Oct 1361 (VQ 7, 364) Petrus Brunelli pays 53 fl., 551 écus, 560 mutones, 62 regales, 6 s. Avin.
18 Jul 1362 (OS 31, 156^r-157^r) quittance to Bertrandus de Moleria for the balance of his composition of 500 fl., in view of the late collector's fraudulent collection of 1000 gold pieces.

252] Dominicus de Campocassio, canon of Genoa, nuncio and collector in Corsica and Genoa.

16 Jan - 24 Mar 1363 (IM 2299) commissioners Guido Scettem, archbishop of Genoa, and Raphael de Turre, report their inquest into the nuncio's spoils; he died with accounts outstanding.

253] Dominicus Grima OP, bishop of Pamiers. Bishop from 1326.

29 Jul 1345 (EFR C1, 1854) reservation in advance of death.
13 Jan 1348 (ibid., 3691) commission.
n.d. (Coll. 30, 283^r) accounts of collector Raymundus Rogerii.
n.d. (Coll. 233, 48^r-91^r) accounts of subcollector Bernardus Sayseti, commissioned by Morerius de Moreriis, rendered to Martinus de Girardo.
after 1353 (Coll. 31, 190^v-191^v) accounts of collector Martinus de Girardo.
1360 x 1363 (Coll. 18, 193^v-203^r) collections by Bertrandus de Castanherio and Aymericus Pelicerii: £106.17.1 Tur.
1360 x 1363 (Coll. 235, 61^r-66^v) arrears collected by Bertrandus de Castanherio.

254] Donusdei Malavolti, bishop of Siena. Formerly canon of Siena, notarius apostolicus; bishop from 1317.

9 Mar 1332 (EFR J1, 56621) licentia testandi.
17 Apr 1350 - (RA 108, 21^r-56^v) process by commissioner Andreas de Tuderto.
27 Dec 1350 (EFR C2, 2364) commission.
15 Feb 1351 (ibid., 2389) instructions.
4 Apr 1351 - 17 Jan 1352 (Coll. 246, 91^r) executors pay composition of 1000 fl. in three terms.

255] Draconetus Artaudi de Montauban, bishop of Gap. Formerly bishop of S. Paul-Trois-Châteaux from 1310; of Gap from 1328.

10 Jun 1328 (EFR J2, 3605) licentia testandi.
11 Jun 1333 (EFR J1, 60521) licentia testandi.
12 Mar 1349 (EFR C1, 4103) commission to Guillelmus de Balma, dean of Avignon, collector of Arles.
10 May 1349 (ibid., 4163) instructions.
2 Mar 1350 (VQ 5, 433) collector makes payment.
6 Mar 1350 (ibid., 434) he pays 140 fl. from sales.
1 Sep 1350 (ibid., 439) he pays 400 fl.
12 Dec 1351 (ibid., 602) he pays arrears.
28 Feb 1354 (VQ 7, 48) he pays 300 fl.
16 Feb 1356 (Coll. 497, 57^v) successor obligated to a composition of 40 fl.

256] Durandus Braxerie, canon of Embrun and Aix.

31 Mar 1332 (VQ 1, 516) nephew pays 250 fl., the sentence against him for receiving reserved spoils.

257] Durandus de Capellis de Lescamel, bishop of Maguelonne. Formerly cantor of Rouen; bishop of Couserans from 1345; of Rieux from 1348; of Maguelonne from 1353.

14 Nov 1360 (Coll. 231, 106ᵛ; VQ 7, 302) nephew Geraldus de Lescamel pays composition of 6000 fl. (cf. OS 23A, 104ᵛ).
n.d. (Coll. 149, 167ᵛ-168ʳ) collector Guillelmus Guilaberti gives the nephew 803 fl. from spoils.

258] Durandus Laurentii, bishop of Lamego, died before 1363. Formerly canon of Lamego; bishop from 1349.

17 Jul 1363 (OS 31, 181ᵛ-182ʳ) composition of successor Laurentius, 300 fl.
20 Jul 1363 (OS 31, 182ʳᵛ) orders dean and chapter to release spoils to successor.
12 Nov 1364 (IM 2339, 24; IE 303, 24ᵛ) successor Laurentius pays 150 fl. of a composition of 300 fl. for spoils and vacancy.

259] Eblo de Bironis, dean of Psalmody, diocese of Nîmes.

8 Jun 1347 (Coll. 497, 32ᵛ) abbot Guillelmus obligated to a composition of 900 fl.
18 Jun 1347 (VQ 5, 390) he pays 847 fl.

260] Eblo de Mederio, bishop of Vaison, died before 27 Jan 1380. Formerly archdeacon of S. Serène, diocese of Cahors, clerk of the Camera, papal chaplain and familiar; bishop from 1371.

24 Jul 1380 (Coll. 359, 48ʳ) successor to be supported with 230 fl. until the new fruits.

261] Elias de Champeriis, abbot of Grasse OSB, diocese of Carcassonne, died 14 Oct 1362. See *Gall. Christ.* 6:958D-959C.

16 Feb 1363 (IE 303, 9ᵛ-10ʳ) Jordanus de Haya, procurator fiscal substitute, and Deodatus Boffias, commissioners, pay 1809 fl., 1200 écus.
18 Feb 1363 (OS 31, 169ᵛ-170ʳ) itemized quittance for silverware assigned to the Camera.
25 Feb 1363 (Coll. 497, 82ᵛ) successor Raymundus Folcaudi obligated to a composition of 50 fl.
25 Feb 1363 (OS 31 169ʳᵛ) gives the composition as 200 fl.
28 Feb 1363 (VQ 6, 23) Anglicus Grimoard receives 37 m. 7 unc. of silverware from the spoils, as in an inventory by Joannes Palaysini, as part-payment for the fruits of Avignon.
20 Apr 1363 (OS 31, 175ʳᵛ) obligation of the successor for half of the spoils.

19 Apr 1363 (ibid., 175ᵛ-176ʳ) commission to Raymundus Folcaudi to collect the spoils, less a debt owed to Rigaldus de Champeriis.

28 Nov 1363 (ibid., 207ʳᵛ) second successor Guido obligated to the composition owed by Raymundus.

17 Jun 1364 (IE 303, 20ᵛ) Rigaldus de Champeriis pays 400 fr., 347 agni, etc.

Jun 1364 (IM 2339, 15) Rigaldus de Champeriis, knight, pays 400 fr., 347 mutones of a composition of 1900 fl. offered during the abbot's last illness.

262] Elias de Donzenaco, bishop of Castres, died 30 May 1383. Archdeacon in the church of Constance, nobilis, notary apostolic; bishop of Padua from 1371; of Castres from 1373.

8 Nov 1383 (Coll. 360, 62ᵛ-63ʳ) camerarius directs Raymundus de Senancio, collector of Rodez, to give to Archambaudus, viscount "de Combornio" 200 fr. de cygno, a horse and a mule.

2 Jan 1384 (ibid., 70ʳᵛ; IM 3165) camerarius orders the collector to turn over the spoils to the bearers, Guido Bonafes and Izarnus Cauderiem sergeants at arms.

1 Apr 1385 (Coll. 360, 232ᵛ-234ʳ) quittance for goods to Guido Bonafes.

1386 (Coll. 84, 214ᵛ) collector declares that the subcollector has not accounted to him for the goods.

263] Elias Magnan, abbot of S. Salvator de Blaye, diocese of Bordeaux and collector of Bordeaux, died before 6 Nov 1363. See *Gall. Christ.* 2:880.

1363 (IM 2281) inventory witnessed by Petrus de Villarerio and Guillelmus de Ruppe.

29 Feb 1364 (OS 31, 130ʳᵛ) commission to Petrus Barreti, canon of Bordeaux.

4 Jun 1365 (Coll. 363, 46ᵛ-47ʳ) quittance for books received by the Camera.

264] Elias Ortici, archdeacon and canon of Périgueux.

18 Dec 1384 (Coll. 37, 11ʳ-12ʳ, 21ʳᵛ) commissioner Petrus de Moreriis reports that he cannot collect the spoils, that Petrus de Mornazo, seneschal of Périgord, has confiscated them because they were willed to the archdeacon's nephew in English territory in Bordeaux, a rebellious act; the collector has suffered opprobrium for opening a general process against the holders of the goods, and the seneschal has threatened to arrest him and take him to Paris in chains.

265] Elias de Podio, abbot of S. Martial, diocese of Limoges. See *Gall. Christ.* 2:563E-564A

1 Oct 1361 (Coll. 497, 76ʳ) successor Aymericus obligated to a composition of 100 fl. (attributed by error to the monastery of Psalmody).

3 Dec 1361 (OS 31, 254^v-256^r) spoils released to Guido de Brolio, abbot of Psalmody, agent of the successor, and executor Jacobus de Sperabe, for 500 fl. composition.

12 Jan 1362 (ibid., 77^v) executor obligated to a composition of 500 fl.

18 May 1362 (VQ 7, 403) Ranulphus de Perussia, marshal of justice, assumes the executor's composition and pays 495 fl.

266] Elias de Pons, bishop of Angoulême, died before 20 Jun 1380. Formerly canon of Angoulême.

1380 (IM 4746) camerarius demands accounts.

267] Elias de Salignac, archbishop of Bordeaux. Formerly bishop of Sarlat from 1359; of Bordeaux from 1361.

15 Jul 1378 (Coll. 393, 67^v-68^v) treasurer dictates the disposition of legacies to Elias Peleti, collector of Bordeaux.

268] Elias Servient, bishop of Périgueux, died before 22 Mar 1387. Formerly archdeacon of Périgueux; bishop from 1384.

30 Jul 1387 (Coll. 359, 230^v) camerarius Franciscus de Conzia directs Petrus de Moreriis to collect, observing the *moderatio*, especially in regard to a debt due to Picardus, canon of Périgueux.

31 Oct 1387 (Coll. 37, 16^v) successor Petrus is conceded the *moderatio* of Gregory XI, here copied in full.

n.d. (ibid., 23^v-26^v) collections and expenses.

269] Elias de Tolosa, died in curia.

14 May 1348 (VQ 5, 406) executor pays composition of 50 fl.

270] Eliziarius de Glandava, bishop of Toulon, died 1324. Formerly provost of Toulon; bishop from 1317.

20 Apr 1326 (IM 971) camerarius Gasbert de Valle cites the successor Anselmus to answer for the spoils.

28 Apr 1326 (EFR J1, 26465) commission.

271] Eliziarius de Ponteves OFM, bishop of Apt, died Dec 1361. Bishop from 1358.

6 Apr 1362 (Coll. 497, 80^r) the successor is obligated to a composition of 114 saumata of grain.

272] Eliziarius de Villanova, bishop of Digne, died 7 Oct 1341. Bishop from 1327.

8 Oct 1341 (EFR B2, 894) reservation of the vacancy.

15-23 Oct 1341 (Coll. 471, 1^r-24^v) accounts rendered by Durandus de Serris.

273] Elmerius Dangolmonsier, prior of Sancerre OSB, diocese of Bourges, papal legate to Flanders.

1 Dec 1389 (IM 3418) inventory of books, received by collector Joannes Francisci from subcollector Joannes Bondierii.

274] Emmingus Laurentii, archbishop of Uppsala, died 15 May 1351. Archbishop from 1342.

17 May 1351 (Coll. 497, 74^v) Benedictus Joannis and Henricus Arturi, clerics of Uppsala, confess to receiving 410 m. in the name of the chapter.
1 Jul 1351 (EFR C2, 2455) commission.
25 Feb 1356 (Coll. 97, 42^r-49^v) accounts.

275] Engelbertus de Dolen, archbishop of Riga, died in curia 9 Sep 1347. Former provost of Dorpat; bishop of Dorpat from 1323; archbishop of Riga from 1341.

9 Sep 1332 (EFR J1, 58307) licentia testandi.
1353 (RA 122, 250^{rv}) goods in the papal treasure.

276] Engerranus de Stella, archbishop of Capua, died before 18 Feb 1334. Formerly canon of Sisteron; archbishop from 1312.

13 Oct 1325 (EFR J1, 23549) licentia testandi.
17 Jun 1346 (EFR C2, 1025) commission.
10 May 1347 (ibid., 1378) faculty to receive goods from the archbishop's brother Ricarius de Stella, deposited in various merchant banks.
2 Dec 1364 (OS 23A, 90^r) Franciscus, elect of Termoli, is obligated to the Camera for two-thirds of the spoils, taken by Ricarius de Stella as heir.
2 Dec 1364 (Coll. 353, 24^v-25^v) the camerarius commissions Stephanus Alberti, abbot of S. Victor, Marseille, and nuncio in Italy, to recover the spoils from Ricarius de Stella.

277] Ermengaudus, abbot of Villemagne, diocese of Béziers. See *Gall. Christ.* 6:409.

20 Aug 1368 (Coll. 156, 31^v) the successor Pontius pays 25 fl. of a composition to Joannes Garrigie.
before 1377 (Coll. 157, 152^v) he pays 100 fr.

278] Ermengaudus, abbot of "Villabertrandi" OCSA, diocese of Gerona.

26 Nov 1347 (Coll. 497, 36^r) the successor Dalmacius is obligated to a composition of 800 fl.

5 Feb 1348 (VQ 5, 400) he pays 400 fl.
2 Jun 1348 (ibid., 408) he pays 400 fl.

279] Ermetus Sancii, archdeacon of Segovia, died in curia before 1370.

n.d. (Coll. 116, 79^r) a *Decretum* sold at Segovia for £27.10.

280] Evenus Begaynon OP, poenitentiarius apostolicus, bishop of Tréguier. Bishop from 1362.

4 Apr 1371 (EFR G1, 135) commission to Guido de Ruppe, canon of Tours.

281] Eximinus de Luna, archbishop of Toledo, died before 13 May 1338. Formerly sacristan of Zaragoza; archbishop of Zaragoza from 1296; of Tarragona from 1317; of Toledo from 1328.

28 Jul 1317 (EFR J1, 4530) licentia testandi.
21 Jan 1330 (ibid., 48206) licentia testandi.
4 Jun 1338 (EFR B3, 1837) commission.
before 4 Jul 1338 (Coll. 229, 14^r-24^r) accounts of the commissioner Almeracius de Cabrespina.
2 Aug 1338 (EFR B3, 1937).
1 Dec 1338 (VQ 4, 137) the commissioner pays 8390 1/2 duple etc.
30 Nov 1339 (ibid., 149) the successor Aegidius, obligated to a composition of 3000 fl., paid in full.

282] Eximinus Sancii de Ripavelosa, bishop of Huesca, died 19 Dec 1368. Lic.Decr.; formerly provost of Gerona; bishop of Huesca from 1364.

n.d. (Coll. 116, 115^v) his heir pays a composition of 300 fl. for the remaining goods; the spoils "pro maiori parte fuerant deraubata per magnos homines."

283] Fernandus, bishop of Astorga, died before 1 Jul 1370. Formerly secular abbot of S. Marcellus, diocese of Leon; bishop from 1358.

n.d. (Coll. 119, 98^r) report of the collector Arnaldus de Vernolio.

284] Fernandus Martini de Burgis, portionarius of Seville, died in curia.

7 Oct 1353 (RA 122, 337^r) goods in the papal treasure.
18 Nov 1353 (VQ 7, 18) Balduinus Ricardi, sigillifer auditoris Camerae, pays 7 fl. 3 s. Avin.

285] Ferrandus Garciae, archdeacon of Burgos.

17 Aug 1358 (VQ 7, 223) Joannes, bishop of Jaen, pays a composition of 200 fl.

286] Ferrandus Vargas, bishop of Burgos. Formerly bishop of Calahorra from 1352; of Burgos from 1362.

6 Oct 1366 (OS 23A, 92^r) successor pays a composition of 1000 fl.
n.d. (Coll. 119, 98^r) goods, to the value of 1000 fl., released to the successor.
14 Nov 1366 (Coll. 353, 76^v-77^r) the collector Arnaldus de Vernolio is ordered to collect the value of the spoils.

287] Ferrarius de Abella OP, bishop of Barcelona, died 21 Dec 1344. Formerly bishop of Patrai from 1323; of Mazzara from 28 Sep 1330; of Barcelona from 1334.

29 Dec 1344 (EFR C1, 1371) commission.

288] Ferrarius Colon, bishop of Lerida, died 3 Dec 1340. Bishop from 1334.

13 Dec 1340 (EFR B3, 2972) commission to Almeracius de Cabrespino.
19 Jan 1341 (ibid., 2986) judicial powers to the commissioner.
14 Aug 1341 (VQ 4, 181-182) commissioner Almeracius de Cabrespino makes various payments.
1340-1342 (Coll. 229, 60^v-75^v, 116^v-119^r) the commissioner's accounts.
12 Jan 1347 (EFR C2, 1294) further faculties to the commissioner.

289] Fortanerius Vassalli OFM, patriarch of Grado and administrator of Ravenna, died Oct 1361. Minister general OFM; archbishop of Ravenna from 1347; patriarch of Grado from 1351. Created cardinal 17 Sep 1361, but died at Padua before entering the curia. See AFH 59 (1966): 231-234.

17 Aug 1370 (EFR U2, 3191) commission to Bernardus, bishop of Rimini, mentioning the composition arranged with the archbishop of Ravenna.
24 Dec 1372 (Coll. 358, 132^v-133^r) the executors are directed to compound for 500 fl. against the goods held by cardinal Elias Talleyrand of Périgord.

290] Fortius de Auxia, bishop of Poitiers, died 8 Mar 1357. Formerly canon of Poitiers; bishop from 1314.

9 Nov 1316 (EFR J1, 1782) licentia testandi.
11 Apr 1364 (EFR U2, 883) commission to Sancius Vaquerii to recover the goods taken by Geraldus de Bordis and his wife.

291] Franciscus, bishop of Acqui, died 1380. Formerly prior of Foligno; bishop from 1373.

1380 (IM 4746) the camerarius Petrus de Croso demands accounts.

292] Franciscus, bishop of Castro, died before 9 Aug 1361. Formerly rector in the diocese of Lettere; bishop from 1347.

7 Sep 1361 (Coll. 169, 130ᵛ) accounts.

293] Franciscus, bishop of Korone in Achaia, died before 21 Oct 1359.

9 May 1354 (RA 128, 598ᵛ) licentia testandi.
26 Nov 1361 (Coll. 130, 153ʳ) the subcommissioner Jacobus, abbot of Torcello, Crete, pays 3280 ducats 49 s. 4 d.

294] Franciscus, abbot of Peneclaria OSB, diocese of Ancona.

late 1368 (Coll. 353, 129ʳ-130ʳ) this case is used as occasion to apply the *moderatio* to all cases of spoils.

295] Franciscus, plebanus of Lancilla, diocese of Florence, died 8 Mar 1367.

12 Apr 1367 (Coll. 248, 30ᵛ) the collector Lucius, bishop of Cesena, collects 18 fl., £55 of Pisan money for goods from Philippus, subcollector of Florence.
5 Aug 1368 (ibid., 31ʳ) his cousin Simon de Lancilla pays a composition of 40 fl.

296] Franciscus de Aretio OP, bishop of Limassol, Cyprus, died 13 Jul 1351. Bishop from 1346.

29 Nov 1352 (EFR C2, 2703-2704) commission.
23 Sep 1353 (IM 1952) the exceptions of Albertus to the process of commissioners Odo bishop of Paphos and Monaldus de Campo.
28 Sep 1353 (IM 1953) further exceptions.
n.d. (RA 346, 243ʳ-244ᵛ) fragmentary record of the process.
10 Sep 1355 (Coll. 497, 55ᵛ) the successor Elias is obligated to a composition of 283 fl.
10 Aug 1358 (IM 4594, 10ᵛ) nephew Conradus de Margato pays £3000.

297] Franciscus Capograsso, bishop of Policastro. Formerly dean of Capua; bishop from 1353.

16 Jun 1361 (Coll. 169, 130ʳ) accounts of Guillelmus, former rector of Benevento, nuncio.

298] Franciscus de Cardillaco OFM, bishop of Cahors. M.Theol., D.Decr.; formerly bishop of Cavaillon from 1366; of Cahors from 1388.

1389 (*Gall. Christ.* 1:143) licentia testandi.
1398 or 1399 (IM 4781) testament, lacking beginning and end.

2 Jun 1404 - (Coll. 91, 325ʳ-330ʳ) collector Petrus Berengas narrates the course of the spoils process; total receipts of £701.14.2.

299] Franciscus Cavallerius de Brundisio, bishop of Ostuni, died before 1 Apr 1362. Formerly canon of Ostuni; bishop from 1337.

30 Jun 1362 (Coll. 169, 136ʳ) accounts.

300] Franciscus Crispi de Messana OESA, archbishop of Manfredonia, died before 16 Nov 1354. Archbishop from 1351.

31 Dec 1354 (Coll. 169, 51ᵛ) spoils collected by subcommissioner Joannes, abbot of S. Sebastiano, Naples.

301] Franciscus Eximenis OFM, patriarch of Jerusalem, administrator of Elne, died 23 Jan 1409. M.Theol., patriarch and administrator from 1408. See AFH 60 (1967): 469; 61 (1968): 497-499.

1409 (Coll. 469B, 17ʳ-30ʳ) books collected as spoils.

302] Franciscus Graziani, bishop of Perugia, died 1352. Formerly archpriest of Perugia; bishop from 1339.

3 Nov 1352 (EFR C2, 2699) commission.
21 Dec 1353 (EFR I1, 676) commission to Petrus Costuti, mentioning that the reservation of spoils was made by Clement VI during the bishop's lifetime.
27 Sep 1354 (Coll. 497, 53ʳ) successor Andreas is obligated to a composition of 4000 fl.

303] Franciscus de Lanceo, advocate in the Roman curia.

19 Mar 1351 (VQ 5, 444) executors pay 100 fl. composition to Balduinus Riccardi, sigillifer auditoris Camerae.

304] Franciscus de Mara, archbishop of Cosenza, died before 29 Jan 1354. Formerly bishop of Anglona from 1325; archbishop of Cosenza from 1330.

16 Mar 1354 (Coll. 169, 51ʳ) subcommissioner Armandus de Gretuilla pays for spoils.

305] Franciscus de Marziis OFM, bishop of Lacedogna. Bishop from 1345. See AFH 55 (1962): 258-259.

14 Dec 1351 (Coll. 169, 45ᵛ) spoils collected by subcommissioner Petrus, bishop of Trevico, for Petrus, archbishop of Benevento: 6 unc. 4 car.

306] **Franciscus de Monteolivo, bishop of Elne, died 12 Oct 1354. Former prior of Tortosa; bishop from 1352.**

21 Nov 1354 (EFR I1, 1204) commission to Bertrandus de Abbate.
1357-1359 (Coll. 154, 213^r) accounts.
ca. 1359 (Coll. 159, 238^v) collector receives 270 fl. Aragon.

307] **Franciscus de Montfaucon, bishop of Lausanne. Formerly dean of S. Jean de Maurienne; bishop of Lausanne from 1347.**

8 Apr 1354 (EFR I1, 877) commission to Geraldus de Arbento.
4 Oct 1354 (ibid., 1136) the same.
9 Jun 1355 (VQ 7, 94-95) collector pays 1000 fl.
1375 (Coll. 479A, 8^r) collector finds lawbooks.

308] **Franciscus de Neapoli, protonotary apostolic, papal secretary, died in curia.**

2 Feb 1358 (VQ 7, 216) executors pay 2000 fl. of a 4000-fl. composition; cf. OS 23A, 93^r.

309] **Franciscus de Oliveriis, rector of B. M. "de Castellione de Surriana," diocese of Tortosa.**

11 Jun 1346 (EFR C2, 1008) commission to Almeracius de Cabrespino.
9 Jul 1348 (ibid., 1686) commission to Petrus Venrelli.
2 Oct 1349 (VQ 5, 579) Bernardus Alanyani, collector of Zaragoza and Tarragona, pays from the spoils.

310] **Franciscus Oscii OESA, bishop of Civita Castellana, died before 15 Dec 1348. Bishop from 1331.**

24 Nov 1350 (EFR C2, 2338) commission.

311] **Franciscus Petri, prior of S. Cruz OCSA, diocese of Coimbra.**

22 Sep 1350 (EFR C2, 2307) commission to Petrus de Marcello, archdeacon of Lisbon.
11 Nov 1350 (ibid., 2331) the same.
27 Mar 1353 (EFR I1, 208) collector is directed to release the spoils to the successor Alfonsus, "excepto thesauro furto subtracto."
27 Mar 1353 (ibid., 209) the successor is granted powers to collect the spoils.
3 Apr 1353 (Coll. 497, 49^r) successor Alfonsus is obligated to a composition of 4000 fl.
n.d. (IM 4592, 2^r) collector Joannes Garrigie accounts for 1000 fl. of the composition.
24 Nov 1360 (IM 2199) collector Guillelmus Piloti pays Joannes Garrigie the last 711 3/4 fl. of the composition.

11 Oct 1362 (Coll. 497, 50ʳ) note that the composition has been paid in full.

312] Franciscus de Silanis OFM, bishop of Valva-Sulmona. Bishop from 1350.

18 Jan 1368 (IM 2501) inventory of goods assigned by Nicolaus de Isornia to Guillelmus Maurelli, receiver general.
22 Jun 1368 (IE 325, 21ᵛ-22ʳ) proceeds from sales at Rome.

313] Franciscus Silvestri, bishop of Florence, died 21 Oct 1341. Bishop of Sinigaglia from 1318; of Rimini from 1321; of Florence from 1323.

22 May 1326 (EFR J1, 15440) licentia testandi.
6 Dec 1341 (EFR B3, 3243) commission.
31 Dec 1341 - 25 Apr 1342 (Coll. 244, 57ᵛ-64ʳ) accounts of the collector Joannes de Pererio.
25 Jan - 27 Apr 1342 (Coll. 244, 94ʳ-102ʳ) expenses and the storage of spoils.
5 Jun - 2 Sep 1350 (Coll. 246, 93ʳ) quittances to the collector Andreas de Tuderto.

314] Franciscus de Sistarico, canon of Vence.

27 Nov 1331 (OS 12, 147ʳ; VQ 1, 523) commissioner Raymundus Naulonis pays 97 fl. etc.

315] Franciscus de Stella, bishop of Termoli, died before 3 Sep 1372. Bishop from 1364.

7 Dec 1372 (Coll. 358, 117ʳ) the *moderatio* of Urban V is conceded to the successor Jacobus de Senis.

316] Franciscus de Tuderto, canon of Angers, died in curia.

13 Oct 1361 (VQ 7, 362) Nicolaus, bishop of Melfi, executor, pays 200 fl. composition.

317] Fredericus, bishop of Bisignano, died Jun 1339. Formerly canon of Bisignano, bishop from 1331.

9 Sep 1345 (EFR C2, 772) commission.

318] Fredericus de Ceva, bishop of Albenga, died before 18 Feb 1350. Bishop from 1329.

9 Sep 1345 (EFR C2, 2273) commission.

319] Fredericus de Pernstein OFM, archbishop of Riga, died in curia 1340: see AFH 42 (1949): 22-36. **Poenitentiarius apostolicus; archbishop from 1304.**

3 May 1319 (EFR J1, 9369) licentia testandi.
18 Jun 1324 (ibid., 20473) commission.
31 May 1325 (ibid., 23339) license to dispose of his books.
25 Jun 1332 (ibid., 57578) the same.
7 Mar 1341 (VQ 4, 171) Petrus Orlandi pays a loan of 12 fl.
7 Mar 1341 (ibid., 171-173) Joannes Maurelli, sigillifer auditoris Camerae, assigns some silverware.
10 Mar 1341 (EFR B3, 3018-3019) the Dominican convent of Riga is ordered to pay 4000 fl. and other goods.
22 Mar 1341 (ibid., 3031) orders the bishop of Prague to recover 1600 m. of silver from the archbishop's nephew Dirslaus, provost of Prague.
15 Jul 1341 (ibid., 3123-3124) quittance to the Acciaioli company of Florence for moneys paid.
22 Nov 1341 (VQ 4, 185) silver sold by Antonius, bishop of Lombez for 90 fl. 1 s. 1 d.
11 Jan 1343 (Coll. 289, 39^{rv}) goods in the papal treasure.
13 Jun 1343 (VQ 5, 337) Aymon de Durchia, citizen of Lyon, pays 100 fl.
8 Sep 1343 (EFR C1, 397).
16 Sep 1343 (VQ 5, 338-339) 4500 fl., deposited in the Dominican convent of Riga, is paid to the Camera by the Teutonic Knights through merchants of Asti at Bruges.
13 May 1346 (ibid., 369) Aymon de Durchia pays 100 fl.
24 May 1346 (ibid., 370) Joannes de Durchia pays 100 fl.
18 Aug 1346 (ibid., 376) the same.
2 Jan 1347 (ibid., 379-380) the same.
8 Oct 1347 (ibid., 395) executors pay 800 fl. sent.
18 Feb 1348 (ibid., 402) Aymon de Durchia pays 100 fl.
23 Sep 1348 (ibid., 411) Joannes de Durchia pays 100 fl.
1 Aug 1349 (ibid., 428) the same.
28 Aug 1351 (ibid., 448) the same, paying his debt in full.

320] Fredolus, abbot of S. Pierre de Nanty OSB, diocese of Vabres.

24 Apr 1346 (Coll. 497, 27^r) successor Bernardus is obligated to a composition of 800 fl.
8 Jun 1347 (ibid., 32^v) the same note.

321] Fredolus de Lautrico, abbot of Moissac OSB, diocese of Cahors, died 27 Jul 1375. See *Gall. Christ.* 1:170A.

n.d. (Coll. 236, 323^v-324^r) accounts of the collector Aymericus Pelicerii.

1375 (Coll. 235, 142ʳ-144ʳ) accounts of the subcollector Petrus de Reno: 1271 fl. assigned to the Camera, 233 fl. remaining.

322] Fulco Pererii, collector of Aragon.

6 Apr 1371 (EFR G1, 137) commission to Arnaldus Andreae to secure certain immovable properties for the Camera.
6 Nov 1372 (Coll. 358, 124ʳ) commissioner Bertrandus Raffini receives £1290.8 Barc., 47 fl. Fr., 35 nobles, 293 fr., etc.
11 Aug 1384 (Coll. 360, 157ᵛ) instructions to Arnaldus Andreae.

323] Gabriel de Malaspinis, bishop of Luni, died before 25 Feb 1363. Formerly canon of Luni; bishop from 1351.

5 Sep 1371 (Coll. 358, 12ᵛ) commission to Lucius, bishop of Cesena.

324] Galganus, bishop of Salpe. Formerly canon of Bari; bishop from 1351.

18 Dec 1345 - 22 Sep 1346 (Coll. 168, 52ʳ-53ᵛ) sales by Guillelmus de Roseriis.

325] Galganus de Pagliaricci OP, bishop of Massa Maritima. Poenitentiarius apostolicus; bishop from 1332.

22 Apr 1349 (EFR C2, 1984) commission to Andreas de Tuderto.
8 Aug 1349 - 17 Feb 1350 (Coll. 245, 131ᵛ-132ᵛ) accounts.

326] Galhardus, abbot of Psalmody OSB, diocese of Nîmes, died 1331. See *Gall. Christ.* 6:477.

26 Sep 1332 (VQ 1, 525) successor Raymundus pays 400 fl. of a composition of 800 fl.
14 Feb 1333 (ibid.) he pays the remaining 400 fl.

327] Galhardus de Fargis, bishop of Bazas. Formerly archdeacon in the church of Burgos; bishop from 1334.

17 Feb 1348 (EFR C1, 3745, 3747) commission to Petrus Joannis, rector of S. Remi, diocese of Avignon and Morerius de Moreriis.
25 May 1349 (ibid., 4171) orders officiales of Agen, Bazas and Condom to collect spoils.
1 Jun 1360 (Coll. 497, 72ʳ) nephew obligated to a composition of 3000 fl.; cf. OS 23A, 98ᵛ, where the figure is given as 300 fl.

328] Galhardus Niger, commensal chaplain, died in curia before 27 Apr 1360.

28 May 1360 (Coll. 231, 85ʳ; VQ 7, 295-296) heirs pay 300 fl. composition.

329] Galhardus de Podio, bishop of Saintes, died before 16 May 1362. Formerly archpriest of Orléans, LL.D.; bishop from 1351.

3 Jun 1362 (VQ 7, 408) commissioner Petrus Heraudi, prior of S. Eutropius OClun, diocese of Saintes, pays 1260 regales.
22 Jun 1362 (OS 31, 151^{rv}) commission by the camerarius to Petrus Ayraudi.
22 Jun 1362 (ibid., 152^{rv}) composition of Petrus Ayraudi for 2000 écus.
14 Dec 1362 (ibid., 163^v-164^r) commission to the collector of Saintes to take 2000 écus from the spoils of the late Petrus Ayraudi to pay his composition.
4 Jan 1365 (Coll. 353, 26^r-27^v) the heir of collector Vitalis Vassali pays money collected.

330] Galhardus de Preyssac de Saumate, archbishop of Arles, died 31 Jul 1323. Formerly papal chaplain, notary apostolic; bishop of Toulouse from 1306; of Riez from 1317; of Maguelonne from 1317; archbishop of Arles from 1318.

29 Jul 1323 (EFR J1, 17822) licentia testandi.
1326 - 1335 (IE 83, 188^r-201^v) accounts of Arnaldus de Verdala.
14 May 1327 (VQ 1, 526) he pays 928 fl., 322 agni, etc.
27 Dec 1331 (OS 12, 137^r-138^r) quittance to Arnaldus de Verdala.
30 Nov 1335 (EFR B2, 122) general quittance.
30 May 1336 (Coll. 147, 27^r) accounts of Raymundus Flori.

331] Garsias Arnaldi de Caupene, bishop of Dax, died 8 Jan 1327.

31 May 1312 (Regestum Clementis Papae V, 8122) licentia testandi.
For this unusually long process, see these printed sources:
EFR J1, 26460, 29699, 40474, 42402, 41246, 50750.
EFR J2, 3139, 3228-3230, 3269, 3311, 3394, 3751, 4035, 4068.
VQ 1, 518.
VQ 4, 98, 100, 106, 108, 112.
and manuscript sources:
OS 12, 83^{rv}, 90^v-91^r, 93^r, 100^v, 112^r, 116^v-117^r, 136^r.
Coll. 29, 198^{rv}.
Coll. 145, 17^r.
RA 116, 389^v.
and cf. *Gall. Christ.* 1:1049D-1050C; Rymer, *Foedera* (1740) 4:559; A. Degert, *Histoire des évêques de Dax* (Paris, 1903), 148-161.

332] Garsias Fabri, bishop of Aire. Formerly canon of Aire; bishop from 1328.

5 May 1349 (EFR C1, 4157) commission to Martinus de Girardo.
21 Apr 1350 (VQ 5, 435) executor Raymundus de Podio, priest of Aire,

pays to the Camera the money deposited with him: 30 fl. Fl., 61 fl. Pied., 25 regales; he still owes 255 fl.

26 Jan 1351 (Coll. 497, 46ʳ) the executor is obligated to a composition of 5000 fl.

14 Mar 1351 (EFR C1, 4924) commission to Guillelmus Raymundi de Fabro.

1 Jan 1352 (VQ 5, 450) executors pay 300 fl.

after 1352 (Coll. 31, 190ᵛ, 192ʳ) receipts by Martinus de Girardo: 1449 écus, 392 fl., etc.

before 1355 (Coll. 114, 68ʳ) accounts of Martinus de Girardo.

24 Nov 1373 (EFR G1, 3136) commission to Monaldus de Grueria, after the death of commissioner Guillelmus Raymundi de Fabro.

333] Gasbertus de Luganh, clericus Camerae.

Feb 1385 (IM 3203, 6) his servant Durandus Monnarii pays 380 fl. of a composition of 500 fl.

334] Gasbertus de Serici, prior of S. Saturnin OClun, diocese of Uzés.

12 Apr 1358 (Coll. 497, 75ᵛ) successor Stephanus de Vassinhaco is obligated to a composition of 1000 fl.; the Camera is to receive gold and silver, books, grain and wine; the gifts *inter vivos* are to stand.

17 May 1359 (VQ 7, 263-264) successor pays 250 fl.

18 Jul 1359 (ibid., 265) he pays 100 fl.

335] Gasbertus de Valle, camerarius, archbishop of Arles, translated to Narbonne and his goods reserved Oct 1341. Formerly bishop of Marseille from 1319; archbishop of Arles from 1323. See also the following entry.

22 May 1336 (EFR B2, 8983; B1, 3735) licentia testandi.

27 Nov 1341 (Coll. 472, 2ᵛ-3ʳ) commission to the vicecamerarius Jacobus de Broa.

1-21 Dec 1341 (Coll. 26, 2ʳ-14ʳ) inventory of goods at Arles.

19 Oct 1342 (VQ 5, 472) Raymundus de Moreriis, collector of Arles, commissioned to collect the goods and debts at Arles at the time of the translation.

28 Jan 1343 (ibid., 473) record of sale of wine.

n.d. (Coll. 472) accounts of Raymundus de Moreriis and Pontius de Pereto.

336] Gasbertus de Valle, camerarius, archbishop of Narbonne, died 3 Jan 1347. See also the preceding entry.

19 Aug 1344 (EFR C1, 1037) licentia testandi.

5 Jan 1347 (Coll. 152, 1ʳ-8ʳ) inventory of utensils by Joannes Regis.

7 Jan 1347 (IM 1724) Joannes Regis published his letters of commission at Narbonne.

11 Jan 1347 (EFR C1, 3048) Stephanus Cambaruti appointed camerarius, succeeding Gasbertus de Valle.

4 Feb 1347 (ibid., 3098-3099) Elias de Nexonio is ordered to collect all moneys from nephew Joannes de Valle, and to give the brother and nephews 5000 fl. as a free alms.

10 Feb 1347 (ibid., 3112-3115) legacies.

12 Feb 1347 (VQ 5, 382) commissioner pays receipts.

20 Feb 1347 (ibid., 383) executor Raymundus de Valle pays 6000 fl., 600 écus.

21 Feb 1347 (EFR C1, 3128) the church of Narbonne is allowed to recover 3000 fl. lent to the king.

23 Feb 1347 (ibid., 3134-3135) commission to Elias de Nexonio and orders to Joannes Regis.

28 Mar 1347 (VQ 5, 383) Elias de Nexovio pays for goods at Narbonne.

14 Apr 1347 (ibid., 383-384) payment by executors.

19 May 1347 (ibid., 384) payment by Joannes Regis.

20 Jun 1347 (ibid.) payment by executors.

22 Jun 1347 (ibid., 385) payment by executors.

4 Dec 1347 (ibid., 385-386) payment by Joannes Regis.

26 Aug 1348 (ibid., 410) Joannes Regis died 23 Aug; his cousin pays.

1348 (Coll. 150, 81^r-131^v; Coll. 154, 207^r-208^r) accounts of Bernardus de Abbate.

before 1356 (Coll. 114, 80^v) collector Bernardus de Abbate reports receipts.

1366 (Coll. 157, 224^v, 231^r, 238^r) report of debts paid.

1368 x 1374 (Coll. 157, 21^r) list of uncollectable debts.

337] Gaucelmus de Deux, treasurer, bishop of Maguelonne, died 9 Aug 1373. Former abbot of Psalmody; bishop of Nîmes from 1362; of Maguelonne from 1367. See *Gall. Christ.* **6:791C-793B.**

9 Aug 1373 (EFR G1, 1316) commission to Joannes, abbot of Mas de Garnier and Arnaldus Andreae.

10 Aug 1373 (ibid., 1199) treasurer Petrus de Vernolis is directed to collect goods from Petrus Scatisse and Guillelmus Rolandi, knights, and Enguerrardus de Parvocellario, citizen of Paris.

10 Aug 1373 (EFR G2, 2068) treasurer and Bertrandus Raffini are directed to observe the *moderatio*.

16 Aug 1373 - 11 Jan 1374 (Coll. 137, 143^r-319^r) inventories and accounts at Avignon and Montpellier.

17 Sep 1373 (IM 2808) commission to Joannes Rosseti.

18 Sep 1373 (EFR G1, 1355) camerarius ordered to compel the holders of the goods to surrender them.

10 Nov 1373 (IM 2814) Joannes Rosseti reports his sale of salt for 352 fl. and expenses.

Mar 1375 (IM 2877, 2) Petrus de Cassanhis, cubicularius, buys a "patena argenti ad dandam pacem" for 4 fl. 3 s. 6 d.
23 Aug 1375 (ibid., 5; OS 42, 65^v) Petrus de Vernolis, successor in the treasury and Maguelonne, pays 1000 fl. of a composition of 4000 fl. for salt.
31 May 1376 (IM 2924, 4; OS 42, 65^v) he pays 1000 fl.
26 Sep 1376 (Coll. 358, 177^v) utensils granted, with those of Raymundus de Pradella, archbishop of Nicosia (q.v. below), to Guillelmus de Beaufort, viscount of Turenne.
3 Apr 1377 (OS 42, 99^r) Camera pays a 35-fr. debt of Gaucelmus to Guillelmus de Gaudiaco, LL.D.

338] Gaucelmus Joannis, bishop of Carcassonne. Bishop from 1338.

16 Apr 1339 (EFR B1, 7033) licentia testandi.
21 Mar 1347 (EFR C1, 3186) commission.

339] Georgius Joannis, bishop of Coimbra. Lic.Decr., former canon of Astorgas; bishop from 1333.

8 Apr 1356 (Coll. 352, 97^v) note that a commission was expedited to the collector of Portugal, Guillelmus Piloti.
24 Nov 1360 (IM 2199) Guillelmus Piloti pays £2584.18.8.
ca. 1370 (Arm. 33 to. 18, 84^r-85^r) receipts by collector Bertrandus de Macello: £130.17.8 Portugal.

340] Georgius de Serluchiis, archdeacon in the diocese of Tours, papal chaplain.

8 Jul 1344 (EFR C1, 952) commission.
3 Nov 1345 (VQ 5, 362) nephew Thomas de Serluchiis pays 100 fl. of a composition.
temp. Urban V (OS 23A, 103^v) note that half the composition of 2000 fl. is still owed.

341] Geraldus, bishop of Agde. Formerly canon of Cahors, notary apostolic and papal familiar; bishop of Agde from 1332.

25 Oct 1339 (EFR B2, 657) commission to Almeracius de Cabrespino.
1339-1340 (Coll. 229, 36^r-45^r) accounts of the commissioner.
7 Jan 1340 (EFR B3, 2637) commissioner ordered to assign books.
22 Feb 1340 (VQ 4, 155) commissioner pays £810.10.1.
4 Mar 1340 (ibid., 156) he pays 200 fl.
11 Mar 1340 (ibid.) he pays 25 fl. Fl., 9 fl. Pied., and a ring.
4 Apr 1340 (ibid., 156) he pays £40.5.
17 Aug 1340 (ibid., 162) he pays 122 coron., 107 écus, etc.
4 Nov 1340 (ibid., 165) he pays 28 duple, 8 fl. 13 s. 2 d. for 3580 saumatae of salt.

4 Dec 1340 (ibid., 166) Raymundus de Amacio, domicellus of Agne, pays a debt he owed to the bishop.

342] Geraldus, archbishop of Benevento. Formerly canon of Limoges; papal familiar; archbishop from 1360.

9 Apr 1362 (OS 31, 141^{rv}) *moderatio* on behalf of the successor Guillelmus Bourgeois.

343] Geraldus, bishop of Sisteron, died 9 Dec 1369. Formerly prior of "Nemorevicenarum" OGrandmont, diocese of Paris, D.Decr.; bishop from 1362.

1370 (Coll. 19, 295^r-304^v) accounts of the collector Geraldus Mercaderii.
17 Jul 1370 x 1373 (IM 6067) successor Rainulphus pleads for help for the bishop's nephews, whose support as scholars was removed by spoils.

344] Geraldus, abbot of Tournus OSB, diocese of Chalon-sur-Saône. See *Gall. Christ.* 4:973.

29 Aug 1344 (EFR C1, 1199) commission.
4 Feb 1345 (Coll. 497, 24^v) successor promises to surrender all the goods.
13 Mar 1345 (EFR C1, 1556).
18 Mar 1345 (ibid., 1577).
6 Sep 1345 (VQ 5, 360) commissioner Joannes Regis pays 600 fl.
28 Apr 1346 (ibid., 368-369) successor Archambaudus pays 878 fl. of a composition of 1000 fl.
2 Sep 1346 (ibid., 376) nephew Bertrandus de Asserio pays 200 fl. of a composition of 800 fl.

345] Geraldus OSB, abbot of S. Michel-en-l'Erm, diocese of Luçon.

13 Jan 1366 (EFR U2, 1507) commission to Petrus Domandi.
ca. 1366 (Coll. 92, 30^r) he collects 1482 nobles, 390 regales.

346] Geraldus de Arbento, collector of Lyon, Vienne, Tarentaise, Besançon and Trier, died between Mar 1360 and Nov 1361.

15 Jan 1362 (OS 31, 219^{rv}) commission to Joannes Rosseti to collect spoils from Joannes de Taleni.
26 Sep 1363 (ibid., 192^v) quittance to Joannes Rosseti for 1105 fl. paid to the Camera.
11 Mar 1365 (IM 2391) Joannes Rosseti renders accounts to Aubricus Radolphi.
n.d. (Coll. 66, 9^v-11^v) the composition arranged between Joannes Rosseti and servitor Martinus Novelli is collected by Aubricus Radolphi.

347] Geraldus Artaudi OClun, prior of Piolenc, diocese of Orange.

3 Mar 1334 - (Coll. 28, 1^r-15^v) inventory by commissioner Pontius de Pereto.
10 Mar 1334 - (ibid., 16^r-23^v; 26^v-34^v) expenses; assignments.

348] Geraldus Dominguez, bishop of Evora, died 5 Mar 1321. Formerly bishop of Porto from 1300; of Palencia from 1307; of Evora from 1313.

26 Feb 1308 (Regestum Clementis Papae V, 2664) licentia testandi.
9 Aug 1322 (VQ 1, 478) Petrus Danrocha and Arnaldus de Roseto pay 8012 duple, 1108 fl., etc.
26 Sep 1322 (Coll. 351, 49^r) note of commission.
10 Jan 1327 (OS 12, 103^v-104^r) Petrus de Brunia pays for this and other commissions.
10 May 1336 (EFR B3, 869) the archbishop of Braga may absolve from excommunication the holders of these and other spoils, upon restitution.

349] Geraldus de Ehrenberg, bishop of Speyer, died 28 Dec 1363. Bishop from 1350.

22 Feb 1365 (Coll. 353, 33^r) successor obligated to a composition of 5000 fl., payment delayed until Easter.
3 Apr 1365 (ibid., 36^r) payment delayed until midsummer.
7 Jun 1365 (ibid., 39^v) payment delayed until Easter 1366.
26 Feb 1366 (ibid., 59^r) payment delayed until Michaelmas.
Jan 1372 (IM 2676, 3) successor pays 450 fl. of 3000 fl. owed.
Aug 1372 (ibid., 66) he pays 158 fl.

350] Geraldus Guiscardi, sacristan of S. Felix, Gerona and canon of S. Agricol, Avignon.

2 Aug 1397 (IE 374, 33^r) cardinal Guido de Malosicco pays 100 fl. for himself and the executors.

351] Geraldus de Languisello, bishop of Nîmes, died 23 Apr 1337. Formerly bishop of Apt from 1330; of Nîmes from 1331.

18 Sep 1335 (EFR B1, 1683) licentia testandi.
2 May 1337 (EFR B2, 288) commission to Pontius de Pereto.
2 May - Jul 1337 (IM 5095) commissioner's accounts.
3 Jul 1337 (VQ 4, 120) commissioner pays £351.7.7.

352] Geraldus de Marcenaco, canon of Chartres, collector of Reims.

19 Apr 1364 (EFR U2, 897) commission to Sancius Vaquerii, Joannes Mauberti and Joannes de Sirano.

353] Geraldus Maurelli, vicetreasurer, magister hospitii Papae.

12 Feb 1370 (IM 2576, cited in Renouard, *Relations* 331) a partial list of goods and money received in the treasury at Rome by Gaucelmus de Pradello from the scribe Raymundus Macelli.

354] Geraldus Paute, abbot of S. Benoît, Fleury-sur-Loire OSB, diocese of Orléans.

20 Jul 1380 (Coll. 359, 47^r-48^r) nuncios Joannes bishop of Geneva, Petrus Gerardi, and the subcollector of Orléans are ordered to pay a 281-fr. debt to Petrus de Grat and Stephanus de Vaucois.

355] Geraldus de Portali, bishop of Rimini and rector of the church of Miremont, diocese of Toulouse, died before 13 Nov 1366. Bishop from 1366.

n.d. (Coll. 235, 169^{rv}) accounts of spoils at Toulouse: 2 fl. received, 44 fl. remaining.
1371 (Coll. 18, 261^r-264^r) accounts of Aymericus Pelicerii: 481 fl. 7 gr. received, 46 fl. 10 gr. remaining.
1 Oct 1373 (Coll. 236, 147^v, 156^v) the same report.

356] Geraldus de Posilhaco, archbishop of Aix, died 23 May 1379. Formerly provost of Embrun; archbishop from 1368.

1379 (Coll. 480, 3^r-11^v) accounts of collector Geraldus Mercaderii.
1380? (IM 4746) camerarius Petrus de Croso demands accounts.
4 Jul 1380 (Coll. 359, 45^r) the collector is ordered to give certain books, acquired outside the benefice, to Bernardus de Monterotundo.

357] Geraldus Rogerii, bishop of Limoges, died in curia 1324. Bishop from 1312.

4 Oct 1324 (EFR J2, 2226-2227) commission.
14 Oct 1324 (ibid., 2235).
11 Jul 1324 (ibid., 2540).
13 Aug 1324 (ibid., 2580).
1324-1328 (IE 67, 74 fols.) accounts by commissioner Petrus Danrocha of the arrears of debts due to the mensa.
Sep 1325 (VQ 1, 499) he pays 1500 fl., 1280 agni.
27 Apr 1326 (VQ 1, 500) he pays 90 fl., 50 agni, £343.0.16.
17 Mar 1327 (ibid.) he pays 300 fl.
16 May 1329 (EFR J2,).
2 Aug 1330 (ibid., 4265).
23 Sep 1339 (EFR B2, 646) commission to Joannes Bertrandi to collect the remaining goods.

358] Geraldus la Tremoliera, administrator of the Pinhota, died 1348.

12 Jan 1349 (VQ 5, 416) Petrus de Frigidavilla, executor and successor, pays a composition of 100 fl.

359] Geraldus de Valle, nuncio in the kingdom of Naples. Former canon of Naples, papal chaplain.

6 Dec 1341 (EFR B3, 3244) commission.
1 Feb 1342 (VQ 4, 189) guarantor Betinus Bonacursi makes posthumous satisfaction of 3170 1/2 fl.

360] Geraldus de Wippingen, bishop of Basel, died 17 Mar 1325. Formerly bishop of Lausanne from 1301, of Basel from 1309.

Mollat in RHE 29 (1933): 321 cites Riezler, *Vatikanische Akten*, n. 460 for an attempt to secure his spoils, 25 Mar 1325.

361] Germanus, scriptor Papae, sealer in the episcopal court of Avignon, died in curia.

8 Jul 1361 (VQ 7, 341) executor pays 194 fl. 19 s. 8 d.

362] Gibba, pope's barber, died in curia.

13 Oct 1340 (VQ 4, 164) Guillelmus Bos, clericus Camerae, pays 26 fl.

363] Gilbertus, abbot of S. Chaffre, diocese of Le Puy, died 3 Oct 1388. See *Gall. Christ.* 2:768.

3 Oct 1388 (Coll. 8A, fasc. 3, 12^r-33^r; Coll. 85, 111^r-128^v) an inventory, including the spoils of priors of dependent monasteries listed as debts; a note of the successor's composition of 300 fl.
Apr 1389 (IM 3337, 49) successor Dragonetus pays 100 fl. of a 300-fl. composition.
Nov 1389 (IM 3337, 60) he pays the last 100 fl.

364] Gilbertus de Cantabrio OSB, bishop of Rodez, died 12 Mar 1348. D.Decr., abbot of S. Gilles OSB, then of S. Victor, Marseille; bishop of Rodez from 1339. See *Gall. Christ.* 1:692 and 218B-E.

Feb 1339 (Coll. 143, 109^r-165^v) inventory of goods left at S. Victor, Marseille when Gilbertus was elevated to Rodez.
17 Mar 1349 (EFR C1, 4107) commission to Guido Fayditi.
10 Jun 1349 (VQ 5, 426) commissioner makes payments.
17 Jul 1349 (EFR C1, 4211) mention of a licentia testandi; the commissioner assigns 1208 fl. to the Camera, of which 400 fl. is a legacy to the Apostolic See.

27 Jul 1349 (VQ 5, 428) executors obligated to a composition of 2000 fl.; they still owe 792 fl. (in VQ: 15 s. 2 d.!).
4 Jan 1350 (ibid., 432) they pay 396 fl.
22 May 1355 (VQ 7, 91) they pay 396 fl.

365] Gilbertus Flamingi, auditor sacri palatii.

11 Oct 1348 (VQ 5, 413) his familiar Ricardus de Raol pays 20 écus.

366] Gilbertus Griffa de Bulla OCist, bullator, died in curia.

1 Aug 1367 (IM 2488, 4 fols.) inventory of goods in his house in Avignon; 200 fl. assigned to Joannes Garrigie and Joannes Rosseti.

367] Gilbertus Joannis, bishop of Carcassonne, died before 14 Nov 1354. Former archdeacon in the church of Cahors; bishop from 1347.

15 Nov 1354 (EFR I1, 1197) commission to Bernardus de Abbate.
16 Nov 1354 (ibid., 1198) commission to Petrus Peselli, canon of Rouen, without prejudice to the earlier commission.
1357-1359 (Coll. 154, 209^r) accounts of Guillelmus Guilaberti.
15 Feb 1364 (OS 31, 131^{rv}) commissioner Petrus Ruffi paid the bishop's debt to cardinal Gaucelmus Joannis, and the money is now disposable by the cardinal's heirs.

368] Gilbertus de Lestrangiis, provost of Toulouse.

24 May 1387 (Coll. 362, 40^r) commission.
15 Sep 1387 (ibid., 81^r) the camerarius releases 300 fl. for pious uses.

369] Gilbertus de Mendagachis, bishop of Lodève, died 21 Jul 1361. Formerly abbot of S. Aphrodise, Béziers; bishop of S. Pons de Thomières from 1348; of Gap from 1353; of Lodève from 1357.

27 Aug 1361 (OS 31, 155^{rv}) quittance for silver, jewels, etc. to Galhardus de Balazaco, subcollector.
24 Dec 1361 (VQ 7, 379-380) successor Aymericus pays composition of 300 fl. (cf. OS 23A, 110^r).
28 Nov 1362 (IE 303, 8^r) commissioner Galhardus pays 88 fl., 11 regales, 9 fr.
before 1377 (Coll. 157, 184^v) collector Arnaldus Andreae reports no receipts, because a composition was made in Camera.

370] Gilbertus de Septemfontibus, died in curia.

14 Jul 1348 (VQ 5, 409) a mule is submitted by executor in payment of a composition of 100 fl.

371] Goffridus OSB, bishop of Grasse, died 1343. Formerly monk of S. Germain, Auxerre; bishop from 1299.

23 Jan 1344 (VQ 5, 343) commissioner Joannes de Amelio pays.

372] Goffridus, bishop of Le Mans, died 20 Jul 1347. Bishop from 1338.

22 Jun 1344 (EFR C1, 918) commission in advance of the bishop's death.
1 Jul 1348 (ibid., 3909-3911) a composition of 2000 fl. in subsidy against the Turks is paid by heirs and executors.
14 Jul 1348 (VQ 5, 409) composition paid.

373] Goffridus, bishop of Tarazona from 1346.

4 Oct 1353 (EFR I1, 579) commission to Fulco Pererii.
12 Oct 1353 (ibid., 599) the same; the reservation was by Clement VI.
1354 (Coll. 497, 75^v) successor Petrus obligated to a composition of 3000 fl.
26 Jan 1355 (VQ 7, 87) he pays 1000 fl.
26 Jan 1356 (ibid., 128) he pays 1000 fl.
1358 x 1361 (Coll. 117, 176^r) he pays 500 fl.

374] Goffridus de Coetmoisan OSB, bishop of Dol. Formerly abbot "de Cultura," diocese of Le Mans; bishop of Quimper from 1352; of Dol from 1357.

7 May 1381 (Coll. 359, 65^{rv}) successor Guido is granted sufficient funds from the spoils for repairs.
7 Jun 1381 (Coll. 359, 64^v-65^r) Guido de Ruppe, collector of Tours, or the subcollector of Dol, ordered to observe the *moderatio*.
22 Sep 1381 (ibid., 85^r-86^v) they are ordered to pay the funds for repairs to the successor.

375] Goffridus David Pauteix, bishop of Autun, died before 22 Apr 1377. Formerly archdeacon in the diocese of Lyon, Lic.Decr.; bishop of Autun from 1361.

5 Sep 1379 (Coll. 359, 158^{rv}) Guillelmus de Lacu, collector of Lyon and Joannes Bullandi, commissioner, ordered to pay the bishop's debt of 700 fl. to Joannes Rosseti.

376] Goffridus Isnardi, bishop of Riez, died in curia 26 Jul 1348. Formerly bishop of Cavaillon; of Riez from 1334.

26 Jun 1331 (EFR J1, 54100) licentia testandi.
6 Jan 1344 (EFR C2, 598) licentia testandi.

377] Goffridus de Jandraco, procurator, died in curia.

8 Apr 1361 (Coll. 231, 130ʳ; VQ 7, 335-336) Balduinus, sigillifer auditoris Camerae, pays 40 fl.

378] Goffridus de Veyrols, archbishop of Toulouse, died 10 Mar 1377. LL.Lic., former chancellor of Cahors; bishop of Lausanne from 1342; of Carpentras from 1347; of Carcassonne from 1357; archbishop of Toulouse from 1361. See *Gall. Christ.* 13:41D-42B.

10 Jan 1378 (OS 42, 116ʳ) collector Aymericus Pelicerii pays 1200 fr. by letter of exchange.
after 1378 (Coll. 235, 146ʳ-160ᵛ) inventory and accounts: 5161 fl. received, 7452 fl. remaining due.
1380 (IM 4746) the camerarius demands accounts.
11 May 1380 (Coll. 359, 33ᵛ) he orders the collector to observe the *moderatio*.
n.d. (Coll. 236, 323ᵛ, 324ʳ) collector reports receipts and remains.

379] Goffridus de Weisseneck, bishop of Passau, died 15 Sep 1362. Bishop from 1344.

20 Feb 1364 (OS 23A, 95ᵛ) successor Albertus is obligated to pay within 16 months a composition of 10,000 fl. for the spoils and vacancy.
2 Dec 1365 (IE 303, 32ʳ) the successor pays 600 fl. Cam.
23 Jan 1366 (Coll. 353, 56ᵛ-57ʳ) payment and excommunication delayed until All Saints.

380] Gomecius Manrique, archbishop of Toledo, died 19 Dec 1375. Formerly dean of Leon; bishop of Tuy from 1348; archbishop of Compostela from 1351; of Toledo from 1362.

26 May 1377 (OS 42, 104ʳ) executors pay 15,000 duple of a composition of 20,000, through Fulco Pererii.

381] Gregorius OSB, bishop of Mazzara, died before 19 Apr 1363. Formerly monk of S. Nicola dei Arenis, diocese of Catania; bishop from 1357.

ca. 1375 (Coll. 222, 192ʳ) successor Rogerius and Henricus de Marzuco owed goods, but all were destroyed in the sack of Mazzara.

382] Gregorius, abbot of Issoire OSB, diocese of Clermont.

15 Aug 1351 (EFR C1, 5030) commission to Petrus Gervasii.
30 Aug 1352 (VQ 5, 458) successor Petrus agrees with collector Petrus Gervasii for a composition of 600 fl.

383] Gregorius, abbot of S. Gregorius in Concha OSB, diocese of Rimini.

1370 x 1377 (Coll. 129, 234ʳ) oeconomus of the monastery pays a composition of 88 ducats.
19 Mar 1372 (Coll. 358, 33ʳ) successor Jacobus de Faytanis is granted Cameral authority to compel holders of the spoils to pay for repairs of the monastery's buildings.

384] Guido OCSA, bishop of Maillezais, died before 4 Jun 1380. Formerly abbot of S. Amand OCSA, diocese of Sarlat; bishop of Luçon from 1354; of Maillezais from 1359.

4 Aug 1380 (Coll. 359, 48ᵛ-49ʳ) collector Petrus Domandi, or subcollector, ordered to observe the testament and the *moderatio*.
1380? (IM 4746) camerarius demands accounts.

385] Guido, abbot of Sauve-Majeur OSB, diocese of Bordeaux, died 24 Jun 1362.

17 Jan 1363 (OS 31, 166ʳ-167ʳ) successor Hugo de Marchenaco compounded for 500 fl. for the spoils and 500 fl. for the fruits of the vacancy, but the Camera still reserves 1300 fl. held by Arnaldus de Lagrelleyra.

386] Guido, abbot of Sassovivo, diocese of Foligno, died in curia at Montefiascone.

6 Apr 1359 (Coll. 202, 3ʳ) one magister Angelus pays 202 fl. 6 s. 10 d.

387] Guido, abbot of N. D. de Charon OCist, diocese of Saintes, papal chaplain of honor.

5 Mar 1375 (Coll. 356, 64ᵛ-65ʳ) Petrus Domandi is ordered to proceed against Joannes, abbot of Grenda OCist, diocese of Saintes, for wounding, torturing in prison and killing Guido, and keeping his spoils; the accused is to appear before the pope or, after his departure, in the court of the treasurer at Avignon.

388] Guido de Canilhaco, abbot of Aniane OSB, diocese of Maguelonne, died 3 Mar 1331. See *Gall. Christ.* 6:846.

28 Mar 1332 (VQ1, 530) Arnaldus de Verdala pays 1920 fl. from the composition of the successor Guillelmus.
ca. 1 Apr 1333 (IE 83, 155ʳᵛ) he pays 3100 fl.
3 Feb 1334 (ibid., 371ʳ) he pays 700 fl. Piedmont.
30 Nov 1335 (EFR B2, 122) general quittance to Arnaldus de Verdala.

389] Guido Cattano OP, archbishop of Oristano, Sardinia, died before 23 Oct 1340. Archbishop from 1312.

18 Apr 1341 (EFR B3, 3061) commission.

390] Guido de Guardia, camerarius of the monastery of S. Gilles OSB, diocese of Nîmes.

6 Oct 1347 (EFR C1, 3499) commission.
13 Oct 1347 (Coll. 497, 35^v) successor Guillelmus de Alterio is obligated to a composition of 2000 fl. for spoils and 250 fl. for the vacancy.
21 Dec 1347 (VQ 5, 398) successor pays 550 fl. of composition.
7 Jun 1348 (ibid., 408) he pays 100 fl.
5 Nov 1348 (ibid., 414) he pays 200 fl.
8 Jan 1349 (ibid., 415) he pays 100 fl.

391] Guido Guidonis, died in curia.

12 Jan 1361 (Coll. 231, 119^v; VQ 7, 331) executor pays composition of 50 fl.

392] Guido de Ibolino OP, bishop of Limassol, Cyprus, died 29 Mar 1367. Bishop from 1357.

Apr 1367 (IM 2467) inventory.
n.d. (IM 2469) note of £1548 still due.
n.d. (IM 5274) note of sales.

393] Guido de Io, prior "de Prato" OClun, diocese of Auxerre, died in curia.

9 Jan 1348 (Coll. 497, 36^v-37^r; OS 23, 4^{rv}; VQ 5, 400) Hugo, abbot of Cluny, pays 200 fl. of a composition of 450 fl.
26 Apr 1348 (VQ 5, 405) he pays 250 fl.

394] Guido de Nobilibus (Farnese), bishop of Orvieto and rector of the Patrimony of S. Peter in Tuscany, died 1328. Bishop from 1302.

16 Jun 1333 (VQ 1, 468) commissioner Petrus de Artusio pays 253 fl. etc.
30 Jul 1335 (EFR B3, 462) the bastard Ninus Guittonis may retain 200 fl. and be absolved from excommunication if he repays the rest of the goods that he holds.
30 May 1339 (ibid., 2396) orders Hugo Cornuti, treasurer of the Patrimony, to collect.
20 Jul 1339 (ibid., 2444) permission to the treasurer to compound with the heirs and holders of goods.
20 Mar 1365 (IM 2393) the chapter of Orvieto petitions for return of goods which were collected as the spoils of later bishops.

395] Guido de Prangins, bishop of Lausanne, died 11 Jun 1394. J.U.Prof.; bishop from 1375.

5 Oct 1385 (Coll. 361, 9^v) commission to Guillelmus de Lacu.
13 Jan 1386 (ibid., 24^{rv}) directions to the subcollectors of Geneva and Lausanne.

396] Guido de Ribieyra, canon of Nevers, paneterius and scribe of the Chancery.

24 Sep 1363 (OS 31, 191^v) camerarius orders Petrus Andoyni, canon of Nevers, to release the spoils to the executors.

397] Guido Rolandi, notarius sedis apostolicae.

1362 x 1370 (OS 23A, 117^v) his brother Guillelmus is obligated to a composition of 100 fl.

398] Guido de Ruppe, bishop of Lavaur, died before 12 Jul 1395.

? (RV 308, 194^v, cited by Favier, *Finances Pontificales* 252 n. 1) commission.

399] Guido Scettem, archbishop of Genoa. Formerly archdeacon of Genoa; archbishop from 1358.

1 Feb 1368 (Coll. 353, 107^v-108^r) camerarius Arnaldus Alberti in Rome directs treasurer Gaucelmus de Deux in Avignon how to proceed.
1368 (Coll. 132, 59^v) accounts of collector Raphael de Turre: £198 received.
19 Dec 1368 (ibid., 123^v-124^r) permits the successor Raphael de Turre to press Guido's widowed mother for the 400 fl. that she owes.
10 Mar 1369 (ibid., 194^v-195^r) orders the collector to pay 31 fl. for wine sold to the archbishop.
28 Jun 1371 (coll. 358, 9^v) collector pays £198.
1371 (Coll. 132, 100^r) collector fears that £100 owed cannot be paid because of war.

400] Guido de Terrena OCarm, bishop of Elne, died 21 Aug 1342. Formerly prior general OCarm; bishop of Mallorca from 1321; of Elne from 1332.

5 Jun 1321 (EFR J1, 13590) licentia testandi.
30 Apr 1333 (ibid., 60190) licentia testandi.
18 Dec 1346 (VQ 5, 379) executors pay composition of 1000 fl., legacy of 100 fl.

401] Guido de Vassinhaco, abbot of S. André OSB, Villeneuve, Avignon, died 5 Aug 1380.

14 Aug 1380 (Coll. 359, 53ᵛ-54ʳ) infirmarian appointed administrator; spoils and vacancy reserved.

402] Guido de Ventadour, bishop of Vabres. Formerly archdeacon of Brussels; bishop of Cambrai from 1342; of Vabres from 1349.

14 Oct 1352 (EFR C1, 5423) commission.
1353 (OS 23A, 104ᵛ) note that the executors paid a composition of 100 fl. during 1 Innocent VI.

403] Guido Vigerii, rector "de Cassano," diocese of Uzés, died in curia; familiar of the camerarius Gasbertus de Valle.

13 Aug 1344 (VQ 5, 351) Galhardus de Riparia pays 6 fl. Fl., 3 fl. Pied., etc.

404] Guidotus de Tervisio, scriptor Papae, died in curia.

14 May 1361 (VQ 7, 338) Balduinus Riccardi, sigillifer auditoris Camerae, pays the executors' composition of 30 fl.

405] Guigo, provost of Pignans OCSA, diocese of Fréjus.

1347 x 1348 (OS 23A, 103ʳ) note that his successor Hugo paid a composition of 1500 fl.

406] Guigo de S. Germano, bishop of Montecassino. Papal chaplain, LL.D, notary apostolic, papal familiar; rector of the Patrimony of S. Peter in Tuscany; bishop of Montecassino from 1340.

2 Jul 1324 (EFR J1, 19873) licentia testandi.
Jan 1340 (EFR B1, 7927) licentia testandi.
28 Aug 1341 (VQ 4, 182) Lucas de Abbatibus pays 451 fl. 18 s. 10 d. which he had received for Guigo from the Bonacorsi.
19 Oct 1341 (ibid., 183) Martellus Neyio, Guigo's almoner, pays 131 fl. Fl., 19 fl. Pied.
24 Jan 1342 (ibid., 188) Jacobus de Plumbayrola, monk of Cassino, surrenders 250 fl. stolen from Guigo's goods.
11 Apr 1342 (ibid., 194) Bernardus de Lacu assigns to the Camera books and various goods.
15 Mar 1344 (VQ 5, 345) Guillelmus Gisberti pays 96 fl.; Petrus Arnaldi, domicellus, pays 107 1/2 fl.; Jacobus Cambafortis pays 81 fl.
18 Jun 1347 (ibid., 390) Angelus Geoli, stationarius, pays 18 fl. for an *Inventarium juris*.
30 Jun 1347 (ibid., 391) Joannes Maurelli pays 168 fl. from goods found in the curia.
27 Apr 1349 (Coll. 497, 41ʳ) Jacobus Cambafortis undertakes to render accounts.

407] Guillelmus OSB, bishop of Alet, died before 5 Jul 1363. Formerly, abbot of S. Gilles, Cendras, diocese of Nîmes; bishop from 1355.

22 Nov 1363 (Coll. 156, 198ᵛ; IM 2279, 20; IE 303, 15ᵛ) commissioner Bertrandus Barrerie assigns to the Camera 612 fl. Fr., 463 fr.

1363 x 1364 (OS 13A, 112ᵛ) Stephanus, bishop of Vabres, is obligated to a composition of 600 fl. Fr.

6 Jul 1364 (Coll. 156, 199ʳ; IM 2339, 17; IE 303, 21ʳ) he pays 480 fl. Fr.

before 1368 (Coll. 156, 240ʳ) debts to 984 fl. for spoils and vacancy paid.

408] Guillelmus, bishop of Aquino. Former archpriest of Montesarchio, diocese of Benevento; bishop from 1354.

16 Dec 1359 (VQ 7, 269) commissioner Reginaldus, bishop of Capua, pays 110 fl. from spoils.

14 Nov 1360 (ibid., 302; Coll. 231, 107ᵛ) Florentine merchants send a letter of credit to the Camera for 1510 fl. Cam. for these spoils and those of Petrus, archbishop of Benevento.

409] Guillelmus, bishop of Cotrone, died before 5 Nov 1348. Bishop from 1346.

28 Dec 1357 (Coll. 352, 118ᵛ) commission dated 14 Dec, dispatched by hand of Reginaldus de Lupchaco to himself and Petrus, archbishop of Benevento.

410] Guillelmus, bishop of Isola Capo Rizzuto.

27 Jun 1348 (Coll. 168, 73ᵛ) Guillelmus de Roseriis collects goods to the value of 8 unc.

411] Guillelmus, bishop of Massa Maritima.

22 Apr 1349 (EFR C2, 1984) commission to Andreas de Tuderto.

412] Guillelmus OFM, bishop of Nice, died before 5 Apr 1323. Poenitentiarius apostolicus, papal familiar; bishop from 1317.

15 Jul 1323 (VQ 1, 480) executors pay 266 fl., 34 ducats.

413] Guillelmus, bishop of Nice. Former canon of Nice; bishop from 1335.

5 Sep 1348 (EFR C1, 3948) commission.

414] Guillelmus, bishop of Umbriatico, died before 4 May 1362. Bishop from 1347.

7 Jul 1362 (Coll. 169, 137ʳ) goods received by the subcollector.

415] Guillelmus, abbot of Joucou OSB, diocese of Alet. See *Gall. Christ.* 6:289C.

19 Oct 1361 (VQ 7, 363) Arnaldus de Planzolis pays 200 fl. composition.

416] Guillelmus, abbot of S. M. de Gualdo, diocese of Benevento, collector in the kingdom of Naples.

9 Nov 1350 (EFR C2, 2328) commission.
12 Nov 1353 (Coll. 169, 52^v) successor Nicolaus pays 10 unc. for spoils.

417] Guillelmus, abbot of S. Sophia OSB, diocese of Benevento.

24 Apr 1333 (EFR J1, 60136) licentia testandi.
29 Nov 1339 (EFR B1, 8287) quittance for the expenses of making an inventory.
15 Dec 1339 (EFR B3, 2627) replaces the late commissioner Petrus Vasconis with Arnulphus Marcellini.
8 Jun 1340 (ibid., 2787) orders Arnulphus Marcellini, vicerector of Benevento, to investigate and collect spoils.
29 Jun 1340 (ibid., 2816) permission to compound for grain in view of a famine.
7 Jun 1340 (VQ 4, 161-162) executor pays 216 fl.
11 Mar 1344 (EFR C1, 718).

418] Guillelmus, abbot of "Venticanum," diocese of Benevento.

early 1362 (Coll. 169, 135^r) accounts.

419] Guillelmus, abbot of S. Romain de Blaye OCSA, diocese of Bordeaux.

26 Aug 1365 (EFR U2, 1932) commission to Sancius Vaquerii.

420] Guillelmus, abbot of Sauve-Majeure, diocese of Bordeaux.

17 Jan 1363 (OS 23A, 94^r) successor Hugo, obligated to a composition of 1000 fl., paid.

421] Guillelmus OSB, abbot of Le Vigeois, diocese of Limoges. See *Gall. Christ.* 2:596D.

10 Nov 1372 (Coll. 358, 109^v-110^r) treasurer Petrus de Vernols orders collector Petrus Chauneti to leave the spoils to the successor Guido for the service of the monastery.

422] Guillelmus, abbot of S. Sauveur OSB, diocese of Lodève.

20 Oct 1361 (VQ 7, 363) subcollector pays 38 fl. etc.

9 Nov 1361 (Coll. 497, 76ᵛ) successor Petrus Castanhi is obligated to a composition of 80 fl.

1 Feb 1362 (VQ 7, 389) successor pays 80 fl. sent.

1368 x 1377 (Coll. 157, 185ʳ) collector Arnaldus Andreae reports no receipts because the successor made a composition in the Camera.

423] Guillelmus, abbot of Psalmody OSB, diocese of Nîmes, died before 25 Jul 1348.

late 1348 (RA 101, 47ʳ-51ʳ) inventory by commissioner Raymundus de Salerio.

6 Dec 1348 (Coll. 497, 39ᵛ) successor Gaucelmus obligated to a composition of 100 fl.

18 Feb 1349 (VQ 5, 418-419) he pays 100 fl.

27 Oct 1349 (Coll. 497, 42ʳ) he assumes the obligation of Guillelmus for the spoils of Raymundus de Serinhaco, former abbot (q.v.).

2 April 1351 (VQ 5, 445) he pays 100 fl.

1357 x 1359 (Coll. 154, 211ᵛ-212ᵛ) accounts of Guillelmus Guilaberti.

n.d. (Coll. 149, 164ʳᵛ; Coll. 155, 236ʳᵛ) he reports debts received to the sum of 82 fl. 19 s. 8 d.

424] Guillelmus, abbot of Psalmody OSB, diocese of Nîmes.

Jun 1375 (IM 2877, 4) Arnaldus Andreae, collector of Narbonne, pays 107 fl. Cam. 15 s. 2 d. for silver vessels sold.

23 Oct 1375 (Coll. 356, 60ᵛ) Bertrandus Jordani commissioned to collect the remains.

22 Aug 1376 (OS 42, 83ʳ) quittances to Arnaldus Andreae for payments: 100 fr. on 16 Jun 1375; 86 m. 9 d. on 20 Jun 1375.

26 Sep 1378 (ibid., 131ᵛ) he pays 80 fr.

425] Guillelmus, abbot "de Pinu" OSB, diocese of Poitiers.

11 Mar 1371 (RA 182, 209ʳ) goods released by reason of the monastery's poverty.

426] Guillelmus, abbot of S. Paolo fuori le Mura, Rome, died in curia at Rome.

3 Jul 1368 (Coll. 433, 3ʳ-4ᵛ; EFR U2, 2786; IM 2508) commission to Gaucelmus de Pradallo.

8 Aug 1368 (IM 2512) publication of the bull of commission.

1368-1378 (Coll. 433, 3ʳ-151ᵛ; Coll. 492, 10ʳᵛ) accounts of commissioner Gaucelmus de Pradallo.

427] Guillelmus, priest, died in the Pinhota.

Apr 1389 (IM 3337, 49) Geraldus Mistralis, governor of the Pinhota, pays 9 fl. Cam. 5 s. 6 d.

428] **Guillelmus de Alsona OSB, bishop of Alet, died 6 Jan 1355. Formerly abbot of Grasse, diocese of Carcassonne; bishop from 1333.**

EFR C1, 1271, 4324, 4964, 4978: preparations for spoils in anticipation of the bishop's death, in view of his large debts to the Camera.
5 Nov 1354 (EFR I1, 1177) commission to Bernardus de Abbate in anticipation.
Dec 1354 (Coll. 102, 25 fols.) donations inter vivos.
Jan 1355 (RA 128, 81^r-121^v) inventory by commissioner Petrus Chamboneti.
3 Feb 1355 (VQ 7, 88) Bernardus de Abbate, collector of Narbonne, pays to the Camera through Petrus Chamboneti: 228 écus, 252 fl., 38 georgii, etc.
11 Jul 1355 (ibid., 96) Petrus Chamboneti pays 454 écus.
5 Mar 1356 (ibid., 130) Bernardus de Abbate pays 266 fl., 74 mutones, 197 écus.
1357 x 1359 (Coll. 154, 209^r) accounts of Guillelmus Guilaberti.

429] **Guillelmus Amici, patriarch of Jerusalem and administrator of Fréjus, died 9 Jun 1360. Formerly provost of Lavaur, LL.D., papal chaplain; bishop of Apt from 1341; of Chartres from 1342; patriarch and administrator from 1349.**

8 Sep 1332 (EFR J1, 58291) licentia testandi.
23 Jul 1360 (Coll. 231, 96^r; VQ 7, 297) executors pay a composition of 500 fl.

430] **Guillelmus Arnaldi de Clerico, sacristan of Bordeaux.**

15 Apr 1330 (EFR J2, 4166) commission.
29 Feb 1331 (OS 12, 138^v; VQ 1, 524) Raymundus de Clerico pays 455 fl.

431] **Guillelmus Audebert, bishop of Périgueux, died before 8 Jun 1347. J.U.Prof., papal chaplain; bishop of Apt from 1336; of Périgueux from 1341.**

11 Mar 1339 (EFR B1, 7031) licentia testandi.
22 Nov 1349 (Coll. 289, 28^v) silver vessels in papal treasure.

432] **Guillelmus d'Auxonne, bishop of Autun, died before 27 Oct 1344. Former canon of Paris, LL.D., bishop of Cambrai from 1336; of Autun from 1344.**

5 Nov 1344 (EFR C1, 1228) commission.
1 Mar 1345 (ibid., 1507).
11 Mar 1345 (ibid., 1553) cites a licentia testandi and yields the spoils to the executors.

433] Guillelmus de Balma, prior of Tarascone, diocese of Avignon, and collector of Arles, died in curia.

17 Jul 1361 (VQ 7, 341) commissioner Nicolaus Cortesii pays 112 fl. 20 s.
19 Oct 1361 (ibid., 363) he pays 11 fl.
22 Sep 1362 (Coll. 231, 143^v) he pays 114 fl.

434] Guillelmus Barralhi, provost of N. D. des Doms, Avignon.

3 Jul 1363 (OS 31, 180^{rv}) commission to Arnaldus Len, canon of Lodève.

435] Guillelmus Batemann, bishop of Norwich, died in curia 6 Jan 1355. LL.D., papal chaplain, former dean of Lincoln; bishop from 1344.

1 Oct 1340 (EFR B1, 7933) licentia testandi.
9 Feb 1355 (VQ 7, 88) nephew-executor Simon de Suberio, auditor sacri palatii, pays 1000 fl. of a composition of 2000 fl.
7 Sep 1355 (ibid., 97) he pays 1000 fl. (cf. OS 23A, 107^r).

436] Guillelmus de Baylivia, bishop of Pamiers, died 31 Oct 1365. Formerly archdeacon in the church of Paris, papal familiar; bishop from 1351.

10 Dec 1365 (EFR U2, 2060) commission to Aymericus Pelicerii.
1365- (Coll. 235, 125^v-137^r, 162^v-168^v) accounts.
1371 (Coll. 18, 226^v-260^v) accounts of Aymericus Pelicerii: 149 fl. 5 gr. collected.
1 Oct 1373 (Coll. 236, 147^v, 156^v) and £1842.18.2 1/2 remaining.

437] Guillelmus de Benevento, archdeacon of Ardennes in the church of Liège, clericus Camerae, died before 25 Jul 1361: Baix, "Notes," 38 n. 13.

14 Jan 1362 (VQ 7, 385) executor pays 338 fl. for a composition and 100 fl. for a legacy.
14 Jan 1362 (OS 31, 216^v-217^r; 217^r-218^r; 220^r-221^r) spoils released to executors.

438] Guillelmus Berilhonis, scriptor and abbreviator litterarum apostolicarum, died in curia.

27 Aug 1364 (IE 303, 22^r) executor Aymericus Pellicerii pays 30 fl.

439] Guillelmus Bernardi, chancellor of Paris, died in curia.

27 May 1336 (VQ 4, 107) Jordanus and Arnaldus Rocelli, heirs, pay 300 fl. composition.

440] Guillelmus Bernardi de Cieychello.

12 Oct 1353 (EFR I1, 598) commission to Joannes de Palmis.

441] Guillelmus Bernardi de Pinu, bishop of Bayonne, died before 20 Jun 1371. Bishop from 1357.

31 Mar 1372 (Coll. 358, 33^r) successor Petrus is granted cameral power to compel the holders of spoils to repair buildings.

442] Guillelmus de Bordis, archbishop of Embrun, died before 18 Jun 1361. Formerly archdeacon of Mende, notary apostolic, papal familiar; archbishop from 1361.

15 Sep 1361 (VQ 7, 356) successor Raymundus orders 300 fl. exchange from banker Lucas de Abbatibus, and himself pays 289 fl. composition.
22 Sep 1361 (ibid., 357) brother Stephanus de Bordis pays 1000 fl. of a composition of 2000 fl. (cf. Coll. 231, 142^r).
16 Mar 1362 (ibid., 393) he pays 1000 fl.
26 Mar 1362 (ibid., 394-395) he pays 62 fl. exchange premium.

443] Guillelmus de Bordis, bishop of Lectoure, died before 6 Mar 1346. Bishop from 1311.

22 Sep 1311 (Regestum Clementis Papae V, 7318) licentia testandi.
4 Mar 1346 (EFR C1, 2342) commission in anticipation of death.

444] Guillelmus Borrelli, collector of Bordeaux.

10 Mar 1378 (Coll. 359, 3^r) quittance to successor Elias Peleti.

445] Guillelmus de Broa OP, bishop of Cahors, died in curia. Bishop from 1317.

20 Jun 1324 (EFR J1, 19788) licentia testandi.
15 Jul 1324 (EFR J2, 2143-2144) John XXII limits a legacy to the Dominican convent of Cahors to 2000 fl.

446] Guillelmus de Cadolla, abbot of Montmajour OSB, diocese of Arles, died before 15 Nov 1328. See *Gall. Christ.* 1:612.

6 Feb 1329 (VQ 1, 538) domicellus pays 72 m. 1 1/2 unc. silver.
28 Jun 1329 (ibid.) he pays 400 fl.
17 Nov 1329 (ibid.) nephews pay 28 fl.

447] Guillelmus Calloie, canon of S. Denis, diocese of Angers, died in curia.

17 Apr 1347 (VQ 5, 387-388) canons of Angers pay spoils.

448] Guillelmus de Camareto, prior of Sauxillanges OClun, diocese of Clermont.

1 Mar 1327 (EFR J1, 28059) licentia testandi.
4 Jul 1330 (EFR J2, 4246) commission.
3 Dec 1330 (VQ 1, 564) merchants pay debts.
13 Dec 1330 (ibid.; OS 12, 133^v) merchants pay debts.

449] Guillelmus de Campigio, auditor sacri palatii.

7 Jul 1349 (VQ 5, 427) executor pays composition of 160 fl.

450] Guillelmus Capodiferro, bishop of Chieti, died 1352. Notary apostolic, papal familiar; bishop from 1340.

15 Mar 1341 (EFR B1, 8768) licentia testandi.
2 Sep 1344 (EFR C1, 1071) commission in anticipation of death.

451] Guillelmus Caprarii, canon and cantor of Tours.

23 Dec 1365 (EFR U2, 1065) commission to Guido de Ruppe; the spoils "fuerunt reservata diu ante infirmitatem ex qua decessit."
24 Jan 1367 (Coll. 353, 78^v-79^r) commissioner ordered to release goods to the heirs as the canon's *peculium*: "erat magnus advocatus et multas habebat pensiones a multis nobilibus partium illarum pro advocatione sua."

452] Guillelmus de Cardalhaco OSB, bishop of Montauban, died before 10 Jun 1355. Formerly abbot "de Pessano" OSB, diocese of Auch; bishop from 1317.

14 Mar 1329 (EFR J1, 44732) licentia testandi.
21 Aug 1355 (Coll. 497, 55^r) the heirs Bernardus Fabrefortis and Bernardus Hugonis obligated to a composition of 200 fl.
1 Oct 1373 (Coll. 236, 251^r) Aymericus Pellicerii reports 47 fl. remaining of a composition.

453] Guillelmus de Cardalhaco OSB, bishop of S. Papoul, died 15 Feb 1347. Formerly abbot of S. Victor, Marseille; bishop from 1328.

6 Jan 1347 (EFR C1, 3039) bishop is summoned to the curia.
19 Feb 1347 (ibid., 3127) commission.
4 Mar 1347 (ibid., 3160) faculty to the archbishop of Toulouse to absolve Gerardus de Montefalcone and others who captured and robbed the late bishop, after restitution; the king had released him from prison to face judgement in the curia.

454] Guillelmus de Cavanhaco, clericus Camerae.

17 Sep 1361 (OS 31, 213ᵛ-214ʳ) quittance to brother Geraldus.
27 Sep 1361 (VQ 7, 357-358) Geraldus pays 200 fl. for composition and legacy.
12 Oct 1361 (OS 31, 252ᵛ-253ʳ) commission to Rigaldus Tornamira to collect debts for Geraldus de Cavanhaco.

455] Guillelmus de Colterio de Aragonia OP, bishop of Terralba, Sardinia, died before 13 Sep 1364. Bishop elect of Castres by mistake (the see was not vacant); bishop of Terralba from 1356.

n.d. (Coll. 116, 29ᵛ-30ʳ) subcollector pays £2250.6.10 and notes a composition of £100 for goods at Vich, where the bishop died.

456] Guillelmus de Cornhaco, clericus Poenitentiariae Papae, died intestate in curia.

25 Jan 1356 (VQ 7, 170) commissioner Petrus Ruffi pays 1700 fl., 300 écus.

457] Guillelmus de Duroforti, bishop of Lombez. Formerly archdeacon of S. Antoine, Rodez; LL.Lic.; papal chaplain, auditor sacri palatii; bishop from 1363.

n.d. probably ca. Apr 1379 (OS 42, 158ᵛ-159ʳ) commission to Aymericus Pellicerii under the general reservation of Gregory XI; two copies of the inventory are to be sent to the Camera.
May 1379 (Coll. 235, 145ʳ) the collector owes 112 fl. for spoils.

458] Guillelmus Emergavi OFM, bishop of Kisamos, Crete, died in curia. Bishop from 1349.

25 Oct 1352 (Coll. 497, 79ᵛ) successor Joannes is obligated to a composition of 200 fl.

459] Guillelmus de Fabrica, scriptor Poenitentiariae, died in curia.

30 Oct 1360 (Coll. 231, 103ᵛ; VQ 7, 300-301) executors pay a composition of 400 fl. to Balduinus Ricardi, sigillifer auditoris Camerae.

460] Guillelmus de Flavacuria, archbishop of Auch, died before 3 Jul 1359. Formerly archdeacon of Rouen; bishop of Viviers from 1319; of Carcassonne from 1322; archbishop of Auch from 1323; of Rouen from 1357. Only his goods at Auch were in view in this process.

1 Feb 1323 (EFR J1, 16899) licentia testandi.
12 Apr 1325 (ibid., 21984) licentia testandi.

11 May 1372 (EFR G1, 773) commission to Joannes Alamandi, subcollector of Auch.

461] Guillelmus de Fonnans, subcollector of Besançon, died ca. 28 Jul 1382.

2 Nov 1382 (Coll. 360, 24^r-25^r) Guillelmus de Lacu commissioned.

462] Guillelmus Fredoli OSB, bishop of Béziers, died 20 Nov 1349. Formerly abbot of S. Tiberius, diocese of Agde; bishop from 1313.

3 May 1324 (EFR J1, 19502) licentia testandi.
19 Feb 1344 (Coll. 71, 104^v) licentia testandi.
22 Nov 1349 (EFR C1, 4319-4320) commission to Bernardus de Abbate.
22 Nov 1349 - (Coll. 71, 104^r-129^v) commissioner's accounts.
27 Aug 1350 (Coll. 497, 44^v) executors undertake to render full accounts.
30 Aug 1350 (VQ 5, 438) they pay 1676 fl., £20.6.1 for goods sold.
before 1356 (Coll. 114, 81^r) commissioner receives 221 fl. 16 s.
1357 x 1359 (Coll. 154, 209^v) commissioner's accounts.
ca. 1359 (Coll. 156, 16^r) 25 fl. Fr. debt paid.
before 1377 (Coll. 157, 152^v) 140 fr. collected.

463] Guillelmus Fulci, prior of Mons Ebrodonis, diocese of Maguelonne.

3 Dec 1344 (EFR C1, 1297) commission.

464] Guillelmus Furnerii de Marcossay, bishop of Geneva. Formerly bishop of Gap from 1362; of Geneva from 1366.

20 Mar 1378 (Coll. 393, 65^r-66^r) commission by treasurer to Guillelmus de Lacu.

465] Guillelmus Galaberti, subcollector of Bourges.

Feb 1386 (Coll. 85, 314^r-326^v) goods collected against a debt to the Camera.

466] Guillelmus Garsiae Manrique, bishop of Oviedo, died 17 Feb 1412. Formerly bishop of Siguenza from 1388; of Oviedo from 1389.

Jan 1412 - Mar 1413 (ASV Indice 254, 114^r) collector Jeronimus, bishop of Elne, receives 6980 fl. 10 s. 6 d.

467] Guillelmus de Gennep, archbishop of Cologne, died 15 Sep 1362. Formerly treasurer of Cologne; archbishop from 1349.

13 Jan 1364 (EFR U1, 1029) the pope orders the camerarius to proceed against the canons who have opposed the commissioner Petrus Begonis.

16 May 1364 (IM 2339, 12; IE 303, 19^v; IE 305, 34^r: Kirsch, *Kollektorien* 392-393) commissioner Florentius, bishop of Münster, pays 3761 fl. for goods "ante eius obitum ... reservata et per ipsum quondam archiepiscopum predicte Camere relicta."

6 Aug 1364 (IE 303, 21^v-22^r) commissioner Petrus Begonis pays 3716 fl. Cam. by note of exchange.

30 Oct 1365 (Coll. 353, 52^r) the chapter of Cologne is absolved for holding the goods.

468] Guillelmus Gilberti, collector of Narbonne.

21 Oct 1361 (VQ 7, 366) successor Joannes de Lacmolio pays money held by Guillelmus, including his personal spoils of 177 fl.

469] Guillelmus de Gimiel, bishop of Cartagena, died in curia before 12 Dec 1383. Formerly archdeacon in the church of Clermont, LL.D., papal chaplain, auditor sacri palatii; bishop from 1372.

14 Jan 1384 (Coll. 360, 73^v) the camerarius orders collector Fulco Pererii to provide for the new bishop Fernandus until the next fruits, "de antiqua et approbata consuetudine."

470] Guillelmus Grandini, died in curia 1361.

17 Sep 1361 (VQ 7, 357) Eblo de Mederio, clericus Camerae, pays 50 fl. from goods.

471] Guillelmus de Grenlaw, collector of Scotland.

8 Dec 1374 (EFR G2, 3019) commission to Joannes de Plebis.

472] Guillelmus de Guarrico, subcollector of Coimbra.

ca. 1370 (Arm. 33, to. 18, 85^v) Bertrandus de Macello receives £1172.4.3.

473] Guillelmus Guitardi OSB, bishop of Lisieux, died in curia before 19 Nov 1358. Formerly abbot of S. Taurinus, diocese of Evreux; bishop of S. Paul-Trois-Châteaux from 1348; of Lisieux from 1349.

30 Jun 1359 (VQ 7, 264) goods collected worth 2241 fl., of which 500 fl. are assigned to the thirtieth subsidy and 1000 fl. to spoils.

27 Jul 1361 (ibid., 354) commissioner Bertrandus bishop of Comminges pays 405 fl. 15 s.

474] Guillelmus Isnardi OFM, archbishop of Benevento. Formerly bishop of Alba from 1321; archbishop of Brindisi from 1333; of Benevento from 1344. See AFH 47 (1954): 224.

6 Jun 1326 (EFR J1, 25565) licentia testandi.
18 Jan 1334 (ibid., 62481) licentia testandi.

25 Aug 1346 (IM 1710) inventory of goods at Naples.
26 Aug 1346 - 20 Apr 1347 (Coll. 168, 61^r-72^v) books sent to the Camera, sales to the sum of 989 unc. 9 tari 2 gr. by Guillelmus de Roseriis.
9 Sep 1346 (EFR C2, 1204) commission to Guillelmus de Roseriis, bishop of Montecassino.
13 Sep 1346 (IM 1710) further inventory at Naples by Guillelmus de Roseriis.
19 Sep 1346 (IM 1714) bill of lading for animals and grain to Avignon.
12 Oct 1346 (EFR C2, 1235-1238) orders to Petrus Vitalis.
7 Apr 1347 (IM 1736) commissioner reports further collections of money.
3 Jun 1350 (EFR C2, 2212) faculty to Andreas de Tuderto to compound with the Buonacursi company.

475] Guillelmus Joannis, prior "de Securo" OClun, diocese of Albi.

4 Aug 1375 (Coll. 356, 45^r) instruction to the collector Guillelmus Amarinti: if the prior died after 4 Jul 1375, when a new abbot was provided to Moissac, that abbot gets the spoils by custom.

476] Guillelmus de Judice, cardinal priest of S. Clemente, died 28 Apr 1374. Created cardinal 20 Sep 1342.

17 Jan 1375 (EFR G2, 3099) the collector of Hungary and Poland is to collect the spoils.

477] Guillelmus de Lacu, bishop of Lodève (not in Eubel); formerly provost of Geneva, LL.Lic., collector of Lyon.

31 Jan 1404 (RA 320, 93^v-94^r: Favier, *Finances* 252 n. 6) spoils reserved before death.

478] Guillelmus de Landore, abbot of Ile-Barbe OSB, diocese of Lyon. Formerly prior of Villanova, diocese of Montauban; abbot from 1354. See *Gall. Christ.* 4:230D-E.

20 Jun 1371 (EFR G1, 269) commission to Aubricus Radolphi.

479] Guillelmus de Leschemel, abbot of La Celle, diocese of Troyes, died 1348?

22 Nov 1349 (Coll. 289, 28^r) silver vessels in the inventory of the papal treasure.
13 Feb 1350 (ibid., 42^v) note of obligation for 50 fr. by the heir of a debtor.

480] Guillelmus de Lionbart, camerarius of cardinal Guillelmus de Gordonio, died in curia.

30 Aug 1357 (VQ 7, 181) executors pay a composition of 20 fl.

481] Guillelmus Lombardi, rector of the church of Montguiscard, diocese of Toulouse.

8 Sep 1344 (EFR C1, 1084) commission to Jacobus de Broa.
13 Jul 1345 (ibid., 1825) orders Arnaldus de Baucio, seneschal of Toulouse, to restore goods to the commissioner.
6 Apr 1346 (VQ 5, 366-367) Guillelmus had spent the proceeds of grain from the monastery of Barjols, diocese of Fréjus, which belonged to the Camera; his procurator Raymundus pays a composition of 500 fl.

482] Guillelmus Lombardi, rector "de Bellopodio," diocese of Mirepoix.

1 Oct 1373 (Coll. 236, 251^v) collector Aymericus Pelicerii reports that the heirs have made a composition for 150 fl., of which 5 fl. 2 1/2 gr. remain to be paid.

483] Guillelmus de Mandagoto, bishop of Uzés, died 21 Apr 1344. Formerly sacristan of Nîmes; bishop of Lodève from 1313; of Uzés from 1318.

30 Oct 1316 (EFR J1, 1672) licentia testandi.
18 Apr 1323 (ibid., 17208) licentia testandi.
22 Dec 1344 (VQ 5, 353) Bremundus, prior of S. Didier, Uzés, pays 3000 fl. of a composition of 4000 fl.
23 Jan 1345 (ibid., 359) successor Elias pays his composition of 1500 fl. in full.
28 Jan 1345 (ibid., 354) Bremundus pays 300 fl. of his composition.
4 May 1345 (ibid., 357) he pays 700 fl., and it is noted that 1000 fl. remain to be paid.
1362 x 1370 (OS 23A, 105^v) note that 3400 fl. were paid, but that a balance still remains.

484] Guillelmus Martel, bishop of Belley.

29 Aug 1362 (OS 31, 159^{rv}) commission to Aubricus Radolphi and Joannes Rosseti to collect and hold the spoils for further orders.

485] Guillelmus Méchin, bishop of Dol, died 15 Mar 1328. Formerly bishop of Troyes from 1317; of Dol from 1324.

3 Jun 1324 (EFR J1, 19684) licentia testandi.
28 Apr 1328 (EFR J2, 3560) commission.

486] Guillelmus de Molendino, died in curia.

16 May 1348 (VQ 5, 406) Petrus Lacadre pays 10 écus.

487] Guillelmus Morerii, papal chaplain of honor, hebdomedarius de Insula, diocese of Avignon, died in curia 1397.

before 1405 (Coll. 160, 122^v) Joannes de Ripis Altis, collector of Elne, collects £43.19.

488] Guillelmus de Patau, bishop of Urgel, died 29 Jun 1364. Formerly dean of Urgel; bishop from 1362.

4 Feb 1365 (EFR U2, 1549) commission to Fulco Pererii and Guillelmus de Villareto.
n.d. (Coll. 116, 54^v) collections of £715 Barc.
15 Jan 1369 (Coll. 353, 162^v-163^r) Fulco Pererii is ordered to release 425 fl. from spoils to the successor Petrus de Luna.

489] Guillelmus Piloti, cantor of Lisbon, collector of Portugal.

1 Aug 1368 (Arm. 33, to. 18, 3^r-20^r; Coll. 179, 3^r-20^r) accounts of commissioner Bertrandus de Macello.

490] Guillelmus Pinchon, provost of Mainz.

1368? (IM 6427, ed. above, Appendix C) advocate Bertrandus de Macello argues for the right of cardinal Raymundus de Canilhaco to take the spoils, because he paid the composition and succeeded as provost, and so has a better right than the executors.

491] Guillelmus de Plessis, abbot of S. Trinité, Vendôme OSB, diocese of Tours, died 21 Jul 1384. See *Gall. Christ.* 7:1373D-E.

29 Jul 1385 (RA 242, 71^r; Coll. 361, 16^v-17^r) commission to Armandus Jusserandi, collector of Tours.
n.d. (Coll. 277, 143^v) subcollector Nicolaus de Senelayo receives £40.

492] Guillelmus de Prohins, bishop of Mirepoix, died 1377. Formerly archdeacon in the church of Lectoure, clericus Camerae. Bishop since 3 Jul 1377.

30 May 1381 (Coll. 358, 190^v-191^r) camerarius orders clergy to cite the heirs before the Camera.

493] Guillelmus Ribati OCarm, bishop of Vence, died before 29 Oct 1361. Formerly papal chaplain; bishop of Segni from 1348; of Vence from 1348.

17 Feb 1362 (OS 31, 210^{rv}) camerarius orders the officiales of Vence and Nice to investigate a debt owed by Amadeus, bishop of Grasse, transferred by testament to the pope.

23 Apr 1362 (ibid., 142^{rv}) commission to successor Stephanus Digne, to collect spoils.
28 Apr 1362 (ibid., 142^v) *moderatio* allowing Stephanus half of the net spoils for his maintenance.

494] Guillelmus de Rivoforcato, archdeacon of Toledo, died in curia.

8 Jul 1336 (VQ 4, 110) Stephanus Benerii pays moneys to be held pending judgement in the heir's action against the Camera.
9 Aug 1336 (ibid., 110) Ludovicus de Petragrossa, procurator fisci, pays 25 fl. for the sale of a house in Avignon "confiscati per mortem cuiusdam clerici in Romana curia."
n.d. (IM 5331) arguments of the advocatus Camerae against the heir's claim.
30 Nov 1338 (VQ 4, 135) spoils received: 125 duple, 130 fl., £12.9.

495] Guillelmus de Roffilhaco, bishop of Fréjus, died 3 Nov 1364. LL.D., secular prior "Ahentensis," diocese of Limoges; bishop from 1361. See *Gall. Christ.* 1:437B-D.

1364 (Coll. 107, 187^r-240^v) accounts of Joannes Rosseti.
28 Feb 1365 (Coll. 353, 33^{rv}) successor Raymundus Draconis is granted a delay in paying his composition of 700 fl. Piedmont.
9 Jun 1365 (IM 2378, 23; IE 303, 29^v) Joannes Rosseti pays 217 fl., £160 Avin.
31 Jul 1366 (Coll. 353, 72^v-73^v) quittance to Joannes Rosseti for assignments of 28 Dec 1364; silver and vestments are itemized.

496] Guillelmus de Roseriis OSB, bishop of Tarbes. D.Decr.; former nuncio and collector in the kingdom of Naples, rector of Benevento; abbot of Ss. Sergius and Bacchus, diocese of Angers; archbishop of Trani from 1343; of Brindisi from 1344; bishop of Montecassino from 1346; of Tarbes from 1353.

7 Nov 1360 (Coll. 231, 105^r; VQ 7, 301-302) commissioner Raymundus Rogerii pays 665 fl. 13 s. 10 d.
8 Nov 1361 (VQ 7, 369) Guillelmus de Roffilhaco, elect of Fréjus, buys goods from Eblo de Mederio, clericus Camerae: cross, mitre, and rings for 231 fl.
4 Jun 1365 (Coll. 353, 46^r-47^r) quittance for books.
1 Nov 1375 (Coll. 34, 82^r-83^v) accounts of collector Arnaldus de Peyraco of spoils collected by his predecessor Sancius Vaquerii.

497] Guillelmus Ruffi, canon of Mende, collector of northern Bourges.

5 Oct 1348 (EFR C1, 3973) commission.

498] Guillelmus de Ruppe, rector of S. Columbe, diocese of Mende.

11 Jul 1372 (EFR G1, 847) commission to Joannes Deodati, canon of Le Puy, papal chaplain, nuncio.

499] Guillelmus de Sabrano OSB, bishop of Digne, died before 17 Nov 1327. Former abbot of S. Victor, Marseille; bishop of Digne from 1324.

12 Jan 1328 (OS 12, 83^v; VQ 1, 522-523) successor Elziarius pays 1000 fl. through Arnaldus de Villanova.

500] Guillelmus de Sallone OFM, bishop of Aversa, died before 21 Feb 1326. Formerly bishop of Pozzuoli, ca. 1317; bishop of Aversa from 1324. See AFH 49 (1956): 496.

1 Mar 1317 (EFR J1, 3068) licentia testandi.
1324 x 1332 (Coll. 221, 151^v) Geraldus de Valle received 493 unc. 3 tari 7 gr. 1 d. from these spoils and those of Petrus de Bolonesio.

501] Guillelmus de Sandreux OSB, bishop of Sarlat from 1334.

4 Jun 1338 (EFR B2, 446; Coll. 30, 61^r) commission to Raymundus de Chameraco.
1338-1339 (Coll. 30, 61^r-76^v) accounts of commissioner.
1 Dec 1339 (VQ 4, 151) he pays £450.
13 Oct 1340 (ibid., 165) he assigns rings.
23 May 1341 (EFR B2, 842; EFR B3, 3087) commission to Raymundus Flori.
25 Jun 1342 (VQ 5, 462) report of the commissioner.

502] Guillelmus de Sonheto, prior of S. Marcel OSB, diocese of Chalon-sur-Saône.

22 May 1385 (Coll. 361, 7^r-8^r) camerarius orders Guillelmus de Lacu, directing clerk of the Camera in Lyon, Vienne, etc., and Petrus de Perpelaria, subcollector of Chalon, to collect the spoils under the general reservation.
22 May 1385 (ibid., 9^{rv}) instructions to Robertus Camerarii, canon of Geneva, collector of Lyon and Vienne.

503] Guillelmus Stephani, bishop of Gap, died 29 Aug 1328. Bishop from 1318.

19 Aug 1328 (EFR J1, 42214) licentia testandi.
31 Oct 1328 (OS 12, 98^v; VQ 1, 539) heir and executors pay 1000 fl. of a 2000-fl. composition.
13 Jan 1329 (OS 12, 101^r; VQ 1, 539) they pay 1000 fl.

29 Mar 1329 (OS 12, 104ᵛ; VQ 1, 539) successor Draconetus Artaudi pays 500 fl. of a composition of 1000 fl.
19 Jun 1329 (OS 12, 108ʳ; VQ 1, 540) he pays 500 fl.

504] Guillelmus de Sure, archbishop of Lyon, died 20 Sep 1340. Formerly archdeacon of Lyon; archbishop from 1332. See *Gall. Christ.* 4:163E-164D.

17 Sep 1340 (EFR B2, 783) commission to Joannes Ogerii, dean of Beaune, diocese of Autun.
18 Dec 1340 (EFR B1, 8345; IM 1543) directs the officiales of Lyon and Mâcon to warn the royal bailli of Mâcon to remove the king's hand.
9 Jan 1341 (EFR B1, 9176; IM 1547) the response of the lieutenant of the officialis of Mâcon.
23 Mar 1341 (VQ 4, 173-175) Joannes Ogerii, commissioner, pays some money, silver vessels, and two books.
30 May 1341 (ibid., 177-178) he pays 200 fl. Pied. to close accounts.
Jun 1343 (Coll. 289, 40ᵛ-41ʳ) goods in the papal treasure.
28 Feb 1344 (EFR C1, 701) directions on the execution of the testament.

505] Guillelmus de Thurey, archbishop of Lyon, died 12 May 1365. Formerly dean of Lyon; bishop of Autun from 1356; archbishop from 1358.

28 May 1365 (EFR U2, 1794) commission to Aubricus Radolphi de Lingonis, primicerius of Verdun.
Jul 1366 (IM 2435, 13) Joannes Rosseti, commissioner, pays 245 fl. 6 s. 6 d. for the sale of a silver cross.
6 Nov 1366 (IM 6632, 9ʳ-10ʳ) camerarius orders the officiales of the suffragan sees to cooperate with the collection of the archbishop's debts.
Dec 1366 (IM 2435, 19) he pays 160 fl. 1 s. 7 d. for silver vessels.

506] Guillelmus le Tort, bishop of Marseille, died 15 Nov 1403. LL.D., former canon of Cambrai; bishop of Marseille from 1396. See *Gall. Christ.* 1:661C-D.

1403-1496 (Coll. 23, 200ʳ-212ᵛ) inventory and accounts by Simon de Pratis.

507] Guillelmus Turpini, bishop of Angers, died 31 Jan 1371. Formerly dean in the diocese of Orléans, LL.Prof., papal chaplain and familiar; bishop from 1359.

1371 x 1372 (Coll. 257, 443ʳ) the collector Guido de Ruppe reports: he was told in the Camera to collect the spoils, though they had not been reserved and he was given no letters. He published an executory notice, but accomplished nothing by it. The bishop had been poor, and his goods had been raided by his nephew and others, so that they were not enough to pay for the necessary repairs.

18 Mar 1372 (Coll. 358, 32ᵛ) the successor Milo is granted a letter to compel the heir or holders of goods to repair the houses, mills and other buildings of the mensa.

508] Guillelmus de Ulmo OSB, abbot of Chaise-Dieu, diocese of Clermont, died before 11 May 1378. Lic.Decr., former prior of Aubignac, diocese of Limoges; vicar general of Clermont. See *Gall. Christ.* 2:345A-E.

9 Dec 1378 (OS 42, 138ʳ) successor Andreas pays 300 fr. of a composition for 600 fr.

509] Guillelmus Valelha, vicar in the diocese of Avignon, died in curia.

24 May 1364 (IM 2339, 12; IE 303, 19ᵛ-20ʳ) Petrus Thomae, lieutenant of the auditor of the Camera, commissioned to collect spoils in curia, pays 100 fl.

510] Guillelmus Vaquerii, archdeacon of Mallorca, commensal chaplain, camerarius of cardinal Petrus Rogerii de Beaufort, died in curia.

21 Jun 1354 (VQ 7, 54) the executors are obligated to a composition of 1000 fl., of which their procurator assumes 800 fl. and pays 100 fl.

511] Guillelmus de Veyraco, canon of Salisbury, LL.D., papal chaplain, registrator litterarum apostolicarum.

11 Jul 1334 (EFR J1, 63521) licentia testandi.
n.d. (RA 54, 501ʳ-502ʳ; EFR B1, 8387) copy of testament, naming his brother Guibertus his heir.
12 Dec 1347 (RA 137, 48ʳ-51ᵛ) inventory by Petrus Chautardi, sigillifer auditoris Camerae.
1 Jan 1348 (OS 23, 1ʳ) quittance to Petrus Chautardi.
23 Jun 1349 (EFR C1, 4196) goods released to the heir, with the faculty to execute the testament.
1 Jul 1349 (ibid., 4201) the abbot of Marsillac, diocese of Cahors, is ordered to collect goods in the name of the heir, who still owes a loan of 2500 fl. and a composition of 1500 fl. to the Camera.
1 Apr 1350 (OS 25, 212ʳ) the heir pays 2500 fl.
3 Dec 1359 (VQ 7, 269) he pays 100 fl. of the composition.

512] Guillelmus de Vesencay, abbot of S. Maixent, diocese of Poitiers, died before 19 Mar 1380. See *Gall. Christ.* 2:1258E-1259A.

30 Mar 1380 (IM 3038, IM 3039) inventory by Petrus Domandi, collector of Poitiers.
1380? (IM 4746) camerarius demands accounts.

513] Guillelmus de Villareto, subcollector of Urgel.

1376 (Coll. 121, 8ᵛ-9ʳ) Bernardus Vallesii, subcollector of Barcelona, notes that he made the inventory and collected goods and debts to a sum of £1312.7.6 Barc.

514] Guillelmus de Volta OSB, bishop of Albi, died before 24 Oct 1392. Formerly bishop of Toulon from 1364; of Marseille from 1368; of Valence-Die from 1379; of Albi from 1383.

21 Nov 1392 (Coll. 366, 70ʳ) quittance to Raymundus de Senancio and subcollector Guigo Salvagii for goods delivered to the papal palace.

515] Gundisalvus, bishop of Osma. Formerly archdeacon "de Soria"; bishop of Osma from 1348.

30 May 1354 (EFR I1, 966) commission to Tellius Garsiae, Laurentius Petri and Blasius Martini.
28 Jul 1354 (Coll. 497, 53ʳ) the prior and sacristan of Osma are obligated to a composition of 1400 fl.
9 Jan 1355 (ibid., 53ᵛ) nullifies the earlier obligation; Petrus Fernandi and Bartholomeus Sancii are obligated to a composition of 2500 fl.
9 Jun 1355 (VQ 7, 94) they pay 1250 fl.

516] Gundisalvus de Aquila, archbishop of Toledo. M.Theol.; former bishop of Cuenca from 1341; of Siguenza from 1342; archbishop of Compostela from 14 Aug 1348; of Toledo from 1351.

4 Mar 1353 (EFR I1, 169) commission to Franciscus Ruffacii, canon of Barcelona.
1353 (Coll. 497, 75ʳ) executor obligated to a composition of 12,000 fl.
31 Mar 1353 (IM 1937, IM 6344; EFR I1, 212-213) goods granted to the executors, cardinal Aegidius de Albornotio; Nicolaus Fernandi, dean of Cartagena; Joannes Joannis, archdeacon "de Molinis," diocese of Siguenza; Joannes Eliae, cantor of Leon; and Petrus Martini, canon of Siguenza.

517] Gundisalvus Gundisalvi OFM, bishop of Cadiz, died before 9 Mar 1384. Bishop from 1364.

1 Jul 1386 (Coll. 122, 179ᵛ) Alphonsus Roderici, canon of Cadiz, pays 1000 maravedis of a composition to the archbishop of Toledo.

518] Gundisalvus Nunii de Naboa, bishop of Orense, died 1332.

29 Jul 1334 (EFR J1, 63916; VQ 1, 603-604) commissioner Gundisalvus, archbishop of Braga, pays 26 fl.

519] Gundisalvus Pereira, archbishop of Braga. Bishop of Lisbon from 1322; archbishop of Braga from 1326.

22 Aug 1323 (EFR J1, 17974) licentia testandi.
10 Jan 1348 (EFR C2, 1553) commission.
23 Jan 1349 (ibid., 1912) collector Guillelmus Piloti pays £1333.1.10.
n.d. (Coll. 116, 142^v) Rodericus Velasci de Pereira, knight, loses the income of a chapel, to pay for silverware that he took from the spoils.
n.d. (ibid., 145^r-146^r passim) obligations of the heirs and executors.

520] Gundisalvus Petri, collector of Portugal.

15 May 1366 (Coll. 116, 142^v) Petrus Beranerii, subcollector of Braga, orders the heirs and executors to account for funds belonging to the Camera.

521] Henricus, bishop of Troia, died in curia. Bishop from 1341.

7 Jun 1361 (Coll. 169, 129^{rv}) spoils collected.

522] Henricus, abbot of S. Andrea di Brosano, diocese of Genoa.

28 Jan 1371 - 1373 (Coll. 125, 57^v) successor Hugolinus pays 190 fl. of a composition of 300 fl.
28 Jun 1371 (Coll. 358, 9^v) collector Raphael de Turre pays £137.10.

523] Henricus de Ast, advocate in the Roman curia, died in curia.

3 Nov 1360 (VQ 7, 301) executor pays 200 fl. legacy and composition.

524] Henricus de Bosco, bishop of Dol, died Mar 1348. Bishop from 1340.

3 Nov 1352 (EFR C1, 5449) commission.

525] Henricus de Cigno OP, poenitentiarius Papae.

3 May 1345 (EFR C1, 678) the bishop of Basel and Hugo Monachi, Dominican prior of Basel, are ordered to secure the goods for the Camera; Henricus absconded with them from the curia.
1 Jun 1345 (Coll. 497, 10^{rv}) books returned to the Dominican procurator general by Joannes Maurelli, sigillifer auditoris Camerae.

526] Henricus Hermann, bishop of Abo, Finland, died before 8 Nov 1367. Formerly provost of Abo; bishop from 5 Oct 1366.

29 Jan 1369 (Coll. 353, 147^r-149^r) collector is ordered to enforce the *moderatio*, the text of which is enclosed in a letter to the successor Joannes.

527] Henricus de Marco de Caserta, bishop of Muro Lucano. Formerly canon of Caserta; bishop from 1344.

8 Nov 1348 (Coll. 168, 76^r) Laurentius, archbishop of Conza, pays 13 unc. for these and other spoils.

528] Henricus de Monte OP, bishop of Acerra, died before 27 Oct 1348. Bishop from 1344.

25 Jun 1349 (Coll. 168, 74^v) Guillelmus de Roseriis collects 33 fl. 6 unc. 20 car.

31 Dec 1354 (Coll. 169, 51^v) the collections of subcommissioner Joannes, abbot of S. Sebastiano, Naples.

529] Henricus de Pictavia, bishop of Troyes, died 25 Aug 1370. Formerly dean of Le Puy; elect to Gap 1349; bishop of Troyes from 1353.

31 Jan 1371 (EFR G1, 30) the officialis of Troyes and Carolus de Pictavia, knight, are allowed to receive the spoils, notwithstanding the testament and commission, but they should pay the legacies and just debts.

24 Dec 1371 (Coll. 357, 51^r) camerarius Petrus de Croso certifies the 1000-fr. debt of Carolus de Pictavia; a marginal note of 1 Jul 1372 says that it was paid.

29 Dec 1371 (ibid., 52^r-55^v) copy of an instrument describing the execution by Carolus de Pictavia.

530] Henricus de Rallo, dean of Trento, died in curia.

11 Jul 1352 (VQ 5, 457) Silvester Lupi of Florence pays 20 fl. from the spoils; he is to release the balance of 66 fl. to the executors.

531] Henricus Rocha Anglicus, died in curia.

17 Sep 1361 (VQ 7, 357) Eblo de Mederio, clericus Camerae, pays 30 fl.

532] Henricus de Salviniaco, abbot of S. Paul, Besançon, died 20 Jan 1362. See *Gall. Christ.* 15:223E-224A.

ca. 1362 (Coll. 66, 82^r) collector Aubricus Radolphi receives 448 fl.

533] Henricus de Seneri, bishop of Rodez. Formerly prior of Romainmoutier OClun, diocese of Lausanne; bishop of S. Jean de Maurienne from 1381; of Rodez from 1385.

28 Nov 1396 (IE 374, 8^r) commissioner Joannes de Villanova pays 725 fl. 10 s.

534] Henricus Sessa, bishop of Como, died between 19 Jun and 9 Aug 1380. J.U.D., bishop of Pesaro from 1357; of Ascoli Piceno from 1358; of Brescia from 1362; of Como from 1369.

30 Sep 1372 (EFR G2, 1045) commission to Raymundus, abbot of S. Nicola di Lido, Venice, in anticipation of death.

535] Henricus Ulcebi of Lincoln, canon of Ravenna, died in curia.

14 Jan 1352 (VQ 5, 451) Balduinus Ricardi, sigillifer auditoris Camerae, pays 21 fl.

536] Hermannus de Osenbrügge, bishop of Ösell, died before 24 Jul 1363. Former canon of Ösell; bishop from 1338.

Sep 1363 (OS 31, 198^r-199^r; IM 2279, 16) successor Conradus pays 1500 fl. composition for spoils and vacancy.

537] Homodeus, archbishop of Tarsus from before 1328.

2 Sep 1344 (EFR C1, 1074) commission.
6 Sep 1345 (EFR C2, 767) orders Odo, bishop of Paphos, to pay 5250 silver bezants to Franciscus Baralli, merchant of Avignon.
9 Sep 1345 (VQ 5, 360) Franciscus de Pisis, archdeacon of Tarsus, pays a composition of 1000 fl.

538] Hugo, abbot of S. Vivant, Vergy, diocese of Autun.

30 Mar 1384 (Coll. 359, 209^v-212^r) quittance to Guillelmus de Lacu.

539] Hugo, abbot of S. Petrus extra Muros, Chalon-sur-Saône. See *Gall. Christ.* 4:964A.

12 Jan 1362 (OS 31, 218^v-219^r, 221^v-222^v) instrument of the obligation of the successor Jocerandus to a composition consisting of 50 saumata of grain and 6 barrels of Beaune wine, with an executive letter by the camerarius to Joannes Rosseti.
27 Jan 1362 (Coll. 497, 77^r) note of the above obligation.

540] Hugo, abbot of SS. Nicola and Cataldo, diocese of Lecce.

10 Feb 1354 (Coll. 169, 50^r) successor Nicolaus pays for the spoils.

541] Hugo, abbot of S. Pierre de Sauve OSB, diocese of Nîmes.

6 Apr 1357 (IM 6277) minute of a commission to Bernardus de Abbate, provost of Mirepoix, collector of Narbonne.
1357 (Coll. 114, 81^r) he notes receipt of 105 fl.
9 May 1357 (VQ 7, 175-176) he pays cash and goods worth 617 fl. 5 s. 6 d.
16 Aug 1357 (ibid., 180) he pays 163 fl.

542] Hugo, abbot of Terrason OSB, diocese of Sarlat.

28 Jan 1372 (Coll. 358, 25^v) commission to Arnaldus Garini, collector of Sarlat.

543] Hugo Alberti, bishop of Albi, died before 18 May 1379. Archdeacon of Noyon in 1353, despite defect of age (18 years: EFR I1, 177); notary apostolic; bishop of Albi from 1354.

1380 (IM 4746) camerarius Petrus de Croso demands accounts.
5 Feb 1382 (Coll. 359, 167^{rv}) the bishop's debt to his former ward Joannes Vergerii is to be paid from the spoils.

544] Hugo Aymerici, bishop of S. Paul-Trois-Châteaux, died between 3 Jun and 5 Aug 1348. Formerly dean of S. Ruf, Avignon; bishop of Orange from 1324; of S. Paul from 1328. See *Gall. Christ.* 1:719D-721A.

1 Nov 1326 (EFR J1, 26888) licentia testandi.
5 Aug 1348 (EFR C1, 3926) commission to Joannes de Babuis, canon of S. Frontin, Périgueux.
3 Oct 1348 (Coll. 497, 39^v) successor Guillelmus obligated to a composition of 150 fl. for grain.
1353 (RA 125, 229^r) successor Guillelmus Guitardi died as bishop of Lisieux; 150 fl. of his spoils (q.v.) are reckoned to pay this composition.

545] Hugo de Bacho, bishop of Urgel, died 20 Feb 1361. Formerly abbot of Ripoll OSB, diocese of Vich; bishop from 1351.

12 Feb 1362 (OS 23A, 96^r) successor Guillelmus obligated to a composition of 2500 fl. for spoils and vacancy.
2 May 1362 (OS 31, 146^{rv}) note of an additional composition of 500 fl.

546] Hugo Barroti, precentor and canon of Narbonne.

17 Dec 1356 (Coll. 352, 50^r) note of the expedition, by the courier Bernardus Stephani, of a commission to Petrus Stephani and Arnaldus de Villario, dated 9 Dec 1356.

547] Hugo de Bonovillari, bishop of Lectoure, died before 21 Oct 1370. LL.Lic.; former archdeacon in the church of Auch; bishop from 1369.

8 Nov 1370 (IM 2616) inventory of goods in the house of the procurator of the bishop of Avignon.
23 Jan 1372 (Coll. 357, 63^{rv}) Raymundus Bernardi de Bonafonte is obligated to a composition of 660 fl. Fr.
Feb 1372 (IM 2676, 7) the executor, Paganus de Bellopodio, is obligated to a composition of 3000 fl., and pays 387 fl.

n.d. (IM 2332) partial accounts of the spoils and vacancy by Paganus de Bellopodio.

16 Jul 1375 (OS 42, 26ʳ) Arnaldus de Peyraco, collector of Auch, pays 290 fl. 4 s. 1 d. for silver vessels from these spoils and those of Bernardus de Mornaco, bishop of Tarbes (q.v.).

1 Feb 1376 (Arch. dép. de Vaucluse G, 81: Briefs of Joannes Surelli, 16ʳ-17ʳ) receipt of books by Petrus Praderii, canon of Rieux, usufructuary under the testament.

after 1385 (Coll. 35, 262ᵛ-263ʳ) accounts of Sicardus de Brugayrosio.

548] Hugo de Castellione, bishop of S. Bertrand de Comminges, died 4 Oct 1352. Bishop from 1335.

21 Jan 1353 (EFR I1, 78) commission to Bernardus de Abbate, supplanting that by Clement VI to Martinus de Girardo.

7 Jun 1353 (ibid., 331) commissioner is instructed to collect the remaining goods.

before 1356 (Coll.114, 81ʳ) commissioner reports receipts of 600 écus, 400 fl.

1357-1359 (Coll. 154, 213ᵛ) acounts of commissioner Guillelmus Guilaberti, collector of Narbonne.

27 Feb 1359 (VQ 7, 260) nephew executor Albertus de Castellione pays 100 fl. of a composition for 500 fl.

2 Jan 1360 (ibid., 330) he pays 100 fl.

2 Jan 1361 (Coll. 231, 117ᵛ) he pays 100 fl.

n.d. (OS 23A, 109ʳ) note of the payment of 500 fl. in full.

549] Hugo Caychendi de Calciata.

16 Mar 1351 (VQ 5, 444) his brother pays 2 fl. composition, on his oath that there are no goods beyond those of a modest inventory.

550] Hugo de Croso, abbot of Déols OSB, diocese of Bourges. See *Gall. Christ.* 2:152C.

2 Nov 1384 (Coll. 359, 212ᵛ-213ʳ) camerarius orders Joannes Francisci to release certain rings to Albertus de Tineria, lord of Cortina, the late abbot's nephew.

1 Dec 1384 (Coll. 360, 196ʳᵛ) camerarius releases spoils to successor Robertus at the petition of Joannes, duke of Bourges, except 200 fl. worth of vessels and rings.

5 Mar 1385 (ibid., 214ᵛ-215ʳ) he releases 600 fr. worth of goods to Dalphina de Croso, the lady of Murat.

551] Hugo de Engolisma, canon of Saintes, paneterius to John XXII, died in curia before 25 Apr 1342.

22 May 1328 (EFR J1, 41242) licentia testandi.

28 Nov 1343 (EFR C1, 552) a *Decretum*, assigned by the Camera under Benedict XII to Bernardus Fornerii, succentor of Narbonne, is not to go to Hugo's heirs with the rest of his goods which the Camera has restored to them.

552] Hugo Fenollet, bishop of Valencia, died 21 Jun 1356. Formerly canon of Elne; bishop of Vich from 1346; of Valencia from 1348.

30 Jun 1356 (Coll. 352, 85^v) note of the expedition of a commission dated 28 Jun to Fulco Pererii.
6 Dec 1356 (Coll. 114, 163^r-165^r) accounts of the vacancy from the date of Hugo's death to the date of his successor's provision.
n.d. (Coll. 116, 63^r) accounts of spoils: £106.11.4 collected.
n.d. (Coll. 119, 124^v) Fulco Pererii is accused of giving valuable books to his own nephew.
n.d. (Coll. 430A, 76 fols.) a badly mutilated account of the legal process in the Camera.

553] Hugo Gauberti, almoner of the Pinhota, died in curia.

11 May 1341 (VQ 4, 177) Petrus Natalis pays 6 fl. 4 s.

554] Hugo Geraldi, bishop of Cahors, died 18 May 1317. Formerly archdeacon in the church of Rouen, papal chaplain; bishop from 1313. Condemned and burned for a plot on the life of John XXII.

30 Jul 1313 (Regestum Clementis Papae V, 9756) licentia testandi.
1 Apr 1325 (EFR J2, 2452) commission.
16 Mar 1328 (OS 12, 88^v-89^r) quittance to commissioner Durandus Payrola.
25 Jan 1331 (ibid., 139^v) commissioner Hugo Lasserra pays 21 fl. etc. from a debt.

555] Hugo de Harlam, canon of Chester, diocese of Coventry-Lichfield.

26 Jan 1378 (Coll. 393, 63^v-64^r) treasurer commissions Geraldus Mercaderii to collect the spoils.

556] Hugo Laporta, archdeacon in the church of Tours, died in curia.

4 Sep 1360 (VQ 7, 299) Balduinus Ricardi, sigillifer auditoris Camerae, pays 20 fl.

557] Hugo de Mandagoto, provost of Embrun. Formerly canon of Aix.

23 May 1327 (EFR J1, 28781) licentia testandi.
29 Jan 1363 (Coll. 497, 81^v) executor obligated to a composition of 100 fl.

558] Hugo de Marchenaco, abbot of Sauve-Majeure, diocese of Bordeaux, died 12 May 1371. See *Gall. Christ.* 2:874.

20 May 1372 (Coll. 358, 48^v-49^r) successor Raymundus made a composition for 800 fr.; his terms and rights are described, including a period of vacancy in 1371. The collector is ordered to compel payment of debts to Raymundus.

9 Jul 1372 (Coll. 358, 66^r) Nicolaus Chautardi, canon of Paris, and Fr. Arnaldus de Greylero, prior "de Noveyo," diocese of Reims, are commissioned to collect debts.

559] Hugo de Peyraco, rector of S. Pierre, Avignon.

13 Oct 1348 (VQ 5, 413) executors pay 500 fl. composition.

560] Hugo Rigaldi, familiar of cardinal Galhardus de Mota.

28 Aug 1347 (VQ 5, 394) heirs and executors pay a composition of 15 fl.

561] Hugo Rogerii, abbot of S. Sernin OCSA, diocese of Toulouse, died between 1356 and 1359. See *Gall. Christ.* 13:97B-C.

15 May 1324 (EFR J1, 19564) licentia testandi.
8 Jan 1360 (Coll. 497, 71^v) successor Joannes obligated to a composition of 3000 fl.

562] Hugo de Roqua, abbot of Pébrac OCSA, diocese of S. Flour. See *Gall. Christ.* 2:462.

17 Dec 1384 (Coll. 85, 110^v) successor Dalmatius pays a composition of 80 fr.

563] Hugo de S. Francisco OFM, bishop of Sessa Aurunca, died before 21 Apr 1344. Bishop from 1340.

28 Apr 1343 - 30 Jun 1344 (Coll. 168, 37^v) accounts of Guillelmus de Roseriis.

564] Hugo de Vaucemain, magister generalis OP, died in curia.

17 Aug 1341 (EFR B2, 877; B3, 3169) the Dominican provincial of France, Petrus de Parma, is ordered to collect the spoils.

565] Hugolinus, abbot of S. Pietro, Perugia.

4 Nov 1363 (OS 23A, 94^v) successors Capulus and Philippus were obligated in turn to a composition of 450 fl.
20 Jan 1368 (Coll. 353, 106^{rv}) the commune of Perugia is liable for a debt of 2000 fl.; on their appeal, sentence of interdict is suspended for 2 months.

566] Hugolinus Malabranca OESA, patriarch of Constantinople and administrator of Rimini, died 1373. M.Theol.; patriarch and administrator from 10 Feb 1371.

1373 (Coll. 129, 234ʳ) spoils yield 573 ducats 18 s. 4 d.
28 Dec 1373 (EFR G2, 2385) commission to Franciscus, elect of Acqui, and the abbot of S. Nicola di Lido, Venice.

567] Humbertus de Montauro, archbishop of Naples, died 3 Jul 1320. Formerly canon of Naples; archbishop from 1308.

1324 x 1332 (Coll. 221, 151ʳ) Geraldus de Valle collects 1463 unc. 13 tari 17 grani 3 d. for spoils and vacancy, half to be paid to the duke of Calabria.

568] Humbertus Piloti, provost of S. André, Grenoble.

15 Mar 1373 (EFR G1, 1152) the governor of the Dauphiné is ordered to remove impediments to the collection of spoils.

569] Humbertus de Villeta, archbishop of Tarentaise, died Apr 1379. Formerly prior of Tarentaise, Lic.Decr.; archbishop from 15 Jan 1379.

1380? (IM 4746) camerarius demands accounts.
12 Jun 1387 (Coll. 362, 48ᵛ-49ʳ) he directs Antonius, patriarch of Jerusalem and legate, to collect debts.

Ingeramnus: see Engerannus.

570] Itericus de Mirmande, abbot of Cluny, diocese of Mâcon, died 20 Feb 1347 in curia. See *Gall. Christ.* 4:1152.

2 Apr 1347 (VQ 5, 386) successor Hugo pays 300 fl. from spoils for annates.
8 Apr 1347 (EFR C1, 3217-3218) spoils composition.
23 Jan 1348 (VQ 5, 408-409) successor pays 1000 fl.
18 Apr 1349 (ibid., 424) he pays 1000 fl.
22 Nov 1349 (Coll. 289, 28ᵛ) goods in inventory of papal palace.
n.d. (OS 23A, 96ʳ) note of final payment of successor's composition.

571] Jacobus, bishop of Malta, died before 15 Jun 1356. Formerly bishop of Sebaste in Armenia from about 1330; of Malta from 1346.

28 Dec 1368 (Coll. 353, 132ᵛ-133ʳ) camerarius orders Dominicus de Sassenorio, collector of Sicily, to collect 36 unc. silver from Nicolaus de Calathagirono.

572] Jacobus, bishop of Sora, died before 4 Sep 1355. Former canon of Sora; bishop from 1323.

mid-1362 (Coll. 169, 136ᵛ) spoils collected from successor Andreas.

573] Jacobus, archbishop of Taranto, died 1378. Formerly archbishop of Corinth from 1340; of Taranto from 1349.

1 Aug 1389 (Diversa cameralia 1, 127^r) quittance to Fr. Michael, abbot of S. Salvator de Septimo, for goods assigned to the Roman Camera.

574] Jacobus, abbot of S. Giovanni in Venere, diocese of Chieti.

ca.Feb 1362 (Coll. 169, 134^{rv}) spoils collected.
27 Feb 1363 (IE 303, 10^r) 40 fl. paid for a mitre, included in the successor's composition.

575] Jacobus, abbot of S. Maria de Arbona, diocese of Chieti.

mid-1362 (Coll. 169, 136^v) spoils collected from successor Bernardus.

576] Jacobus, abbot of Sassovivo OSB, diocese of Foligno.

29 Sep 1345 (EFR C1, 2000; Coll. 232, 151^{rv}) premature reservation.
4 Nov 1350 (EFR C2, 2327) commission.
1 May 1353 (EFR I1, 261) orders goods restored to successor Guido in consideration of a composition.

577] Jacobus, archimandrite of the monastery of S. Salvator, Messina, died 10 Mar 1373.

ca. 1375 (Coll. 222, 173^v) the archbishop of Messina is liable to pay 4 unc. for a ring, cape, and shoes which he received by custom.
ca. 1375 (ibid., 175^r) the monks, who divided the spoils, are liable for a total of 134 fl. 17 unc. 15 car.

578] Jacobus, provost of Toulouse.

11 May 1375 (Coll. 235, 144^v) executor Guillelmus de Rua is obligated to a composition of 125 fl., paid.
n.d. (Coll. 236, 323^v-324^r) accounts of collection of remains by Aymericus Pelicerii.

579] Jacobus de Abbatisvilla, commensal chaplain to cardinal Guillelmus de Judicis, died in curia.

22 Sep 1360 (Coll. 231, 100^v; VQ 7, 299) executor pays 50 fl. composition.

580] Jacobus de Albenoriis, sacristan of Pamiers, died in curia.

20 Jun 1336 (VQ 4, 109) Bernardus Faycheti, canon of Pamiers, pays 100 regal., 64 agn., 15 Paris. auri, 47 fl. 12 d.

581] Jacobus Annibaldi OFM, bishop of Assisi, died before 29 Jan 1369. Formerly poenitentiarius apostolicus, bishop of Fondi from 1363.

5 Mar 1369 (Coll. 353, 176^r-177^r) the spoils are to be collected subject to the *moderatio*.

582] Jacobus Arnaldi, archdeacon of Conflans, diocese of Elne, canon and officialis of Mallorca.

3 Jul 1375 (Coll. 356, 31^{rv}) the subcollector is ordered to hand over the excess of goods, patrimonial property, etc. to the executor and heir. The full canonical justification of this procedure is given, following Giovanni d'Andrea.

1 Sep 1375 (ibid., 53^r) executors obligated to a composition of 400 regal. and execution in full: letter to Petrus Borrerii, collector of Aragon.

583] Jacobus Artaudi, bishop of Gap, died Aug 1399. Formerly canon of Die, LL.B.; bishop of S. Paul-Trois-Châteaux from 1364; of Gap from 1366.

1403-1406 (Coll. 23, 198^r-199^r) inventory of goods recovered from a robbery.

584] Jacobus Ayas OP, bishop of Suelli, Sardinia from 1384.

21 Mar 1399 (Coll. 486, 5^v-19^v) inventory by Mattheus de Rapacio, collector of Corsica and Sardinia, in Spanish.

585] Jacobus Barrani, collector of Saintes and Tulle.

4 Jan 1365 (Coll. 353, 26^r-27^v) accounts of Vitalis Vassali, late collector.

586] Jacobus de Broa, archdeacon of Lunez, diocese of Béziers, treasurer to Benedict XII, died between 19 May and 1 Jun 1348.

1 Jun 1348 (EFR C1, 3895) commission to Bernardus Raymundi, almoner of Béziers.

2 Jul 1348 (AA Arm. C, to. 18) inventory of goods at Narbonne and Béziers by Eustacius Piscis, canon of Béziers.

587] Jacobus de Caussanis, abbot of Cluny, diocese of Mâcon, died in curia 6 Jul 1383. See *Gall. Christ.* 4:1155E-1156B.

13-23 Jul 1383 (Coll. 484, 38 fols.) an inventory with its first folio missing, by Guillelmus de Lacu and Petrus Meleti.

30 Mar 1384 (Coll. 359, 209^v-212^r) quittance to Guillelmus de Lacu.

588] Jacobus de Columna, bishop of Lombez from 1328.

27 Aug 1341 (EFR B2, 891) commission.

28 Jun 1346 (EFR C1, 2621) Clement VI orders the commissioners to carry out the mandates of Benedict XII.

589] Jacobus de Corvo OP, bishop of Toulon, died 1341. Formerly bishop of Zagreb from 1322; of Quimper from 1326; of Toulon from 1330.

29 Sep 1345 (EFR C1, 2001) commission to Joannes Regis.
21 Oct 1345 (ibid., 2057) Jacobus Aloys and Petrus de Corvo, the bishop's familiars, are cited as holders of the goods.
29 Oct 1345 (ibid., 2075) Joannes Regis is permitted to compound with those condemned in the bishop's court for their debts.
5 Apr 1346 (VQ 5, 366) he pays 250 fl.

590] Jacobus Falconerii de Neapoli, bishop of Bitonto, died before 14 Dec 1357. D.Decr.; bishop of Aquino from 1342; of Bitonto from 1348.

28 Dec 1357 (Coll. 352, 118^v) expedition by hand of Reginaldus de Lupchaco, cantor of Auxerre, to himself and Petrus archbishop of Benevento, of a commission dated 14 Dec 1357.

591] Jacobus Fornerii OCist, bishop of Pamiers, whose spoils were reserved when he was translated to Mirepoix 3 Mar 1326. Formerly abbot of Fontfroid, diocese of Narbonne; bishop of Pamiers from 1317; later Pope Benedict XII, 1334-1342.

22 Feb 1326 (EFR J1, 24464) licentia testandi.
1 Aug 1326 (EFR J2, 3073-3074) directions about the disposition of spoils at Pamiers.
14 Nov 1326 (ibid., 3073-3074) collections and payment of debts at Pamiers.
7 Jan 1327 (VQ 1, 525-526) Arnaldus de Verdala pays 1615 fl. 2000 gr., £9.11.8.
14 May 1327 (ibid., 526) he pays 208 agni, 114 regal.
ca. 1329 (IE 83, 60^r-64^r) accounts of the vacancy.
27 Dec 1331 (OS 12, 137^r-138^r) quittance to Arnaldus de Verdala.
30 Nov 1335 (EFR B2, 122) general quittance to Arnaldus de Verdala by Benedict XII for various collections, including his own spoils.
3 Mar 1336 (Coll. 147, 26^v) Raymundus Flori pays his collections of debts totaling 46 s. 4 d.

592] Jacobus de Longofonte, prior of S. M. "de Ariberto," diocese of Liège.

Apr 1389 (IM 3337, 49) Joannes Eraclei, prior "de Ispaniaco," diocese of Mende, pays a composition of 107 fl.

593] Jacobus de Malavoltis, bishop of Siena, died 8 Nov 1371. Formerly canon of Siena, D.Decr., auditor sacri palatii, papal chaplain; bishop from 1371.

7 Jul 1372 (Coll. 358, 64^{rv}) collector Lucius bishop of Cesena is ordered to pay the church's debts out of the spoils and allow support for the successor at 4 fl. per day.

594] Jacobus de Milas, advocatus sacri palatii.

28 Jul 1347 (VQ 5, 393; IM 6455,1) executors pay a composition of 1000 fl.

595] Jacobus Muto, bishop of Spoleto, died before 24 Nov 1372. LL.D., auditor sacri palatii; former canon of Ostia, papal chaplain; bishop of Marsi from 1363; of Arezzo from 1365; of Spoleto from 1371. Vicar in Rome 1369-1371.

3 Dec 1372 (Coll. 358, 117^v-118^r) instructions to Geraldus, receiver general in Italy: the bishop had license to dispose of the goods which he acquired before translation to Spoleto; the executors are to receive back the goods taken by the collectors, "prout in partibus illis et presertim in Urbe Romana unde ... episcopus originem traxit ipse antequam ad aliquam ecclesiam assumptus fuit et erat homo magne scientie, magni consilii et etiam magne industrie."

4 Dec 1372 (ibid., 117^r) successor Galhardus is to have the benefit of the *moderatio*.

596] Jacobus Queraldi, papal chaplain of honor, chaplain "de Sereto," diocese of Elne, died in curia 1398.

before 1405 (Coll. 160, 123^r) Joannes de Ripis Altis receives £108.4 from fruits.

597] Jacobus Sion, bishop of Tortosa, died 18 Oct 1351. Former canon of Lerida; bishop of Lerida from 1341; of Tortosa from 1348. See J. de Zunzunegui, "La percepcion de los espolios del obispo de Tortosa Don Jaime Cyon (1348-1351)," *Anthologica Annua* 13 (1965): 361-390.

27 Oct 1351 (EFR C2, 2517) commission.
18 Jun 1352 (ibid., 2652) commission to Fulco Pererii.
n.d. (Coll. 98, 20 fols.) inquest of Fulco Pererii.
ca. 1354 (Coll. 100, 44^r-106^v) inquest into the rights of Franciscus bishop of Elne.

598] Jacobus de Sirano, canon of Narbonne.

18 Jul 1377 (OS 42, 107^v) almoner of Narbonne pays a composition.
18 Jul 1377 (Coll. 393, 60^v-62^r) quittance by treasurer.
18 Jul 1377 (ibid., 61^v-62^r) he orders the officialis of Narbonne to secure the goods for the almoner.

599] Jacobus de Urrea OCSA, canon of Zaragoza.

27 Mar 1354 (EFR I1, 847) commission to Fulco Pererii.

600] Jacobus de Villa, procurator curiae Romanae.

Jun 1350 (VQ 5, 437) executors pay a composition of 90 écus to Balduinus Ricardi, sigillifer auditoris Camerae.

601] Jacobus de Vinariis, prior of Monserrat, diocese of Barcelona.

Jul 1376 (Coll. 121, 3ᵛ-5ʳ) accounts of the subcollector of Barcelona.

602] Jacobus Zatria, bishop of Gerona, died 30 Mar 1374. B.Decr., archdeacon of Mallorca; bishop from 1369.

mid-1375 (Coll. 121, 7ʳ-8ᵛ) subcollector of Barcelona receives £87.17.9 Barc. from debts.
21 May 1376 (IM 2924, 4; OS 42, 68ʳ) Albertus de Trilhia, domicellus, pays 100 fl. of a 300-fl. composition.
6 Aug 1376 (OS 42, 68ʳ) he pays 200 fl.

603] Jambertus de Livrono, abbot of Montmajour OSB, diocese of Arles. Formerly abbot of S. André, Villeneuve, diocese of Avignon; of Montmajour from 1353 (Gall. Christ. 1:613C). For his testament on the day of his death, 13 Jun 1361, see Baluze-Mollat 2:442.

8 Feb 1362 (OS 31, 226ᵛ) releases goods to his unnamed executors.

604] Joannes, bishop of Andria.

28 Feb 1362 (Coll. 169, 133ᵛ) accounts.

605] Joannes OSB, bishop of Lodève, died before 27 Aug 1375. Former abbot of Ménat OSB, diocese of Clermont; bishop of Lodève from 1371. His surname may have been Gastelli: *Gall. Christ.* 2:368A.

before 1377 (Coll. 157, 184ᵛ) goods sold for 812 fr.

606] Joannes, bishop of Lugo. Not in Eubel.

5 Mar 1375 (EFR G2, 3200) commission to Bartholomeus de Lausuta OP, lector of Aosta.
Oct 1375 (IM 2877, 8) Thomas de Ammanatis, elect of Limassol, nuncio, pays 294 fl. 18 s. for goods received from the lector of Aosta.

607] Joannes, bishop of Maillezais, died before 20 Feb 1359.

Jul 1359? (IM 2150) inquest into the spoils, which were mostly lost in an English sack before the death of the bishop.

608] Joannes, bishop of Mondoñedo, died before 27 Feb 1329. Formerly archdeacon of Calahorra; bishop from 1327.

30 Dec 1329 (VQ 1, 501) Gundisalvus, archbishop of Braga, pays 9605 fl. 11 s.

609] Joannes OP, archbishop of Otranto. Formerly archbishop of Korfu from 1320; of Otranto from 1330.

1 Apr 1324 (EFR J1, 19240) licentia testandi.
29 Mar 1345 (Coll. 168, 47^v) goods collected by Guillelmus de Roseriis.
15 Jan 1346 (EFR C2, 881) commission to Guillelmus, archbishop of Brindisi.

610] Joannes, bishop of Rapolla, died before 17 Nov 1346. Formerly bishop of Lavello; of Rapolla from 1342.

1 Dec 1346 (Coll. 168, 59^r-60^r) collections and sales by Guillelmus de Roseriis.

611] Joannes, bishop of Rieux. Former succentor of Béziers, LL.Lic.; bishop of Rieux from 1371.

1 Oct 1373 (Coll. 236, 147^r, 155^v) collector Aymericus Pelicerii reports 232 fl. collected, £1865.18.10 remaining.
n.d. (ibid., 253^{rv}) he notes four debts, total £15.7.6 and 34 fl.
26 Feb 1375 (EFR G1, 1817) commission to Raymundus de Casilhaco and Joannes de Caffris.
3 Apr 1375 (EFR G1, 1846) thanks to Petrus Raymundi de Rapistagna, seneschal of Toulouse, for his help to commissioners.
11 May 1375 (Coll. 356, 21^r-22^v) a series of letters from the camerarius Petrus de Croso: Joannes de Caffris is not to collect from the servants because the successor has made a composition; the successor is empowered to collect goods from familiars; quittance to familiars.
28 May 1375 (OS 42, 14^r) Arnaldus Bernardi, knight, is quit for 160 fl. for goods that he received.
2 Jun 1375 (Coll. 356, 23^{rv}) quittance to familiars.
Jun 1375 (IM 2877, 4) commissioners pay 214 fl. 8 s.
Sep 1375 (ibid., 7; OS 42, 43^v) Aymericus Pelicerii pays 117 fl. 14 s.
Oct 1375 (IM 2877, 8; OS 42, 43^v) successor Joannes pays 1000 fr. of a 4000-fr. composition.
3 Oct 1375 (Coll. 356, 57^v) his next term is changed from 22 Jul to 30 Nov.
10 Dec 1375 (OS 42, 44^v) Bernardus de Quimballo pays 40 fl. of an 80-fl. composition.

612] Joannes, bishop of Rieux, died 1381.

1381 (Coll. 235, 144^v) collector reports nothing received: goods worth about 100 fl., debts to 1500 fl. Marginal note: "Non propter hoc debuisti cessare a factione inventarii."

613] Joannes, bishop of Salpe, died before 14 Dec 1357.

28 Dec 1357 (Coll. 352, 118ᵛ) dispatch by hand of Reginaldus de Lupchaco, cantor of Auxerre, of a commission to himself and Petrus, archbishop of Benevento, dated 14 Dec 1357.

614] Joannes OESA, archbishop of Split. Formerly bishop of Zengg from 1333; archbishop of Split from 1348.

27 Dec 1348 (EFR C2, 1884) commission.
3 Mar 1349 (Coll. 245, 132ᵛ) receipts by collector Andreas de Tuderto.

615] Joannes, bishop of Vesprem, died before 18 Dec 1357. Bishop from 1346.

24 Dec 1357 (Coll. 352, 101ᵛ) dispatch by hand of the courier Raymundus de S. Michele, sergeant at arms, to Arnaldus de Lacausina, collector of Poland and Hungary, of a commission dated 18 Dec 1357.

616] Joannes, bishop of Viseu, died before 2 Jul 1365. Formerly cantor of Viseu; bishop from 1349.

15 Apr 1371 (Arm. 33, to. 18, 196ʳ-197ᵛ) balance of spoils collected by Bertrandus de Macello.

617] Joannes, abbot of S. Lupo, diocese of Benevento.

25 Sep 1348 - 10 Jan 1349 (Coll. 168, 75ʳ) Guillelmus de Roseriis collects 10 car.

618] Joannes, abbot of Jaucels OSB, diocese of Béziers.

6 Nov 1361 (Coll. 497, 76ᵛ) successor Petrus is obligated to a composition of 100 fl.
1 Feb 1362 (VQ 7, 389) successor pays 100 fl.
1368 x 1377 (Coll. 157, 185ʳ) collector Arnaldus Andreae reports no receipts, because the successor made a composition in the Camera.

619] Joannes, abbot of Maubec OSB, diocese of Bourges.

3 Mar 1381 (Coll. 358, 173ᵛ) Guillelmus de Riomo, operarius of Déols OSB, diocese of Bourges, is commissioned to make an inventory and pay the Camera.

620] Joannes, abbot of S. Maria della Vittoria OCist, diocese of Marsi.

12 May 1362 (Coll. 169, 135ᵛ) accounts.

621] Joannes, abbot of S. Maria de Irachio OSB, diocese of Pamplona.

14 Mar 1383 (Coll. 360, 39^r-40^r) camerarius commissions Martinus bishop of Pamplona to collect the composition from certain holders of the goods.

622] Joannes, chaplain of S. Vitale, Bologna.

1372 (Coll. 129, 227^v) the nuns of the convent pay 143 ducats.

623] Joannes Ademari, canon of Lodève.

1368 x 1377 (Coll. 157, 184^v) Raymundus Ademari pays a composition of 47 fr.

624] Joannes Alfonsi, bishop of Evora, died before 28 Nov 1356. Formerly canon of Evora; bishop from 1352.

4 Aug 1357 (Coll. 352, 66^v) dispatch of commission to Guillelmus Piloti, canon of Braga.
ca. 1360 (Coll. 116, 144^r) Alfonsus Aegidii is obligated to a composition of £200 Barc.

625] Joannes Amalrici, bishop of Sorra from 1342, nuncio in Sardinia.

26 Aug 1344 (EFR C1, 1056) commission.
2 Sep 1344 (ibid., 1072).
30 Sep 1344 (ibid., 1136).
14 Oct 1344 (ibid., 1167).
28 Feb 1353 (RA 125, 262^r) goods in papal treasure.

626] Joannes Arnaldi, rector in the diocese of Carcassonne, died in the Comtat-Venaissin.

12 Aug 1387 (Coll. 362, 61^v-62^v) commission to Guillelmus de Viridimonte, clericus Camerae.

627] Joannes Artaudi OP, bishop of Marseille, died Jul 1335. Former bishop of Nice from 1329; of Marseille from 1334.

29 Jun 1335 (EFR B1, 1680) licentia testandi.
1335 (Coll. 143, 5^r-73^v) accounts.
Nov 1335 (Coll. 398, 11^r-69^r) claims to spoils by various plaintiffs before the Camera.
21 Oct 1336 (VQ 4, 112) commissioner Hugo Roqua pays 13 fl.
23 Dec 1339 (ibid., 114) 76 fl. for the sale of a horse.
18 Nov 1339 (ibid., 149) commissioner Bartholomeus Berbignerii pays £40.
4 Jul 1340 (ibid., 160) successor Joannes pays 359 fl.

628] Joannes Aubriot, bishop of Chalon-sur-Saône from 1345.

24 Dec 1350 (EFR C1, 4841) commission to Joannes de Caola.
28 Apr 1351 (Coll. 497, 47^v) heirs obligated to a composition of 500 fl.

629] Joannes Bauphes, bishop of Lerida, died at Marseille about Nov 1403. J.U.D., former cantor of Evreux; bishop of Dax from 1375; of Vich from 1391; of Huesca from 1393; of Lerida from 1403.

Nov 1403 (RA 325, 196^{rv}) accounts of Joannes Lobera, clericus Camerae.

630] Joannes Bellihominis, scriptor Papae.

Aug 1372 (IM 2676, 66) Raymundus de Valle and Guido Garini, executors, pay a composition of 100 fl.

631] Joannes Bisaci, prior of S. Victor, diocese of Uzés.

1403 x 1406 (Coll. 159, 439^{rv}) Joannes Martini, collector of Narbonne, receives £39.2 from spoils.

632] Joannes Bonivini, abbot of S. Victor, Marseille, died 1405. See *Gall. Christ.* 1:693-694.

4 Apr 1405 (EFR B1, 8365; RA 54, 358^r-366^v) inventory by Petrus Olivarii, subcollector of Marseille.
1405 x 1405 (Coll. 23, 214^r-217^r) accounts of collector Simon de Pratis.
1405 (IM 5204, 13^r-19^v) quittance to Simon de Pratis.

633] Joannes de Borbonio, bishop of Verdun. LL.Lic., former dean of Autun; bishop from 1362.

20 Mar 1372 (EFR G1, 702) commission to Joannes, bishop of Toul.

634] Joannes Boutin, abbot of S. Croix de Talmont OSB, diocese of Luçon.

13 Sep 1365 (EFR U2, 1964) commission to Petrus Domandi.
ca. 1366 (Coll. 92, 30^r) successor pays a composition of 100 nobles.

635] Joannes de Campeto, canon of S. Ademaro, diocese of Muro Lucano, died in curia.

11 Aug 1351 (VQ 5, 448) Balduinus Ricardi, sigillifer auditoris Camerae, pays 15 écus, 6 fl.

636] Joannes de Cardone OCSA, archbishop of Arles, died before 14 Aug 1348. Formerly sacristan of Maguelonne; archbishop from 1341.

8 Sep 1348 (EFR C1, 3951) commission.

12 Oct 1354 (Coll. 497, 53ʳ) heirs of the debtor Guillelmus Costa are obligated to a composition of 600 fl.
6 Oct 1355 (VQ 7, 98) they pay 37 fl. 12 s.
29 Jan 1354 (Albanès, *Gallia Christiana Novissima*: Arles, n. 1562, cols. 664-665) Joannes Bonifilii, canon of Arles, orders all chaplains of the diocese to warn Jacoba, widow of Jacobus Joannis, now wife of Guido de Brossa, to pay to himself as commissioner £30 owed by her late husband, or to answer the complaint of the procurator fiscal before the camerarius at Avignon on 5 February.
27 Jan 1356 (ibid., n. 1563, col. 665; n. 1595, col. 682) commissioner's quittance to Petrus and Joannes Brossani for 50 s.
18 Aug 1360 (VQ 7, 297-298; Coll. 231, 95ʳ) the heirs of Guillelmus Costa pay 37 fl. 12 s.
22 Aug 1360 (ibid., 298) they pay 50 fl.

637] Joannes de Castello OFM, bishop of Mariana, Corsica, died in Genoa. Bishop from 1353. See AFH 47 (1954): 224.

Feb - 6 Jun 1364 (Coll. 132, 42ᵛ) accounts of Raphael de Turre.
7 Jun 1364 (Coll. 353, 12ʳ) quittance to Raphael de Turre for books.
23 Aug 1372 (Coll. 358, 85ᵛ-86ʳ) the Camera's rights in a debt of £200 Gen. is transferred to the governor of Corsica for a certain composition.

638] Joannes de Castro, bishop of Tuy, died before 20 Jul 1384. Formerly dean of Leon; bishop from 1351.

1384 x 1386 (Coll. 122, 72ᵛ-73ʳ) collector Guillelmus Boudrevillae's accounts of sales.

639] Joannes de Castronovo, collector of Reims.

18 Nov 1362 (Coll. 171, 122ʳ-126ʳ) inventory and accounts.
Dec 1362 (Coll. 66, 80ʳ-82ʳ) Aubricus Radolphi describes his recovery of the goods from the castle of Montague, diocese of Besançon.
2 Mar 1364 (OS 31, 128ᵛ-129ʳ) commissioners Aubricus Radolphi and Ricardus de Montemaiano are not to trouble Girarda, widow of Stephanus Mercereti de Sabinis for a Bible from the spoils, which she has restored.
27 Mar 1364 (Coll. 353, 5ʳ-6ʳ) obligation of Stephanus de Finis, knight, to pay a loan of 3158 écus.
9 Oct 1364 (Coll. 353, 18ᵛ) Stephanus's debt prorogued to 24 Jun 1365, and he is absolved from excommunication; he should pay earlier 700 écus as a draft on the royal treasury at Nîmes.
15 Dec 1364 (Coll. 353, 23ᵛ-24ʳ) quittance to collector Aubricus Radolphi for books and clothing.

11 Jul 1369 (Coll. 354, 71^{rv}) treasurer orders the citation of Bisantius Petit on account of 400 fl. which he borrowed from the late collector to pay for the celebration of his M.D. degree.

640] Joannes de Cavanhaco, canon of Chartres, cantor of Coimbra, collector of south Bourges.

2 April 1364 (EFR U2, 871) commission to Guillelmus Amarinti.
24 Apr 1364 (Coll. 353, 8^{rv}) commission.
7 May 1364 (EFR U2, 939) commission to Hugo de Lamanhania and Arnaldus de Vernolio.
17 Jun 1364 (ibid., 1020) commission to Guillelmus Piloti.
ca. 1370 (Arm. 33, to. 18, 85^v) Bertrandus de Macello receives at Coimbra £330 Port. His unfinished letter of commission is IM 2282.

641] Joannes de Champdorat OSB, bishop of Le Puy, died 15 Sep 1356. Formerly abbot of Chaise-Dieu, diocese of Clermont; bishop of Le Puy from 1342. J.U.D.: *Gall. Christ.* 2:725B-E.

14-15 Sep 1356 (Coll. 8A, fasc.2) testamentary dispositions and an inquest of spoils.
14 Jan 1357 (VQ 7, 170) executors pay 1000 fl. of an 1800-fl. composition.
12 Jul 1357 (ibid., 177-178; cf. OS 23A, 106^v) they pay 800 fl.
Mar 1363 (IM 2279, 6) 658 fl. Fr. paid for silverware.
Dec 1363 (ibid., 22) Aymericus Chatti de la Joussac, bishop of Bologna, pays 339 fl. for a mitre and crozier.

642] Joannes de Chissey, bishop of Grenoble. Bishop from 1337.

2 Sep 1350 (EFR C1, 4689-4690) commission and instructions to Joannes de S. Petro de Valonis.
13 Apr 1351 (VQ 5, 445) successor Radolphus pays 100 fl.

643] Joannes de Cojordano, bishop of Mirepoix, died between 9 Oct and 17 Dec 1361. Former archdeacon of Lunez, diocese of Béziers, papal familiar; bishop of Avignon from 1336; of Mirepoix from 1349.

20 Dec 1333 (EFR J1, 62347) licentia testandi.
n.d. (Coll. 66, 44^r) Aubricus Radolphi, collector of Lyon and Vienne, recounts his recovery of goods taken by (nephew?) Joannes de Cojordano.
3 Jan 1362 (OS 31, 214^v-215^r) recognition of a composition by successor Arnaldus de Villario.
23 May 1362 (OS 31, 150^{rv}) commission to the officialis of Carcassonne to collect debts owed to Joannes and to the king of France.
24 Apr 1364 (Coll. 353, 11^{rv}) quittance to the collector.

644] Joannes de Cori OP, bishop of Tivoli, died Aug 1342. Former bishop of Knin from 1334; of Tivoli from 1337.

17 May 1344 (EFR C1, 828-829) commission.
24 Oct 1344 (ibid., 1180).

645] Joannes Cortoys, provisor of the Pinhota.

17 Mar 1348 (IM 1754) inventory by Petrus Chautardi.
4 Aug 1348 (RA 101, 18^r-25^v) inventory by Petrus Chautardi.
22 Sep 1348 (VQ 5, 411) executor pays a debt of 100 fl.
5 Mar 1349 (ibid., 419) executor Jacobus de Villa pays 200 fl. of a composition; cf. OS 23A, 96^v.

646] Joannes de Craon, archbishop of Reims, died 26 Mar 1373. Formerly archdeacon in the church of Le Mans; bishop of Le Mans from 1347; archbishop of Reims from 1355.

7 Apr 1374 (EFR G1, 1588) commission to Bernardus Cariti and Joannes Mauberti.
25 May 1374 (ibid., 1605) faculties granted to Joannes Mauberti.

647] Joannes Cros, cleric, died in curia.

22 Mar 1352 (VQ 5, 453) Marcus de Corona, merchant, pays 50 fl.

648] Joannes Deodati, canon of Le Puy, subcollector in Le Puy and Clermont, died in curia.

28 May 1375 (Coll. 356, 20^{rv}) commission to Joannes de Cabrespino and Joannes de Caffris.
29 May 1380 (Coll. 359, 38^r-40^v) heirs make a composition in the Camera.

649] Joannes Fabri, bishop of Carcassonne, died before 27 Jun 1371. Formerly abbot of Grandmont OSB; bishop of Le Puy from 1356; of Tortosa from 1357; of Carcassonne from 1362.

9 Jan 1372 (Coll. 358, 24^v-25^r) collector Bertrandus Raffini is directed to pay the bishop's nephew a debt from the spoils.
4 Nov 1372 (ibid., 107^v) he is directed to turn the utensils over to the successor.

650] Joannes Fabri, clavarius of Châteauneuf-du-Pape, diocese of Avignon.

17 Jul 1361 (VQ 7, 341) payments by commissioner Nicolaus Cortesii, 313 fl. 7 s. 2 d.
22 Sep 1362 (Coll. 231, 143^r) further payments.

651] Joannes Fernandi de Sotomayor, bishop of Tuy, died 14 Jun 1323. Bishop from 1286.

16 Jul 1323 (EFR J1, 18197) reservation of spoils: the bishop died intestate.
10 Jan 1327 (OS 12, 103ᵛ-104ʳ) payments by Petrus de Brunia.

652] Joannes de Fisco, abbot of S. Maria, Florence.

15 Oct 1339 (Coll. 244, 34ʳ-35ᵛ) accounts of Joannes de Pererio.
6 Jun 1341 (EFR B3, 2983) commission.

653] Joannes Francisci, LL.Lic., canon of Chartres, collector of Bourges.

15 Jun 1397 (IE 374, 28ᵛ) goods yield 25 fl. 4 s.
30 Sep 1397 (ibid., 37ᵛ-38ʳ) they yield 29 fl. 22 s.

654] Joannes Galtini, magister medicinae, died in curia.

4 Sep 1360 (VQ 7, 299) Balduinus Ricardi, sigillifer auditoris Camerae, pays 10 fl.

655] Joannes Garrigiae, collector of Narbonne.

11 Sep 1369 (IM 2566) nuncupative testament.
17 Sep 1369 (Coll. 354, 78ᵛ) commission to Guillelmus Amarinti.
Jan 1372 (IM 2676, 3) collector Bertrandus Raffini pays 61 fl., £137.12.1.
Feb 1372 (ibid., 7) he pays 262 fr. 3 s. 3 d.
Aug 1372 (ibid., 51) he pays 15 fl. 30 fr.
Mar 1375 (IM 2877, 2) Petrus de Cassanhis, cubicularius, pays 22 fl. 23 s. 4 d. for a chalice.
before 1377 (Coll. 157, 153ᵛ-154ʳ) summary accounts by the successor Arnaldus Andreae: 1262 fr. 4 gr. received, 58 1/2 fr. remaining.

656] Joannes Gasconis, bishop of Marseille, died 10 Sep 1344. Bishop from 1335.

13 Jul 1327 (EFR J1, 29272) licentia testandi.
5 Sep 1344 (*Gall. Christ.* 1:657C-D) testament.
28 Jan 1345 (VQ 5, 354) executors pay 200 fl. of a 400-fl. composition.
19 Mar 1345 (ibid., 355) they pay 200 fl.

657] Joannes Gasconis, bishop of Nîmes, died 27 Aug 1369.

17 Sep 1371 (Coll. 357, 48ʳᵛ) executors Petrus and Raymundus Gasconis are obligated to a composition of 3000 fl.
19 Sep 1371 (IM 2661) camerarius Petrus de Croso instructs the commissioners Bertrandus Pelherii and Raymundus Pegole to assign to the executors the value of the goods in their inventory.

May 1372 (IM 2676, 40; Coll. 357, 48ᵛ) the executors pay 500 fl.
7 May 1373 (Coll. 358, 130ᵛ) the officialis, archdeacon, and subcollector of Nîmes are ordered to force debtors to pay the executors.
28 May 1372 (Coll. 357, 48ᵛ) the executors have paid their composition of 3000 fl. in full.

658] Joannes Godivosten Anglicus, died in curia.

Sep 1375 (IM 2877, 7) spoils yield 80 fl.

659] Joannes Gometii de Chaves, bishop of Evora, died 10 Mar 1368. Bishop from 1356.

8 Sep 1368 (Arm. 33, to. 18, 46ʳ-62ʳ) accounts of Bertrandus de Macello: £2803.15.2 Port. received.
15 Mar 1369 (Coll. 353, 195ᵛ-196ʳ) camerarius orders collector to observe the *moderatio*.

660] Joannes Grand Furstat, archbishop of Bremen, died in curia 30 May 1327. Formerly archbishop of Lund from 1290; of Bremen from 1310.

1 Sep 1319 (EFR J1, 10028) licentia testandi.
26 May 1327 (ibid., 29730) commission.
after 29 May 1327 (ibid., 29706 = IM 1327, caps. 22, n. 14) inventories of goods.
9 Jun 1327 (VQ 1, 521) commissioner Guillelmus Girberti assigns to Camera 7339 fl., 204 d. ad massam, etc.
16 Apr 1334 (ibid., 374-375) books sold for 450 fl.; other assignments by commissioner.

661] Joannes Graphei OFM, bishop of Patti-Lipari, died before 28 Nov 1373. Bishop from 1360. See AFH 48 (1955): 205.

n.d. (IM 7205) Bertrandus de Macello, receiver general in Sicily, records the wealth and income of the mensa.
1375 (Coll. 222, 173ᵛ, 177ᵛ, 183ʳᵛ, 186ʳ, 187ʳ, 192ᵛ, 197ʳᵛ, 202ʳᵛ, 206ʳ, 208ʳᵛ) records of debts due.
1375 (ibid., 210ʳ-211ʳ) goods and cash held by persons in Lipari.
1375 (ibid., 229ᵛ) Bertrandus de Macello collects 30 fl. etc.
1375 (ibid., 238ᵛ-242ʳ) note of the remains to be collected.

662] Joannes Guilaberti, dean of Dorpat, died in curia.

20 Jul 1363 (OS 31, 187ᵛ) composition by successor.
9 Aug 1364 (Coll. 353, 15ʳ-16ʳ) Henricus Biscop, provost of Bremen, reports 330 fl. received.
5 Sep 1364 (IE 303, 22ᵛ; IE 311, 61ʳ, ed. Kirsch, *Kollektorien* 394) successor

Gotfridus Warendorp compounded for 400 fl. as in an instrument by Joannes Palaysini; paid 150 fl.; he was granted until 20 Jun 1365 to pay the remaining 250 fl.

663] Joannes Guilhamini, D.Decr., rector "de Sarrenco," diocese of Lombez, died in curia.

11 Mar 1362 (Coll 497, 77^v) his father Stephanus obligated to a composition of 700 fl. Pied.
17 Mar 1362 (VQ 7, 393-394) father and brother pay 500 fl.
18 May 1362 (ibid., 402) they pay 200 fl.

664] Joannes de Hoya, bishop of Toul, died 19 Aug 1372. Former archdeacon of Toul; bishop from 1363.

6 Jun 1373 (EFR G1, 1251) commission to Joannes de Vitriaco.
8 Apr 1375 (Coll. 356, 11^v) commissioner directed to release goods to successor Joannes in consideration of a composition.

665] Joannes de Isoduno Anglicus OCSA, died before 1 Apr 1348.

15 Dec 1349 (VQ 5, 431-432) commissioner Joannes de Balafaso pays 40 fl., £32.
25 Feb 1351 (ibid., 444) sale of a house yields 52 fl. 10s.

666] Joannes Joannis, dean of Sigüenza.

23 Aug 1375 (Coll 356, 48^{rv}) the chapter is ordered to surrender goods to the collector of Castile.

667] Joannes de Jourens, bishop of Le Puy, died before 5 Nov 1361. LL.D., former papal chaplain, auditor of contradicted letters, bishop of Riez from 1348, of Valence-Die from 1352, of Luçon in 1354, of Elne from 1354.

20 Mar 1363 (OS 31, 200^{rv}) quittance for goods in an inventory to commissioner Petrus Gervasii.
31 Mar 1363 (IE 303, 11^r) Guillelmus Dominici pays for Petrus Gervasii 658 fl. Fr. etc.
3 Jun 1363 (OS 31, 177^v) quittance for a white horse to the collector and courier.
3 Jul 1363 (OS 31, 180^v) orders Petrus Gervasii to surrender goods to the new commissioner Bertrandus de Cosnaco, bishop of Comminges.

668] Joannes Laurentii, subcollector of Langres.

ca. 1360 (Coll. 66, 38^v) collector Aubricus Radolphi receives 7 fl.
26 Sep 1363 (OS 31, 192^v-197^r) quittance to collector Joannes Rosseti for 300 fl.

669] Joannes de Lieux, bishop of Poitiers, died Aug 1362. Formerly papal chaplain, bishop since 1357.

13 Feb 1365 (Coll. 353, 29^v) camerarius orders collector to release spoils, earned by the bishop's own industry and left to his heir.
20 Jun 1365 (ibid., 43^v; OS 23A, 90^v) obligation of Michael Casse, canon of Poitiers, to pay 170 regales auri and 3 m. silver.
Apr 1366 (IM 2435, 5) Petrus de Virgina, canon of Poitiers, pays 379 fl.
ca. 1366 (Coll. 92, 29^v) payments by several debtors for spoils.
23 Jun 1366 (Coll. 353, 69^r-70^v) composition by the chapter for spoils and vacancy.

670] Joannes de Luna, bishop of Catania, died before 4 Dec 1355. Formerly canon of Toledo; bishop from 1348.

12 Apr 1356 (Coll. 352, 117^r) dispatch of a commission dated 25 Jan 1356 to fr. Martialis, bishop of Catania, nuncio in Sicily.

671] Joannes de Magnavia, bishop of Orvieto, died before 29 Oct 1364. LL.Lic., formerly canon of Agen, nuncio in the March of Ancona; bishop of Orvieto from 1361.

21 Jan 1365 (Coll. 478, 1^r-7^v) inventory of spoils.
18,20 Mar 1365 (IM 2393) successor Petrus requests the return of goods collected as spoils, which belonged to the church.
n.d. (IM 2585) collector pays 256 fl. and reports expenses.

672] Joannes de Mardonia, rector "de Castoneto," diocese of Toulouse, died in curia.

12 Aug 1382 (Coll. 360, 16^r) goods released to executors for a composition of 600 fl.

673] Joannes de Marescalla, commensal chaplain, died in curia.

31 Jan 1355 (VQ 7, 88) Balduinus Ricardi, sigillifer auditoris Camerae, pays 367 fl.

674] Joannes Marignollae de Florentia OFM, bishop of Bisignano, died before 22 Mar 1359. Bishop from 1354.

9 May 1367 - 18 Dec 1370 (Coll. 248, 30^v-31^v) Lucius, bishop of Cesena, collects 65 fl. for goods left deposited in Florence.

675] Joannes Martini, prior "de Sermasia" OGrandmont, diocese of Saintes.

1383 x 1386 (Coll. 277, 142^v) subcollector Nicolaus de Senelayo collects £294.6 from sale of wine.

676] Joannes Martini de Barcelona OCSA, bishop of Huesca. Former archdeacon of Zaragoza, D.Decr.; bishop of Segorve from 1362; of Huesca from 1369.

19 Sep 1371 (EFR G2, 303) commission to Arnaldus Andreae.

677] Joannes Martini de Solhaes, archbishop of Braga, died 1 May 1325. Former bishop of Lisbon from 1294; archbishop of Braga from 1313.

1297 (EFR Registres de Boniface VIII, 3013) licentia testandi.
17 Nov 1328 (VQ 1, 486) Petrus de Brunia pays.
10 May 1335 (EFR B3, 869) orders Gonsalvus Petri, archbishop of Braga, to absolve holders of the spoils after restitution.

678] Joannes Maurelli, bishop of Vaison, died before 7 Oct 1370. Formerly canon of Sens, provost of Liège; bishop of Vaison from 1362.

1359 (RA 140, 17^r) licentia testandi, rubric.
1370 (Coll. 19, 307^v-320^v) accounts of Geraldus Mercaderii.
Aug 1372 (IM 2676, 66) he pays 400 fr.

679] Joannes de Mellato, bishop of Clermont, died before 2 Jan 1376. Formerly archdeacon in the church of Toul, papal chaplain; bishop of Chalon-sur-Saône from 1353; of Clermont from 1357.

13 Mar 1381 (Coll. 358, 174^v-175^r) the executors' petition for return of the goods is granted.

680] Joannes Mercerii, dean of Auxerre.

26 Jul 1383 (Coll. 360, 54^r-55^r) the camerarius directs Armandus Jusserandi, collector of Sens and Rouen, to cite the executor Adam Sapiens, canon of Auxerre, to answer in the Camera for the spoils.
27 Jul 1383 (ibid., 55^r-56^r) Adam, nephew of the executor, is granted license to depart from the curia to collect the necessary documents.

681] Joannes de Merulo, vicar of Noves, diocese of Avignon.

25 Oct 1359 (VQ 7, 267) his successor Jacobus Seguini pays 30 fl.

682] Joannes Morosini OESA, bishop of Cittanova d'Istria, died before 15 Mar 1359. Bishop from 1347.

14 May 1360 (Coll. 130, 150^v) successor pays 40 ducats composition.

683] Joannes Mottula de Neapoli, bishop of Caiazzo, died 21 Apr 1356.

4 Jun 1362 (Coll. 169, 135^v) accounts.

684] Joannes Natimbene OESA, bishop of Trivento, died before 28 Feb 1344. Formerly bishop of Avellino from 1326; of Trivento from 1334.

15 Jun - 28 Dec 1344 (Coll. 168, 38^r-39^r) goods collected by Guillelmus de Roseriis.

685] Joannes Nicolai, canon of Reims, papal chaplain.

16 Apr 1373 (EFR G1, 1202) commission to Joannes Mauberti and Radolphus Jaquetelli, canons of Reims.

686] Joannes de Nogareto, abbot of S. Sernin OCSA, diocese of Toulouse, died 12 Aug 1361.

24 Mar 1362 (Coll. 497, 78^r) successor Radulphus is obligated to a composition of 3000 fl.
1 Jan 1363 (Coll. 235, 78^r) collector Bertrandus de Castanherio notes receipt of 1000 fl., remains of 1000 fl.
1364 (ibid., 121^v) 613 fl. received, 69 fl. remaining.
1371 (Coll. 18, 214^v) the successor's composition is given as 1312 fl.; Bertrandus de Castanherio and Aymericus Pelicerii received 970 fl. 8 gr.
1 Oct 1373 (Coll. 236, 147^v, 156^r) Aymericus Pelicerii reports 870 fl. 8 gr. 3 barc. collected, 341 fl. 9 gr. 9 barc. remaining.

687] Joannes de Novocastro, bishop of Nevers, whose spoils were reserved when he was translated to Toul 27 Aug 1372. D.Decr., former treasurer of Besançon; bishop of Nevers from 1371. Later created cardinal in 1383, died 1398.

23 May 1375 (EFR G1, 1908) quittance to Raymundus de Casilhaco, preceptor of the hospital "de Canaheriis," diocese of Rodez, Joannes de Caffris, canon of Nevers, and Arnaldus Beraldi, lord "de Sessaco," diocese of Cahors.

688] Joannes Ogerii, dean of Beaune, diocese of Autun, collector, died before 4 Mar 1350.

689] Joannes le Parity, bishop of Vannes from 1312.

30 May 1335 (EFR B2, 63; B3, 332) commission to Bernardus de Casis.
3 Jan 1336 (EFR B2, 132; B3, 729) goods released to the executors.
26 Jun 1337 (EFR B3, 1378) orders Henricus de Bellomonte to collect the wealth not legitimately spent by the late bishop's coadjutors during his last illness.

690] Joannes Peissoni, archbishop of Aix, died 10 Oct 1368. Formerly canon of Béziers, papal chaplain and familiar; bishop of Digne from 1341; archbishop of Aix from 1361.

14 Oct 1368 (Coll. 478, 9^r-37^v) inventory by notary Joannes Lordati.
before 1370 (Coll. 19, 258^r-279^v) accounts of collector Geraldus Mercaderii.
Feb 1372 (IM 2676, 7) he pays 440 fr.
7 Apr 1375 (Coll. 356, 12^r) 220-fl. debt of Ludovicus de Falquaquerio is forgiven.

691] Joannes Pelegrini de Vignerio, secular abbot of S. Genès de Thiers OSB, diocese of Elne.

17 Nov 1393 (RA 272, 146^r) spoils said to have been reserved before death: Favier, *Finances* 252 n. 5.
1393 x 1405 (Coll. 160, 123^r) Joannes de Ripis Altis, collector of Elne, receives a composition of £55 from successor Jacobus Bonamie.

692] Joannes de Pererio, canon of Fréjus, nuncio in the kingdom of Naples, died between 5 Aug and 11 Sep 1343.

11 Sep 1343 (EFR C1, 398).
12 Dec 1343 (Coll. 168, 2^r) executors pay 50 unc.
23 Jan 1344 (ibid., 1^r) executor Raymundus de Cartayrata pays 10 fl.
24 Feb 1344 (EFR C1, 689) 1600 fl. paid.
15 Mar 1344 (VQ 5, 344-345) executor pays.

693] Joannes Picardi, servitor Camerae.

28 Feb 1385 (Coll. 360, 212^{rv}) camerarius Franciscus de Conzia releases spoils to the executors in consideration of 250l. composition.

694] Joannes Pilusfortis de Rabastens, abbot of Mas d'Azil, diocese of Rieux. See *Gall. Christ.* 13:203E.

11 Mar 1367 (Coll. 18, 290^v) composition by Petrus de Belloforti, prior of Montauban, and Guillelmus Bonis, prior of S. Manfred, diocese of Cahors, for 700 fl. Fr.
1 Oct 1373 (Coll. 236, 148^r, 156^v) collector Aymericus Pelicerii reports 700 fl. paid.

695] Joannes de Pinu, abbot of Cluny, diocese of Mâcon, died 27 Dec 1374. See *Gall. Christ.* 4:1155C-E.

8 Mar 1375 (Coll. 356, 3^v-5^r) successor is granted all the goods except the books at Paris in consideration of a composition.
8 Nov 1375 (IM 2877, 9; OS 42, 41^v) successor Jacobus pays 200 fl. of a 3000-fl. composition.

4 Apr 1376 (IM 2924, 3; OS 42, 66^{rv}) he pays 200 fl.
8 May 1376 (OS 42, 103^{rv}) he pays 500 fl.
28 Oct 1376 (ibid., 103^v) he pays 321 fl., 12 s.
8 Mar 1378 (ibid., 121^r) he pays 300 fl.
16 Jan 1379 (ibid., 143^r) he pays 500 fl.

696] Joannes de Pomerolio, archdeacon in the church of Toulouse.

9 Apr 1375 (Coll. 356, 12^v-13^r) commission to Aymericus Pelicerii.

697] Joannes de Ponte, abbot of S. Jovin de Marnes OSB, diocese of Poitiers. See *Gall. Christ.* 2:1275.

16 Oct 1384 (IM 5529) inventory by Petrus Guidonis, subcollector of Poitiers, for Joannes Francisci, collector.

698] Joannes de Porta, archbishop of Capua, died before 14 Dec 1357. Formerly archbishop of Brindisi from 1348; of Capua from 1353.

29 Dec 1357 (Coll. 352, 118^v) dispatch of a letter of 14 Dec asking information on spoils, by hand of Reginaldus de Lupchaco, to himself and Petrus, archbishop of Benevento.
23 Jun 1358 (ibid., 119^v) dispatch by hand of Raymundus de Albofolio of instructions to the commissioners, dated 3 May 1358 and accompanied by the bull *Quamquam fabricam militantis*, limiting the collection of spoils.

699] Joannes de Potgula OESA, bishop of Massalubrense from 1351.

12 Feb 1362 (Coll. 169, 131^r) accounts.

700] Joannes de Pratis, bishop of Castres. Former abbot of S. Pierre, diocese of Le Puy; bishop of Coimbra from 1333; of Castres from 1317.

18 Mar 1338 (EFR B1, 5824) licentia testandi.
5 Aug 1348 (EFR C1, 3926) commission.
16 Apr 1349 (VQ 5, 424) the executor, cardinal Petrus de Pratis, pays 300 fl. composition.
24 Nov 1360 (IM 2199) Guillelmus Piloti, collector of Portugal, pays £68.6.8 from spoils at Coimbra.
And see Samaran-Mollat, *Fiscalité* 218-219 for complaints against the activity of the collector Joannes de Palmis in this case; but according to his own accounts (Coll. 74, 73^r-162^v) he collected only vacancies in Castres in 1348.

701] Joannes de Prato OP, bishop of Evreux, died before 30 Jul 1333. M.Theol.; bishop from 1328.

1 Aug 1331 (EFR J1, 54402) licentia testandi.
18 Feb 1343 (EFR C1, 1491) cites licentia testandi.

6 Nov 1343 (ibid., 509) orders executor Michael Salverii to render accounts of vacancy and spoils.

23 Oct 1345 (ibid., 2061) orders Bertrandus Cariti to place goods under the hand of the Camera, because the executors are in disagreement.

13 Apr 1348 (ibid., 3806) Bertrandus Cariti is ordered to sell the goods at auction.

702] Joannes Prima, servitor of the Pinhota.

18 Jun 1344 (VQ 5, 350) 10 fl. received from spoils.

703] Joannes Raymundi, collector of Bourges and Limoges.

20 Sep 1362 (OS 31, 159^v-160^r) commission to five agents: the abbot of S. Ambroise OCSA, Ademarus Chautardi, Seguinus Elie, Joannes Bertrandi and Joannes Laurentii.

704] Joannes Raymundi, prior of La Carità OClun, Venice.

8 Apr 1372 (Coll. 358, 28^{rv}) Raymundus, abbot of S. Nicola di Lido, collector of Lombardy, is ordered to restore the spoils unless the prior was a papal officer in debt to the Camera.

705] Joannes Recuperi, canon of Pisa, papal chaplain, subcollector of Pisa.

30 Sep 1344 (EFR C1, 1137) commission.

706] Joannes Revelli OP, bishop of Orange, died 30 Sep 1367. Bishop from 1349.

15 Jan 1368 (Coll. 353, 102^v-104^v) camerarius Arnaldus Alberti at Rome dictates to the treasurer at Avignon the handling of legacies and the acceptable composition.
before 1370 (Coll. 19, 165^r) accounts of Geraldus Mercaderii.

707] Joannes Rigaldi OFM, bishop of Tréguier, died before 16 Sep 1323. Former poenitentiarius apostolicus; bishop from 1321. See AFH 64 (1971): 611; 66 (1973): 493.

15 May 1322 (EFR J1, 15424) licentia testandi.
15 Mar 1330 (IM 1146; EFR J1, 50753) commission.

708] Joannes Rigaldi, auditor sacri palatii.

5 Nov 1348 (VQ 5, 414) Raymundus Lachaminada, sigillifer auditoris Camerae, pays 43 fl.
14 Feb 1351 (ibid., 444) Guillelmus de Bordis, notary, pays 20 fl. for a *Decretales*.

709] Joannes de Riparia, cleric of Pamiers, rector of the March of Ancona.

14 Feb 1350 (EFR C2, 2138) commission to Berengarius, elect of Lucca.
20 Feb 1350 (ibid., 2140-2141) commission to Andreas de Tuderto, and orders to obey the specific instructions of camerarius Stephanus Cambaruti about the debts owed by the late rector.

710] Joannes de Rocca Guillelmi, bishop of Chieti. Formerly canon of Naples, papal chaplain. The surname Crispani appears in EFR B3.

4 Jan - Aug 1335 (IM 1322, 1326, 5012, 5353, 7183) documents in the spoils process before deputies of Geraldus de Valle, nuncio in the kingdom of Naples.
6 Jan 1336 (EFR B3, 736) note that the testament contained a legacy to the Apostolic See.
24 May 1336 (EFR B2, 183; B3, 904) commission to Geraldus de Valle to seize immovables to pay a legacy of 30,000 fl. and 300 m. silver.
25 May - 14 Jun 1336 (EFR B3, 4012).
14 Jul 1336 (ibid., 4015).
20 Sep 1336 (EFR B2, 220; B3, 1083) urges Geraldus de Valle to intensify the process against holders of the goods; commends him to King Robert of Naples.

711] Joannes Ronsel, priest of Lincoln, died in curia.

10 Jan 1360 (VQ 7, 291) Balduinus Ricardi, sigillifer auditoris Camerae, pays 24 fl.

712] Joannes Rousselli OP, bishop of Maillezais, whose spoils were reserved when he was translated to Osimo 27 May 1382. Bishop since 4 Jun 1380.

4 Jul 1382 (Coll. 359, 128^v-129^v) goods reserved to the value of 538 fl. for unpaid services; commission to Petrus Domandi, collector of Poitiers.

713] Joannes Saie, bishop of Albi, died 11 Oct 1383. LL.Bacc., former canon of Bordeaux; bishop of Lombez from 1362; of Dax from 1363; of Agen from 1375; of Albi from 1382.

1364 (RA 157, 47^r) licentia testandi, rubric.
14 Nov 1383 - (Coll. 84, 156^r-181^r) accounts.
2 Jan 1384 (IM 3165; Coll. 360, 70^{rv}) camerarius orders collector Raymundus de Senencio to give the goods to the bearers of this letter, Guido Bonafes and Isarnus Cauderiae, sergeants at arms.
4 Jan 1384 (Coll. 360, 71^{rv}) collector is ordered to find and prosecute the holders of the goods.

10 Jan 1384 (Coll. 359, 198ᵛ-199ʳ) collector is quit of certain goods which he gave to Isarnus Cauderiae.
30 Jan 1384 (IM 3152) collector assigns jewelry to the sergeant.
1 Apr 1385 (Coll. 360, 232ᵛ-234ʳ) quittance to Guido Bonafes.
1386 (Coll. 84, 156ʳ-181ʳ) collector's accounts.
16 Sep 1387 (Coll. 362, 82ʳᵛ) camerarius orders sergeant to pay Radolphus de Letrangiis, domicellus, 20 m. silver.
16 Sep 1387 (ibid., 82ᵛ-83ʳ) he directs Radolphus to retain his pledges, since the Camera cannot pay his loan of 500 fr.

714] Joannes de Salagny, bishop of Mâcon, died 1359. Bishop from 1330.

1360 (Coll. 66, 17ᵛ-18ʳ) accounts of Joannes Rosseti and Aubricus Radolphi.
2 Sep 1360 (IM 2196) commission to Geraldus de Arbento and Joannes Rosseti.
2 Sep 1362 (IM 2261) successor Philippus receives goods of the church from Joannes Rosseti.
31 Jul 1366 (Coll. 353, 73ᵛ-74ʳ) note that Joannes Rosseti paid goods to the treasure, 20 Feb 1365.

715] Joannes Salamonis OP, archbishop of Nazareth, died before 4 Feb 1381. Archbishop from 1369.

4 Sep 1381 (Coll. 359, 79ʳ) clerics and the subcollector of Nantes are ordered to recover the goods.

716] Joannes Sancii de Majorali, archdeacon of Darocha, diocese of Zaragoza.

n.d. (Coll. 116, 95ᵛ) Lupus, archbishop of Zaragoza, collects £265 Barc.
ca. 1369 (Coll. 119, 125ʳ) collector Fulco Pererii is accused of misusing the spoils.

717] Joannes de S. Cirico, prior of S. Firmin, diocese of Maguelonne.

27 May 1362 (OS 31, 148ʳ) camerarius orders collector Joannes de Lacmolio to release goods to the successor Pontius.
5 Aug 1365 (OS 23A, 122ʳ) subcollector pays collector Joannes Garrigie 115 m., 400 fl.

718] Joannes de S. Justo, bishop of Chalon-sur-Saône, died before 18 Jun 1369. Formerly canon of Chartres, papal chaplain; bishop from 1361.

28 Jun 1369 (Coll. 354, 74ᵛ-75ʳ) note of a bull of commission.
14 Mar 1371 (RA 182, 205ʳ-208ʳ) Aubricus Radolphi is ordered to receive 600 fl. composition from Stephanus, abbot of Savigny, diocese of

Lyon; and a debt of 500 fr., 130 fl. owed to the late cardinal Hugo Rogerii.

719] Joannes de S. Quentino, scriptor Papae.

27 May 1351 (VQ 5, 447) Balduinus Ricardi, sigillifer auditoris Camerae, pays 16 fl.

720] Joannes Scarlatto, archbishop of Pisa, died Feb 1362. Former archdeacon in the church of Astorga, papal chaplain; elect to Korone 30 Aug 1346; archbishop of Pisa from 1349.

1 Mar 1363 (IM 2279, 6; Coll. 497, 82^r; IE 303, 10^r) executor pays a composition of 400 fl.

721] Joannes Schadland OP, bishop of Augsburg and administrator of Constance, resigned 1373; died at Koblenz before 1 Apr 1373.

12 Apr 1373 (EFR G2, 1682) commission to Elias de Vodronio.
12 Apr 1373 (ibid., 1683) faculty to the bishops of Worms and Speier and the collector to seize goods.

722] Joannes Serrani, bishop of Sigüenza. Former prior of Guadalupe, diocese of Toledo; bishop of Segovia from 1388; of Sigüenza from 1389.

6 Jul 1402 (IM 4626, 13-16) spoils inquest.
n.d. (IM 4626, 26) list of letters and documents in the case.
14 Nov 1402 (IM 4624) quittance for goods given to officials of the church.

723] Joannes Sicci Herriotti de Teramo, bishop of Sarno, died before 24 Nov 1372. Formerly canon of Teramo.

4 Dec 1372 (Coll. 358, 117^r) successor is conceded the *moderatio* of Urban V.

724] Joannes Sierra, bishop of Segovia, died 16 Feb 1374. Former dean of Salamanca, D.Decr., bishop of Orense from 1367; of Segovia from 1370.

13 Mar 1374 (EFR G2, 2531) commission to Arnaldus de Bernolio and Jacobus de Sirano.

725] Joannes Stephani, bishop of Toulon. Formerly archdeacon of Figeac, diocese of Cahors, notary apostolic, papal familiar. Bishop from 1368; but Toulon was administered from 1385 by Jacobus Faysenqui OFM, M.Theol.

9 Mar 1394 (Coll. 366, 149^v-151^r) quittance to Petrus Merle, collector of Provence.

30 Sep 1397 (IE 374, 38ʳ) Joannes Lavernha, treasurer, pays 16 fl. to the Camera for a missal.

726] Joannes Strote OP, bishop of Skoplje, suffragan bishop of Cologne.

5 Mar 1351 (EFR C2, 2402) commission.

727] Joannes Supponi, preceptor of S. Antonii, diocese of Chalon-sur-Saône.

20 Jul 1325 (EFR J2, 2547) commission.

728] Joannes de Texandria OFM, bishop of Rieux. Formerly bishop of Lodève from 1322; of Rieux from 1324. See AFH 47 (1954): 224.

4 Mar 1345 (EFR C1, 1520) premature commission to Morerius de Moreriis.
5 Nov 1347 (ibid., 3576) another, to the same commissioner.
14 Aug 1348 (RA 101, 37ʳ-40ᵛ, 41ʳ-46ᵛ) inventory by the chapter.
21 Aug 1348 (EFR C1, 3936) commission to Petrus de Sparzellos, nuncio.
1-4 Oct 1348 (RA 101, 57ʳ-70ᵛ) inventory.
n.d. (Coll. 30, 281ʳ) accounts of commissioner Raymundus Rogerii.
ca. 1350 (Coll. 233, 1ʳ-37ᵛ) accounts of Martinus de Girardo, collector of Auch and Toulouse.
31 Jan 1353 (VQ 7, 2) commissioner Petrus Hugonis pays 10 coron.
after 1353 (Coll. 31, 190ᵛ-191ʳ) accounts of Martinus de Girardo.
1360 x 1363 (Coll. 235, 54ʳ-57ʳ) arrears of debts collected by Bertrandus de Castanherio.
1371? (Coll. 18, 187ʳ-190ᵛ) accounts of debts collected by Bertrandus de Castanherio and Aymericus Pelicerii: £408.5.1.
18 Jun 1375 (OS 42, 23ᵛ-24ʳ) Bernardus Martini pays 440 fr. for Bartholomeus Reginaldi, a composition for money which he held in deposit.

729] Joannes de Tournefort, bishop of Nice, died before 17 Oct 1403. Formerly abbot of S. Honoré, diocese of Grasse; bishop from 1382; but Jacobus Isnardi was appointed vicar, 17 Sep 1396.

1403 - 1406 (Coll. 23, 195ʳ-197ʳ) inventory of provisions remaining after seizures by the governor of Nice.

730] Joannes de Treal, abbot of Redon OSB, diocese of Vannes, died 5 Mar 1371.

4 Apr 1371 (EFR G1, 136) commission to Guido de Ruppe.
1371 x 1372 (Coll. 257, 443ᵛ) collector Guido de Ruppe received the successor's obligation to a composition of 700 fr.

731] Joannes Turrini, canon of Bourges.

11 May 1352 (EFR C1, 5300) commission.
1 Feb 1354 (EFR I1, 746) orders the chancellor of Bourges and Guillelmus de Roffilhaco, canon of Limoges, to arrest and send to the curia Henricus Turrini as a holder of reserved goods.
30 Apr 1354 (Coll. 497, 51^v) Henricus de Vusione, canon of S. Pierre, Bourges, obligated to a composition of 1000 fl.
9 May 1355 (VQ 7, 94) nephew pays 200 fl.
12 Jan 1364 (IM 2339, 1; IE 303, 16^v) nephew Henricus de Vusione pays 100 fl.
12 May 1365, 18 Aug 1366 (Coll. 79, 111^r, 236^v) he pays 184 fl.

732] Joannes de Ursinis, archbishop of Naples, died before 3 May 1358. Formerly archdeacon in the church of Coutances, papal chaplain; archbishop of Naples from 1327 (at age 25).

23 Jun 1358 (Coll. 352, 119^v) dispatch by Raymundus de Albofolio of a commission to Petrus, archbishop of Benevento and Reginaldus de Lupchaco, dated 3 May 1358 and accompanied by the bull *Quamquam fabricam militantis*, limiting the collection of spoils.
4 Mar 1361 (Coll. 169, 126^r) collections to the sum of 12 car.
8 Apr 1361 (VQ 7, 336) 769 fl. paid by letter from Raymundus, archbishop of Vapua, commissioner.
24 Jun 1362 (Coll. 169, 126^r) 1 unc. 10 car. collected.

733] Joannes de Ursinis, bishop of Padua, died in curia before 12 Jun 1359. Formerly sacristan of Urgel; bishop from 1353.

1359 (RA 140, 17^r) licentia testandi, rubric.
6 Mar 1360 (VQ 7, 293) his brother, cardinal Reginaldus de Ursinis, pays 300 fl.

734] Joannes de Utica, bishop of Nîmes, died before 20 Jun 1380. LL.D., papal subdeacon and familiar; former provost of Cavaillon; bishop from 1372.

1380? (IM 4746) camerarius demands accounts.

735] Joannes Vaceti, abbot of B. M. d'Arles OSB, diocese of Elne, died 25 Mar 1394.

before 1405 (Coll. 160, 122^{rv}) Joannes de Ripis Altis notes receipt of a composition from the monks, £16.1 — the abbot of less than half a year was "pauperissimus"; the clerk of the Camera notes in the margin, "Doce de potestate componendi sine auctoritate domini Camerarii."

30 Jun 1406 (IM 4613, 74 fols.) inquest by Petrus, bishop of Maguelonne, governor of Avignon and the Comtat-Venaissin.

736] Joannes Vaquerii, bishop of Glandèves, died Mar 1402. J.U.D., former officialis of Auch for archbishop Arnaldus Alberti, 1368; canon of Agen; bishop from 1375.

1403 - 1406 (Coll. 23, 167^r-188^r) accounts of Simon de Pratis; the goods were placed *sub manu regis* by Charles, prince of Tarentaise.

737] Joannes de Vernhio, registrator litterarum apostolicarum.

28 Feb 1383 (Coll. 360, 36^r) camerarius directs Petrus de Siris, subcollector of Couserans, to give the executors the books deposited with the chapter, in consideration of a composition.

738] Joannes de Vernhola, provost of Barjols, diocese of Fréjus, died in curia.

6 Jul 1344 (VQ 5, 350) receipt of 300 fl. from nephews.
7 Jul 1344 (EFR C1, 950) commission.

739] Joannes de Vienne, archbishop of Reims, died 14 Jun 1351. Formerly dean of Le Mans; bishop of Avranches from 1328; of Thérouanne from 1330; archbishop of Reims from 1334.

21 Oct 1348 (VQ 5, 413) Petrus Hugonis and Bartholomeus de Visper pay the spoils.
12 Jul 1351 (EFR C1, 5006) note of debt to the Camera.
24 Jul 1351 (ibid., 5010) orders Joannes de Castronovo to recover from the executors and heirs £14,500 Tur. parv., arrears of *visitationes ad limina* for 9 years.

740] Joannes de Vischhusen, bishop of Dorpat, died before 5 Sep 1373. Formerly canon of Dorpat; bishop from 1346.

16 Dec 1374 (Coll. 354, 18^r) successor Henricus is granted a delay in paying his composition.
25 Jul 1375 (OS 42, 25^{rv}) he pays 470 fl.
2 Feb 1376 (ibid., 50^v) he pays the last 827 fl. of a composition of 1500 fl.

741] Joannes de Watrelos OCist, bishop of Viseu, died before 8 Jul 1349. Bishop from 1333.

24 Nov 1360 (IM 2199) collector Guillelmus Piloti pays £458.15.

742] Joannes Windloch, bishop of Constance, died 21 Jan 1356. Bishop from 1353.

7 Jul 1357 (Coll. 497, 62^r) successor Henricus obligated to a composition of 10,000 fl.
18 Dec 1357 (VQ 7, 185) he pays 5000 fl.

743] Jordanus, bishop of Squillace, died before 12 Dec 1345.

26 Sep - 14 Oct 1346 (Coll. 168, 58^v-59^r) Guillelmus de Roseriis collects 100 unc.

744] Lambertinus Balduini, bishop of Brescia, died 3 Sep 1349. Formerly cantor of Nicosia, papal chaplain; bishop of Limassol from 1337; of Brescia from 1344.

26 Feb 1341 (EFR B1, 8766) licentia testandi.
15 Sep 1349 (EFR C2, 2064) commission to Raymundus, abbot of S. Nicola di Lido, Venice.
30 Nov 1351 (Coll. 130, 87^v) subcollector of Brescia pays 125 fl. 46 s. to Raymundus de Treve, abbot of S. Nicola di Lido.

745] Lambertus de Born, bishop of Speyer, collector of Germany, whose goods were reserved when he was translated to Strassburg, 28 Apr 1371. Earlier abbot of Gengenbach; elect of Brescia; bishop of Speyer from 1364. Later bishop of Bamberg 1374-1399.

24 Apr 1372 (RV 275, 38^v: Tihon, *Lettres de Grégoire XI* 2, n. 1565) Elias de Vodronio and Sigerus de Novolapide are ordered to collect the spoils.

746] Lancelinus Viliarii, collector of Embrun.

27 Mar 1364 (IE 303, 18^r) 40 fl. restored by the heiress of Antonius Bochardi for a house purchased by the collector on 7 Apr 1359.

747] Landulphus, bishop of Valva-Sulmona, died before 17 Jan 1350. Formerly provost of Valva; bishop from 1348.

3 Jul 1354 (Coll. 169, 52^r) successor Franciscus pays 40 fl.

748] Lapus, abbot of S. Miniato, Florence.

5 Sep 1366 (Coll. 248, 30^r) the collector Lucius, bishop of Cesena, sells a *Rosarium* to Mattheus de Castello, vicar of Florence, for 20 fl.

749] Laurentius, archbishop of Conza, died before 17 Jun 1351. Formerly bishop of S. Angelo dei Lombardi; archbishop of Conza from 1346.

31 Dec 1353 (Coll. 169, 51^v) successor Philippus pays spoils.
13 Aug 1354 (ibid., 52^v) he pays 13 unc. 15 car.

750] Laurentius, abbot of S. Biagio di Mirabella, diocese of Frigento.

9 Apr 1345 (Coll. 168, 51ʳ) successor Henricus pays Guillelmus de Roseriis 1 unc.

751] Laurentius de Albiaris, bishop of Tulle, died before 8 Aug 1369. Formerly archpriest in the diocese of Cahors; bishop of Vaison from 1355; of Tulle from 1361.

11 Jan 1373 (Coll. 358, 133ᵛ-134ᵛ) camerarius orders collector to surrender the spoils to Petrus Fabri.
6 Apr 1375 (Coll. 356, 10ᵛ) he orders the return of a crozier and mitre to the church.

752] Laurentius de Berra, abbot of S. Pons OSB, Nice, died Oct 1372. See *Gall. Christ.* 3:1299B.

2 Jul 1373 (Coll. 480, 2ʳ) his brother Honoratus de Berra LL.D., knight, pays a composition of 450 fl. through the collector Geraldus Mercaderii.

753] Laurentius Pictoris, bishop of Nice, died 12 Apr 1371. Former provost of Nice; bishop from 1360.

28 May 1371 (Coll. 492, 3ʳᵛ) successor Roccasalva compounded for 1000 fl., from which the subcollector paid the funeral expenses and debts, leaving 590 fl.
Aug 1372 (IM 2676, 66) collector Geraldus Mercaderii paid Camera 260 fl.
1372-1375 (Coll. 480, 1ʳᵛ) the collector pays 596 fl.

754] Laurentius Roderici, bishop of Lisbon, died 19 Jun 1364. Formerly cantor of Coimbra; bishop of Idanha from 1347; of Coimbra from 1356; of Lisbon from 1358.

1364 - (Coll. 275, 113ʳ-161ᵛ) accounts of Velascus Dominici, commissioner.
17 Apr 1368 (IE 325, 20ᵛ-21ʳ) he pays 121 fl. Cam. 8 s. 6 d.
See Glénisson in *Mélanges* 59 (1947): 98-99: the collector entered pleas before the king to release confiscated goods, and got a papal bull dated 25 Jun 1369, threatening excommunication and interdict. When the king yielded, his treasure proved empty.
11 Jan 1370 - (Arm. 33, to. 18, 21ʳ-23ʳ) the remains collected by Bertrandus de Macello, including a pension on a royal property to pay a debt of £3200 Port.
n.d. (ibid., 176ʳ-180ʳ) remains of spoils at Idanha.

755] Laurentius Roderici, subcollector of Silves.

26 May 1380 (Coll. 359, 39ᵛ) Petrus, bishop of Silves, collector of Portugal, is ordered to hold the goods pending the subcollector's accounts.

756] Leodegarius, bishop of Famagusta, died before 17 Dec 1365. Formerly dean of Nicosia; bishop from 1348.

30 Jan 1366 (Coll. 353, 58^{rv}) successor Arnaldus makes a composition.

19 Mar 1371 (RA 182, 223^v-225^r) the camerarius orders collectors to release the goods in consideration of a 2000-fl. composition by the successor, and to compel the holders of the spoils to surrender them to him.

19 Nov, 5 Dec 1372 (IM 4604, 19 fols.) inquest before Aymericus de Valle, canon of Nicosia and vicar of Raymundus, bishop of Nicosia, collector.

Dec 1372 (IM 2676, 79) successor pays 600 fl. of his composition.

24 Apr 1376 (IM 2924, 3; OS 42, 70^r) he pays 100 fl.

6 Aug 1376 (OS 42, 70^r) he is granted a delay to 6 Jan to pay the remainder.

757] Leonardus, bishop of Monteverde.

8 Nov 1348 (Coll. 168, 76^r) Laurentius, archbishop of Conza, pays 13 unc. for these and other spoils.

758] Leonardus Ammavengo, bishop of Aquino, died before 30 Jul 1340. Formerly canon of Aquino; bishop from 1313.

16 Oct 1340 (EFR B1, 8332) commission.

25 Oct 1340 (ibid., 8334) inventory.

26 Oct 1340 (IM 1532) inventory by Guillelmus de S. Paulo.

2 Nov 1340 (IM 1535-1537) he describes an attack by the people of Aquino against himself.

28 Feb 1341 (EFR B3, 3030) orders Guigo de S. Germano, elect of Montecassino and others to pursue the holders of the spoils.

30 Apr 1341 (IM 7195) inventory in the accounts of Raymundus de Cameraco and Pontius de Pereto.

12 Nov 1341 (VQ 4, 184-185) they pay through the Buonacursi 491 fl., 344 ducats; through the Acciaiuoli 454 fl., 467 ducats.

26 Mar 1342 (ibid., 192) further payments.

27 Nov 1343 (VQ 5, 340) further payments.

759] Lichotus de Narnia, auditor sacri palatii.

2 Sep 1349 (VQ 5, 429) executor pays 20 fl. composition.

760] Ligus de Urbeveteri, bishop of Nola, died between 13 Jun and 25 Aug 1348. Formerly canon of Reims, papal chaplain; bishop from 1340.

24 Aug 1346 (IM 7193, 1^r) licentia testandi.

22 May 1353 (EFR I1, 303) orders Petrus, archbishop of Benevento, to restore to the church its own goods, and to sell the rest for the Camera.

n.d. (IM 7193) the general reservation in the kingdom of Naples was overcome by the executor, cardinal Bertrandus de Deux.

761] Lombardinus de Turre, bishop of Vercelli, died 9 Apr 1343. Formerly papal chaplain; bishop from 1328.

7 Jan 1339 (EFR B1, 5831) licentia testandi.
18 Jun 1343 (EFR C2, 193) commission.
1 Oct 1343 (VQ 5, 339) his brother Ludovicus de Turre pays 746 fl., 1024 fl. Pied., 220 ducats, 10 Gen.
19 Nov 1343 (Coll. 497, 23^r) Ludovicus de Turre, bishop of Elne, undertakes to render full accounts.
11 Feb 1344 (EFR C2, 387) successor Manuel de Flisco is accused of holding goods without right.
15 Jul 1350 (VQ 5, 437) the brother pays 313 fl.

762] Lombardus, procurator in the Roman curia, died in curia.

24 Oct 1357 (VQ 7, 183) payment of 15 fl. composition.

763] Lucanus, bishop of Massa Maritima.

22 Apr 1349 (EFR C2, 1984) commission to Andreas de Tuderto.

764] Lucas Manuelli OP, bishop of Fano, died before 8 Nov 1362. Formerly bishop of Zeitun in Greece from 1344; of Osimo from 1347; of Fano from 1358.

16 Jan 1365 (Coll. 353, 27^v-28^r) commission to the treasurer and collector of the March of Ancona to collect the spoils, up to the sum of 375 fl. due for services.

765] Ludovicus, bishop of Valence-Die, died 3 Sep 1377. Former archdeacon of Lyon; bishop of Valence-Die from 1354, in administration of Vienne from 1363.

19 Nov 1377 (OS 42, 114^v-115^r) collector Guillelmus de Lacu pays from the spoils the balance owed for the tenth in Vienne.
1380? (IM 4746) camerarius demands accounts.

766] Ludovicus de Bolena, abbot of Montmajour OSB, diocese of Arles, died before 13 Oct 1363. See *Gall. Christ.* 1:613.

before 1370 (Coll. 19, 165^r) accounts of Geraldus Mercaderii.

767] Ludovicus de Hessen, bishop of Münster, died 18 Aug 1357. Formerly canon of Mainz; bishop from 1310 (aged 28).

21 Sep 2357 (Coll. 352, 29^r) commission, dated 13 Sep 1357, is given to

Hermannus Isslechore, dean of S. Moritz, Münster, collector of Münster, Osnabrück, and Minden.

768] Ludovicus de Monteviligardo, archbishop of Besançon, died 25 Jul 1362. Formerly dean of Besançon; archbishop from 1361.

n.d. (Coll. 66, 79^v) report of Aubricus Radolphi: debts consumed some of the spoils, and the archbishop's father, the count of Montfaucon, has the rest.

769] Lupus, bishop of Burgos, died 12 Oct 1351. Formerly bishop of Calahorra from 1348; of Burgos from 8 Jun 1351.

6 Jun 1351 (EFR C1, 2443) premature commission.
5 Nov 1351 (ibid., 2521) commission.
20 Dec 1352 (Coll. 497, 49^v) successor Lupus is obligated to a composition of 3200 fl.
10 Jan 1353 (EFR I1, 40) commission to Joannes Bonifatii.
5 Sep 1353 (Coll. 497, 75^v) Garcias Petri, canon of Burgos, assumed an obligation to a composition of 3200 fl.
5 Sep 1353 (IM 1947; EFR I1, 543) the canons of Burgos are commissioned to collect the remaining spoils.
8 Jan 1354 (EFR I1, 708) Petrus king of Castile and Leon is ordered to release the reserved goods; IM 6277 is a preliminary draft of the letter.
31 Mar 1354 (VQ 7, 49) the procurators of Garcias Petri and the canons of Burgos pay 1000 fl. of the composition.
9 Jun 1355 (ibid., 94) they pay 600 fl.
30 Oct 1355 (ibid., 99) they pay 100 fl.
23 Jan 1356 (ibid., 170) they pay 100 fl.

770] Luzonus de Lemps, provost of S. Lorenzo Uleten., diocese of Turin.

16 Jan 1364 (OS 31, 128^{rv}) the successor Joannes Bigoti makes a composition for 2000 fl.
30 Apr 1364 (IE 303, 19^r) he pays 500 fl.
5 Mar 1364 (IE 303, 17^v) he pays 1500 fl.
24 Jul 1366 (OS 23A, 92^v) note of payment of the composition in full.

771] Magdalusius, abbot of the hospital "de Plan.," diocese of Treviso.

1361 (Coll. 130, 151^r) successor Franciscus de Padua pays a composition of 300 ducats.

772] Magnus Joannis, bishop of Ribe, died before 7 Nov 1369. Formerly bishop of Aalborg from 1354; of Ribe from 1365.

7 May 1371 (EFR G2, 144) commission to Henricus, bishop of Schleswig.

773] Manuel de Flisco, bishop of Vercelli, died before 22 Sep 1348. Formerly canon of York, papal chaplain; bishop from 1343.

16 May 1336 (EFR B1, 3381) licentia testandi.
23 Sep 1348 (VQ 5, 411) a small sum paid by Hubertus, abbot of Monteverde, diocese of Volterra.
28 Sep 1348 (EFR C2, 1719-1720) commission and instructions to Lazarinus de Flisco.
28 Feb 1349 (VQ 5, 419) Lazarinus, elect of Albi, pays 20 fl. for goods at Avignon.
15 Oct 1349 (EFR C2, 2085) commission to Fr. Lazarinus, bishop of Albi, and Pampinianus de Flisco.
19 Oct 1349 (VQ 5, 430) executors pay 550 fl. of a 1050-fl. composition.
21 Jun 1351 (EFR C2, 2570) Lazarinus and Papinianus de Flisco, executors, pay 300 fl. of the composition.
24 Dec 1352 (ibid., 460) they pay 200 fl.

774] Marcholinus, bishop of Fossombrone, died before 11 Dec 1363.

1374 x 1376 (Coll. 129, 182^v) Raymundus, bishop of Padua, collector, receives 141 ducats 25 s. for the sale of horses, and 230 ducats composition from nephew Benedictus, OServ.

775] Marinus, archbishop of Manfredonia, died before 8 Nov 1361. Formerly archdeacon of Manfredonia; archbishop from 1354.

mid-1362 (Coll. 169, 136^v) accounts.

776] Marinus de Judice, bishop of Teano, whose spoils were reserved in anticipation of his translation to Amalfi, 16 Apr 1361.

28 Dec 1357 (Coll. 352, 118^v) dispatch, by hand of Reginaldus de Lupchaco, cantor of Auxerre, of a commission dated 14 Dec 1357 to himself and Petrus archbishop of Benevento.

777] Martinus, bishop of Orense. Former bishop of Plasencia; of Orense from 1375.

25 May 1380 (Coll. 359, 37^r) Paschasius Garsiae, collector of Castile, is ordered to pay the servants' wages, and to observe the *moderatio*.

778] Martinus Alfonsi, bishop of Evora from 1341.

1 Jun 1340 (EFR B1, 7931) licentia testandi.
12 Oct 1347 (EFR C2, 1516-1517) commission.

779] Martinus Cande, bishop of Segovia. Formerly dean of Toledo; bishop from 1364.

before 3 Oct 1370 (Coll. 215, 2^{rv}) inventory by the chapter of Segovia, turned over to canon Paulus Petri for safekeeping.

16 Jan 1372 (Coll. 358, 25^r) note of a direction sent to the collector of Castile, that he should sell the books.

Jul 1372 (IM 2676, 51) successor Joannes pays 916 fl. for spoils.

780] Martinus de Castris, scriptor litterarum apostolicarum.

19 Jul 1375 (OS 42, 39^v) executors pay 100 fl. composition.

781] Martinus de Girardo, collector of Toulouse and Auch.

24 Sep 1362 (OS 31, 160^{rv}) maintenance granted to nephew Bertrandus Guinerii pending settlement of the spoils.

28 Sep 1362 (OS 31, 160^v-161^r) commission to Bertrandus de Castanherio to realize 1124 fl. due to the Camera.

1 Oct 1373 (Coll. 236, 253^v) Aymericus Pelicerii, collector of Toulouse, reports 813 fl. still due from heirs to balance accounts.

782] Martinus Logicus, bishop of Idanha, died before 10 Oct 1322. Bishop from 1319.

1323 (VQ 1, 486) receipts.

783] Martinus de Tuderto, died in curia.

21 Jul 1338 (VQ 4, 132) executor pays 52 fl.

784] Mattheus OFM, bishop of Civitate, died before 21 Oct 1360. Formerly bishop of Urgentsch; of Civitate from 1348.

28 Feb 1362 (Coll. 169, 133^v) accounts.

785] Mattheus, abbot of SS. Narbone and Felice, Bologna, died 17 Apr 1370.

1374 (Coll. 129, 227^v) collector Raymundus, bishop of Padua, collects small sums.

786] Mattheus, abbot of S. Paolo, Bologna.

1373 (Coll. 129, 228^v) goods sold for 354 ducats 9 s. 4 d.

787] Mattheus, abbot of Ripoll, diocese of Vich.

11 Nov 1366 - 23 Jun 1367 (Coll. 248, 30^v) 100 fl. collected from members of the order of Altopasso as spoils.

788] Mattheus de Alagno, bishop of Castellamare. Formerly canon of Amalfi; bishop from 1331.

20 Feb 1362 (Coll. 169, 132ᵛ-133ʳ) accounts.

789] Mattheus de Porta de Cumis OFM, archbishop of Palermo, died 28 Jan 1377. M.Theol.; archbishop from 1366. See AFH 47 (1954): 224; 49 (1956): 40.

28 Jan 1377 (RA 203, 1ʳ-18ᵛ) inventory by Mattheus de Floreto.
n.d. (Indice 254, 97ʳ-101ᵛ) accounts of collector Benedictus de Consule, and strictures by the Camera.

790] Mattheus Ribaldi, bishop of Verona, died in curia 1 May 1348. Formerly canon of Constance; bishop of Pavia from 1342; of Verona from 1343.

30 Aug 1350 (VQ 5, 438) Geraldus Raconisini is obligated to a composition for 500 fl., pays 150 fl.
n.d. (OS 23A, 101ʳ) note, temp. Urban V, that the balance was still unpaid.

791] Mattheus de Urbeveteri, receptor bonorum of the monastery of S. Joannes in Lamis OCist, diocese of Manfredonia.

1324 x 1332 (Coll. 221, 152ʳ) Geraldus de Valle receives 166 unc. 17 tari 7 grani silver; 23 unc. 12 carats gold.

792] Mauritius de Darpel, advocatus in curia, died in curia.

16 Jan 1358 (VQ 7, 215) composition of 12 fl. paid.

793] Mauritius Fabri, rector "de Goronio," diocese of Le Mans.

16 Jan 1358 (VQ 7, 215) his brother Stephanus pays 20 fl.

794] Maurus, abbot of S. Renato, diocese of Sorrento.

27 Apr 1346 (Coll. 168, 56ʳ) Guillelmus de Roseriis collects and sells goods for 21 car.

795] Melior Bevilaqua, archbishop of Palermo, died before 15 Jan 1365. Formerly canon of Verona; archbishop from 1363.

ca. 1375 (Coll. 222, 202ʳ, 234ᵛ) collector Dominicus de Saxonorio compounds with Joannes de Claromonte for 500 fl.

796] Michael de Brachia, bishop of Le Mans, died before 25 Oct 1367. Formerly archdeacon in the church of Chartres, M.Theol.; bishop of Le Mans from 1355.

before Feb 1369 (IM 2557, 1ʳ) collector Guido de Ruppe estimates the net spoils at 600 fr.
1369 x 1372 (Coll. 257, 439ᵛ-442ᵛ) net spoils reported at 11 s. 5 1/2 d.

797] Michael Ricomanni, bishop of Barcelona, died 7 Jun 1361. Formerly canon of Valencia and clerk of the Camera; bishop of Vich from 1345; of Barcelona from 1346.

9 Jul 1337 (EFR B1, 4695) licentia testandi.
18 Jun 1362 (Coll. 497, 78ᵛ; VQ 7, 409) Bertrandus bishop of Comminges and Joannes de Cabrespino are obligated to a composition of 400 fl.; Fulco Pererii pays his 400-fl. composition.
n.d. (Coll. 116, 43ʳ) total collections, £84.11.6.
n.d. (Coll. 119, 123ᵛ) Petrus Francisci, subcollector of Tarragona, says Fulco Pererii received £100 which he did not report.

798] Michael Sancii de Asiain, bishop of Pamplona, died Jan 1364. Bishop from 1356.

28 Mar 1364 (EFR U2, 866) Fulco Pererii is ordered to proceed against the holders of the spoils.
24 Nov 1364 (IM 2339, 24; IE 303, 24ᵛ) Jordanus de Haya, commissioner, pays 100 fl.
6 Nov 1372 (Coll. 358, 124ʳ) commissioner Bertrandus Raffini accounts for £380.19.6 of the goods included in the inventory of Fulco Pererii.
before 1376 (Coll. 118, 144ᵛ) Guillelmus de Broa, subcollector of Pamplona, receives £17 in debts and some books.
n.d. (Coll. 116, 106ᵛ-107ʳ) accounts : £1037.2.6.

799] Monaldus de Monaldeschis OFM, archbishop of Benevento, died before 26 Dec 1331. Formerly bishop of Savona from 1298; archbishop of Benevento from 1303. See AFH 47 (1954): 224; and Mollat in *Revue des sciences religieuses* 19 (1939): 50-57.

1 Feb 1332 (Coll. 413, 14ʳᵛ; IE 140, 29ᵛ-30ʳ) Petrus de Artusio, rector of the Patrimony, and Stephanus Lascoutz is commissioned.
1 May 1332 (Coll. 413, 22ᵛ-25ᵛ; IM 1211; EFR J1, 58225) inquest.
6 May 1332 (IM 1212; EFR J1, 58226).
16 Aug 1332 (IE 140, 60ʳᵛ) a valuable cope is to be restored to the archbishop and chapter of Benevento, as church property.
9 Sep 1332 (EFR J1, 58312-58313) nephew Tramus, bishop of Orvieto, is granted two terms to pay debts.
11 Jan 1336 (EFR B3, 742) orders Rogerius de Vintono, rector of Campania and Maritima, to compel holders to surrender goods.
27 Aug 1337 (ibid., 1462) permits the rector to compound for spoils.
30 Mar 1339 (ibid., 2397) orders Hugo Cornuti, treasurer of the Patrimony, to collect.

6 Mar 1344 (EFR C2, 432) orders Bernardus, elect of Viterbo and rector of the Patrimony, to absolve Monaldus Berardi, nephew, excommunicated for holding goods.
7 Jul 1349 (EFR C1, 4209) orders the rector to collect from the nephew 1200 fl. at 100 fl. per year.
1 Dec 1350 (EFR C2, 2355) orders Pontius, bishop of Orvieto, to receive 800 fl. from the goods of Hermannus de Monaldeschis.

800] Morerius de Moreriis, collector of Narbonne, died Aug 1348.

17 Aug 1348 (EFR C1, 3934) commission.

801] Nerses, archbishop of Nicosia. Formerly archbishop of "Manazguardien." in Armenia [Anazarbos?] from 1338; of Nicosia from 1363.

12 Jan 1364 (OS 31, 258^v) a mitre, staff, chalice and books are ordered restored to Dominicus OESA, his successor in Armenia.

802] Nicolaus, bishop of Bovino from 1349.

11 Feb 1354 (Coll. 169, 50^v) subcommissioner Pontius, bishop of Treviso, pays.

803] Nicolaus, bishop of Lacedogna, died before 21 Oct 1330.

15-16 Jun 1331 (IM 7188, 8 fols.) inventory by Petrus Regis for Geraldus de Valle.
1331 x 1332 (Coll. 221, 152^r) Geraldus de Valle collects 14 unc. 14 car.
20 Dec 1344 (Coll. 168, 45^v-46^v) Guillelmus de Roseriis collects 28 unc. 17 car. and vestments.

804] Nicolaus, bishop of Nola, died between 22 Aug and 17 Sep 1340. Bishop of Bisignano from 1319; of Nola from 22 Oct 1331.

17 Sep 1340 (EFR B3, 2901; IM 7192, 3^r) commission to Arnulphus Marcellini.
Oct 1340 - Mar 1341 (IM 7192) inquest of Arnulphus Marcellini.
27 Apr 1344 (VQ 5, 347) he pays 220 fl.

805] Nicolaus OCist, bishop of Penne and Atri, died before 8 Oct 1352. Formerly bishop *nullius*; bishop of Penne-Atri from 1326.

18 Oct 1352 (Coll 169, 46^{rv}) accounts of commissioner Petrus, archbishop of Benevento, and subcommissioner Joannes de Aquila: more than 600 fl. in sales.
8 Jan 1353 (ibid., 48^v) Joannes de Pinu, prior of Articella OSB, diocese *Aquensis*, brother and subcommissioner of Petrus de Pinu, archbishop of Benevento, recovers a chest of 4424 fl.

20 Feb 1353 (ibid., 49ʳ) subcommissioner Joannes, bishop of Ariano, recovers money and seven books.

4 May 1353 (EFR I1, 265) commissioner is ordered to pay 4500 fl. from these spoils to Joannes archbishop of Naples and Angelus Tavernini, treasurer of the Patrimony.

806] Nicolaus, archbishop of Rouen, died 3 Apr 1347. Formerly abbot of Grasse OSB, diocese of Carcassonne; archbishop from 1343.

7 Mar 1345 (EFR C1, 1531) licentia testandi.

13 Jun 1347 (ibid., 3315) permits cardinals Hugo Rogerii and Nicolaus de Bessia to proceed to execute the testament.

1 Dec 1347 (ibid., 2623) orders all debtors to pay to the executors.

807] Nicolaus, abbot "de Brondulo" OCist, diocese of Padua.

May 1360 - Mar 1361 (Coll 130, 151ᵛ) the spoils of the abbot, killed by his own monks, yield 350 ducats.

808] Nicolaus, abbot of S. Andrea, Rimini.

1370 x 1376 (Coll. 129, 234ʳ) priors pay 72 ducats.

809] Nicolaus Aegidii, collector of Elne, died 12 Nov 1393.

n.d. (Coll. 160, 122ʳ) successor Joannes de Ripis Altis receives the composition of the heirs, £165 and goods.

810] Nicolaus Andreae, bishop of Catanzaro, died before 27 Apr 1369. D.Decr., formerly canon of S. Pietro in Vaticano, Rome.

5 May 1369 (Coll. 353, 219ᵛ-220ʳ) camerarius orders the collector of Calabria to observe the *moderatio*.

811] Nicolaus de Aquila, bishop of Cartagena, died before 24 Nov 1371. Lic.Decr., former dean of Cartagena; bishop from 1361.

1 Dec 1372 (EFR G2, 1228) commission to Arnaldus Andreae.

812] Nicolaus de Aquila, advocatus Camerae, D.Decr., died in curia before 7 Oct 1353.

25 Sep 1354 (VQ 7, 57) Tancredus Francisci de Florentia pays a debt of 1292 fl. 6 s. 4 d.

20 Jun 1355 (ibid., 95) Petrus de Perusio pays 50 fl.

813] Nicolaus Canali, archbishop of Patrai. Formerly plebanus of Venice; bishop of Bergamo from 1342; archbishop of Ravenna from 1342; of Patrai from 1347.

25 Oct 1349 (EFR C2, 2092) commission to Raymundus, abbot of S. Nicola di Lido, Venice, nuncio, and Bonincontrus, abbot of S. Felix de Aymonis.

30 Jan 1350 (ibid., 2384) the same, to abbot Raymundus alone.
18 May 1351 (VQ 5, 446) successor Sirellus pays 450 fl.
7 Oct 1351 (EFR C2, 2506) commission to Georgius, bishop of Modon.
20 Nov 1351 (ibid., 2552) commission to nuncio Raymundus to collect the spoils and fruits of the vacancy.
27 Jan 1354 (EFR I1, 740) orders Joannes de Sela, nuncio, to transfer 800 fl. to nuncio Raymundus.

814] Nicolaus Carpentorii, canon of S. Petrus, diocese of Ario in Crete.

14 Oct 1362 (OS 31, 167^r) quittance to Bertrandus de Tiarno, archdeacon of Passey, diocese of Sens, for 4 marks of silverware.

815] Nicolaus de Genestra de Camera, canon of S. Donato, diocese of Genoa.

27 Mar 1349 (EFR C2, 1963) commission to Martinus de Burgaria for these and other spoils.

816] Nicolaus de Graneriis, canon of Geneva, died in curia.

26 Jan 1397 (IE 374, 13^v) executors pay 160 fl. composition.

817] Nicolaus de Gulczewo, bishop of Plock, died before 1368.

12 Nov 1372 (Coll. 358, 155^{rv}) spoils to be collected from successor Stanislaus de Gulczewo.

818] Nicolaus de Luxemburgo, patriarch of Aquileia, died 29 Aug 1358. Formerly archdeacon in the church of Prague, papal chaplain; bishop of Naumburg from 1349; patriarch from 1350.

ca. 1360 (Coll. 130, 150^r, 168^v-170^v) accounts.
5 May 1362 (VQ 7, 400) collector Geraldus, abbot of S. Giorgio, Venice, pays 600 ducats for the sale of a mitre.
ca. 1 Apr 1363 (OS 31, 171^v-172^r) quittance to Geraldus, lacking inventory.

819] Nicolaus Martini OP, bishop of Recanati-Macerata, died before 19 Feb 1369.

Jul 1369 (Coll. 353, 248^v-249^r) commission with *moderatio*.

820] Nicolaus Matthei de Augina, canon of Anagni, scriptor Papae, died in curia.

25 Aug 1354 (RA 128, 599^r) licentia testandi.
8 Feb 1360 (VQ 7, 292) Balduinus Ricardi, sigillifer auditoris Camerae, pays silverware and cash to the sum of 400 fl. 14 s. 9 d.

821] Nicolaus Mauri, scriptor Papae, died in curia.

2 Aug 1352 (VQ 5, 457) Balduinus Ricardi pays 50 fl. composition from executors.

822] Nicolaus de Nantolio, abbot of Fécamp OSB, diocese of Rouen, died in curia.

6 Apr 1358 (VQ 7, 219-220) successor Joannes and Joannes de Campis, notary of the Camera, pay 2586 fl. 3 s. 11 d.
15 Sep 1358 (ibid., 224) Bernardus Bartholomei of Avignon and his wife Agnes pay a loan debt of 170 écus.
30 Apr 1362 (ibid., 399) Nicolaus Grimaldi de Luca pays debts to a sum of 1808 fl. 9 s. 9 d.

823] Nicolaus de Parma, procurator, died in curia.

6 Oct 1357 (VQ 7, 183) executors pay a composition of 358 fl.

824] Nicolaus Policis, plebanus of Brumstberg, diocese of Worms, died in curia.

23 Jun 1345 (VQ 5, 359) Otto, canon of Worms, pays 14 fl. Pied.

825] Nicolaus Rubei, papal chaplain of honor.

1358 x 1371 (Coll. 130, 149^v) collector receives 200 ducats.

826] Nicolaus de Senelayo, archpriest "de Ruppella," diocese of Saintes, subcollector, died between 17 Aug 1392 and 8 Feb 1393.

8 Feb 1393 (IM 3562) copy of testament dated 17 Aug 1392.

827] Nunius, archbishop of Seville, died in curia before 18 Jun 1361. Formerly secular abbot of S. Anderius, Burgos; bishop of Astorgas from 1346; archbishop of Seville from 1349.

20 Mar 1363 (Coll. 497, 82^v) Joannes Fernandi, canon of Burgos, is obligated to restore the goods to the chapter.

828] Octavianus de Labro, archbishop of Palermo, died before 20 Dec 1363. Formerly canon of Girgenti; bishop of Girgenti from 1350; archbishop of Palermo from 1362.

ca. 1375 (Coll. 222, 195^r) successor Mattheus de Porta made a composition for 100 fl.

829] Odo, bishop of Cuenca, died 1338. Formerly bishop of Oviedo from 1323; of Cuenca from 1328.

14 May 1333 (EFR J1, 60346) licentia testandi.
28 Dec 1340 (EFR B3, 2980) commission to Almeracius de Cabrespino.

30 Jan 1341 (ibid., 2992) orders Petrus Girardi to take up the process from Almeracius.

1340-1341 (Coll. 229, 60^r) accounts of Almaracius de Cabrespino.

14 Aug 1341 (VQ 4, 181-182) payments by Almeracius.

25 Aug 1342 (VQ 5, 237-238) successor Gundisalinus pays 865 1/2 fl.

830] Odo, bishop of Lescar, died between 10 and 29 Jul 1402. Formerly sacristan of Aire; bishop from 1363.

10-29 Jul 1402 (Coll. 487, 1^r-12^v) donations inter vivos and post-mortem inventory.

831] Odo, bishop of Paphos, died before 13 Apr 1357. Formerly treasurer of Nicosia, LL.D.; bishop from 1337.

12 May 1357 (Coll. 352, 95^r) dispatch by hand of nuncio Petrus Domandi de Argendonio of a commission to himself and Gaufridus Pasiata, dated 13 Apr 1357.

11 Sep 1357 (IM 4594, 1^r-12^r) inventory and accounts; sales to the sum of £380.1.7, 226 ducats, 115 fl.

27 Mar 1360 (Coll. 497, 71^v) successor Elias is obligated to a composition of 5000 fl.; payment is delayed until 25 Dec.

4 Dec 1361 (VQ 7, 375) he pays 2000 fl.

13 Aug 1362 (ibid., 418) he pays 1000 fl.

2 Oct 1362 (OS 31, 161^v-162^r) successor absolved from excommunication, and the last two terms are prorogued.

2 Oct 1362 (ibid., 162^{rv}) orders Petrus Domandi to collect the composition of the successor Elias.

832] Odo, prior of S. Martin, diocese of Chartres, condemned for heresy.

5 Jul 1322 (VQ 1, 476) Bertrandus Cariti and Raymundus de Parisiis pay 3542 fl., 79 cathedrae.

5 Jan 1324 (ibid.) they pay 500 fl.

25 Sep 1328 (OS 12, 96^v) quittance to commissioner Raymundus.

18 Nov 1329 (ibid., 116^v; VQ 1, 476) Bertrandus Cariti and Guillelmus Dultoni pay 70 fl.

833] Olafus, archbishop of Trondheim, died before 22 Oct 1371. Formerly abbot of S. Maria OSB, Trondheim; archbishop from 1350.

23 May 1372 (EFR G2, 752) commission to Henricus, bishop of Schleswig.

25 May 1372 (ibid., 756) commendation of the collector to king Aquinus (Haakon) of Norway.

29 May 1372 (ibid., 760) the collector is directed to cite the successor Trondo before the Camera if he does not surrender the goods.

834] Oliverius de Sarzeto, auditor sacri palatii, papal chaplain, died in curia.

24 Nov 1356 (VQ 7, 137) executors pay a composition of 260 fl.

835] Opicinus de Canistris, cleric of Pavia, scriptor Poenitentiariae, died in curia before 21 Aug 1355.

21 Aug 1355 (VQ 7, 96; OS 23A, 105^v) Joannes de Papia pays 120 fl. of a composition of 150 fl.

836] Ortolphus de Weisseneck, archbishop of Salzburg, died 12 Aug 1365. Formerly provost of Salzburg; archbishop from 1343.

31 Jan 1372 (IM 2676, 3; IE 336, 4^v, in Kirsch, *Kollektorien* 403) successor Pelegrinus pays 200 fl.

837] Pandulphus, bishop of S. Agata dei Goti, died 1342. Bishop from 1327.

20 Aug 1343 (EFR C2, 256) commission.
16 Apr 1347 (Coll. 168, 60^r) successor Jacobus pays 12 unc. to Guillelmus de Roseriis.

838] Pandulphus de Sabello, provost of S. Maria de Monterodono, diocese of Rieux, papal notary.

13 Jun 1318 (EFR J1, 7486) licentia testandi.
1335 (Coll. 29, 199^v) accounts of Arnaldus de Verdala.

839] Paschalis, bishop of Cuenca, died before 21 Aug 1322. Bishop from 1299.

1299 x 1303 (EFR Registres de Boniface VIII, 3989) licentia testandi.
14 Aug 1324 (VQ 1, 490) commissioner Raymundus Ebrardi pays for the vacancy.
23 Mar 1333 (EFR J1, 59883-59884) arranges the composition.

840] Paulinus de Venetiis OFM, poenitentiarius apostolicus, bishop of Pozzuoli from 1324. See Alberto Ghinato, *Fr. Paolino da Venezia OFM, vescovo di Pozzuoli* (Studi e Testi Francescani 1; Rome, 1951) and D. Franceschi, "Fra Paolino da Venezia OFM, +1344," *Atti della Accademia delle scienze di Torino, classe di scienze morali, storiche e filologiche* 98 (1963-4): 109-152.

22 Jun - 28 Dec 1344 (Coll. 168, 39^v-41^r) accounts of Guillelmus de Roseriis.

841] Paulus, patriarch of Constantinople, administrator of Patrai, died before 10 Feb 1371. Formerly bishop of Smyrna from 1345; archbishop of Thebes from 1357; patriarch from 1366, in administration of Patrai from 1367.

6 Jun 1372 (Coll. 358, 66^{rv}) Raymundus, abbot of S. Nicola di Lido, collector of Lombardy and the Romagna, ordered to audit again the accounts of Joannes de Nomaco, canon of Patrai.

842] Paulus, abbot of S. Savino OSB, Pisa, papal chaplain.

15 Mar 1340 (EFR B3, 2732) commission.
17 Apr 1340 - 29 Mar 1341 (Coll. 244, 36^r-37^v) accounts of the collector Joannes de Pererio.
Apr 1342 (Coll. 244, 97^r-102^r) account of the safeguard of spoils.

843] Paulus de Gabrielibus, bishop of Lucca, died 10 Sep 1380. D.Decr., papal chaplain and familiar; bishop from 1374.

12 Feb 1390 (Diversa cameralia 1, 160^r) books assigned to the Camera at Rome.

844] Pelegrinus, rector of S. Biagio di Funiculo, diocese of Benevento.

1372 (Coll. 129, 227^v) debt of 14 ducats 14 s. collected.

845] Perinus de Bolonia OCarm, poenitentiarius Papae.

26 Mar 1348 (VQ 5, 404) executor pays a composition of 100 fl.

846] Perinus Francisci, canon of S. Thibaut, diocese of Metz, died in curia.

17 May 1354 (VQ 7, 52) Balduinus Ricardi, sigillifer auditoris Camerae, pays 30 fl. 7 s. 4 d.

847] Petrus, bishop of Ascoli Satriano, died before 29 Jan 1354.

11 Feb 1354 (Coll. 169, 50^v) subcommissioner Pontius, bishop of Trevico, pays for spoils.

848] Petrus OCist, archbishop of Cagliari, died before 18 May 1352. Formerly abbot of Benifazano OCist, diocese of Tortosa; archbishop from 1348.

4 Jul 1352 (EFR C2, 2661).
1353 x 1355 (Coll. 168, 111^r-132^v; 141^r-152^v) executors' inventory and commissioners' accounts.

849] Petrus, archbishop of Conza from 1332.

6 Aug - 1 Dec 1346 (Coll. 168, 56^v-58^v) accounts of Guillelmus de Roseriis.

12 Oct 1346 (EFR C2, 1233) commission to Guillelmus de Roseriis, bishop of Montecassino.

850] Petrus, bishop of Dax from 1359.

31 Mar 1359 (VQ 7, 261) Joannes de Gardana, subcollector of Bayeux, pays 50 fl. 12 s.
14 May 1359 (Coll. 497, 68^r) Guillelmus Crimelleris et al. are obligated to a composition of 83 fl., 19 écus.
30 Nov 1359 (VQ 7, 268) successor Petrus pays 333 fl.

851] Petrus, bishop of Elne, died 18 Sep 1346. Bishop from 1342.

19 Sep 1346 (EFR C1, 2810) no accounts rendered for the spoils of his predecessor.
12 Oct 1346 (VQ 5, 525) Almeracius de Cabrespino, collector of Tarragona and Zaragoza, pays £137 Barc.
Nov 1346 (Coll. 497, 30^v) successor Bernardus is obligated to a composition of 1100 fl.
12 Jan 1347 (VQ 5, 380) executors pay 1000 fl. composition.
10 Feb 1347 (ibid., 381) successor pays 550 fl.
5 Jun 1347 (ibid., 389-390) he pays 550 fl.
before Oct 1348 (Coll. 113, 89^r-98^r) debts collected by Almeracius de Cabrespino in the accounts of his nephew Joannes.

852] Petrus, bishop of Lettere from 22 Sep 1327.

before 1332 (Coll. 221, 151^v) Geraldus de Valle received 10 unc. 25 tari 14 grani.

853] Petrus, bishop of Périgueux. Formerly bishop of Viterbo from 1348; of Verona from 1348; of Périgueux from 1349.

4 May 1372 (EFR G1, 766) commission to Arnaldus Garini, canon of Saintes.
4 May 1372 (ibid., 768) letter commending the commissioner to the seneschal of Saintes.

854] Petrus, archbishop of Sorrento, died before 14 Dec 1357. Former bishop of Beirut; archbishop of Sorrento from 1348.

28 Dec 1357 (Coll. 352, 118^r) dispatch by hand of Reginaldus de Lupchaco, cantor of Auxerre, of a commission dated 14 Dec 1357 to himself and Petrus, archbishop of Benevento.
30 Oct 1360 (Coll. 231, 106^r; VQ 7, 301) Reginaldus, archbishop of Capua, pays 342 fl. by a letter of exchange through merchants of Lucca.

855] Petrus, bishop of Teano. Formerly archdeacon of Lunez, diocese of Béziers; bishop from 1338.

29 Jun 1340 (EFR B3, 2818) commission.
23 Mar 1353 (Coll. 497, 49^r) executors are obligated to a composition of 200 fl.

856] Petrus, abbot of S.Lorenzo OSB, diocese of Aversa.

21 Aug 1364 (IE 303, 22^r) Paulus Matthei pays 137 fl. Cam. 24 s. for spoils.

857] Petrus, abbot of S. Sophia, Benevento, died in the diocese of Piacenza.

1375 (Coll. 129, 228^r) goods in Bologna yield 558 ducats 12 s.

858] Petrus, abbot of S. Jacques, diocese of Béziers. See *Gall. Christ.* 6:415.

31 May 1348 (EFR C1, 3894; IM 1764) commission to Bertrandus Raymundi, almoner of Béziers.
20 Jun 1348 (ibid., 3905) orders Eustachius Piscis, canon of Béziers and Aymericus Charierras, canon of Cambrai, to collect goods gathered by the late almoner.

859] Petrus, abbot of S. Satur, diocese of Bourges.

16 May 1382 (IM 1667-1668) commission to Joannes Francisci.
27 May 1382 (IM 3111) instructions to collector.
29-30 May 1382 (IM 3110; IM 3113) camerarius orders the collector to observe the *moderatio*, citing the petition of the monks.
n.d. (IM 3125) accounts.
18 Nov 1383 (Coll. 360, 63^{rv}) successor is granted a delay in paying his composition of 1000 fl.
10 Apr 1384 (ibid., 86^v) another delay.

860] Petrus, abbot of S. Benigne de Dijon OSB, diocese of Langres.

24 Nov 1354 (EFR I1, 1218) commission to Geraldus de Arbento.
28 Dec 1354 (VQ 7, 62) he pays 240 fl., 200 écus.
2 Mar 1355 (Coll. 497, 54^v) successor Petrus is obligated to a composition of 1200 fl.
28 Apr 1356 (VQ 7, 132) successor pays 400 fl.
17 Apr 1357 (ibid., 175) he pays 200 fl.
7 Apr 1358 (ibid., 220) he pays 200 fl.
5 Oct 1359 (ibid., 267) he pays 200 fl.
2 Jan 1360 (ibid., 331; Coll. 231,118^r) he pays 200 fl.

861] Petrus, abbot of Aniane OSB, diocese of Maguelonne.

5 Aug 1365 (OS 23A, 122^r) subcollector pays the collector Joannes Garrigiae 80 m. silver.

862] Petrus, abbot of S. Petrus foras Portas OSB, diocese of Vienne.

12 Jan 1362 (OS 31, 218^v-219^r; Coll. 497, 77^r; VQ 7, 397) the successor Imbertus pays 200 fl. of a composition of 500 fl.; the balance is to be paid to Joannes Rosseti at Vienne.
26 Sep 1362 (OS 31, 192^v-197^r) collector Joannes Rosseti received 300 fl.

863] Petrus, prior of Bigorre, Cérisy-la-Forêt, diocese of Bayeux.

5 Feb 1344 (EFR C1, 650).
6 Sep 1345 (VQ 5, 507) Bertrandus Cariti, collector of Rouen, assigns £1023.10.6 Tur.
30 Sep 1345 (ibid.) he pays 73 écus 20 d. Tur. gr.
26 May 1346 (VQ 5, 370) Petrus, abbot of S. Pierre de Dijon, pays the second half of his composition of 1500 fl.

864] Petrus de Agrifolio, bishop of Avignon, died before 20 Nov 1369. Formerly abbot of Chaise-Dieu OSB, diocese of Clermont; bishop of Tulle 1347; of Vabres from 1347; of Clermont from 1349; of Uzés from 1357; of Mende from 1366; of Avignon from 1368.

1359 (RA 140, 17^r) licentia testandi: rubric.
30 Nov 1369 (RA 274, 532^r-535^r) inventory by Bernardus Ariberti.

865] Petrus Alamanni, bishop of Fréjus. Formerly dean in the diocese of S. Flour, notary apostolic; bishop from 1346.

1 Aug 1333 (EFR J1, 60885) licentia testandi.
21 Nov 1348 (EFR C1, 4000) commission to Bartholomeus Galhardi, canon of Fréjus.
12 Dec 1348 (RA 101, 74^r-81^v) accounts of commissioner Bartholomeus Galhardi.
6 Feb 1349 (VQ 5, 417) Pontius Alamanni pays 500 fl. for goods.
21 Jan 1350 (ibid., 578-579) commissioner pays £276.
22 Mar 1351 (ibid., 603) Raymundus Naulonis, collector of Aix, pays on arrears of spoils.

866] Petrus Alfonsi, bishop of Porto, died before 26 Oct 1355. Formerly archdeacon of Lisbon; bishop of Silves from 1331; of Astorga from 1333; of Porto from 1342.

22 Feb 1356 (Coll. 497, 57^v) successor Alfonsus is obligated to a composition of 3000 fl.
10 May 1357 (VQ 7, 176) successor pays 1250 fl.

3 Oct 1358 (ibid., 226) he pays 580 fl.
24 Jan 1359 (ibid., 259) he pays 50 fl.
24 Nov 1360 (IM 2199) collector Guillelmus Piloti pays £500.

867] Petrus Alrici, collector of Venice.

10 Jun 1340 (VQ 4, 159) Bernardus de Lacu assigns books to the Camera.

868] Petrus Amelii, subcollector of Béziers.

before 1377 (Coll. 157, 152^v) 5 fl. Fr. paid for goods.

869] Petrus Andreae, bishop of Cambrai, died 13 Sep 1368. Formerly canon of Paris; bishop of Noyon from 1340; of Clermont from 1342; of Cambrai from 1349.

16 Mar 1369 (Coll. 353, 189^r) camerarius Arnaldus Alberti asks the Cameral council to advise him on the donations inter vivos which the bishop made in his last illness.

870] Petrus de Antra, abbot of Toussaints OCSA, diocese of Châlons-sur-Marne, died between Jul 1350 and May 1352.

11 May 1352 (EFR C1, 5299) commission.

871] Petrus Anzelerii, bishop of Lectoure. Formerly cantor of Amiens, LL.D.; bishop from 1351.

1364 (RA 157, 47^r) licentia testandi: rubric.
6 Jan 1365 (EFR U2, 1492) commission to Sancius Vaquerii.
1 Nov 1375 (Coll. 34, 103^v-104^r) accounts of Arnaldus de Peyraco, collector of Auch.

872] Petrus de Aquila OFM, bishop of Trivento. Formerly bishop of S. Angelo dei Lombardi from 1347; of Trivento from 1348.

25 Apr 1361 (Coll. 169, 126^v) spoils yield 4 car.
10 Nov 1361 (ibid.) 597 fl. 5 unc. 36 car. 20 grani.
11 May 1362 (ibid., 127^r-128^r) list of goods collected.

873] Petrus Artaudi OP, bishop of Fréjus, died before 27 Aug 1361. Formerly bishop of Alba from 1334; of Sisteron from 1349; of Fréjus from 1360.

1359 (RA 140, 17^r) licentia testandi: rubric.
12 Nov 1361 (VQ 7, 369) commissioner Petrus Crachati pays 100 fl. from goods at Sisteron.
20 Nov 1361 (ibid., 371) he pays 12 fl. for a mule.

19 Sep 1361 (OS 31, 247^{rv}) commission to Raymundus Naulonis, collector of Aix, and Petrus Torchari, subcollector of Sisteron.
10 Feb 1363 (IE 303, 9^v) successor Geraldus pays 110 fl. "pro quadam antra de argento munita de certis lapidibus et perlis."
17 Feb 1363 (ibid., 10^r) Geraldus pays 195 fl. for goods in an inventory.

874] Petrus Aureoli OFM, archbishop of Aix, died 10 Jan 1322. M.Theol.; archbishop from 1321.

11 Apr 1326 (VQ 1, 500) Hugo de Caluberiis, provost of Aix, commissioner, pays £65.6.2.

875] Petrus Petrus Ayme, bishop of Auxerre, died 2 Sep 1372. Formerly succentor of Beauvais, LL.D., papal familiar; bishop from 1362.

11 Sep 1372 (EFR G1, 909) commission to Bernardus Cariti and the subcollector of Auxerre.
19 Sep 1372 (Coll. 358, 186^v) note of dispatch of letters to Bernardus Cariti.
18 Nov 1372 (ibid., 112^{rv}) Bernardus Cariti, collector of Sens, is ordered to release the goods found outside Avignon to the heirs and executors.

876] Petrus de Aynardo OP, bishop of Sénez 1362-1369.

20 Sep 1369 (Coll. 354, 79^v-80^r) successor compounded by proxy for 400 fl., and the spoils are released to him.

877] Petrus Ayraudi, prior of S. Eutropius OClun, diocese of Saintes.

14 Dec 1362 (OS 31, 163^v-164^r) commission to the collector of Saintes to realize 2000 écus from the spoils to pay the late prior's composition for the spoils of Galhardus de Podio, bishop of Saintes.

878] Petrus Bardonerii, magister capellae Papae.

20 Nov 1350 (VQ 5, 441-442) executor Raymundus de Laglada pays 20 fl. composition; from other sources, 11 fl., £12.3.2.

879] Petrus de Bellejotto, prior of Charité-sur-Loire OClun, diocese of Auxerre.

30 Jan 1335 (EFR B2, 88) arranges composition.
24 Dec 1335 (VQ 4, 105) successor Guillelmus de Pictavia pays 3000 fl., one half of the spoils and arrears of annates.
3 Oct 1336 (ibid., 111) he pays 500 fl.
28 Nov 1336 (ibid., 114) he pays 2500 fl.

880] Petrus de Benhaco, bishop of Castres, died before 27 May 1364. LL.D., bishop of Castres from 1348.

29 Jan 1365 (IE 303, 26^v) commissioner Guillelmus Amarinti pays 408 fl. Fr.

2 May 1365 (OS 23A, 119^v) nephew Raymundus Arnaldi is obligated to a composition of 1500 fl.

2 May 1365 (Coll. 353, 37^r-39^r) collector Guillelmus Amarinti is ordered to release goods to a nephew in consideration of the composition.

before 1368 (Coll. 80, 257^r) collector notes that he made an inventory and received 2658 fl. Fr.

16 Jun 1368 (IE 325, 21^v) composition of 800 fl. received.

Jan 1372 (IM 2676, 3) nephew pays 300 fl.

881] Petrus Beraldi, bishop of Agde, died 22 Feb 1354. LL.Lic., former archdeacon of Paris; bishop from 1342.

22 Apr 1354 (Coll. 497, 51^v) executors are obligated to a composition of 700 fl.

11 May 1354 (VQ 7, 52) commissioner Petrus Ruffi pays 20 fl.

14 Jun 1354 (ibid., 53) nephew executor Joannes Beraldi pays 676 fl. 16 s. in goods and cash.

7 Oct 1355 (ibid., 98-99) bailiff pays debt of 50 fl.

882] Petrus Burgundionis, bishop of Sarlat, died 1 Feb 1341. Formerly treasurer of Laon, papal chaplain; bishop from 1338.

1 Feb - 1 Oct 1341 (Coll. 197, 3^r-10^r) accounts of Joannes Bertrandi and Guillelmus Ruffi, commissioners.

10 Feb 1341 (EFR B2, 811) commission to Raymundus Flori.

14 May 1341 (EFR B1, 9202; IM 1572) warning of Raymundus Flori against the holders of goods.

20 May 1341 (IM 1572) response returned to Raymundus Flori: the holder of the goods was prevented by war from coming before the collector.

n.d. (Coll. 492, 1^r) list by brother Lancelmus Burgundionis of the goods in his possession.

25 Jun 1342 (VQ 5, 462) collector's report.

883] Petrus de Bolonesio, bishop of Aversa, died before 1 Jun 1324. Formerly canon of Beauvais, magister capellae to the king of Naples; bishop from 1309.

1324 x 1332 (Coll. 221, 151^v) Geraldus de Valle received 493 unc. 3 tari 7 grani 1 d. from the spoils and vacancy.

884] Petrus Borserii, provost of S. Salvy OCSA, diocese of Albi, D.Decr.

22 Jun 1329 (VQ 1, 529) commissioner Guillelmus de Bos pays 61 fl.

28 Nov 1330 (OS 12, 136ʳ) Raymundus de Chameraco pays 62 reg., 56 fl.
8 Feb 1332 (VQ 1, 529) he pays £82.3.
1335 (Coll. 29, 199ʳ) accounts of Arnaldus de Verdala.
21 Oct 1340 (VQ 4, 165) Geraldus Colle pays 5 fl.

885] Petrus Bruni OP, bishop of Couserans from 1342.

25 Oct 1345 (EFR C1, 2064) commission.

886] Petrus de Brunia, canon of Braga, nuncio in Portugal, died between 17 Nov 1328 and 8 Oct 1329.

8 Oct 1329 (EFR J2, 3987) commission to Arnaldus de Verdala.
Oct 1329 - (IE 83, 51ʳᵛ) accounts of Arnaldus de Verdala.
18 Nov 1329 (EFR J2, 4023) commission to Bernardus de Taxeriis.
15 Jan 1330 (VQ 1, 351) Arnaldus de Ruppe pays debt of 30 fl.
27 Feb 1330 (OS 12, 121ʳ) quittance to Arnaldus de Ruppe and Guillelmus de Cadonheto for 30 fl.
30 Nov 1335 (EFR B2, 122) general quittance to Arnaldus de Verdala.

887] Petrus Buccaplanula OFM, archbishop of Cosenza, died 1319. Archbishop from 1298.

4 Jun 1320 (EFR J1, 12158) orders Guillelmus de Balaeto, rector of Benevento, to inquire whether Petrus had a licentia testandi, and if not to collect the spoils from the executors.
23 Dec 1320 (ibid., 12771) orders him to deliver vestments to the church of Cosenza.
22 Sep 1321 (ibid., 16080) orders him to recover goods not legitimately given away during the last illness.
24 Dec 1322 (VQ 1, 310) Raymundus de Balaeto assigns books for his brother Guillelmus, rector of Benevento and Campagna.

888] Petrus de Cabilone, bishop of Chalon-sur-Saône, died before 21 Mar 1345. Formerly canon of Chalon, archdeacon of Autun; bishop from 1342.

21 Aug 1341 (EFR B1, 8770) licentia testandi.
24 Mar 1345 (EFR C1, 1594) commission.

889] Petrus de Calasso, bishop of Montauban, died 22 Nov 1379. Formerly provost of Nîmes; bishop from 1368.

23 Dec 1379 (Coll. 359, 6ʳ-7ᵛ) nephew Elias Jacobi is obligated to a composition of 3000 fl.
19 Jan 1380 (Coll. 359, 162ʳᵛ) executors are to pay half of their composition by 2 Feb.

21 Nov 1380 (Coll. 235, 144ᵛ) composition of 3750 fl. paid by Elias Jacobi, Guillelmus de Lacu and Petrus Jacobi.
17 Dec 1380 (Coll. 358, 173ʳ) holders of goods are absolved of their excommunication.
1380? (IM 4746) camerarius demands accounts.
n.d. (Coll. 236, 323ᵛ) note of spoils and remains by Aymericus Pelicerii.

890] Petrus de Calciata, prior "de Sazo," diocese of Avignon, died in curia.

7 Jan 1348 (VQ 5, 400) Petrus Chautardi pays 32 s. 6 1/2 d.

891] Petrus de Camiada, abbot of S. Croix, diocese of Bordeaux, died 31 Oct 1375. See *Gall. Christ.* 2:863D.

28 Jun 1376 (OS 42, 84ʳ) successor Raymundus pays 400 fr. of a composition of 800 fr.
26 Dec 1376 (ibid., 96ʳ) he pays 300 fr.
29 Mar 1378 (ibid., 121ᵛ) he pays 192 fr.
9 Oct 1378 (ibid.) he pays 8 fr.

892] Petrus de Canilhaco OSB, bishop of Maguelonne, died 7 Jul 1361. Formerly abbot of Montmajour, diocese of Arles; bishop of S. Pons from 1353; of Maguelonne from 1361.

31 Oct 1361 (VQ 7, 367; OS 23A, 108ᵛ) his brother Raymundus de Canilhaco, cardinal of Palestrina, pays 1000 fl. composition.
1364 (Coll. 156, 63ʳ-65ᵛ) accounts of collector Joannes Garrigiae.

893] Petrus de Capra, provisor of the Pinhota.

12 Jan 1349 (VQ 5, 416) Petrus de Frigidavilla, administrator of the Pinhota, pays 415 fl. and other moneys.

894] Petrus de Casa OCarm, patriarch of Jerusalem and administrator of Vaison, died before 2 Mar 1349. Prof.Theol., magister generalis OCarm; bishop of Vaison from 1341, patriarch of Jerusalem from 1342.

17 Jan 1350 (EFR C2, 2121) commission to Odo bishop of Paphos.
11 Jan 1356 (VQ 7, 127) executor pays legacy of 100 fl.

895] Petrus de Castellus, bishop of Valence-Die, died between 1 Dec 1351 and 28 Feb 1352. Formerly abbot of Cluny; bishop from 1342.

26 Jul 1343 (EFR C1, 299-300) premature commission.
16 May 1350 (ibid., 4510) commission to Geraldus de Arbento.
28 Feb 1352 (ibid., 5227) commission to Guillelmus de Balma.

15 Mar 1352 (OS 28, 145ᵛ-148ʳ) commissioner Guillelmus de Balma pays goods to Camera.
30 Jan 1354 (VQ 7, 46; OS 23A, 102ᵛ) successor Joannes pays the last 250 fl. of a composition for 500 fl.

896] Petrus de Castronovo, bishop of Rodez, died 19 May 1334. Formerly archdeacon in the church of Rodez; bishop from 1319. See *Gall. Christ.* 1:217A-C.

16 May 1334 (Coll. 210, 87ʳ-93ᵛ) nuncupative testament, made at Paris.
1334 - (Coll. 210, 94ʳ-) accounts of Pontius de Pereto and Raymundus de Cameraco, commissioners.
1334-1335 (Coll. 145, 252ʳ-332ᵛ) commissioners' accounts of the vacancy.
18 Jan 1335 (EFR B2, 14) orders the vicars to be cited before the curia.
22 Apr 1335 (ibid., 46) orders the vicars to send an inventory and to hold the goods pending instructions.
23 Jul 1335 (ibid., 86) commission to Raymundus de Cameraco and Pontius de Pereto.
29 Oct 1335 (ibid., 113-116) commissioners pay 600 fl., 600 agni, 7200 regal.
29 Oct 1335 (VQ 4, 103) they pay £6525 Tur. parv. for spoils and vacancy.
18 Feb 1337 (ibid., 119) they pay £5370.10.
27 Jun 1338 (ibid., 131) commissioner Amanevus de Ramafortis pays £1132.6.8.
23 Dec 1338 (ibid., 136) Pontius de Pereto pays £1270.
29 Dec 1338 (ibid., 167-168) payment by Raymundus de Cameraco.
27 Nov 1343 (VQ 5, 340) further payment.
25 Jun 1342 (ibid., 462) payment by collector Raymundus Flori.
18 Mar 1347 (EFR C1, 3177) orders Ademarus de Laobraria, canon of Tournai, to pay £1900 Tur. parv. legacy to the bishop's sister Barrana and her daughters Galharda and Alasia.

897] Petrus de Castroparro, abbot of S. Polycarpe OSB, diocese of Alet. See *Gall. Christ.* 6:190A-B.

3 Dec 1383 (Coll. 360, 65ᵛ-66ʳ) brother Joannes de Castroparro is ordered to appear before the Camera to answer for the goods.

898] Petrus de Caunis, abbreviator, died 1347.

3 Jun 1336 (EFR B1, 3382) licentia testandi.
7 Feb 1349 (VQ 5, 418) executors pay 100 fl. of a 250-fl. composition.
n.d. (OS 23A, 97ʳ) note, temp. Urban V, that the whole composition was paid.

899] Petrus de Clasquerin, archbishop of Tarragona and patriarch of Antioch, died 10 Jan 1380. LL.D., former archdeacon of Barcelona; bishop of Huesca from 1348; archbishop of Tarragona from 1357, and patriarch of Antioch from 1375.

1380? (IM 4746) camerarius demands accounts.

1386 (Coll. 152, 181ʳ-183ᵛ) goods among those of Arnaldus Andreae, collector of Narbonne.

900] Petrus de Clusello OP, bishop of Concordia, died before 15 Feb 1361. Formerly bishop of Chioggia from 1346; of Melfi from 1347; of Concordia from 1348.

Mar - Apr 1361 (Coll. 130, 150ᵛ) collector sells goods for 20 ducats 34 s. 6 d.

901] Petrus de Colle, sacristan of Tortosa.

23 Dec 1343 (EFR C2, 359) commission.

902] Petrus de Combeton, abbot of S. Benigne de Dijon OSB, diocese of Langres, died 18 Apr 1379. See *Gall. Christ.* **4:690B.**

1380? (IM 4746) camerarius demands accounts.

903] Petrus Cornarii de Venetiis OFM, archbishop of Patrai, died at Tarragona 1397 x 1401. Formerly bishop of Korone from 1367; archbishop of Patrai from 1386.

28 Feb 1402 (Coll. 123, 47ʳ) collector Joannes de Ripis Altis receives £16.10 from the subcollector of Tarragona.

904] Petrus de Cosnaco, bishop of Tulle.

before 5 Apr 1407 (Coll. 91, 337ʳ) collector reports that the goods were seized by royal officials.

905] Petrus de Cuellac, bishop of Segovia, died before 30 May 1351. Bishop from 1342.

6 Jun 1351 (EFR C2, 2443) commission.

906] Petrus Curtis, chaplain of honor, provost of S. Michel de Cuxà OSB, diocese of Elne.

1393 x 1405 (Coll. 160, 123ʳ) Joannes de Ripis Altis, collector of Elne, receives £30.

907] Petrus de Dacia OP, poenitentiarius Papae, died in curia.

20 Aug 1347 (VQ 5, 394) executors pay a composition of 60 fl.

908] Petrus Fabri de Leschemel, bishop of Riez, died Dec 1369. Formerly cantor of Orléans; bishop from 1352.

7 Oct 1365 (EFR U2, 2003) premature commission to Raymundus Naulonis and Jacobus de Sala to collect the goods of "episcopi Regensis, nuper extra curiam defuncti."
1370 (Coll. 19, 281^r-293^r) accounts of Geraldus Mercaderii.
7 Apr 1375 (Coll. 356, 12^r) 120 fl. debt of Ludovicus de Forcalquerio is forgiven.

909] Petrus Ferri, bishop of Chieti, died 17 Nov 1336. Formerly bishop of Anagni from 1320; of Marsi from 1327; of Chieti from 1336.

10 Jul 1336 (EFR B1, 3387) licentia testandi.
24 Aug 1339 (EFR B3, 2495) commission.

910] Petrus Fretaldi, archbishop of Tours, died 21 May 1357. Formerly archdeacon in the church of Tours; archbishop from 1335.

20 Apr 1344 (EFR C1, 791) premature commission.
11 Dec 1354 (EFR I1, 1229) commission to Petrus Belmondi, in anticipation of death.
26 Aug 1357 (Coll. 497, 62^v) executors are obligated to a composition of 2000 fl.
ca. 1358 (Coll. 255, 128^r) 1400 fl. of composition is paid.

911] Petrus de Frigidavilla, administrator of the Pinhota.

30 Jun 1361 (VQ 7, 340) executors Guillelmus Amici and Ademarus Deodati pay a composition of 800 fl.
13 Sep 1362 (Coll. 231, 141^r) note of the same payment.
Apr 1363 (IM 2279, 11) grant of the executors' portion of 258 fl. found after the composition was settled.
9 Apr 1363 (IE 303, 11^r) executors pay 129 fl., etc.

912] Petrus Gabrieli, bishop of Gubbio. Formerly canon of Gubbio; bishop of Fossombrone from 1317; of Gubbio from 1327.

6 Jul 1345 (EFR C1, 1815) commission to Berengarius Blasini, treasurer of the Duchy of Spoleto.
12 Jul 1345 (Coll. 232, 142^r-144^v) accounts and compositions.
30 Aug 1345 (EFR C1, 1934) orders the podestà, governors and council of Gubbio to assist the commissioner.

913] Petrus de Galganis, archbishop of Cosenza, died 3 Nov 1362. Formerly archdeacon of Manfredonia; archbishop of Reggio from 1328; of Cosenza from 1354.

4 May 1329 (EFR J1, 45099) licentia testandi.
5 Aug 1354 (RA 128, 599^r) licentia testandi.
28 Dec 1357 (Coll. 352, 118^v) dispatch of an anticipatory commission

dated 14 Dec 1357, by hand of Reginaldus de Lupchaco, to himself and Petrus, archbishop of Benevento.

914] Petrus Gasconis, rector of Benevento.

15 Dec 1339 (EFR B3, 2627) Arnulphus Marcellini is substituted for the late Petrus Gasconis.

23 Apr 1340 (EFR B1, 8292) quittance for an inventory sent to the curia by Guillelmus de S. Paulo.

915] Petrus Germani, archdeacon in the church of Sens, registrator supplicationum, died 1355.

2 Dec 1355 (VQ 7, 100) executors pay 300 fl. of a 400-fl. composition.

29 Dec 1355 (ibid., 101) they pay 100 fl.; cf. OS 23A, 108^r.

916] Petrus Gervasii, canon of Le Puy, collector of Le Puy.

14 Apr 1375 (Coll. 356, 14^r-16^r) letters of commission and instruction to Joannes de Cabrespino.

28 May 1375 (OS 42, 22^r) commissioner pays 320 fl. Cam. 17 s. 3d.

28 May 1375 (Coll. 356, 25^v-26^v) goods released to executors in consideration of a composition.

917] Petrus Goffridi OESA, bishop of Toulon, died before 18 Jun 1361. Bishop from 1355.

9 May 1364 (Coll. 353, 11^r) subcollector is directed to pay a legacy of 300 fl. to the Augustinian convent of Limoges.

918] Petrus de Golardo, bishop of Condom, died before 3 Dec 1369. Formerly prior "de Neraco" OSB, diocese of Condom; bishop from 1340.

1 Nov 1375 (Coll. 34, 143^r-148^r) accounts of Arnaldus de Peyraco.

after 1385 (Coll. 35, 323^r-325^r) remains collected by Sicardus de Brugayrosio.

919] Petrus Gometii de Barroso de Albornotio, cardinal archbishop of Seville, died 1 Jul 1390. Formerly dean of Toledo, LL.D.; bishop of Siguenza from 1348; of Coimbra from 1358; of Lisbon from 1364 ; archbishop of Seville from 1369, and cardinal priest of S. Praxedis 30 May 1371.

30 Jan 1392 (IM 3537) collector Fulco Pererii receives 80,000 maravedis.

920] Petrus de Gongolio, bishop of Le Puy. Formerly bishop of Le Mans from 1312; of Le Puy from 1326.

11 Feb 1327 (EFR J2, 3138).
13 Feb 1327 (ibid., 3141).
12 Sep 1332 (VQ 1, 522) composition of 5000 fl. received from nephew-executors.
12 Sep 1322 (RA 44, 653^r, ed. Mollat in RHE 29 [1933]: 338) the pope declares the testament unlicensed and invalid.

921] Petrus de Grassinis OP, bishop of Anagni, died before 30 Oct 1362. Formerly bishop of Sorra; of Anagni from 1348.

1 Feb 1369 (Coll. 353, 149^r) camerarius warns Jacobus de Mutis, bishop of Arezzo, that Magnus Vetulus, provost of Anagni, has been granted a judgement against him for 150 fl. taken from the spoils.

922] Petrus Guillelmi, bishop of Orange, died Dec 1341. Formerly rector of the Comtat-Venaissin; bishop of Toulon from 1325; of Orange from 1328.

30 Dec 1341 (EFR B2, 919) commission to Pontius de Pereto.
31 Dec 1341 (EFR B1, 9248; RA 55, 491^r) beginning of a copy of an inventory by Pontius de Pereto.
1 Feb 1342 (VQ 4, 189) commissioner Pontius de Pereto pays 1428 fl., 419 fl. Pied., etc.
4 Mar 1342 (ibid., 191-192) he assigns silver, rings, etc.
3 Dec 1343 (VQ 5, 341) Joannes, bishop of Fréjus, pays 104 fl.

923] Petrus Joannis, prior of S. Remy, diocese of Avignon, collector of Arles, died between 7 Mar and 24 Aug 1348.

8 Sep 1348 (EFR C1, 3950) Guillelmus de Balma OCSA, collector of Arles, is directed to inquire into the payments made by subcollectors who are now dead.

924] Petrus Joannis de Moussey, bishop of Carcassonne, died 17 May 1338. Formerly bishop of Meaux from 1321; of Viviers from 1325; of Bayeux from 1326; of Carcassonne from 1330. See *Gall. Christ.* 6:897B-898A.

1 Sep 1326 (EFR J1, 26369) licentia testandi.
7 Mar 1330 (EFR J1, 48759; Coll. 94, 1^v-2^r) licentia testandi.
20 May 1338 (EFR B2, 440; Coll. 94, 1^{rv}) commission to Amanevus de Rimaforti and Pontius de Pereto.
27 Jun 1338 (VQ 4, 131) commissioner pays £1132.6.8.
28 Jul 1338 (ibid., 132; EFR B2, 479; EFR B3, 1933) commissioner assigns a mitre and crozier.
23 Dec 1338 (VQ 4, 136) he pays £1250.18.4.
1 Dec 1339 (ibid., 150) he pays £555.8.6.
Sep 1340 (Coll. 426, 64 fols.) accounts of Pontius de Pereto.

13 Jul 1341 (VQ 4, 181) he pays 89 fl. etc.
9 Feb 1342 (ibid., 190) he pays £31.12.7 and 24 fl.
8 Jan 1343 (Coll. 289, 37^v) goods in inventory of papal treasure.
17 Apr 1344 (Coll. 289, 37^v) Petrus de Franconia pays 10 d.
5 Jan 1339 (OS 18, 14^v) Pontius de Pereto assigns goods and jewels.
1338-1342 (Coll. 94, 1^r-70^v) accounts of Pontius de Pereto and Amanevus de Rimaforti.

925] Petrus de Lapeirareda OP, bishop of Mirepoix, died 19 Aug 1348. M.Theol.; bishop from 1327.

23 Aug 1329 (EFR J1, 46077) licentia testandi.
23 Aug 1348 (EFR C1, 3939) commission to Petrus Hugonis for these and other spoils.
15 Jun 1350 (Coll. 497, 43^v) executors obligated to a composition of 150 fl.

926] Petrus Lasteyrie, abbot of Psalmody OSB, diocese of Nîmes. See *Gall. Christ.* 6:478D.

1 Feb 1376 (OS 42, 50^v) Petrus de Bonofonte, monk, pays 300 fr.

927] Petrus Leterii, abbot of S. Croix d'Angle OCSA, diocese of Poitiers. See *Gall. Christ.* 2:1347.

12 Feb 1351 (Coll. 497, 46^v) Reginaldus Leterii, prior of Issoire OCSA, diocese of Tours, is obligated to a composition of 1200 fl.
28 Mar 1351 (EFR C1, 4939) commission to Geraldus Judicis, canon of Angers.
6 Apr 1351 (ibid., 4944) commission to Reginaldus Leterii, prior of Issoire, diocese of Tours.

928] Petrus Lobeti, abbot of S. Antoine chef de l'Ordre, diocese of Vienne, died 1369. See *Gall. Christ.* 16:197E-198C.

21 Mar 1354 (RA 128, 598^{rv}) licentia testandi.
25 Nov 1369 (Coll. 354, 83^r) commission by treasurer to Jacobus Golferii.
Jun 1375 (IM 2877, 4) Jacobus Malheti, canon of S.Antoine, pays the last 50 fl. of a 90-fl. debt.

929] Petrus Loherii, prior of S. Etienne de Beaune OSB, diocese of Autun.

10 Sep 1381 (Coll. 359, 64^r) goods to be held for the prior's uncle, cardinal Petrus Amelii.
24 Sep 1381 (ibid., 90^r) orders goods surrendered to the cardinal.

930] Petrus de Luca, archbishop of Bordeaux, died 1345. Archbishop from 1332.

28 Aug 1332 (EFR J1, 58156) licentia testandi.
5 Jan 1346 (EFR C1, 2252) the goods are to be seized pending accounts.
5 Mar 1346 (ibid., 2343) notes seizure of goods by officers of the king of England.
15 Mar 1346 (ibid., 2371-2375) instructions to the collector.
24 Mar 1346 (IM 1664) the collector Elias Magnan protests against holders of the goods, including the successor.
8 Jun 1346 (EFR C1, 2552) orders Radulphus baron of Stamford, seneschal of Gascony, to pay a loan of £40 of Bordeaux.
8 Jun 1346 (ibid., 2553) orders Joannes Bajuli, constable of Bordeaux, to pay 400 modii of salt, 20 startae of wheat and 38 startae of millet.
8 Jun 1346 (ibid., 2553) orders abbot Elias to compel testimony about thefts of goods by familiars.
8 Jun 1346 (ibid., 2555) orders him to seize the accounts of administrators.
13 Apr 1347 (Coll. 497, 32^v) successor Amanevus is obligated to a composition of 1000 fl. for fruits of the vacancy.
3 Nov 1347 (ibid., 35^v-36^r) he is obligated to a composition of 3000 écus for spoils.
11 Nov 1347 (IM 5282) note of the obligation sent to the collector.
9 Jul 1349 (Coll. 497, 41^v) the next successor, Bernardus, adopts the obligations for 1000 fl. and 3000 écus.
3 Oct 1352 (ibid., 49^r) obligation of the next successor, Amanevus.

931] Petrus de Luna, bishop of Urgel, died 1370. Formerly precentor of Gerona, LL.D.; bishop from 1365.

1370 (Coll. 479, 1^r-16^v) inventory and sales by Joannes Andressa, collector of Aragon.
1370 (ibid., 17^r-22^v) accounts of the fruits of 1370 and revaluation of the bishopric.

932] Petrus Lupi de Luna, archbishop of Zaragoza, died 22 Feb 1345. Formerly abbot "de Monte Aragonum" OCSA, diocese of Huesca; archbishop from 1317.

22 Jul 1317 (EFR J1, 4486) licentia testandi.
5 Feb 1319 (EFR J1, 8932) licentia testandi.
12 Jul 1345 (VQ 5, 510) collector Almeracius de Cabrespino pays 352 écus.
3 Sep 1345 (EFR C2, 764) asks the king of Aragon to remove his hand from the goods.
8 Oct 1345 (ibid., 783) arranges composition of 20,000 fl.
1345 (Coll. 229, 197^r) accounts of the collector.

20 Jan 1346 (EFR C1, 2278) half the composition paid.
10 Feb 1346 (VQ 5, 364-365) Lupus de Luna, lord of Segovia, pays half of a composition of 18,200 fl.
1 Mar 1346 (EFR C1, 1506).
17 Jun 1346 (EFR C2, 1024) faculty to Almeracius de Cabrespino to collect 9100 fl. of the composition.
8 Jul 1346 (VQ 5, 374) Lupus de Luna pays the other half of his composition.

933] Petrus de Macello, collector of Portugal, died before 14 Apr 1356.

1356 (IM 4592) accounts of his successor Joannes Garrigiae.
1356 (IM 7288) inventory.
1356 (Arm. 33, to. 19, 34^r-36^r; to. 20, 23^r-24^v) records of sales of spoils.
1356 (RA 191, 477^r-528^v) accounts, pretending to be by Joannes Garrigiae, including his narrative of piracy.
14 Apr 1356 (VQ 7, 173-174) cameral record of goods recovered from the pirate ship *S. Vincent*, Joannes de Lordello of Lisbon, master.
25 May 1356 (Coll. 352, 66^r) dispatch of a letter to Reginaldus, bishop of Châlons-sur-Marne, dated 10 May 1356, "super facto cuiusdam incarcerati in ipsius domini episcopi carceribus pro 6000 fl. subtractis furtive per eum de bonis quondam domini Petri de Marcello"; the prisoner may have been Joannes Garrigiae.
17 Feb 1358 (VQ 7, 217) the pirates pay 400 fl.

934] Petrus de Mandagoto, camerarius of the monastery of S. Gilles, diocese of Nîmes, died before 1334.

11 Jan 1343 (VQ 5, 332) Almeracius de Cabrespino pays 170 fl. for spoils reserved by John XXII.

935] Petrus de Marvilla OP, bishop of Toulon, died 4 Sep 1402. Bishop from 1395.

1403-1406 (Coll. 23, 192^r-193^v) partial inventory and payments by the collector Simon de Pratis.

936] Petrus Matthei, archdeacon of Mutavedre, diocese of Valence-Die.

26 Sep 1328 (EFR J2, 3688) commission; Petrus died in the diocese of Maguelonne.
Oct 1328 (IE 83, 49^v-50^v) accounts of Arnaldus de Verdala.
18 Apr 1329 (OS 12, 106^r; VQ 1, 347) he pays 120 fl. Pied.
27 Dec 1331 (OS 12, 137^r-138^r) quittance to Arnaldus de Verdala.
30 Nov 1335 (EFR B1, 122) general quittance to Arnaldus de Verdala.

937] Petrus de Mesenchis, abbot of Quarante OCSA, diocese of Narbonne, died 1 Sep 1361. See *Gall. Christ.* 6:196C.

9 Feb 1363 (Coll. 156, 15ʳ) successor Stephanus pays a composition of 10 fr.

1368 x 1374 (Coll. 157, 19ʳ) successor pays 150 fl. of a composition for 300 fl.

938] Petrus de Monterebello, bishop of Lectoure, died 1368. Formerly archdeacon in the church of Liège, LL.D., notary apostolic, papal familiar; bishop from 1365.

26 May 1369 (Coll. 353, 226ʳ) camerarius orders the collector to pay the vicar's back wages from the spoils.

before 1370 (Coll. 19, 165ᵛ) accounts of collector Geraldus Mercaderii.

6 Feb 1372 (Coll. 358, 27ʳᵛ) camerarius directs Bertrandus Raffini, collector of Narbonne; Aymericus Pelicerii, collector of Toulouse; Sancius Vaquerii, collector of Auch: the bishop earned his own wealth, and willed money to a college at Toulouse and other pious causes; his executors paid a composition of 4000 fl.; and the goods are to be released to them.

6 Nov 1372 (ibid., 124ʳ) Bertrandus Raffini accounts for a composition of 1837 fl.

1 Nov 1375 (Coll. 34, 104ᵛ-108ʳ) accounts of the vacancy by Arnaldus de Peyraco.

after 1385 (Coll. 35, 261ʳ-262ʳ) remains of spoils collected by Sicardus de Brugayrosio.

939] Petrus de Narbona, bishop of Urgel, died before 13 Jun 1348. Formerly secular abbot of S. Paul, Narbonne; bishop from 1341.

26 Nov 1347 (EFR C2, 1541) commission.

12 Mar 1350 (ibid., 2154) successor Nicolaus is permitted to recover jewels and books, etc.

n.d. (Coll. 116, 54ᵛ) arrears of spoils collected temp. Urban V.

940] Petrus de Olargio OSB, bishop of Vabres, died 1329. Formerly abbot of Vabres; bishop from 1317.

3 Nov 1329 (EFR J2, 4012) commission.

19 Feb 1330 (OS 12, 120ᵛ) successor pays 300 fl. of a composition for 600 fl.

30 Jun 1330 (ibid., 128ʳ) he pays 300 fl.

941] Petrus de Palude OP, patriarch of Jerusalem and administrator of Couserans, died in Apulia 31 Jan 1342. M.Theol.; patriarch from 1329, in administration of Couserans from 1336.

13 Jul 1329 (EFR J1, 45696) licentia testandi.

10 Apr 1342 (VQ 4, 194) Geraldus Latremoliera, administrator of the Pinhota, assigns money and rings.

1342 (Coll. 30, 146ᵛ-150ᵛ) Raymundus de Cameraco collects spoils at Couserans.

17 Jan 1345 (Coll. 168, 46ᵛ-47ʳ) goods collected in Apulia by Guillelmus de Roseriis.

942] Petrus de Pinosio, prior of Tortosa, died in curia.

17 Oct 1346 (EFR C2, 1240) commission to Almeracius de Cabrespino to collect the fruits of the vacancy "a tempore quo fuit suspensus Petrus de Pinosis."

8 Feb 1347 (ibid., 1314) faculty to collect spoils.

943] Petrus de Pinu, archbishop of Benevento, died 12 Sep 1360. Formerly elect of Fréjus; bishop of Viterbo from 1348; archbishop of Benevento from 1350.

1360 (Coll. 169, 106ʳ) gives date of death.

14 Nov 1360 (Coll. 231, 107ᵛ; VQ 7, 302) commissioner Reginaldus, archbishop of Capua, sells goods to Florentine merchants; their letter of exchange for 1510 fl. Cam. for these spoils and those of Guillelmus, bishop of Aquino.

944] Petrus de Plana Cassanha OFM, bishop of Rodez and patriarch of Jerusalem, died 6 Feb 1319. Bishop of Rodez from 1302 and patriarch from 1314. See *Gall. Christ.* 1:215E-217A.

15 Sep 1309 (Regesta Clementis V, 4290) licentia testandi.
1 Feb -18 Mar 1319 (Coll. 210, 3ʳ-51ʳ) inventory.
12 Jul 1317 (ibid., 82ᵛ-85ʳ) testament.
12 Nov 1319 (EFR J2, 960) commission to Petrus de Rocha.
21 Feb 1320 (ibid., 999) he is directed to cite the vicars and other holders of goods.
26 Feb 1320 (EFR J1, 12067) instructions to Guillelmus de Balaeto and Stephanus de Pinu (dispatched in March: Coll. 350, 15ᵛ-16ʳ) regarding certain goods left in the care of Ivo, archbishop of Nazareth.
15 Jun 1320 (VQ 1, 471) Petrus Danrocha pays £5029 Tur. gr.
17 Aug 1320 (EFR J1, 26349) regarding the succession to patriarchal goods.
3 Feb 1329 (IM 1088; EFR J1, 46251) quittance to Petrus de Manso and Arnaldus de Fabricis of Cyprus.
23 Jul 1335 (EFR B1, 2484) interpretation of the licentia testandi.
29 Oct 1335 (EFR B2, 115) directs Raymundus de Cameraco and Pontius de Pereto to pay reasonable legacies.
29 Dec 1340 (VQ 4, 167-168) payment by Raymundus de Cameraco.
27 Nov 1343 (VQ 5, 340) another payment.

945] Petrus de Podio, abbot of Marmoutier OSB, diocese of Tours, died 6 Aug 1363. See *Gall. Christ.* 14:231A-B.

29 Oct 1363 (OS 31, 203^{rv}) camerarius limits commissioner Rigaldus Rogeti to a spoils claim of 12,000 fl.

1 Apr 1364 (EFR U2, 870) directs Petrus Berimondi, Olricus Alberici and Petrus Bori to cite the successor, cousin Geraldus de Podio, to appear within 30 days to answer for the spoils.

26 Apr 1364 (IM 2339, 9; IE 303, 18^v) he pays 1100 fr. of a composition.

15 May 1364 (ibid., 12; 19^r) he pays 3000 fl.

23 Jul 1364 (ibid., 17; 21^v) he pays 923 fl.

21 Nov 1364 (ibid., 24; 25^r) he pays 1000 fl.

21 Feb 1365 (IM 2378, 9; IE 303, 26^v) he pays 850 fr.

7 Apr 1365 (ibid., 14; 27^{rv}) he pays 1125 fl.

5, 31 May 1365 (ibid., 21; 29^{rv}) he pays 1967 fl. and 2110 fl. to complete payment of 12,000 fl.; cf. OS 23A, 112^r.

946] Petrus de Porta, archbishop of Messina, died before 23 Dec 1355. Formerly monk "de Bolbona" OCist, diocese of Mirepoix; archbishop from 1349.

23 Jul 1356 (Coll. 352, 118^r) expedition of commission to Fr. Martialis, bishop of Catania, dated 17 May 1356.

1373 x 1375 (Coll. 222, 223^r) note of a debt due to spoils.

947] Petrus Raussen, bishop of S. Flour, died before 14 Jul 1374. Formerly provost of Lerida, J.U.D., notary apostolic; bishop from 1368.

23 Jul 1375 (Coll. 356, 35^r; Coll. 85, 252^r) commission to Stephanus Arnaldi, deacon of S. Flour.

26 Sep - 27 Nov 1375 (Coll. 85, 252^r-259^r) accounts: net proceeds £206.13.

3 Oct 1375 (Coll. 356, 63^v) directs the commissioner to release the grain.

1 Dec 1375 (OS 42, 44^r) he pays 50 fl., 40 fr.

1385 (Coll. 85, 266^r) a *Pontificale* from these spoils assigned to the second successor.

948] Petrus Raymundi de Montebruno, bishop of Tarbes. Formerly provost of Tarbes, LL.D., papal chaplain; bishop from 1339.

16 Mar 1353 (EFR I1, 195) commission to Martinus de Girardo.

949] Petrus Retroncini, papal chaplain.

27 Aug 1372 (EFR G1, 889) commission to treasurer Petrus de Vernolis, abbot of Aniane.

950] Petrus Ricardi, bishop of Città di Castello. Formerly canon of Tours; bishop from 1347.

9 Oct 1357 (Coll. 352, 105^r) dispatch of a commission dated 30 Sep 1357 to Andreas, bishop of Rimini.

951] Petrus de Rocafolio OSB, abbot of S. Guillem du Desert, diocese of Lodève, died 26 Mar 1374. See *Gall. Christ.* 6:597C.

1368 x 1377 (Coll. 157, 185ᵛ) collector Arnaldus Andreae reports no receipts, because the successor made a composition in the Camera.

952] Petrus Roccasalva OP, bishop of Nice, died 31 Aug 1379. Bishop from 1371. Possibly identical with Roccasalva de Soleriis, OP provincial of Provence: *Gall. Christ.* 3:1288A-B.

1379 (Coll. 480, 12ʳ-22ᵛ) inventory and accounts by Geraldus Mercaderii.
1380? (IM 4746) camerarius demands accounts.

953] Petrus Rogerii, bishop of Carcassonne, died at Paris, 25 Dec 1329. Bishop from 1323. See *Gall. Christ.* 6:896A-897B.

1 Apr 1324 (EFR J1, 19251) licentia testandi.
1330 (EFR J2, 4096, 4117, 4135, 4137, 4155, 4200, 4201, 4249) commission and instructions.
1331 (IE 83, 202ʳ-245ᵛ) accounts of Arnaldus de Verdala.
22 Feb 1331 (OS 12, 138ʳ) he pays 1000 agni, 450 fl., etc.
21 May 1331 (EFR J1, 53674) orders the bishop of Carcassonne to absolve the executors who have not fulfilled the testament.
30 Nov 1335 (EFR B2, 122) general quittance to Arnaldus de Verdala.
1336-1338 (ibid., 217, 246, 479) instructions.
1337 x 1339 (Coll. 145, 210ᵛ) collector Guillelmus Medici receives 10 s. debt.
1342 (Coll. 30, 131ʳ) Raymundus de Cameraco collects £74.17.

954] Petrus de Roya, dean of S. Quentin en Vermandois, diocese of Noyon, died before 27 Mar 1378.

25 Oct 1379 (IM 3032) bull of Clement VII ordering the dean's brother Joannes de Roya to answer to the camerarius for goods seized.
2 Jan 1380 (ibid.) the executors of the papal bull, Aegidius de Lorris bishop of Noyon and Petrus Aycelini de Monteacuto bishop of Laon, appoint a subexecutor, Joannes, secular canon of S. Barthélemy.
3 Jan 1380 (ibid.) subexecutor publishes the bull.
4 Jan 1380 (ibid.) publication reported to the camerarius.

955] Petrus de Rupeforti, bishop of Carcassonne, died 31 Mar 1322. Bishop from 1300.

26 Feb 1309 (Regesta Clementis V, 4287) licentia testandi.
11 Nov 1316 (EFR J1, 1814) licentia testandi.
5 Feb 1322 (EFR J2, 1364-1365).

8-10 Mar 1322 (ibid., 1382-1386).
19 Jul 1322 (ibid., 1473-1478).
30 Jul 1322 (ibid., 1842).
8 Aug 1322 (VQ 1, 477) Hugo de Engolisma pays 6257 agni, 5520 fl.
3 Sep 1322 (EFR J2, 1510-1514).
18 Sep 1322 (VQ 1, 477) Hugo de Engolisma pays 20,184 fl., 8935 agni, etc.
30 Oct 1322 (EFR J1, 16521-16525) orders him to collect from the chapter and pay to the executors, restore the books, etc.
10 Jan 1323 (EFR J2, 1583).
15 Jun 1323 (EFR J1, 17702) faculty to Joannes de Belna OP, inquisitor of France, and Bertrandus Auriacho, executors, to sell a house in Paris and found an anniversary Mass at S. Germain-des-Prés from the proceeds.
13 Nov 1324 (EFR J2, 2275).
24 Nov 1324 (ibid., 2282).
1 Aug 1326 (ibid., 2938).
Aug 1326 x 1330 (IE 83, 44^r-45^v) accounts of remains of debts by Arnaldus de Verdala.
21 Aug 1327 (EFR J2, 3321).
27 Dec 1331 (OS 12, 137^r-138^r) quittance to Arnaldus de Verdala.
28 Jul 1332 (EFR B3, 1932).
30 Nov 1335 (EFR B2, 122) general quittance to Arnaldus de Verdala.
10 Dec 1336 (ibid., 246; EFR B3, 1163) commission to Raymundus Flori and Guillelmus Medici to finish the process of Arnaldus de Verdala and Bernardus de Pereto.

956] Petrus de Sabaudia, archbishop of Lyon, died Nov 1332. Formerly dean of Salisbury; archbishop from 1308.

22 Oct 1337 (EFR B3, 1565).
12 Aug 1339 (ibid., 7585).

957] Petrus Sardinae, bishop of Nice, died 8 Mar 1360. Formerly canon of Nice; bishop from 1348.

25-28 Jan 1361 (IM 4270) inventory and inquest by Guillelmus, bishop of Vence, commissioner.

958] Petrus de Sarono, bishop of Oloron, died 4 Dec 1370. Bishop from 1348.

13 Feb 1371 (EFR G1, 70) Gaston count of Foix is asked to aid collector Aymericus Pelicerii.
2 May 1371 (ibid., 196) he is asked to apply pressure on the holders of the spoils.

2 May 1371 (ibid., 198) commission to Arnaldus de Caraigne, canon in the diocese of S. Papoul.

5 Jul 1371 (ibid., 292) the count of Foix is asked to aid the new commissioner; an explanation of the reservation of spoils.

18 Jun 1372 (Coll. 358, 60^{rv}) quittance to the commissioner for goods assigned 2 Jun 1372.

18 Jan 1373 (ibid., 140^r-141^r, 139^r) commissioner ordered to turn over some goods to the count of Foix.

959] Petrus Sicardi, poenitentiarius Papae.

9 Dec 1350 (VQ 5, 443) Balduinus Ricardi, sigillifer auditoris Camerae, pays 6 fl. for goods.

960] Petrus de Stagno OSB, cardinal bishop of Ostia, died Nov 1377. D.Decr., former prior of Canonica, diocese of Mende; bishop of S. Flour from 1361; archbishop of Bourges from 1368; cardinal from 1370.

21 Mar 1380 (Coll. 359, 23^v-24^r) Artaudus, bishop of Grasse, is commissioned to collect the goods, "ut indempnitate dicte Camere curemus obviare."

961] Petrus Stanislai, bishop of Kraków, died 6 Jun 1348. Bishop from 1347.

13 Sep 1349 (EFR C2, 2062) commission.

962] Petrus Stephani Jordani, prior of Auzielle, diocese of Toulouse.

1 Oct 1349 (EFR C1, 4270) commission.

963] Petrus de Tallisata, died in curia 1361.

17 Sep 1361 (VQ 7, 357) Eblo de Mederio, clericus Camerae, pays 50 fl.

964] Petrus de Tegula, died in curia 1361.

17 Sep 1361 (VQ 7, 357) Eblo de Mederio, clericus Camerae, pays 50 fl. from goods.

965] Petrus de Teutonico OFM, bishop of Patti-Lipari, died 21 Jan 1354. Bishop from 1346. See AFH 7 (1914): 339.

12 Apr 1356 (Coll. 352, 117^r) dispatch of commission to Fr. Martialis, bishop of Catania.

966] Petrus Tholoni, provost of Lerida.

4 Feb 1372 (Coll. 358, 26^r) note that the collector of Aragon was ordered to restore to the executors 300 fl. for which they had compounded.

9 Aug 1378 (OS 42, 129ᵛ) quittance to Arnaldus Andreae, collector of Narbonne, for 60 fr. for a *Decretales* which he bought from these spoils in the papal treasure.

967] Petrus Tizonis, bishop of Périgueux, died 11 Aug 1380. Not in Eubel.

Aug-Oct 1380 (Coll. 37, 20ʳᵛ) collector's expenses.
19 Nov 1384 (ibid., 9ᵛ-10ʳ) successor Elias Servient is to receive the spoils in consideration of a composition of 300 fr.; the collector notes that he has not collected any.
2 Jul 1386 (ibid., 12ᵛ-13ʳ) collector ordered to proceed against Laurentius Picardi, canon of Périgueux, who holds goods.
31 Oct 1387 (ibid., 15ᵛ) goods left to successor Elias Servient, now deceased, are reserved to the Camera.
13 Apr 1385 (Coll. 360, 238ᵛ) orders Petrus de Moreriis to collect the remains of spoils for the next successor, who has paid a composition.
25 Aug 1385 (Coll. 359, 216ᵛ-217ʳ) collector is empowered to compel the administrators of the diocese to render accounts.
10 Aug 1386 - (Coll. 428, 21ʳ-41ᵛ) inquest.

968] Petrus Trinci, bishop of Spoleto. Formerly sacristan of Narbonne, procurator of the college of cardinals; bishop from 1307.

9 Feb 1320 (EFR J1, 12062) commission.

969] Petrus de Turre, prior of Charlieu, diocese of Apt, died between 4 Nov 1329 and 3 Aug 1330.

4 Nov 1329 (IM 1135-1137) he is cited to appear before the camerarius for robbery of the clavarius of Noves.
3 Aug 1330 (VQ 1, 536-537; OS 12, 141ᵛ) commissioner Joannes Regis pays 883 fl. Pied., 62 agn. etc.
27 Nov 1330 (OS 12, 134ʳ) successor Cyprianus de Bastita pays 231 fl.
13 Dec 1330 (ibid., 123ᵛ) commissioner pays 350 fl. from the prior's cousin Raymbaudus.
7 Mar 1331 (ibid., 139ᵛ-140ʳ) successor pays 231 fl.

970] Petrus Urgellesii, archdeacon of Tortosa, died in curia temp. Urban V.

1364 (Coll. 119, 124ʳ) charges against the collector Fulco Pererii.

971] Petrus de Uxua OFM, bishop of Leon, died before 5 Mar 1375. M.Theol.; bishop from 1361.

22 Sep 1375 (EFR G2, 3480) asks the king of Navarre not to aid those who seized the goods.

972] Petrus de Valerianis, bishop of Mileto, died before 28 Nov 1373. Formerly canon of Reims; bishop of Mileto from 1348.

10 Mar 1375 (OS 42, 7ᵛ; IM 2877, 2) successor Thomas pays 200 fl. of a 500-fl. composition.

973] Petrus de Valle, physician, died in curia 1361.

17 Sep 1361 (VQ 7, 357) Eblo de Mederio, clericus Camerae, pays 60 fl.

974] Petrus le Vayer, abbot of Bourgeuil OSB, diocese of Angers, died 17 Apr 1371. Lic.Decr.: *Gall. Christ.* 14:663A-B.

1371 x 1372 (Coll. 257, 443ᵛ) collector Guido de Ruppe asks if he should collect the wine, the only movable.

975] Petrus Vera OP, bishop of Bethlehem. Formerly bishop of Zengg from 1346; of Bethlehem from 1347.

2 Aug 1356 (VQ 7, 134) executor Petrus Reconsini, commensal chaplain, pays 50 fl.

976] Petrus de Vernolis, bishop of Maguelonne and treasurer, died 3 Oct 1389. Formerly abbot of Aniane OSB, diocese of Maguelonne; papal treasurer from 1370, and bishop of Maguelonne from 1373.

Nov 1389 (IM 3337, 60) Joannes Joli, collector of Provence, pays 186 fl. Cam. 13 s.; banker Cathalonius de Rocha pays 945 fl. Cam. 6 s. 10 d. for silver vessels.

977] Petrus de Via, bishop of Albi, died 21 Aug 1337. Formerly archdeacon in the church of Narbonne, papal chaplain; bishop from 1334. See *Gall. Christ.* 1:25D-E.

3 Dec 1334 (EFR J1, 64224; Coll. 1, 3ʳᵛ) licentia testandi.
29 Aug 1337 (EFR B2, 360) commission to Raymundus de Cameraco and Pontius de Pereto to collect spoils and fruits of the vacancy.
9 Dec 1337 (ibid., 386) directs them to keep the balance after funeral expenses.
23 Dec 1338 (VQ 4, 137) Pontius de Pereto pays £3172.3.3.
1 Dec 1339 (ibid., 150) commissioners pay £1347.6.7.
13 Jan 1340 (ibid., 153) they pay £265.9.3.
14 Jul 1340 (ibid., 161) Pontius de Pereto assigns six rings.
26 Sep 1340 (ibid., 164) they pay 1 coron., £84.16.1.
27 Nov 1340 (ibid., 166) they pay £309.0.2.
27 Nov 1340 (ibid., 166-167) they pay £200.
29 Dec 1340 (ibid., 167-168) payment by Raymundus de Cameraco.
10 Nov 1341 (ibid., 184) he pays 327 écus.

25 Jun 1342 (VQ 5, 462) Raymundus Flori, collector of Bourges, pays from spoils.
Dec 1342 - Nov 1344 (Coll. 73, 69ʳ-72ᵛ; 105ʳ) Ademarus de Lobera, collector of Bourges, receives 144 fl., 84 écus, 28 agni etc.
27 Nov 1343 (VQ 5, 340) further payments.
1337-1343 (Coll. 1, 210 fols.; Coll. 2, 169 fols.) accounts.

978] Petrus de Vigono, canon of Embrun.

27 Jun 1350 (VQ 5, 438) executor pays 20 fl. of a 30-fl. composition.

979] Petrus Villani Parisius, bishop of Lombez, died before 10 Mar 1389. Formerly dean of Gap; auditor sacri palatii, LL.D., papal chaplain and familiar; bishop from 1382.

Apr 1389 (IM 3337, 49) executors pay the last 210 fl. of a 400-fl. composition.

980] Petrus Vincentii, prior of Peterlingen OClun, diocese of Lausanne.

10 Jan 1388 (Coll. 361, 24ʳ) instructions of camerarius.

981] Petrus Vitalis, primicerius of Lucca and Genoa, collector in Tuscany, died 20 Apr 1348.

3 Jul 1348 (EFR C2, 1681) Andreas de Tuderto appointed collector of Tuscany.
8 Sep 1348 (ibid., 1706) he is directed to investigate deposits with the Buonsignori of Siena.
1 May 1348 (ibid., 1989) he is directed to absolve the Sienese holders of goods.
n.d. (Coll. 114, 34ᵛ) Augerius de Offerans, collector of Castile and Leon, reports collections to a sum of 150 fl.

982] Philippus, bishop of Isernia.

16 Feb 1362 (Coll. 169, 131ᵛ) accounts.

983] Philippus, abbot of Montevergine OSB, diocese of Avellino.

22 Nov 1348 (Coll. 168, 74ᵛ) Guillelmus de Roseriis collects 3 car. for goods.

984] Philippus de Alensona, patriarch of Jerusalem and administrator of Auch, promoted cardinal by Urban VI in 1378 and despoiled by Clement VII in 1379. Formerly archdeacon of Brie, diocese of Mende; bishop of Beauvais from 1356; archbishop of Rouen from 1359; patriarch from 1375. Later captured by Clement VII, ca. 1390; died as collector of Tarbes and Oloron, 1397.

17 Jan 1367/8 (RA 161, 310-316) inventory of books of the archbishop of Rouen.

Jan 1379 (Coll. 359, 18^{rv}) camerarius orders Bertrandus, abbot of Simorre OSB, diocese of Auch, to give the collector the goods and spoils he holds, including those of earlier administrators of Auch.

1379 (Coll. 480, 21^r) Petrus Aegidii, subcollector of Aix, spent 93 fl. 10 gr. to transport 18 bundles of goods to Aix by pack animals, to Avignon by wagon.

31 May 1380 (Coll. 359, 41^{rv}) Arnaldus de Peyraco, collector, and Raymundus Bruni, bishop of Auch, directed to collect goods.

985] Philippus Arboisii, bishop of Tournai. Formerly dean of S. Donatien, Bruges, diocese of Tournai; bishop of Noyon from 1349; of Tournai from 1351.

4 Nov 1364 (IE 303, 23^v-24^r) Petrus Bori pays 700 fl.

28 Jun 1369 (Coll. 354, 74^v-75^r) note of a bull by Urban V reserving spoils, with the *moderatio*.

986] Philippus Blanche, archbishop of Tours, died before 25 Oct 1363. Formerly cantor of Avranches; archbishop from 1357.

Sep 1364 (IM 2339, 22) Petrus Bori, commissioner, pays 700 fl.

9 May 1375 (OS 42, 12^v) executor pays composition of 113 fl. 23 s. 5 d. to Guido de Ruppe, collector of Tours.

987] Philippus de Castilione, archbishop of Reggio in Calabria. Formerly canon of Cosenza; archbishop from 1354.

28 Dec 1357 (Coll. 352, 118^v) dispatch of a commission dated 14 Dec 1357 by hand of Reginaldus de Lupchaco, cantor of Auxerre, to himself and Petrus archbishop of Benevento.

988] Philippus de Gaston, archbishop of Bordeaux, died before 24 Sep 1361. Formerly canon of Tournai, LL.Prof.; bishop of Sion from 1338; of Nicosia from 1342; of Bordeaux from 1360.

13 Jan 1339 (EFR B1, 7030) licentia testandi.

2 Feb 1362 (OS 32A, 75^r) composition by the executors Raymundus and Aymericus de Chambarlaco for 10,000 fl.

7 Feb 1362 (OS 31, 143^r-144^r) note of composition of 10,000 fl. to be paid in three terms by 21 June 1363.

30 Apr 1362 (VQ 7, 399-400) executors pay 1500 fl.

30 Apr 1362 (OS 31, 144^v) quittance to executors for 2500 fl.

18 May 1362 (VQ 7, 403) subcollector Petrus Boraci pays 500 leopardi.

23 Jan 1363 (Coll. 497, 81^v) executors are granted delay of the payment of 5500 fl. of their composition.

5 Aug 1365 (OS 23A, 75ʳ) subcollector pays Joannes Garrigiae 80 m. of silverware.
7 Mar 1367 (Coll. 156, 41ʳ and 133ʳ) the abbot of S. Tiberius, diocese of Agde, pays 330 fl. for silverware.
27 Oct 1368 (IE 325, 24ʳᵛ) executors pay 1885 fl. of composition.
10 Jun 1372 (IM 2676, 40) Fredericus and Marcus de Venetiis pay 500 fl. of the executors' composition.
25 Sep 1375 (Coll. 356, 56ᵛ-57ʳ) executors released from excommunication; the debts were collected as the spoils of Raymundus, bishop of Nicosia.

989] Philippus Hombaldi OP, bishop of Girgenti, died before 12 May 1350. Bishop from 1328.

1 Jul 1354 (EFR I1, 1008) commission to Guillelmus, bishop of Mazzara.
1 Aug 1354 (ibid., 1045) the same commission.
12 Apr 1356 (Coll. 352, 117ʳ) dispatch of a commission to Martialis, bishop of Catania.

990] Philippus de Lancilla, bishop of Florence, died 1363. Formerly secular prior of S. Pietro, Florence; papal chaplain; bishop of Ferrara from 1349; of Florence from 1357.

7 Jan 1368 (Coll. 353, 92ᵛ-93ʳ) the bishops of Siena and Cesena are ordered to release the nephews from excommunication in consideration of their composition for 1500 fl.
5 Aug 1368 (Coll. 248, 31ʳ) Bartholomeus and Nascius, sons of Simon de Lancilla, pay 300 fl. of their composition.
8 Dec 1369 (ibid.) they pay 200 fl.
30 Sep 1370 (ibid., 31ᵛ) they pay 200 fl.

991] Philippus de Lemovicis, notary apostolic, died in curia.

29 Jan 1356 (VQ 7, 128) Geraldus de Podio Falconis, auditor sacri palatii, pays the last 40 fl. of a 45-fl. composition.

992] Philippus de Renestro, scriptor Poenitentiariae, died in curia.

7 Jun 1348 (VQ 5, 408) his clerk Stephanus Florentiae pays 20 fl. etc.

993] Philippus de S. Cruce, bishop of Mâcon, died before 3 Oct 1380. Formerly dean of Mâcon; bishop from 1360.

7 Oct 1380 (IM 5342, 1, 12 fols.) inventory at the order of the dean and chapter.
3-21 Oct 1380 (ibid., 2, 34 fols.) inventory at the order of collector Guillelmus de Lacu.

12 Oct 1381 (Coll. 359, 94ᵛ-95ʳ) collector ordered to receive the composition of the cousin Hugo de S. Cruce, and to observe the *moderatio*.

994] Pictavinus de Montesquieu, bishop of Maguelonne, whose goods were reserved when he was translated to Albi, 27 Jan 1339. Formerly cleric of Bazas; bishop of Bazas from 1325; of Maguelonne from 1334. Later created cardinal, 1350; died 1 Feb 1355.

2 Feb 1339 (EFR B2, 562) quittance to Almeracius de Cabrespino.
29 Mar 1339 (ibid., 582; Coll. 229, 28ʳ-32ᵛ) the same.
17 Dec 1339 (VQ 4, 152) he pays £203.4.8 of debts collected at Maguelonne.
30 Apr 1349 (VQ 5, 570) he and successor Arnaldus bishop of Maguelonne pay 175 fl. etc.

995] Pontius, abbot of Villemagne, diocese of Béziers. See *Gall. Christ.* 6:409A.

21 Jan 1387 (IM 5328) inventory by Raymundus Textoris, subcollector of Béziers.

996] Pontius, abbot of Foix OCSA, diocese of Pamiers.

1371 (Coll. 18, 290ᵛ) successor Bernardus Martini pays 433 fl. of a composition for 466 fl.
1371 (Coll. 235, 139ᵛ-140ᵛ) note of 33 fl. still due.
1 Oct 1372 (Coll. 236, 148ʳ, 156ᵛ) Aymericus Pelicerii reports the composition and remainder.

997] Pontius, provost of Maguelonne.

5 Aug 1365 (OS 23A, 122ʳ) subcollector pays collector Joannes Garrigiae 2 m.

998] Pontius Algeri de Laneis, bishop of Cavaillon, died before 19 Apr 1322. Bishop from 1311.

17 Dec 1322 - 31 Mar 1323 (VQ 1, 479-480) relatives and successor pay spoils.
31 Mar 1323 (EFR J2, 1658).

999] Pontius Beraldi, corrector litterarum apostolicarum.

Apr 1388 (IM 3337, 6) executors pay 80 fl. curr.

1000] Pontius de Canilhaco, abbot of Aniane OSB, diocese of Maguelonne. See *Gall. Christ.* 6:846D-E.

12 Oct 1361 (VQ 7, 361-362) subcollector Bertrandus Cabanerii receives the income of the church of Cellanova as part of spoils.

1001] Pontius Fabri, scriptor Papae, died in curia.

9 Sep 1360 (Coll. 231, 98ᵛ; VQ 7, 299) executors pay a composition of 30 fl. to Balduinus Ricardi, sigillifer auditoris Camerae.

1002] Pontius Ferreoli OCSA, abbot of S. Volusien de Foix, diocese of Pamiers. See *Gall. Christ.* 13:182C-D.

4 May 1339 (EFR B1, 7034) licentia testandi.
4 Nov 1346 (EFR C1, 2929) commission to Morerius de Moreriis.
10 Apr 1347 (Coll. 497, 32ʳᵛ) successor Bernardus is obligated to a composition of 2000 fl.
31 Dec 1347 (VQ 5, 398) he pays 1000 fl.
31 Dec 1348 (Coll. 497, 40ʳ) delay granted in payment of the balance.
15 Apr 1349 (VQ 5, 424) successor pays 300 fl.

1003] Pontius de Gardia OCSA, bishop of Mende, died before 22 Apr 1387. Formerly prior of S. Firmin, diocese of Montauban, notary apostolic; bishop from 1376.

16 Jul 1387 (Coll. 359, 229ʳ-230ʳ) camerarius notes that the nephew is obligated to a composition of 400 fr. for goods in an inventory.
19 Jul 1387 (Coll. 362, 57ᵛ-58ʳ) he directs Pontius de Cros, collector of Le Puy and Mende, to secure the deathbed gifts not mentioned in the inventory.
Mar 1388 (IM 3337, 1) Pontius de Chaldayraco, camerarius of Aniane, nephew and executor, pays 60 fr.
Jun 1388 (ibid., 10) he pays the last 200 fr. of the composition.

1004] Pontius Mitte, abbot of S. Antoine Chef de l'Ordre, diocese of Vienne, died 1374. Formerly precentor of Lyon: *Gall. Christ.* 16:198D-E.

30 Nov 1339 (EFR B1, 7044) licentia testandi.
Oct 1375 (IM 2877, 8) sale of grain yields 342 fl. 24 s.
26 Aug 1376 (IM 2924, 6; OS 42, 87ʳ) successor Bertrandus pays the last 1300 fl. of a 2000-fl. composition.

1005] Pontius Pelaprati, canon of Embrun.

20 Feb 1346 (VQ 5, 509) Stephanus Planterius, collector of Embrun, pays 34 fl Flor., 44 fl. Pied.

1006] Pontius de Pereto, bishop of Orvieto, died in curia before 8 Oct 1360. Formerly archdeacon in the diocese of Chartres.

17 Sep 1361 (VQ 7, 357) Eblo de Mederio, clericus Camerae, pays 396 fl., 21 s.
18 Mar 1365 (IM 2393) successor Petrus requests the return of goods.

18 Jan 1367 (OS 38A, 10^{rv}) camerarius orders Guillelmus de Lordato to force the commune of Orvieto to pay 1500 fl. owed to the late bishop.

1007] Pontius de Ruppeforte de Aurosa, bishop of S. Flour. Formerly dean of S. Brieuc; bishop from 1374.

11 Jan 1383 - (Coll. 85, 260^r-272^v) accounts of subcollector Stephanus Alberti.

1008] Pontius Saturnini, canon of Béziers, administrator operum palatii apostolici.

11 Apr 1349 (VQ 5, 423) Joannes Belli pays 1 fl. for goods.

1009] Pontius de Ulmo, abbot of S. Victor, Marseille, died in curia 1382. See *Gall. Christ.* **1:693D.**

28 Mar 1383 (Coll. 360, 40^r-41^r) camerarius directs subcollector Vitalis Guillelmi and sergeant at arms Begotus de Costa to secure the goods without delay.
4 Mar 1384 (Coll. 359, 200^v-201^r) Vencianus de Croso, camerarius of S. Victor, and the almoner of Montmajour are ordered to observe the *moderatio* and grants to the successor.

1010] Pontius de Villamura, bishop of Couserans, died before 19 Aug 1370. Formerly abbot of S. Antoine de Lésat OClun, diocese of Rieux; bishop from 1362.

1364 (RA 157, 47^r) licentia testandi, rubric.
30 Jul 1372 (Coll. 358, 72^r) goods collected against a 300-fl. condemnation in the audientia sacri palatii.
1 Nov 1375 (Coll. 34, 55^v-69^v) spoils and vacancy, accounts by Guillelmus de Ruppe, subcollector of Couserans.
19 Oct 1379 (Coll. 359, 100^v) Arnaldus de Peyraco sold to Robertus de Ruppe, for 300 fl., the right to the spoils of Pontius and his predecessor; tha Camera confirmed the sale on 20 Dec 1381.
Jan 1382 (ibid., 104^r) the buyer is empowered to collect the spoils.

1011] Pontius de Villanova, abbot of S. Marie d'Arles, diocese of Elne, died 4 Jun 1403. See *Gall. Christ.* **6:1091E-1092A.**

before 1405 (Coll. 160, 123^v) Joannes de Ripis Altis, collector of Elne, made a composition with administrator Petrus Ros for £100 Barc., plus £50 for the fruits of the vacancy.

1012] Prosperus de Pistorio, died in curia.

18 Jun 1347 (VQ 5, 390) commissioner Petrus Chautardi pays 50 fl.

1013] Radolfanus, archdeacon of Sebenico.

1374 (Coll. 129, 247ᵛ) Raymundus, bishop of Padua, collector of Lombardy, pays 12 ducats.

1014] Radolphus, dean of Gaya OClun, diocese of Troyes, died in curia.

5 Jul 1322 (EFR J2, 1465).
18 Aug 1323 (ibid., 1772; VQ 1, 464) Philippus Raynerii of the Bardi company pays 300 fl.; Bertrandus de Narcesio pays 600 fl. for his brother Armandus, the successor, who bought the spoils.
See Mollat in RHE 29 (1933): 337 n. 4.

1015] Radolphus de Castello OESA, bishop of Sinigaglia, died before 5 Jul 1375. M.Theol.; bishop from 1370.

11 Aug 1375 (OS 42, 27ʳ; IM 2877, 5) Philippus de Marsiliis, Florentine merchant at Avignon, pays 620 fr. for the goods left in deposit with him.

1016] Radolphus de Chissiaco, archbishop of Tarentaise, died 1385. Formerly canon of Geneva; bishop of Grenoble from 1350; archbishop of Tarentaise from 1380.

10 Feb 1372! (EFR G1, 648) premature commission to Aubricus Radolphi and Durandus Clavelli to collect the spoils of Radolphus, former bishop of Grenoble.
12 Dec 1385 (Coll. 361, 22ʳᵛ) commission.
28 Dec 1386 (Coll. 362, 20ᵛ) quittance to the prior and chapter for a mitre, crozier and ring.
28 Dec 1386 (ibid., 20ᵛ-21ʳ) quittance to Amblardus de Bellomonte, domicellus, for a debt of 100 fl.
28 Dec 1386 (ibid., 21ʳᵛ) Michael Coqueti de Vermone is obligated to pay a debt of 100 fl.
8 Mar 1387 (ibid., 32ᵛ-33ʳ) 300 fl. of the heirs' composition is released for repairs to the church.
11 Mar 1387 (ibid., 33ᵛ) the composition is reduced to 100 fl.
1 Aug 1387 (ibid., 58ᵛ) Joannes Blasini, canon of Tarentaise, assigns certain goods.
9 Sep 1387 (ibid., 73ᵛ-74ʳ) Joannes Chicoti, collector of Grenoble, is ordered to collect debts there.

1017] Ranulphus Jordani, provost "de Baciaco" OSB, diocese of Saintes.

5 Nov 1331 - (IE 105, 46ʳ-48ᵛ) accounts.
1 Feb 1334 (ibid., 65ʳᵛ) assignments.

1018] Ranulphus de Valignaco, secular abbot of S. Sernin, diocese of Toulouse, died 1376. See *Gall. Christ.* 13:97D.

n.d. (Coll. 236, 323^v-324^r) note of collections by Aymericus Pelicerii.
1376 (Coll. 235, 144^v) successor Petrus is obligated to a composition of 400 fl.

1019] Ratherius de Buscoducis (von Herzogenbusch) dictus Rex, died in curia.

4 Sep 1357 (VQ 7, 182) executors pay a composition of 30 fl.

1020] Ratherius de Penna, provost of S. Sauve, diocese of Albi.

8 Apr 1353 x 8 Apr 1355 (Coll. 73, 230^r) collector Joannes de Palmis receives 10 fl., 10 écus, etc.
before 15 May 1358 (Coll. 76, 75^r) a composition of 150 fl. by Bertrandus de Penna was paid to Joannes de Palmis: account of the collector's successor Geraldus Mercaderii.

1021] Raymundus, bishop of Coimbra, died 15 Jul 1324. Formerly dean of Coimbra; bishop from 1318.

11 Nov 1319 (EFR J1, 10657) licentia testandi.
1 Jan 1327 (OS 12, 103^v-104^r) quittance to Petrus de Brunia.

1022] Raymundus, bishop of Rodez, died before 2 Aug 1361. Formerly abbot of Grasse, diocese of Carcassonne, papal familiar; bishop from 1349.

20 Dec 1361 (VQ 7, 377; OS 23A, 110^r) Fayditus, the bishop's brother, executor and successor, pays a composition of 2000 fl.

1023] Raymundus, abbot of S. Michel de Cuxá, diocese of Elne, died 1357. See *Gall. Christ.* 6:1103C.

n.d. (Coll. 156, 186^r) successor Bertrandus is obligated to a composition of 150 fl.
30 Oct 1358 (VQ 7, 227) he pays 150 fl.

1024] Raymundus, abbot of Sorèze, diocese of Lavaur, died 1361.

1361 (Coll. 235, 78^r) 158fl., etc. received from spoils.
1364 (ibid., 121^r) 190 fl. etc. received.
1371 (Coll. 18, 214^r) successor Philippus pays 181 fl. 4 gr. of a composi-

tion of 341 fl. 6 gr. to Bertrandus de Castanherio and Aymericus Pelicerii.

1 Oct 1373 (Coll. 236, 147ᵛ, 156ʳ) Aymericus Pelicerii reports a balance remaining of 159 fl. 1 gr. 9 Barc.

1025] Raymundus OSB, abbot of S. Guillem du Desert, diocese of Lodève, died 1361. See *Gall. Christ.* 6:597B.

1368 x 1377 (Coll. 157, 184ᵛ) collector Arnaldus Andreae reports no receipts, because successor Petrus made a composition in the Camera.

1026] Raymundus de Argentico, abbot of S. Gilles, diocese of Nîmes. See *Gall. Christ.* 6:500.

18 Nov 1361 (Coll. 497, 76ᵛ) successor Arnaldus is obligated to a composition of 200 fl.

1027] Raymundus Athon OCSA, bishop of Mirepoix, died 25 Feb 1326. Formerly abbot of S. Sernin, Toulouse; bishop from 1318. See *Gall. Christ.* 13:267A-268A.

26 Feb 1325 (EFR J1, 21655) licentia testandi.
7 Mar 1326 (IE 83, 65ʳ-86ᵛ) commission and accounts of Arnaldus de Verdala.
8 Apr 1326 (EFR J2, 2755-2756).
1 Aug 1326 (ibid., 2939-2941).
7 Jan 1327 (ibid., 3115; VQ 1, 526) Arnaldus de Verdala and Joannes Regafredi pay 1476 agni, 135 fl.
27 Mar 1327 (EFR J2, 3195).
30 Nov 1335 (EFR B2, 122) general quittance to Arnaldus de Verdala.

1028] Raymundus de Ayraga, precentor of Arles.

17 May 1327 (VQ 1, 518) Raymundus de Moreriis pays £7.16.4 Tur. gr. etc.

1029] Raymundus Barrani OP, commensal chaplain, died in curia.

11 Oct 1340 (VQ 4, 164) Joannes Maurelli, sigillifer auditoris Camerae, pays 97 fl. etc.

1030] Raymundus de Belleria OSB, bishop of Vich, died 10 Jun 1377. Formerly monk of S. Michel de Cuxá, diocese of Elne; bishop from 1352.

10 Oct 1373 (EFR G2, 2229) premature commission to Jacobus de Sirano and Petrus Cavalerii.
19 Jun and 4-6 Jul 1377 (IM 2971) collector's inquest.

1031] Raymundus de Bernadone, rector "de Ravennaco," diocese of Alet.

15 Dec 1336 (EFR B2, 250) commission.

1032] Raymundus Bernardi de Mota, bishop of Bazas. Formerly canon of Bazas; bishop from 1348.

26 Sep 1354 (RA 128, 599^r) licentia testandi.
19 Feb 1358 (VQ 7, 218) executor pays a composition of 50 fl.
18 Dec 1363 (EFR U2, 721) orders the bishop of Agen and officiales of Auch and Aix to regain the goods from holders.

1033] Raymundus de Biscotio Cambavelha, bishop of Lectoure, died before 9 Oct 1405.

n.d. (RA 325, 197^r-198^r) books distributed by Joannes Romani.

1034] Raymundus Bot, bishop of Apt, died Jan 1330. Formerly operarius of Apt; bishop from 1319.

15 Oct 1326 (EFR J1, 26735) licentia testandi.
27 Jun 1330 (OS 12, 128^{rv}) the executors were obligated to a composition of 831 fl. remaining after legacies; they paid in full.

1035] Raymundus de Bulbone, abbot of Montmajour OSB, diocese of of Arles, died 17 Feb 1348. Formerly camerarius of Montmajour. *Gall. Christ.* 1:613.

20 Jan 1348 (EFR C1, 3693) commission to Petrus Joannis, prior of S. Remi, diocese of Avignon.
28 Feb 1348 (VQ 5, 549) Petrus Joannis pays £10.
15 Apr 1348 (Coll. 497, 37^v; OS 23, 16^r) successor Petrus de Cavilhaco is obligated to a composition of 600 fl.
22 May 1348 (ibid., 412) he pays 300 fl.
24 Sep 1350 (ibid., 439-440) priests of Arles pay 50 fl. for grain.

1036] Raymundus de Cameraco, bishop of Orvieto, vicar in Rome. Formerly canon of Amiens, Lic.Decr., scriptor litterarum apostolicarum; bishop of Rieti from 1342; of Orvieto from 1346; vicar of Rome from 1343.

20 Aug 1348 (Coll. 232, 158^r-173^v) inventory.
26 May 1352 (VQ 5, 454) 220 fl. paid.
18-20 Mar 1365 (IM 2393) bishop Petrus seeks the return of some goods.

1037] Raymundus de Caunis, dean of Tours, collector of Tours.

17 Aug 1352 (EFR C1, 5385) commission to Petrus Belmondi.
n.d. (Coll. 255, 123^r-126^v) goods held by Petrus Belmondi.

1038] Raymundus Draconis OESA, bishop of Pamiers, died in curia. M.Theol.; bishop of Toulon from 1361; of Fréjus from 1364; of Pamiers from 1371.

28 Feb 1380 (Coll. 359, 166^{rv}) Aymericus Pelicerii is ordered to send money to Avignon to pay debts in the curia.

9 May 1380 (ibid., 30^v-31^r) he is ordered to pay Gilbertus de Dittinghem 900 fl.

11 May 1380 (ibid., 31^v-32^v) commission to Audibertus de Fauso, provost of Pignans, with a closed letter to Aymericus Pelicerii.

20 Jun 1380 (Coll. 358, 149^r) commissioner is ordered to pay a debt of 900 fl. to Gilbertus de Dittinghem, papal secretary.

23 Jun 1380 (ibid., 149^v) collector Arnaldus Pelicerii is ordered to collect only 300 fr. and end his execution; the remaining spoils will not cover the debts.

1380 (IM 4746) camerarius demands accounts.

1380 (Coll. 235, 144^v) "nihil fuit receptum quia gentes comitis Fuxi omnia receperunt de facto"; marginal note: "at quare non fuerunt facti processus soliti per Cameram?"

n.d. (Coll. 236, 324^r) "Dominus comes Fuxi debet omnia bona et spolia ... que recepit sine extimatione sua propria auctoritate."

1039] Raymundus de Duroforti, bishop of Périgueux, died 1 May 1341. Formerly archdeacon of Périgueux; bishop from 1314.

11 Mar 1341 (EFR B2, 820) reservation in anticipation of death.

9 May 1341 (EFR B2, 837; B3, 3080) commission to Joannes Bertrandi and Guillelmus Ruffi.

30 May 1341 (EFR B1, 9204) processes by commissioners.

9 Jun 1341 (Coll. 428, 3^r-15^r) inquest by Joannes Bertrandi and Guillelmus Ruffi.

1 May 1341 - (Coll. 197, 12^r-18^v) accounts of vacancy by Joannes Bertrandi and Guillelmus Ruffi.

18 Jul - 28 Jul 1341 (EFR B1, 9211-9216; IM 1575-1582) warning by Joannes Bertrandi and Berengarius Blasini against holders of goods; protest by nephews on the ground of custom.

8 Aug 1341 (EFR B2, 873; B3, 3156) orders executors to hold goods for commissioners.

1 Dec 1341 (VQ 4, 185) nephews' deposits with cardinal Galhardus de Mota paid to the Camera: 3249 regal., 1150 écus.

27 Sep 1342 (ibid., 471) commissioners assign four rings.

28 Oct 1342 (ibid., 464-465) Morerius de Moreriis pays goods deposited at S. Sernin, Toulouse.

1342 (Coll. 30, 151^r-152^r) accounts of Morerius de Moreriis.

1353 (RA 122, 261^v) books in papal treasure.

1040] Raymundus Ebrardi, bishop of Coimbra, died before 3 Jul 1333. Former dean of Coimbra; bishop from 1325.

23 Apr 1327 (EFR J1, 28503) licentia testandi.
10 May 1335 (EFR B3, 869) commission.

1041] Raymundus de Engolisma, elect of Saintes, died in curia before 16 May 1362.

1 Jun 1362 (VQ 7, 407-408) executor Guillelmus de Ruppe pays 500 fl. composition.

1042] Raymundus Fabri, canon of S. Seurin, Bordeaux, papal treasurer.

17 Oct, 20 Nov 1317 (IM 619) inventory of goods at Bordeaux.

1043] Raymundus de Falgueriis, abbot of Joucou OSB, diocese of Alet.

1403 x 1406 (Coll. 159, 94^v-97^r) Joannes Martini, collector of Narbonne, receives £19.2.4.

1044] Raymundus Folcaudi, abbot of Grasse OSB, diocese of Carcassonne. See *Gall. Christ.* 6:959C.

18 Apr 1363 (OS 31, 175^v) camerarius orders collector Joannes Garrigie to yield pontificalia to successor Guido.
28 Nov 1363 (OS 31, 207^{rv}; OS 23A) successor Guido is obligated to a composition of 1500 fl., noted paid; another composition of 1900 fl. also noted paid.
12 Jun 1364 (Coll. 156, 214^v) successor pays 250 fl.

1045] Raymundus Garciae, canon of S. Bertrand de Comminges, subcollector of Comminges.

1 Oct 1373 (Coll. 236, 252^r) Aymericus Pelicerii, collector of Toulouse, reports 10 fl. 4 gr. 52 1/2 écus still to be collected.

1046] Raymundus Gastonis, bishop of Valencia, died 19 Jun 1348. Bishop from 1312.

4 May 1318 (EFR J1, 7120) licentia testandi.
23 Jun 1348 (EFR C2, 1679) orders Petrus de Moncellis and Jacobus Romaci to collect spoils.
29 Aug 1348 (ibid., 1699) commission to Antonius de Alpitato, canon of Valencia.
7 Apr 1349 (VQ 5, 423) commissioners pay 1000 fl.
10 Jul 1350 (EFR C2, 2242) orders Jacobus, bishop of Tortosa, to investigate injuries done to commissioner Antonius by the justice, jury and council of Valencia in the spoils process.
8 Oct 1350 (VQ 5, 440) commissioners pay 6000 fl.
20 Jul 1354 (VQ 7, 55-56; OS 23A, 97^r) they pay the last 1166 2/3 fl.
1358 (Coll. 114, 13^r) accounts of Fulco Pererii.
after 1362 (Coll. 116, 63^r) arrears of spoils collected, £33.6.8 Barc.

1047] Raymundus Gaufridi de Castellane, bishop of S. Paul-Trois-Châteaux, died before 10 Nov 1378. Formerly provost of Aix; bishop from 1367.

8 Mar 1380 (Coll. 359, 23^r) grain granted to Antonius de Ponte, banker.

1048] Raymundus Gauserandi, conversus of Fontfroid OCist, diocese of Narbonne, bullator, died in curia.

8 Apr 1344 (EFR C2, 761) licentia testandi.
28 Jan 1360 (VQ 7, 292) Petrus de Frigidavilla, administrator of the Pinhota, and Hugo de Podio, abbreviator, executors, pay 200 fl., Raymundus's share of a loss by theft from the emoluments of the papal bull during his lifetime.

1049] Raymundus Gileti, bishop of Sulcis and collector of Sardinia, died before 8 Jun 1359. Formerly canon of Cagliari; bishop from 1349.

before 24 Oct 1361 (Coll. 117, 175^v) collector Fulco Pererii receives £158.11 owed by citizens of Barcelona.

1050] Raymundus de Gramat OClun, bishop of Montecassino, died 26 Jul 1340. Formerly prior of Paray-le-Monial; bishop from 1326.

17 Aug 1340 (EFR B3, 2851) commission to Geraldus de Valle and Arnulphus Marcellini.
23 Sep 1340 (EFR B1, 8325; IM 1523) Geraldus de Valle reports resistance by the chapter and interference by Guillelmus de S. Paulo.
5 Dec 1340 (EFR B1, 8280; B3, 2961; Coll. 95, 1^r-2^r) commission to Raymundus de Cameraco and Pontius de Pereto.
12 Dec 1340 (EFR B2, 796; B3, 2967-2968) commission presented by the camerarius.
12 Dec 1340 - (Coll. 95, 72 fols.) accounts of commissioners.
1340 (IM 6598) narrative by successor Guigo de S. Germano of spoils and the election of Jacobus de Plumbarola.
13 Mar 1341 (EFR B2, 824) asks King Robert of Naples to recover goods robbed from commissioners.
17 Mar 1341 (EFR B3, 3029) account of the robbery of spoils.
15 Apr 1341 (EFR B2, 831) thanks the king for recovering goods and punishing the robbers.
28 Jun 1341 (VQ 4, 179-180) commissioners pay through the Buonacorsi company 15,797 fl., 601 ducats etc.; through the Acciaiuoli, 12,998 fl., 601 ducats etc.
28 Aug 1341 (EFR B3, 3172) instructions to Raymundus de Cameraco and Pontius de Pereto.

11 Oct 1341 (EFR B3, 3212) orders them to hold an inquest against accused holders of goods.
26 Oct 1343 (Coll. 168, 14ʳ) debts collected by Guillelmus de Roseriis.
29 Feb 1344 (EFR C2, 422) goods taken by a monk of Cluny.
21 Jul 1345 or 1346 (Coll. 95, 66ʳ) letter of Raymundus de Cameraco, bishop of Rieti and vicar in Rome, disclaiming responsibility for the books.

1051] Raymundus de Jarjaya, prior of S. M. de Mandanays OSB, diocese of Gap.

5 Apr 1351 (EFR C1, 4943) commission.

1052] Raymundus de Lancanta, scriptor Papae, died in curia.

27 Sep 1357 (VQ 7, 182) executors pay a composition of 25 fl.

1053] Raymundus Magistri, scriptor Papae, died in curia.

Jun 1375 (IM 2877, 4) executors pay a composition of 50 fl.

1054] Raymundus Manoelli, Lic.Decr., subcollector of Mende.

1396 (Coll. 85, 330ʳ-371ᵛ) goods collected against debts to the Camera.

1055] Raymundus Monnerii, rector of Tarascon, diocese of Pamiers.

10 Mar 1377 (OS 42, 98ᵛ) Raymundus, bishop of Pamiers, pays the last 50 fr. of a 100-fr. composition.

1056] Raymundus Naulonis, canon and archdeacon of Aix, collector of Aix.

6 Jul 1366 (EFR U2, 2313) commission to Geraldus Mercaderii.

1057] Raymundus de Olarga, bishop of Vabres. Formerly prior "de Vernia" OSB, diocese of Rodez; bishop from 1329.

23 Oct 1347 (EFR C1, 3549) commission to officialis of Vabres and Raymundus de Mayrento, cleric of Saintes.
6 Feb 1348 (VQ 5, 401) Raymundus de Domeyrenco pays.

1058] Raymundus de Oppeda de Avinione, bishop of Sisteron, died before 31 Oct 1328. Formerly canon of Sisteron; bishop from 1310.

12 Mar 1329 (OS 12, 103ʳ) quittance to successor Rostagnus for 500 fl. of a 1000-fl. composition.
21 Apr 1329 (ibid., 105ᵛ) he pays 200 fl.
31 May 1329 (ibid., 107ᵛ) he pays 300 fl.; cf. VQ 1, 539.

1059] Raymundus Pallaysinae, canon of Montroyale, diocese of Carcassonne; rector "de Garmasia," diocese of Narbonne; familiar of the cardinal of Montolieu, Guillelmus de Aura; died in curia.

10 Mar 1350 (VQ 5, 434) Rogerius Picarella, the cardinal's camerarius, commissioner, pays 38 fl. Fl., 30 fl. Pied.
11 Mar 1354 (VQ 7, 48) the goods were said to be confiscated; the arrears of his salary were paid to the Camera by the commissioner.

1060] Raymundus de Podio, bishop of Agde, died 1331. Bishop from 1296.

13 Jul 1312 (Regesta Clementis V, 8239) licentia testandi.
before Easter 1333 (IE 83, 157^{rv}) executors pay Arnaldus de Verdala a composition of £200.
3 Feb 1334 (VQ 1, 371) he pays Camera £200.
30 Nov 1335 (EFR B2, 122) general quittance to Arnaldus de Verdala.

1061] Raymundus de Pradella, archbishop of Nicosia, died in curia. Formerly canon of Gerona; archbishop from 1361.

Aug 1375 (IM 2877, 5) money found in chests with cardinal Petrus de Monteruco: 7285 fl. 15 s. 3 d.
Sep 1375 (ibid., 7) three merchants pay 5823 fl. 49 s.
25 Sep 1375 (Coll. 356, 56^v-57^r) calls for money held by the archbishop as the spoils of Philippus, archbishop of Bordeaux.
Oct 1375 (IM 2877, 8) three payments to Camera, total 403 fl. 35 s. 3 d.
Aug 1376 (IM 2924, 6) sale of silver yields 4124 fl. 6 s. 3 d.
26 Sep 1376 (Coll. 358, 177^v) utensils granted to Guillelmus de Belloforti, viscount of Turenne.
30 Sep 1376 (OS 42, 57^{rv}) Paulus Matthei, Florentine banker, pays 1967 fl. 25 s. Cam., 2333 fl. 8 s. comm. for goods.
12 Apr 1380 (Coll. 359, 25^r) Raymundus bishop of Paphos, collector of Cyprus, is ordered to pay 7000 fl. Cam. to Garnonetus de Abzado, knight.
12 Apr 1380 (ibid., 359^{rv}) he is ordered to pay Fulconetus de Sarvallo, former squire, 200 ducats.

1062] Raymundus de Pratis, bishop of Clermont, died 1 Apr 1340. Formerly bishop of Couserans; of Clermont from 1336.

1 Apr 1340 (EFR B1, 7930) licentia testandi.
9 Apr 1340 (EFR B2, 714) commission.

1063] Raymundus Renouardi, almoner of S. Victor, Marseille.

28 Jul 1350 (Coll. 497, 44^r) successor Bernardus Fabri is obligated to a composition of 300 fl.

31 Oct 1351 (VQ 5, 449) he pays 100 fl.
29 Nov 1352 (ibid., 460) he pays 100 fl.

1064] Raymundus de Roccacorna, bishop of S. Pons de Thomières, died 1345. Formerly abbot of Gaillac OSB, diocese of Albi; bishop of Sarlat from 1318; of S. Pons from 1324.

7 Aug 1319 (EFR J1, 9921) licentia testandi.
21 Jul 1337 (EFR B1, 4697) licentia testandi.
19 Jan 1345 (EFR C1, 1800) commission.
21 Jan 1346 (ibid., 2284) notice to Morerius de Moreriis that the spoils are reserved.

1065] Raymundus de Salgis, patriarch of Antioch, administrator of Agen. Former dean of Paris, D.Decr., papal chaplain; bishop of Elne from 1357; archbishop of Embrun from 1361; patriarch in administration of Elne from 1364.

6 Jun 1375 (Coll. 356, 25^{rv}) commission to Bertrandus Raymundi, subcollector of Uzés, and Joannes, canon of Tulle.
5 Jul 1375 (ibid., 36^v-37^v) heirs are obligated to a composition of 500 fl.
5 Jul 1375 (ibid., 38^{rv}) they are empowered to collect.
20 Aug 1375 (ibid., 43^v) cancels debt of domicellus Arnaldus de Montrial, 108 fr.
24 Jul 1375 (OS 42, 22^v) heir Petrus de Salgnis pays 250 fl. of the composition with books and horses, 117 fl. cash.
n.d. (Coll. 235, 145^r) Aymericus Pelicerii reports that the accounts were not prepared by the late subcollector; marginal note: "non videtur sufficere ista excusio quoniam collector debuisti in hiis diligenter adhibere et supplere illud quod subcollector non potuit facere."
n.d. (Coll. 236, 323^v, 324^r) Aymericus Pelicerii notes collections and arrears.

1066] Raymundus de Salis, domicellus and familiar of Benedict XII, died in curia.

13 Oct 1340 (VQ 4, 164) Guillelmus Bos, clericus Camerae, pays 21 fl.

1067] Raymundus de S. Gemma, bishop of Chartres, died 5 Dec 1374. Formerly dean in the church of Castres, LL.D., notary apostolic; bishop from 1364.

23 Jul 1375 (OS 42, 23^r) Bertrandus Raffini pays 480 fr.
Aug 1375 (IM 2877, 5) Guido, bishop of Poitiers, pays 3 fl. for books.
12 Sep 1376 (ibid., 86^r) executors Raymundus de Senancio and Bertrandus Raffini pay 327 fr. 3 gr.

1068] Raymundus Saqueti, archbishop of Lyon, died before 14 Jul 1358. Formerly dean of Beauvais, LL.D.; bishop of Thérouanne from 1334; archbishop of Lyon from 1356.

2 Jan 1361 (VQ 7, 331) commissioner Bertrandus, bishop of Comminges, pays 80 fl. 17 s. 4 d. for books.

1 Apr 1365 (Coll. 353, 35^{rv}) camerarius orders collector Aymericus Pelicerii to compel payment of 1400 fl. from the spoils to cardinal Aegidius de Monteacuto.

1069] Raymundus de Serinhaco, abbot of Psalmody OSB, diocese of Nîmes.

18 Aug 1317 (EFR J1, 4789) licentia testandi.
19 Jan 1344 (EFR C1, 626) commission.
26 Feb 1344 (Coll. 497, 23^v) successor is obligated to a composition of 2000 fl.
31 Mar 1344 (VQ 5, 346) successor Guillelmus pays 1000 fl. of his composition.
6 Sep 1344 (ibid., 351-352) he pays 500 fl.
18 Dec 1344 (ibid., 353) he pays 500 fl.
n.d. (EFR C2, 534) treasurers are directed to seek information about missing goods.

1070] Raymundus de Valle, canon of Rodez, abbreviator litterarum apostolicarum.

1404 x 1407 (Coll. 91, 337^v) collector Petrus Berengas reports no collections, because the canon had a licentia testandi.

1071] Raymundus de Valle, archdeacon of S. Serenus, diocese of Cahors, notary and familiar, died 9 Aug 1347.

5 Apr 1330 (EFR J1, 49104) licentia testandi.
21 Aug 1347 (VQ 5, 394) heir Raymundus de Valle and executors Arnaldus de Moleria and Gaubertus de Septemfontibus pay 500 fl. composition.
15 Sep 1347 (EFR C1, 3440) commission to Raymundus de Palmis to collect debts, half for the Camera and half for the heirs.
2 May - 14 Jun 1348 (Coll. 74, 74^v-75^v, 156^r) Joannes de Palmis collects £116.19.9.

1072] Raynerius, bishop of Acerra, died before 14 Dec 1357. Formerly cantor of Acerra; bishop from 1348.

28 Dec 1357 (Coll. 352, 118^v) dispatch by hand of Reginaldus de Lupchaco of a commission dated 14 Dec 1357, to himself and Petrus archbishop of Benevento.

1073] Raynerius, prior of S. Salvatore, Bologna.

1374 (Coll. 129, 228ʳ) sales yield 570 ducats 10 s.

1074] Reginaldus, abbot of S. M. La Réau OCSA, diocese of Poitiers.

12 Aug 1384 (Coll. 359, 223ʳᵛ) camerarius directs Joannes Francisci to give the spoils to the successor Joannes in consideration of a composition.

1075] Reginaldus Malibernardi, papal treasurer, bishop of Autun, died 21 Jul 1361. Formerly archdeacon in the church of Lyon; bishop of Palencia from 1353; of Lisbon from 1356; of Autun from 1358.

24 Dec 1361 (VQ7, 379) Nicolaus Grimaldi de Luca pays 3263 fl. 5 s.
20 Jan 1362 (OS 31, 152ᵛ-154ᵛ) accounts and composition by nephew and successor Goffridus David Pauteix.
17 Apr 1363 (EFR U2, 367) the procurator fiscal is ordered to assign the spoils to the successor.
ca. 1370 (Arm. 33, to. 18, 24ʳ) collector Bertrandus de Macello reports receipts at Lisbon of £120, balance due of £146.6.8; cf. Martène, *Thesaurus novus anecdotorum* 2: 1042.
4 Mar 1363 (IE 303, 10ᵛ) successor pays 51 fl.

1076] Reginaldus de Molinis, elect of Nevers, died in curia. Formerly archdeacon in the church of Sens; elect to Nevers 6 Nov 1359.

28 Nov 1360 (Coll. 231, 109ʳ; VQ 7, 302) executor pays a composition of 100 fl.

1077] Ricanus Corvi, condominus of Albagnan.

4 Aug 1362 (OS 31, 158ᵛ) spoils released to his relatives.

1078] Ricardus de Drax Anglicus, advocatus, died in curia.

17 Sep 1361 (VQ 7, 357) Eblo de Mederio, clericus Camerae, pays 187 fl.

1079] Rigaldus, abbot of Bonneval OCist, diocese of Rodez. See *Gall. Christ.* 1:261A.

15 Nov 1381 (Coll. 359, 98ᵛ-99ʳ) collector Guillelmus Amarinti is directed to give the bearer, Michael de Viridario, the 390 fr. 20 s. 18 d. listed in his inventory.
22 Sep 1382 (ibid., 185ʳᵛ) collector Raymundus de Senancio is directed to end his processes and lift excommunication from the successor, prior, and subprior.

1080] Rigaldus Guiscardi, castellanus of Pont-Sorge, diocese of Avignon.

20 Nov 1361 (VQ 7, 371-372) his brother and heir Petrus pays 500 fl. composition.

1081] Robertus, bishop of Tropea, died before 14 Jun 1357. Bishop from 1322.

14 Dec 1360 (Coll. 169, 105^r) goods collected for the nuncio Petrus, archbishop of Benevento.

1082] Robertus de Coos, bishop of Calahorra. Formerly provost of Soissons; bishop of Laon from 1351; of Calahorra from 1362.

25 Sep 1372 (EFR G2, 1029) commission to Arnaldus Andreae.
4 Jul 1381 (Coll. 359, 73^r-74^r) collector is directed to gather 1000 fl. owed to the Camera.

1083] Robertus Darby, rector of a parochial church.

Oct 1375 (IM 2887, 8) 200 fl. paid.

1084] Robertus de Mandagoto, bishop of Marseille, died 1358. Formerly provost of Yzés, D.Decr.; bishop from 1344.

5 Apr 1359 (VQ 7, 261) executor Andreas Saonis pays 600 fl.
1 Jun 1359 (ibid., 264) collector Guillelmus de Balma pays 100 fl.
18 May 1360 (ibid., 295) he pays 300 fl.

1085] Robertus Paynel, bishop of Nantes, died 23 Feb 1366. Formerly canon of Orléans; bishop of Tréguier from 1353; of Nantes from 1354.

16 Apr 1366 (EFR U2, 2202) commission to Guido de Ruppe.
14 Nov 1366 x 20 Oct 1372 (Coll. 257, 439^{rv}) report of the collector Guido de Ruppe: the goods in his inventory were worth less than the debts and *moderatio*; he could find no agent willing to act in the execution, and did not undertake it himself. Marginal note: "de hoc debuisti petere et optinere licentiam a domino Camerario."

1086] Robertus Sustede, advocatus, died in curia.

31 Jul 1375 (OS 42, 27^v) Adam de Eston, monk of Norwich, executor, pays 400 fl. composition.

1087] Robertus de Tresk, advocatus, died in curia.

11 Oct 1350 (VQ 5, 441) Goffridus, servant and heir, pays a composition of 60 fl.

1088] Robertus de Voia, bishop of Lavaur, died before 8 Oct 1383. Formerly provost of Fréjus; bishop of Lodève from 1348; of Lavaur from 1357.

2 Jan 1384 (Coll. 360, 70^v) camerarius orders Sicardus de Brugayrosio, collector of Toulouse, to give the spoils to the bearers, Guido Bonafes and Izarnus Cauderiae, papal sergeants.

12 Aug 1384 (ibid., 163^r-164^r) the camerarius releases the spoils to fulfill legacies to the Dominican convent of Revel, diocese of Lavaur, except 1300 fl. reserved for the studium at Périgord.

1089] Rodericus de Oliveyra, bishop of Lamego from 1311.

26 Aug 1330 (Coll. 112, 88^r-91^v) accounts of Guillelmus de Bos.
3 Feb 1332 (EFR J1, 58224; IM 1210) composition with executors.
17 Mar 1332 (VQ 1, 561) they pay 1650 fl.
26 Aug 1332 (EFR J1, 58252) agreement between the commissioner and executors.
30 Nov 1338 (EFR B3, 2129) commission to Gonsalvus, archbishop of Braga.

1090] Rogerius, bishop of Lombez, died 1361. Formerly provost of Toulouse; bishop from 1352.

1362 (Coll. 235, 67^r-72^v) accounts of Bertrandus de Castanherio, collector of Toulouse.
1364 (ibid., 114^v-115^r) report of estimates of books and remains to be collected.
1371 (Coll. 18, 203^v-209^r) debts collected by Bertrandus de Castanherio and Aymericus Pelicerii, 1060 fl. Fr.
22 Nov 1372 (Coll. 358, 139^v) collector Aymericus Pelicerii is ordered to pay a debt to the bishop's brother Joannes de Noerio, knight.
1 Oct 1373 (Coll. 236, 147^r, 155^v) he reports 1060 fl. collected and 482 fl. remaining to be paid.

1091] Rogerius de Arminiaco, bishop of Lavaur, whose goods were reserved when he was translated to Laon 22 May 1338. Bishop of Lavaur from 1317.

29 May 1338 (EFR B1, 5825) licentia testandi.
1 Sep 1338 - (Coll. 30, 77^r-89^r) accounts of Raymundus de Cameraco.
1 Dec 1339 (VQ 4, 151) he pays £639.10 from debts.
25 Jan 1342 (VQ 5, 462) Raymundus Flori reports collections.

1092] Rogerius Fortis, archbishop of Bourges, died before 2 Apr 1368. Former bishop of Limoges from 1328; archbishop of Bourges from 1343.

n.d. (RA 346, 179ʳ-182ᵛ) record of spoils and goods given to the successor Petrus de Stagno.

1093] Rogerius de Mirapisce, died in curia 1361.

17 Sep 1361 (VQ 7, 357) Eblo de Mederio, clericus Camerae, pays 300 fl.

1094] Rogerius de Turre, abbot of Marsillac, diocese of Cahors. Formerly abbot of Gaillac, diocese of Albi.

15 Oct 1404 (Coll. 91, 332ʳ-336ʳ) inventory and narrative by collector Petrus Berangas.

1095] Romanus, abbot of S. M. de Muro OSBasil, diocese of Lecce.

10 Feb 1354 (Coll. 169, 50ʳ) successor Hilarion pays for spoils.

1096] Romanus, abbot of S. M. de Bondonario OSBasil, diocese of Messina, died 8 Oct 1373.

ca. 1375 (Coll. 222, 173ᵛ) archbishop of Messina owes 4 unc. 7 car. 1 grani for sale of a mare, which he took by custom.

1097] Rostagnus OP, bishop of Nice, died before 9 May 1329. Formerly prior of Marseille; bishop from 1323.

28 Sep 1329 (OS 12, 112ᵛ) successor Joannes pays 300 fl. of a 600-fl. composition.
1 Feb 1330 (ibid., 119ᵛ) he pays 300 fl.

1098] Rostagnus, bishop of Orange, died before 28 Mar 1324. Formerly provost of Avignon; bishop from 1319.

24 Apr 1324 (VQ 1, 487) commissioner Rostagnus de Bonivayleti pays 1000 fl., 37 agni, 4 d. Tur. gr.

1099] Rostagnus Alziacii, provost of Pignans OCSA, diocese of Fréjus, died between 28 Mar and 15 Dec 1338.

9 Feb 1339 (VQ 4, 139) successor Bertrandus pays 900 fl. of a composition for 1800 fl.
14 May 1339 (ibid., 142) he pays 400 fl.
17 Mar 1340 (ibid., 156) he pays 300 fl.
5 Jul 1340 (ibid., 160) he pays 200 fl.

1100] Rostagnus de Lexis, sacristan of Maguelonne.

15 Mar 1373 (EFR G1, 1153) commission to Bertrandus Raffini.

1101] Rostagnus de Merindolio, abbot of S. André OSB, Villeneuve, diocese of Avignon, died in curia ca. Jul 1340.

12 Jul 1341 (VQ 4, 181) commissioner Berengarius Blasini pays 450 fl. etc.
24 Dec 1341 (ibid., 186) 100 fl. paid, due to Guillelmus Cataroni.
14 May 1342 (ibid., 338) Elziarius Cabassole pays 50 fl. owed to Guillelmus Cataroni.
5 Dec 1342 (ibid., 330) Berengarius Blasini pays 230 fl. through Jacobus de Broa.

1102] Rostagnus de Minulis, provost of Pignans OCSA, diocese of Fréjus.

18 Apr 1329 (OS 12, 105^r; VQ 1, 517) successor Rostagnus Alziacii pays 350 fl. of a 700-fl. composition.
31 Aug 1329 (OS 12, 111^r) he pays 350 fl.

1103] Rostagnus de Sandrano OCSA, bishop of Sisteron, died before 28 Jan 1349. Formerly abbot of S. M. de Sabloncelles, diocese of Saintes; bishop from 1328.

16 Dec 1346 (EFR C1, 2998) commission in advance of death to Joannes Regis, scriptor Poenitentiariae.
1 Feb 1349 (VQ 5, 416) commissioner Guillelmus de Broa pays 296 fl. etc.
1 Apr 1349 (ibid., 423) successor Petrus pays 300 fl. of a composition for 600 fl.
2 Jul 1349 (ibid., 427) he pays 300 fl.
3 Sep 1354 (VQ 7, 56-57) procurators of the commune of Fourcalquiers pay 80 fl. owed as a fine in the late bishop's court for a riot against the Jews by priests and laity there.

Rudolphus see Radolphus.

1104] Rufinus de Ficie, J.Civ.Prof., archdeacon of Reims.

17 May 1339 (EFR B1, 7036) licentia testandi, as canon of Reims.
15 Aug 1345 (EFR C2, 755) commission.

1105] Saltarellus, canon of Florence, chaplain of honor.

17 Jul 1363 (OS 23A, 115^v) Bonacursus Lapi Joannis, merchant of Florence, pays a composition of 800 fl.

1106] Sancius, bishop of Oviedo, died before 10 Feb 1371. Formerly secular abbot of S. Hilarius; bishop from 1348.

7 Mar 1371 (RA 182, 204^v-205^r) camerarius orders the collector to observe the *moderatio*.

1107] Sancius Canalis, auditor sacri palatii.

14 Nov 1347 (VQ 5, 397) executors pay a composition of 80 fl.

1108] Sancius Dull, bishop of Segorbe, died 1356. Bishop from 1319.

1358 (Coll. 114, 13^v) Fulco Pererii reports receipts from spoils and vacancy of £323.1.2 Barc., £400 Jac, 400 fl.
14 Jan 1361 (VQ 7, 331-332) spoils collected by Vitalis, bishop of Valencia, 3428 fl.
23 Dec 1361 (ibid., 378-379) he pays 2143 fl. etc.
24 Dec 1361 (ibid., 380) he pays 357 fl. etc.
22 Dec 1362 (IE 303, 8^v-9^r) Vitalis pays 3109 fl. 9 s. and 518 fl. 6 s. 6 d.

1109] Sancius Lupi de Ayerbe OFM, archbishop of Tarragona, died 22 Aug 1357. Bishop of Tarazona from 1343; archbishop from 1346. See AFH 55 (1962): 259.

28 Aug 1357 (IM 6282) commission to Fulco Pererii.
31 Aug 1357 (Coll. 352, 87^r) the same commission, dispatched by hand of Guillelmus Martorerii, canon of Tortosa.
26 Apr 1358 (VQ 7, 220) successor Petrus pays 1000 fl. of a 2000-fl. composition.
20 Jun 1358 (ibid., 222) he pays 600 fl.
n.d. (OS 23A, 108^v) note that the successor paid 1600 fl. of a composition, and collector paid 288 fl.

1110] Sancius Vaquerii, collector of Auch and Bordeaux, died before Oct 1382.

late 1385 (Coll. 35, 61^r-65^v, 64^r, 96^r-97^r, 222^r, 325^r, 345^r-346^r, 366^r) accounts of collector Sicardus de Brugayrosio.

1111] Savaricus Christiani, abbot of S. Victor, Marseille. See *Gall. Christ.* 1:693E.

Jan 1385 (IM 3203, 3) Aldebertus Galterii pays income of the castle of Vernet, diocese of Digne, 42 fl. 24 s.
Jun 1385 (IM 3203, 20) 21 fl. 12 s. paid for a house in Avignon.

1112] Saxius Jumenti de Montesquieu, abbot of Montolieu OSB, diocese of Carcassonne, died 9 Nov 1384. See *Gall. Christ.* 6:995B-996B.

Jan 1385 (IM 3203, 3) successor Bertrandus pays 200 fr. of a composition of 533 fr. for spoils and arrears of other debts.

1113] Scotus de Linariis, bishop of S. Bertrand de Comminges, died 4 Jul 1325. Formerly canon of Toulouse; bishop from 1317.

25 Oct 1325 (VQ 1, 487) nephew pays 212 fl.
5 Sep 1329 (RA 83, 389^{rv}) a book donated to Bon-Pas, diocese of Cahors.
31 Aug 1348 (EFR C1, 3945) commission to Petrus de Sparzelos.

1 Sep 1351 (ibid., 5043) commission to Martinus de Girardo.
7 Oct 1352 (ibid., 5420) the same.

1114] Seguinus Ottonis, abbot of S. Tiberius, diocese of Agde, died before 21 Jul 1361. See *Gall. Christ.* 6:715A-B.

1365 (Coll. 156, 41^v) prior pays 40 fl. 4 gr.
1365 (ibid., 43^v) 20 fl. paid for wine to the Pinhota.
1365 (ibid., 231^r) debts of 46 fl. 4 gr.

1115] Sicardus de Lautrico, bishop of Béziers, died 22 Jul 1383. Formerly provost in the church of Gerona; bishop of Agde from 1354; of Béziers from 1371.

2 Aug 1383 (Coll. 360, 56^{rv}) camerarius directs Arnaldus Andreae, collector of Narbonne, to pay cardinal Guillelmus de Agrifolio 1000 fr. from spoils.

1116] Sigfridus, bishop of Skara, died 1350. Bishop from 1341.

25 Feb 1356 - (Coll. 97, 42^r-49^v) goods among spoils of Emmingus Laurentii, bishop of Uppsala.

1117] Sigfridus Blomenberch, archbishop of Riga, died 30 Jun 1374. Formerly canon of Riga; archbishop from 1370.

5 Apr 1376 (OS 42, 61^v; IM 2924, 3) successor Joannes pays 200 fl. of his composition.
11 Sep 1376 (OS 42, 61^v) he pays 200 fl.

1118] Simon OFM, bishop of Tuy, died Aug 1326. Formerly bishop of Badajoz from 1309; of Tuy from 1324.

3 Dec 1324 (EFR J1, 21158) licentia testandi.
12 Dec 1328 (OS 12, 100; VQ 1, 487) commissioner Berengarius, archbishop of Compostela, pays 120 fl.

1119] Simon, abbot of S. Simphorien, diocese of Metz, died 12 Jul 1366; n.b. *Gall. Christ.* 13:851B-852A.

20 Mar 1366 (EFR U2, 2166) commission to Joannes, elect of Toul.

1120] Simon de Brossa, abbot of Cluny, diocese of Mâcon, died at Paris, 27 May 1369. See *Gall. Christ.* 4:1155B-C.

28 Jun 1369 (Coll. 354, 74^v-75^r) note of a bull of commission.
Jan 1372 (IM 2676, 40) successor Joannes de Pinu pays 300 fl. of a composition for 4000 fl.
May 1372 (ibid., 3) he pays 500 fl.

1121] Simon de Renou OSB, archbishop of Tours, died 2 Jan 1379. Formerly abbot of S. Nicolas, diocese of Angers; archbishop from 1363.

1364 (RA 157, 47^r) licentia testandi, rubric.
11 Jan 1380 (Coll. 359, 11^v-12^r) commission and instructions to Harduinus, bishop of Angers, and the canons.
12 Jan 1380 (ibid., 12^v-13^v) commissioners are to secure the debt to the Camera first: 11,292 1/2 fl.
21 Feb 1380 (ibid., 19^v-20^r) further instructions.
21 Feb 1380 (ibid., 20^{rv}) successor Seguinus is to be supported from the spoils until the next fruits are paid.
12 Apr 1380 (ibid., 24^v-25^r) proceeds are to be given to Joannes bishop of Geneva.
5 Jun 1381 (ibid., 67^r-68^r) successor should be maintained at the rate of 8 fr. per day until 15 Aug.

1122] Sirellus, archbishop of Thebes, died before 15 May 1357. Formerly canon of Patrai; archbishop from 1351.

13 Jul 1357 (Coll. 497, 62^v) successor Paulus is obligated to a composition of 3500 fl.

1123] Stephanus OCarm, bishop of Calvi, died between 22 Jun and 31 Jul 1344. Bishop from 1343.

31 Jul 4 Oct 1344 (Coll. 168, 41^v-43^r) goods collected by Guillelmus de Roseriis.
21 Jan 1345 (EFR C1, 1407) deposit.

1124] Stephanus OFM, bishop of Cuenca, died before 11 Apr 1326. Formerly bishop of Porto from 1310; of Lisbon from 1313; of Cuenca from 1322.

10 May 1335 (EFR B3, 869) orders Gonsalvus Petri, archbishop of Braga, to absolve holders of these and other spoils after restitution.
10 Jan 1327 (OS 12, 103^v-104^r) Petrus de Brunia pays spoils from Lisbon.

1125] Stephanus, bishop of Massalubrense, died before 4 Apr 1343. Bishop from 1322.

6 Apr 1343 (Coll. 168, 37^r) collections by Guillelmus de Roseriis.

1126] Stephanus, abbot of S. Victor OSB, Marseille, died before 1362. This Stephanus was the predecessor of Stephanus Alberti, *Gall. Christ.* 1:693C.

n.d. (IM 4746) collector Geraldus Mercaderii is admonished to collect spoils.

Apr? 1362 (OS 31, 141ᵛ) detailed quittance for silverware to Geraldus Mercaderii.

1127] Stephanus Alberti, abbot of S. Victor OSB, Marseille, died before 25 Jan 1379. See *Gall. Christ.* 1:693C.

22 Feb 1380 (Coll. 469, 160ᵛ-161ʳ) goods from spoils dispersed from papal treasure.
5 Mar 1380 (Coll. 359, 2ᵛ) vicar and prior general granted 60 fl. expenses from spoils.
13 Aug 1380 (ibid., 52ᵛ-53ʳ) Guillelmus Thonerat, magister cerae, is commissioned to collect arrears.

1128] Stephanus de Borgolio, archbishop of Tours, died 7 Mar 1335. Formerly archdeacon in the church of Tours; archbishop from 1323.

9 Feb 1345 (EFR C1, 1482) a query about the testament.
15 Jun 1345 (ibid., 1792) commission to the abbot of Marmoutier to inquire into injuries done to the commissioner, the cantor of S. Martin, Tours, over the pious legacies.
20 Oct 1347 (ibid., 3528) commission to Raymundus de Caunis, cantor of S. Martin, to keep the goods for the Camera, since the executors, including the present archbishop Petrus Fretaldi (n. 910 above), have not executed the legacies and administered the goods in the 12 years since Stephanus died.

1129] Stephanus Cambaruti OSB, archbishop of Toulouse and camerarius, died 15 Mar 1361. Formerly bishop of S. Pons de Thomières from 1346; archbishop of Arles from 1348; of Toulouse from 1350.

31 Mar 1361 (VQ 7, 337; OS 23A, 110ᵛ) Petrus Ayme, bishop of Auxerre, pays 16,000 fl. of a composition of 20,000 fl.
1 Jan 1363 (Coll. 235, 78ʳ) collector Bertrandus de Castanherio, ignorant of the total composition, notes receipts of 1100 fl. from Petrus Ayme, bishop of Auxerre.
26 Aug 1363 (OS 31, 190ʳ) commission to Bertrandus de Castanherio to collect the 4000 fl. remaining of the composition by Petrus Ayme.
5 Mar 1364 (IE 303, 17ᵛ) successor pays 600 fl. of a 3000-fl. composition.
20 Mar 1364 (ibid., 17ᵛ) he pays 400 fl.
22 May 1364 (Coll. 353, 11ᵛ-12ʳ) collector ordered to gather at least 5000 fl. to complete the composition.
26 Jun 1364 (IE 303, 21ʳ) successor pays 500 fl.
1364 (Coll. 235, 120ᵛ) 1276 fl. received from various debtors.
3 Oct 1356 (Coll. 353, 74ᵛ) collector Aymericus Pelicerii is ordered to collect 4000 fl. balance of composition in florins of Florentine weight, not Cameral weight.

1371 (Coll. 18, 213^{rv}) remains of debts collected by Bertrandus de Castanherio and Aymericus Pelicerii: 2039 fl. 9 gr.
1 Oct 1373 (Coll. 236, 147^v, 156^r) Aymericus Pelicerii reports the same receipts, remains of 1276 fl. 11 gr.

1130] Stephanus Digne, bishop of Vence. Formerly canon of Vence, scriptor litterarum apostolicarum; bishop from 1361.

Dec 1372 (IM 2676, 79) the bishop's procurator Hugo de Vinariis pays 50 fr.

1131] Stephanus de Gardia, archbishop of Arles, died 19 May 1361. Formerly archdeacon of Beauvais, papal chaplain; bishop of Lisbon from 1344; of Saintes from 1348; archbishop of Arles from 1351.

1361 - (Coll. 19, 164^{rv}) spoils collected by Geraldus Mercaderii.
Jun 1364 (IM 2339, 15) successor Guillelmus pays 500 fl. of a composition of 3000 fl.
Jan 1365 (IM 2378, 3) he pays 422 fl.
Feb 1372 (IM 2676, 7) he pays 250 fl.

1132] Stephanus Hugonis, subcollector of Reims.

5 Dec 1371 (Coll. 358, 18^r) Joannes Mauberti, collector of Reims, is ordered to collect spoils against debts to the Camera.

1133] Stephanus Joannis, servitor of the Pinhota.

27 Feb 1348 (VQ 5, 403) brother pays a composition of 110 fl.

1134] Stephanus Joannis Tristao, bishop of Idanha, died before 10 Dec 1358. Formerly canon of Coimbra; bishop of Idanha from 1356.

8 Oct 1360 (Coll. 231, 101^v; VQ 7, 300) successor Aegidius pays a composition of 1200 fl.
ca. 1370 (Arm. 33, to. 18, 176^r-180^r) remains of spoils collected by Bertrandus de Macello.

1135] Stephanus de Mazerolis, prior of Veules, diocese of Rouen.

9 May 1355 (VQ 7, 91) Petrus de Labatat, secretary to the king of France, pays 200 fl. composition.

1136] Stephanus Mulceo, bishop of Lerida, died 10 May 1360. Bishop from 1348.

4 Jul 1360 (Coll. 497, 72^v) executors are obligated to a composition of 3000 fl.

29 Aug 1360 (Coll. 231, 100ᵛ; VQ 7, 298) executors pay 1500 fl. of a composition for 3000 fl.
n.d. (Coll. 116, 87ᵛ-89ʳ) report: collections of £2854.19.3 1/2, arrears of £2789.11.6 1/2.

1137] Stephanus de Omale, bishop of Tortosa, died in curia 1356. Formerly abbot of Casa Dei OSB; bishop of Elne from 1350; of Tortosa from 1352.

4 Jan 1357 (VQ 7, 169) commissioner Petrus Ruffi pays 1000 fl.

1138] Stephanus de Pinu, archbishop of Benevento. Formerly auditor Camerae; patriarch of Constantinople; archbishop of Benevento from 1346. See Guillemain, *Cour* 292.

2 Sep 1336 (EFR B1, 3388) licentia testandi.
3 Sep 1350 (EFR C2, 2295) commission to Guillelmus, abbot of S. M. de Gualdo, Benevento.
7 Nov 1350 (ibid., 2325) commission to Guillelmus de Stivalibus.

1139] Stephanus Priosi, rector in the diocese of Châlons-sur-Marne, died in curia.

9 Dec 1361 (VQ 7, 375) executor Joannes Palaysini pays 100 fl. composition.

1140] Sugerius Gometii, archbishop of Compostela, died 29 Jun 1366. Formerly dean of Toledo; archbishop from 1362.

10 Feb 1370 (Coll. 119, 98ʳ) collector Arnaldus de Vernolio receives 300 maravedis from income due in the diocese of Leon.

1141] Tasius, abbot of Donadula, diocese of Forlì.

13 May 1372 (Coll. 129, 237ʳ) grain yields 23 ducats 18 s.

1142] Tedicius, cantor of Badajoz, died in curia.

19 Mar 1375 (OS 42, 8ʳ; IM 2877, 2) Mattheus de Maselis, subcollector of Maguelonne, collects 273 fl. from the commune of Aigues-Mortes, and pays the Camera 68 fl.

1143] Tedicius Aliotti, bishop of Fiesole from 1312.

11 Jun 1335 (IE 145, 2ᵛ) commission to Pontius Stephani.
28 Oct 1336 (EFR B3, 1122-1123) reservation and commission to Pontius Stephani, nuncio in Tuscany.
21 May 1337 (VQ 4, 118) successor Felinus pays 100 fl. of a composition for 200 fl.

21 Feb 1339 - 7 Mar 1341 (Coll. 244, 8^v-10^v) accounts of Joannes de Pererio.

5 Jun 1339 (OS 18, 28^r; IE 145, 57^v) Pontius Stephani pays 100 fl. for goods sold to successor Fulignus.

Apr 1342 (Coll. 244, 97^r-102^r) safeguard of spoils.

1144] Theobaldus de Avalone, canon of Langres.

15 Jun 1375 (Coll. 356, 52^v-53^r) goods granted to Joannes bishop of Clermont in consideration of a composition.

1145] Theobaldus de Castellione, bishop of Lisbon. Formerly bishop of Bazas from 1313; of Saintes from 1318; of Lisbon from 1348. See Yves Renouard, "Un francese del sud-ovest vescovo di Lisbona nel XIV secolo: Tibaldo di Castillon (1348-56)," *Italia e Francia nel commercio medievale* (Rome, 1966), 116-133.

27 Jun 1313 (Regesta Clementis V, 9404) licentia testandi.

15 Jan 1356 (RA 133, 370^r-371^v) inventory by Guillelmus Guilaberti of goods at Montpellier.

14 Apr 1356 (VQ 7, 173-174) goods recovered from pirates received in the Camera.

11 Feb 1357 (RA 133, 445^r-456^v) inventory of goods recovered from a galley at Aigues-Mortes, at order of a royal judge.

1357 (Coll. 275, 100^r-108^v) process to recover goods.

20 Feb - 20 Jun 1357 (RA 137, 28^r-47^v) account of piracy and recovery.

3 Sep 1359 (VQ 7, 266) Petrus de Legantru pays 1000 écus of a composition of 8000 écus.

7 Sep 1359 (ibid.) Guillelmus Peraire pays 100 fl. of a composition of 400 fl.

3 Jul 1360 (ibid., 296-297) Petrus de Legantru pays 6000 fl. for salt to the king's men, and a debt of 3000 fl.

24 Nov 1360 (IM 2199) Guillelmus Piloti pays £1600.7.3.

5 Dec 1360 (Coll. 231, 110^r) debtor pays 2000 fl.

26 Mar 1367 (OS 23A, 104^r) Petrus de Legantru paid 8000 écus.

ca. 1370 (Arm. 33, to. 18, 23^v) collector Bertrandus de Macello receives £120 Port., notes a balance of £96.6.8.

n.d. (IM 4592, 1^v) Joannes Garrigie, collector of Portugal, accounts for receipts: £7750.14.3 1/2.

1146] Theodericus de Bardewine, died in curia.

1 Feb 1354 (VQ 7, 47) Balduinus Ricardi, sigillifer auditoris Camerae, pays 7 écus, 6 fl.

1147] Thomas, bishop of Telese, died before 15 Jul 1345. Formerly archdeacon of Telese; bishop from 1340.

5 Jun 1346 (Coll. 168, 56^v) brother Leonardus pays 3 unc. to Guillelmus de Roseriis.

1148] Thomas, bishop of Terni, died before 14 Dec 1357. Formerly canon of SS. Lorenzo e Damaso, Rome; bishop of Terni from 1323.

28 Dec 1357 (Coll. 352, 118^v) dispatch by hand of Reginaldus de Lupchaco, cantor of Auxerre, of a commission dated 14 Dec 1357 to Petrus, archbishop of Benevento and bearer.

1149] Thomas de Florentia, scriptor Papae, died in curia.

27 May 1352 (VQ 7, 404) Joannes Sinrane, precentor of S. Didier, Avignon, pays 150 fl.
28 May 1352 (ibid., 405) Joannes Petri, archpriest of S. Didier, pays 50 fl. 75 écus, less 10 fl. rent for Thomas's house, owed to the college of S. Didier.

1150] Thomas Guierre, canon of Clermont.

9 Feb 1380 (Coll. 359, 195^v-196^r) 100 fr. composition arranged with the heirs; collector Pontius de Croso is directed to release the spoils.

1151] Thomas de Insula, bishop of Ely, died in curia 23 Jun 1361. Bishop from 1345.

29 Sep 1361 (OS 31, 251^v-252^v) 500 fl. debt from the abbot of Ramsey collected from his sureties.
30 Sep 1361 (VQ 7, 358) Thomas Paxton and Petrus de Holdenesse pay 200 fl. of a debt owed by the late abbot of Ramsey OSB.
20 Dec 1361 (ibid., 377) they pay 300 fl.
23 Jun 1362 (ibid., 410) Thomas Paxton pays 500 fl.

1152] Thomas de Muro, bishop of Ancona, died before 18 Jul 1342. Formerly papal chaplain and subdeacon; bishop of Cesena from 1324; of Ancona from 1326.

31 Oct 1344 (EFR C1, 1207-1208).

1153] Thomasius, abbot of S. Pietro di Piemonte, diocese of Caserta.

31 Dec 1354 (Coll. 169, 51^v) spoils collected by subcommissioner Joannes, abbot of S. Sebastiano, Naples.

1154] Trasmundus, bishop of Alife.

27 Sep 1345 (Coll. 168, 51^v-52^r) heir Joannes de Aspri gives books to Guillelmus de Roseriis.

1155] Valascus, archbishop of Braga. Formerly cantor of Idanha; bishop of Idanha from 1363; of Coimbra from 1346; of Lisbon from 1371; archbishop of Braga from 11 Aug 1371.

16 Jun 1372 (Coll. 358, 55ʳ) familiar Gundisalvus, scholasticus of Coimbra, arrested at Avignon pending his accounting for 800 fl. given him by the late archbishop.
1 Sep 1375 (OS 42, 34ʳ; IM 2877, 7) successor Laurentius pays 3000 fl. of a composition of 7000 fl.

1156] Valascus, bishop of Segovia, died before 13 Feb 1352. Formerly archdeacon in the church of Toledo; bishop from 1351.

28 Jul 1352 (Coll. 497, 48ᵛ) cardinal Aegidius de Albornotio is obligated to a composition of 2000 fl.
17 Nov 1354 (VQ 7, 60) he pays the last 1000 fl. of his composition for the spoils of bishops Petrus and Valascus.
1354 (Coll. 114, 34ᵛ) collector Augerius de Offerans reports collections of 11,000 marks.

1157] Valascus Laurentii, bishop of Silves, died before 5 Nov 1365. Formerly canon of Seville; bishop of Silves from 1350.

6 Jul 1369 (Arm. 33, to. 18, 80ʳᵛ) accounts of Bertrandus de Macello: £1085.9 and three rings.

1158] Valascus Martini, bishop of Lisbon, died between 29 Nov and 17 Dec 1344. Formerly dean of Evora; bishop of Porto from 1328; of Lisbon from 1342.

25 Jan 1327 (EFR J1, 27663) licentia testandi.
17 Dec 1344 (EFR C2, 1340) commission to Gundisalvus, archbishop of Braga.
8 Jan 1345 (VQ 5, 353) procurator at Avignon pays 1000 duple.
1345 (ibid., 371-372).

1159] Valascus Martini, cantor of Braga, died in curia.

20 Mar 1348 (OS 23, 15ʳ) Fernandus Stephani pays 33 1/3 fl. for books.
20 Mar 1348 (VQ 5, 403) legacy of 20 fl. paid to Camera.
12 Apr 1348 (ibid., 405) 33 1/3 fl. received from Fernandus Stephani.

1160] Vincentius de Sassaro OFM, bishop of Ajaccio, died before 19 Dec 1369. Bishop from 1351.

24 Feb 1371 (EFR G2, 60) commission to Bertrandus bishop of Cagliari and Raphael de Turre, canon of Genoa.

1161] Vitalis, abbot of S. Vito de Piço, diocese of Taranto.

10 Feb 1354 (Coll. 169, 50ʳ) successor Nettorius pays for spoils, including spoils of monks who died during the vacancy.

1162] Vitalis de Blanco, bishop of Valencia, died before 5 Mar 1369. Formerly secular abbot of S. Felix, Gerona; bishop from 1356.

n.d. (Coll. 116, 63^r) spoils pay £60.4.7.

1163] Vitalis de Boscomedio, collector of Le Puy and Clermont, etc., died before 6 Jun 1382.

17 Jan 1384 (Coll. 85, 110^r) successor Pontius de Cros reports collections of 294 fr. 6 s. 6 d.

1164] Vitalis de S. Petro de Lavardaco, familiar and scriptor Papae.

25 Jan 1345 (EFR C1, 1418) licentia testandi.
23 Jul 1348 (EFR C2, 1694) commission to Didacus, abbot of S. Facundus OCSA, diocese of Leon and Joannes de Gardaya, scholasticus of Oviedo, nuncios.
7 Feb 1352 (VQ 5, 451) his brother and heir Arnaldus de Banardo, hostiarius, pays 150 fl. of a 300-fl. composition.

1165] Vitalis de Savinhaco, prior of Nayrac, diocese of Condom.

9 Dec 1374 (EFR G1, 1730) commission to Guillelmus Borelli, subcollector of Condom.

1166] Vitalis Vassali, provost of Lerida, collector of Saintes, etc.

2 Apr 1364 (EFR U2, 872) commission to Guillelmus Amarinti.
22 Nov 1364 (ibid., 1384) successor Arnaldus Gavini appointed.

1167] Vitalis de Villanova, provost of Castellion, diocese of Gerona.

9 Apr 1364 (EFR U2, 879) Fulco Pererii, Petrus Rubei, and Jordanus de Haya ordered to cite the bishop of Gerona as holding reserved spoils.
20 Aug 1369 (Coll. 354, 76^v-77^r) treasurer orders the bishop and chapter to pay as spoils a debt of 1000 fl.

1168] Vivianus de Cana OSB, prior of S. George d'Oleron, diocese of Saintes, died in curia before 2 Aug 1361.

31 Aug 1361 (VQ 7, 355-356) commissioner pays 1000 fl.; he reported receipts of 1400 mutones by letter of 2 Aug.
4 Jan 1365 (Coll. 353, 26^r-27^v) heir of collector Vitalis Vassali makes payment.

Anonymous, Arranged in Order of Diocese

1169] _____ , **archimandrite of S. Maria de Terreto OSBasil. (predecessor of Romanus).**

13 Mar 1369 (Coll. 353, 181ᵛ-182ʳ) camerarius orders the *moderatio* observed in collecting spoils.

1170] _____ , cleric, died in the house of Ademarus Alberti.

29 May 1355 (VQ 7, 92) Balduinus Ricardi pays 10 fl. etc.

1171] T_____ , abbot of S. Maria Depositan., diocese of Amalfi.

10 Feb 1349 (Coll. 168, 74ʳ) Guillelmus de Roseriis collects 2 unc. for goods.

1172] _____ , abbot of S. Clemente, Bari.

20 Feb 1346 (Coll. 168, 55ʳᵛ) successor Petrus de Cortuciis pays a composition of 5 unc., and Guillelmus de Roseriis also received a debt of 3 unc.

1173] _____ , abbot of S. Maria de Gualdo, diocese of Benevento.

4 Mar 1345 (EFR C1, 1519) commission.

1174] _____ , abbot of S. Maria de Gualdo, diocese of Benevento. (Possibly Arnaldus, who was alive in 1369.)

5 Jun 1375 (Coll. 256, 24ᵛ-25ʳ) spoils granted to Guillelmus de Belloforti, viscount of Turenne; the monks who hold the goods are cited to appear at Avignon within thirty days.

1175] _____ , preceptor of S. Antonius, diocese of Béziers, died in curia.

10 Sep 1369 (Coll. 354, 82ᵛ) treasurer orders Gaucelmus de Sala to collect spoils and fruits of the vacancy.

1176] _____ , prior of S. Fulgentius OCSA, diocese of Bourges.

22 May 1371 (EFR G1, 241) commission to Audebertus de Gorsis, canon of Bourges.

1177] _____ , abbot of S. Maria de Basilica, diocese of Chieti.

29 Aug 1344 (Coll. 168, 43ᵛ) Guillelmus de Roseriis collects 2 unc. 1 car. 10 grani.

1178] _____ , abbot of S. Riparata de Maradi OVallambrosa, diocese of Faenza.

14 Aug 1372 (Coll. 358, 79ʳ-80ᵛ) collector Lucius bishop of Cesena is ordered to summon the subcollector Girardinus, archpriest of Bologna, to Florence to answer for spoils and vacancy.

1179] _____ , abbot of S. Laurentius in Campo OSB, diocese of Fano (predecessor of Reginaldus Lachiesa).

10 Mar 1371 (RA 182, 231ʳ-232ʳ) camerarius orders the monastery's goods released to the successor.

1180] R_____ , abbot of S. Pedro de Roddis, diocese of Gerona.

1358 (Coll. 114, 13ᵛ-14ʳ) Fulco Pererii reports net receipts of £1635.1.6 Barc.
before 24 Oct 1361 (Coll. 117, 175ᵛ) he collects £150 of the successor's composition for £250.

1181] _____ , abbot of Mons Aragonae OSA, diocese of Huesca.

1 Oct 1358 x 24 Oct 1361 (Coll. 117, 175ᵛ) collector Fulco Pererii receives 100 fl. composition from successor.

1182] _____ , abbot of S. Maria de Caratis, diocese of Lecce.

28 May 1346 (Coll. 168, 56ʳ) Guillelmus de Roseriis sells goods for 50 fl.

1183] _____ , abbot of S. Victorianus, diocese of Lerida.

n.d., probably temp. Urban V (Coll. 116, 87ʳ) successor B. pays a composition and damages of £165 Barc.

1184] _____ Alberti, prior of Bénévent OCSA, diocese of Limoges.

9 Dec 1348 (VQ 5, 415) his brother Audoinus Alberti pays a composition of 400 fl.

1185] _____ , prior of S. Saturninus OSB, diocese of Marseille.

5 Dec 1342 (VQ 5, 331) money and cups paid by Berengarius Blasini.
27 Nov 1343 (ibid., 341) further payment.

1186] _____ , abbot of S. Justina, diocese of Padua.

1361 (Coll. 130, 151ʳ) the successor's composition and sales yield 211 ducats.

1187] _____ , abbot of Charroux OSB, diocese of Poitiers (predecessor of Petrus).

9 May 1369 (Coll. 353, 218ᵛ-219ʳ) camerarius orders collector to observe the *moderatio*.

1188] _____ , abbot of S. Trifone, diocese of Ravello.

early 1362 (Coll. 169, 135ʳ) spoils collected.

1189] _____ , **abbot of Rippealte, diocese of Teano di Puglia.**

16 Apr 1346 (Coll. 168, 55ʳ) Guillelmus de Roseriis collects 10 unc. for goods of the last abbot.

1190] _____ , **abbot of S. Michael della Chiusa OSB, diocese of Turin.**

1380? (IM 4746) camerarius demands accounts.

1191] _____ , **abbot of Pinerolo OSB, diocese of Turin.**

17 Jul 1373 (EFR G2, 2004) orders the castellan of Pinerolo not to impede the collectors.

17 Jul 1373 (ibid., 2005) orders Petrus Gervasii and the sons and treasurer of Amadeus, count of Savoy, to restrain the castellan.

BIBLIOGRAPHY

Printed Sources

See also the Abbreviated Citations above, pp. iv-v.

Boniface VIII. *Liber sextus decretalium Bonifacii VIII*. In *Corpus iuris canonici*, q.v. 2, cols. 933-1124.

Clement V. *Clementis papae V Constitutiones*. In *Corpus iuris canonici*, q.v. 2, cols. 1125-1200.

Codex Justinianus. Edited by Paul Krueger. Vol. 2 of *Corpus iuris civilis*, q.v.

Corpus iuris canonici. Editio lipsiensis secunda, post Aemilii Ludovici Richteri curas, ad librorum manu scriptorum et editionis romanae ed. Emil Friedberg. 2d ed., Leipzig, 1879; 2 vols. Reprint Graz, 1959.

Corpus iuris civilis. 3 vols. Berlin, 1900-1905.

Dubois, Pierre. *De recuperatione terre sancte*: Traité de politique générale. Edited by Charles-Victor Langlois. Paris, 1891. Collection de textes pour servir à l'étude et à l'enseignement de l'histoire, 9.

Extravagantes communes 2, cols. 1237-1312 in *Corpus iuris canonici*, q.v.

Finke, Heinrich. *Acta concilii constanciensis*. 4 vols. Münster, 1896-1928.

Gratian. *Decretum magistri Gratiani*. vol. 1 of *Corpus iuris canonici* q.v.

Gregory IX. *Decretales Gregorii IX*. 2, cols. 1-928 in *Corpus iuris canonici*, q.v.

Guillelmus Durandus senior. *Speculum iuris*. 3 vols. Venice, 1585.

Henry of Susa. *Summa aurea*. Lyon, 1568.

Jean Juvenal des Ursins. *Histoire de Charles VI*. Edited by Théodore Godefroy. Paris, 1853.

Joannes Andreae. *Novella commentaria in decretales*. Venice, 1581; 5 vols. Reprint Turin, 1963.

John XXII. *Extravagantes viginti Joannis papae XXII*. 2, cols. 1201-1236 in *Corpus iuris canonici*, q.v.

Lanhers, Y. et al. *Tables des registres de Clément V publiés par les Bénédictins*. Bibliothèque des Ecoles Françaises d'Athènes et de Rome, série B, 25. Paris, 1948-1957.

Laspeyres, T., ed. *Summa decretalium Bernardi Papiensis*. Ratisbon, 1860.

Luard, Henry Richards, ed. *Matthei Parisii Chronica maiora*. 7 vols. Rerum brittanicarum medii aevi scriptores (Rolls Series), 9. London, 1872-1883.

Lux, Carolus. *Constitutionum apostolicarum de generali beneficiorum reservatione ab anno 1265 usque ad annum 1378 emissarum, tam intra quam extra corpus iuris exstantium, collectio et interpretatio*. STD dissertation, Bresslau, 1904.

Mansi, Giovanni Domenico. *Sacrorum conciliorum nova et amplissima collectio*. 53 vols. in 58. Florence, 1759-1798, reprint Paris, 1901-1927.

Marsiglio of Padua. *The Defensor Pacis of Marsiglio of Padua*. Ed. C. W. Previté-Orton. Cambridge, 1929.

Novellae. Edited by Rudolf Schoell and Wilhelm Kroll. Vol. 3 of *Corpus iuris civilis*, q.v.

Pithou, Pierre. *Preuves des libertéz de l'église gallicane*. 3d ed. 2 vols. Paris, 1731.

Potthast, A., ed. *Regesta pontificum romanorum inde ab anno post Christum natum MCMXCVIII ad annum MCCCIV*. 2 vols. Berlin, 1874-1875.

Les Registres de Benoît XI. Receuil des bulles de ce pape publiées ou analysées de'après le manuscrit original des Archives du Vatican. Edited by Charles Grandjean, Bibliothèque des Ecoles Françaises d'Athènes et de Rome, série B, 15. Paris, 1883–1905.

Les Registres de Boniface VIII (1294–1303). Receuil des bulles de ce pape publiées ou analysées d'après les manuscrits originaux des Archives du Vatican. Edited by G. Digard, M. Faucon, A. Thomas, R. Fawtier. 4 vols. Bibliothèque des Ecoles Françaises

d'Athènes et de Rome, série B, 14. Paris, 1884–1939.
Les Registres d'Urbain IV. Receuil des bulles de ce pape publiées ou analysées d'après les manuscrits originaux du Vatican. Edited by J. Guiraud and S. Clémencet. Bibliothèque des Ecoles Françaises d'Athènes et de Rome, série B, 6. Paris, 1899–1958.
Schroeder, Henry Joseph. *Disciplinary Decrees of the General Councils:* Text, Translation, and Commentary. St. Louis, 1937.
Thomas Aquinas. *Summa theologiae . . . cum textu ex recensione Leonina,* ed. Pietro Caramello. 3 vols. Turin, 1952–1976.

Secondary Works

Boyle, Leonard E. *A Survey of the Vatican Archives and of Its Medieval Holdings.* Toronto, 1972.
Caillemer, Robert. *Confiscation et administration des successions par les pouvoirs publics au moyen âge.* Etudes sur les successions au moyen âge, 2. Lyon, 1901.
Coville, Alfred. *La vie intellectuelle dans les domaines d'Anjou-Provence de 1380 à 1435.* Paris, 1941.
DuCange, Charles du Fresne, sieur. *Glossarium mediae et infimae latinitatis.* 7 vols. Paris, 1840.
Favier, Jean. *Les finances pontificales à l'époque du Grand Schisme d'Occident (1378–1409).* Bibliothèque des Ecoles Françaises d'Athènes et de Rome, 211. Paris, 1966.
———. "Temporels ecclésiastiques et taxation fiscal: le poids de la fiscalité pontificale au XIVe siècle." *Journal des savants* (1964): 102–127.
Fichtenau, Heinrich. *Arenga: Spätantike und Mittelalter im Spiegel von Urkundenformeln.* Graz, 1957.
Glare, P. G. W., ed. *Oxford Latin Dictionary.* Oxford, 1982.
Glénisson, Jean. "Un agent de la Chambre apostolique au XIV- siècle: les missions de Bertrand du Mazel (1364–1378)." *Mélanges d'archéologie et d'histoire* 59 (1947): 89–119.
Guillemain, Bernard. *La politique bénéficiale du pape Benoît XII (1334–1342).* Paris, 1952.
Hayez, A.-M. "Les gabelles d'Avignon d'Innocent VI à Grégoire XI." *Etudes sur la fiscalité au moyen âge* 1.171–206. Actes du 102e Congrès national des sociétés savantes, Limoges, 1977; Section de philologie et d'histoire jusqu'à 1610. Paris, 1979.
Hayez, Michel. Review of Williman, *Records of the Papal Right of Spoil. Bibliothèque de l'Ecole des Chartes* 134 (1976): 210–212.
Hillgarth, J. N. "Inventario de los bienes de Anthoni des Collell, obispo de Mallorca (1349–1363)." *Boletín de la Sociedad Arqueològica Luliana* 31 (1953–60): 504–553.
Jacob, E. F. "Dietrich of Niem." *Essays in the Conciliar Epoch* 24–41. Manchester, 1953.
Laurent, M.-H. "Guillaume des Rosières et la bibliothèque pontificale à l'époque de Clément VI." *Mélanges Auguste Pelzer* 579–604. Louvain, 1947.
Loye, Joseph de. *Les archives de la chambre apostolique au XIVe siècle.* Paris, 1899.
Lunt, William E. *Papal Revenues in the Middle Ages.* 2 vols. Columbia Records of Civilization, 19. New York, 1934.
Mollat, Guillaume. "L'application du droit de dépouille sous Jean XXII." *Revue des sciences religieuses* 19 (1939): 50–57.
———. "A propos du droit de dépouille." *Revue d'histoire ecclésiastique* 29 (1933): 316–347.
———. *La collation des bénéfices ecclésiastiques à l'époque des papes d'Avignon, 1305–1378.* Also printed in the introduction to vol. 8 of EFR *Jean XXII, communes.* Paris, 1921.
———. "Dépouille." *Dictionnaire du droit canonique* 4.1160–1165.
———. *Les papes d'Avignon (1305–1378).* 10th ed. Paris, 1964.
Prochnow, Fritz. *Das Spolienrecht und die Testierfähigkeit der Geistlichen im Abendland bis zum 13. Jahrhundert.* Historische Studien, 136 (Berlin, 1919). Reprinted Vaduz, 1965.
Renouard, Yves. "Intérêt et importance des Archives Vaticanes pour l'histoire économique du Moyen Age, spécialement du XIVe siècle." *Miscellanea archivistica Angelo Mercati* 141–156. Studi e Testi 165. Vatican City, 1952.

———. *La papauté à Avignon*. "Que sais-je" no. 630. Paris, 1962.
Rodano, Guglielmo. *Tractatus de spoliis ecclesiasticis*. Rome, 1585.
Saint-Palais d'Aussac, F. de. *Le droit de dépouille (jus spolii)*. Paris, 1930.
Samaran, Charles. "La jurisprudence pontificale en matière de droit de dépouille (jus spolii) dans la second moitié du XIVe siècle." *Mélanges d'archéologie et d'histoire* 22 (1902): 141–156.
———. Review of Williman, *Records of the Papal Right of Spoil*. *Journal des savants* (1976), no. 2, 151–152.
Samaran, Charles, and Guillaume Mollat. *La fiscalité pontificale en France au XIVe siècle*. Bibliothèque des Ecoles Françaises d'Athènes et de Rome, 96. Paris, 1905.
Schmidt, Clements. Review of Williman, *Records of the Papal Right of Spoil*. *Archivum Franciscanum Historicum* 68 (1975): 559–560.
Valois, Noel. *La France et le Grand Schisme d'Occident*. 4 vols. Paris, 1896–1902.

INDEX TO THE INTRODUCTION

Aix 17
Albi 26
Alexander V 35, 36
Andrea Ghini Malpigli, cardinal 27
Angel de Lordato 27
Angelo dei Ricasoli, bishop of Sora 26
Anglican Church 31
Aragon 25
Arles 26
Arnaldus de Puyana, bishop of Pamplona 23
Arnaldus Cescomes, archbishop of Tarragona 19, 38, 39
Arnaud Aubert, camerarius apostolicus 21, 31
Arnaud Bernard du Pouget 27
Arras 12
Auch 19
Auditio Camerae 22
Aversa 27
Avignon 22, 25
Benedict XI 17
Benedict XII 19, 23, 25, 27
Benedict XIII 1, 23, 32
Bernard of Pavia, *Summa decretalium* 4
Bertrand de Malsang, abbot of Montmajour 24
Bertrand du Mazel, collector of Portugal 22, 40, 43
Bertrand du Pouget, cardinal legate 25
Black Death 30, 33
Boniface VIII 17; *Praesenti* 9, 10, 14, 17, 18, 37
Bordeaux 19
Camera Apostolica 2, 11, 12, 14, 15, 20–22, 23, 25, 27, 33–36
Castile 19
Chancery 11, 17, 26
Charles VI, king of France 14, 32, 34
Cistercian Order 31
Clement V 17, 23; *Frequens* 9, 10, 14
Clement VI 19, 23, 25, 27, 29
Clement VII 31, 32
Colonna family 17
Comtat Venaissin 25
Constance, Council of 1, 9, 35, 37
Corsica 19
Cosenza 12
Cum in officiis 4
Demetrios de Matafaris, bishop of Knin 27
Dietrich of Niem 35–36
Dominican Order 10

Edward II, king of England 15
Ehrle, Franz 14
Empire 25
England 25
Eudes, prior of S. Martin, Chartres 27
Favier, Jean 33
Florence 12, 17
Fortanerio Vassalli 27
France (Northern) 12, 25
Franciscan Order 12, 23
Gallican Church, 14, 31, 34
Gasbert de Laval, camerarius apostolicus 25, 26
Gil Albornoz, cardinal legate 25
Giovanni d'Andrea, *Novella commentaria* 5, 9, 10, 22
Gratian, *Decretum* 3
Gregory I 2, 3
Gregory IX, *Decretales* 4
Gregory XI 19, 27, 29, 31, 37
Guido de Baysio 22
Guillaume Caprarii, cantor of Tours 32
Guillaume de la Jugie, cardinal 27
Guillaume des Rosières, nuncio 30
Guillelmus de Platulis 38, 39
Hayez, Michel 26 n.
Henry of Susa: see Hostiensis
Henry III, king of England 15
Honoré Bonet, prior of Salon 36
Hospitalers 10
Hostiensis 16
Hugues Gérard, bishop of Cahors 27
Hungary 28
Iberia 12
Innocent III 14
Innocent IV 15, 22
Innocent VI 9, 19, 29, 30, 32; *Quamvis in cunctis* 30; *Quamquam fabricam* 30
Italy 12, 25–28
Jacopo Muto, bishop of Spoleto 32
Jean Desprez, bishop of Castres 29
Jean Dupin 30
Jean Juvenal des Ursins 33
Jean de Lieux, bishop of Poitiers 32
Jean des Paumes, collector of Cahors 28, 33
Jean Petit 33
Jesselinus de Cassanis 18
Joannes Andreae: see Giovanni d'Andrea
Joannes Bernardi 10
John XXII 1, 9, 11, 14, 16, 17, 23, 25, 27, 38; *Execrabilis* 17–18; *Ex debito* 17–18

John XXIII 35
Justinian, *Novellae* 3
Justinian, Code of 3
Lambert de Born, bishop of Strassburg 27
Languedoc 12, 25, 26, 34–36
Leon 19
Lodève 36
Lunt, William 15
Mainz 22
Mallorca 19
Marino del Giudice 27
Marsiglio of Padua, *Defensor pacis* 11–12, 25
Matthew Paris, *Chronica maiora* 15
Mollat, Guillaume 14
Naples, 12, 25
Naples, kingdom 19, 30
Narbonne 26
Navarre 19
Opicino de Canistris 25
Oviedo 23
Pamiers 17
Paris, University of 37
Pedro Gomez Albornoz, cardinal 28
Peñiscola 23
Peytavin de Montesquieu, bishop of Montauban 26
Pierre Desprez, cardinal 29
Pierre Dubois 15
Pierre Dupin, archbishop of Benevento 30
Pierre d'Estaing, cardinal 28
Pierre Gérard, bishop of Le Puy 34, 43
Pierre de Monteruc 11
Pierre de Montrebel, bishop of Lectoure 32
Pietro Boccaplanola, archbishop of Cosenza 12
Pisa, Council of 35, 36
Portugal 19
Ramon Lull 15–16, 18, 35
Raymond de Canilhac, cardinal bishop of Praeneste 22, 40
Rhodes 10
Rodano, Guglielmo, *Tractatus de spoliis ecclesiasticis* 13
Roger d'Armagnac 27
Rome 27
Saint-Palais d'Aussac, François de 14–15
Samaran, Charles 14
Sardinia 19
Schism, Great Western 14, 23, 29, 32, 33
Sicily 19
Spoleto 12
Tarragona 19
Theodosian Code 3
Thomas Aquinas, *Summa theologiae* 13
Thomassin, Louis 14, 32
Toulouse 17, 23
Tréguier 12
Trent, Council of 13
Urban IV 15
Urban V 11, 19, 21, 27, 29, 31, 32
Venice 27
Vienne, Council of 10, 15–16
Viterbo 27
Watt, J. A., 16, 18
Wilhelm Pinchon, provost of Mainz 22, 40
Zaragoza 19

ANNUAL INDEX OF SPOILS CASES

The numbers of the individual cases of spoils are printed here, each above the year in which the case began, so that the index also serves as a bar-graph of the frequency of cases. The high count of cases associated with the plague years of 1361, 1348, and 1375 is especially striking.

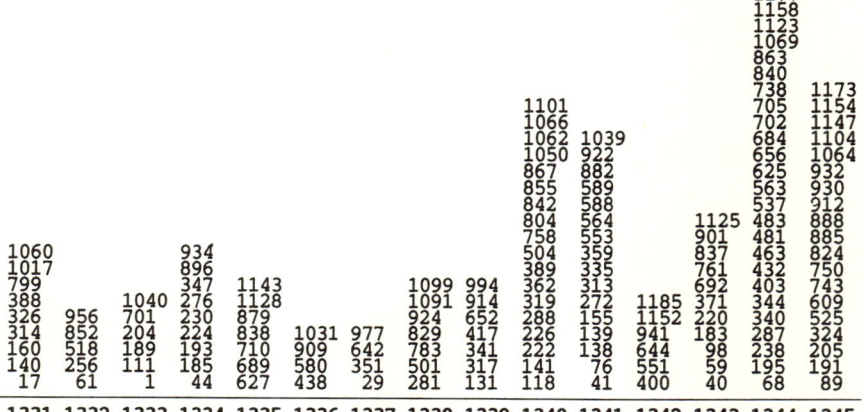

ANNUAL INDEX

1346	1347	1348	1349	1350	1351	1352	1353	1354	1355	1356	1357	1358	1359	1360
		1184												
		1164												
		1159												
		1133												
		1046												
		1036												
		1035												
		992												
		983												
		981												
		961												
		939												
		925												
		923												
		893												
		865												
		858												
		845												
		800												
		790												
		773												
		760												
		757												
		728												
		708												
		700												
		665												
		645												
		636												
		617												
		614												
		586												
		559												
		544												
		528												
		527												
		524												
		519												
		497												
		486												
		479												
		423												
		413												
		410												
		409												
		393										1148		
												1122		
												1109		
												1081		
												1072		
												1052		
	1107	376						1161				1023		1136
	1071	370						1153				1019		1065
	1057	365						1146				950		1048
	1012	364			1138			1095				910		1006
	907	358			1116	1051	1156	965				854		1000
	898	327			1087	927	1149	881				831	1181	957
1189	890	310			1063	905	1037	860				823	1180	943
1182	806	269	1171		1059	895	848	847			1145	776	1134	820
1172	778	253	1103	989	813	821	805	846			1137	767	1084	807
1005	594	250	1008	978	769	731		802		1170	1108	762	1068	784
1002	570	210	962	959	749	647		599		1135	991	698	1032	711
975	560	203	894	878	739	548		540		946	933	615	825	668
942	511	192	763	870	726	535		515		915	834	613	822	654
851	453	172	759	747	719	530		510		866	742	590	818	579
849	447	149	744	709	635	458		367		835	683	541	793	556
796	431	125	741	688	597	450		307		670	641	480	792	523
610	405	123	606	628	549	402		306		624	670	290	732	496
474	390	82	462	600	305	302		304		572	571	223	682	346
443	372	79	449	576	303	117	1020	300		452	561	181	681	429
320	338	60	411	416	296	112	948	249		435	552	144	674	346
309	336	51	332	318	274	101	812	236		428	546	114	607	328
163	275	45	325	311	228	86	516	153		248	456	50	460	257
127	259	39	255	254	218	63	440	113		237	339	48	408	251
77	171	25	148	164	151	38	373	109		167	243	34	386	128
70	161	22	136	126	38	18	284	83		66		27	293	36
46	129	13	55		20	12		74				26	212	23
43	62											158		

ANNUAL INDEX

1361	1362	1363	1364	1365	1366	1367	1368	1369	1370	1371	1372	1373	1374	1375
1186														
1168														
1151														
1139														
1131														
1129														
1114														
1093														
1090														
1080														
1078														
1075														
1026														
1025														
1024														
1022														
1000														
988														
973														
964														
963														
937														
917														
911														
900														
892														
873														
872														
827														
797														
775														
686														
667														
655														
650														
643														
618														
603														
545														
539														
531	1188													1174
521	1126													1144
493	1077													1142
470	1041													1086
468	982													1083
454	921													1061
442	913													1053
437	877													1015
433	862													971
422	815													916
415	814													891
404	788													857
391	781													780
377	768	1105									1178			696
369	764	1044								1179	1155			666
361	720	990								1176	1141			658
316	717	986	1167							1132	1130			648
297	703	945	1166							1106	1082			605
292	699	828	987							996	966			601
289	669	774	985							974	949			582
271	663	770	970							841	875			578
265	639	766	880							833	853			475
235	620	662	871				1092			811	844			424
227	604	565	856				938			753	752			387
219	575	557	801				869	1187	1010	745	723			380
201	574	536	798				817	1175	958	730	704	1191		321
188	532	434	754				690	1169	931	676	687	1100		246
184	484	420	746				659	1162	808	649	664	1096	1165	244
170	467	407	671				623	1160	785	593	633	1045	1117	231
168	418	396	640				490	1120	779	558	630	972	1073	216
162	414	381	637	1157	1140		489	928	678	522	622	786	1067	206
159	397	349	509	997	1119		426	918	547	507	595	740	1013	187
116	385	323	495	861	1085		399	908	529	478	542	721	1004	182
92	379	263	488	836	1056	706	293	876	472	441	498	685	951	178
87	342	258	455	756	787	694	282	864	383	425	421	661	947	174
78	330	252	438	634	748	526	277	819	352	322	315	646	724	152
71	299	247	353	616	520	392	241	810	283	280	202	611	695	132
58	261	233	245	585	355	366	194	772	279	166	121	577	602	120
37	225	229	96	505	345	295	175	751	130	154	104	568	476	73
31	137	106	91	451	286	93	135	718	99	107	84	566	471	56
14	54	35		436	200	49	67	657	94		42	482	179	53
6	95	7	21	4	11	32	47	581	52	64	19	337	169	9
								343	10					

ANNUAL INDEX 259

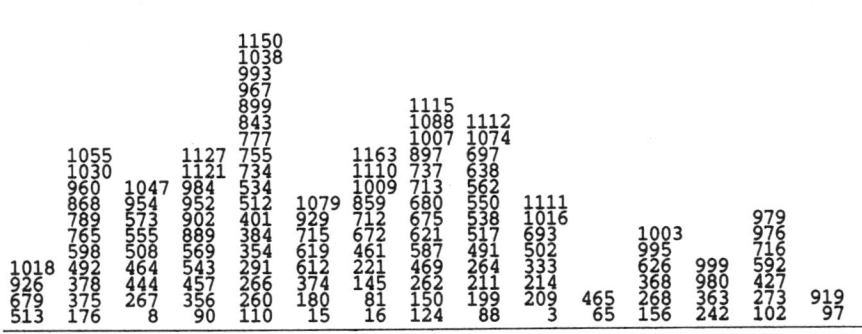

INDEX OF TERRITORIAL INCIDENCE

The cases of spoils are indexed below according to the diocese in which each deceased held his last major benefice. Dioceses are grouped under provinces, either ecclesiastical or civil; and provinces are collected under sovereignties or national regions. Places which changed sovereigns during the period are entered twice, with cross-references. The names of metropolitan sees are italicized.

Following the index, the dioceses are listed in an alphabetical key.

I. Sovereignty of the French Crown
A. Languedoc

(suffragan of *Aix* in Angevin Provence:)
1. Gap 503, 583, 1051 (also VIII.26: Empire to 1349)

(suffragan of *Arles* in Angevin Provence:)
2. S. Paul-Trois-Châteaux 195, 544, 1047
3. *Auch* 24, 62, 64, 75, 460, 984 (also IX.B.1: English France, 1360-1370)
4. S. Bertrand de Comminges 548, 1045, 1113
5. Couserans 72, 134, 232, 885, 941, 1010
6. Lectoure 443, 547, 1033 (also IX.B.6: English France, 1360-1370)
7. Lescar 830
8. Oloron 958

(suffragan of *Bordeaux* in English France:)
9. Agen 26 (also IX.B.9: English France 1360-1369)
10. Angoulême 266 (also IX.B.10: English France 1360-1373)
11. Périgueux 101, 199, 264, 268, 431, 853, 967, 1039
12. Saintes 59, 180, 329, 387, 551, 675, 877, 1017, 1168 (also IX.B.14: English France 1360-1370)
13. Sarlat 94, 196, 501, 542, 882

(suffragan of *Bourges* in Northern France:)
14. Albi 2, 28, 71, 74, 102, 475, 514, 543, 713, 884, 977, 1020
15. Cahors 103, 200, 298, 321, 445, 554, 1071, 1094
16. Castres 29, 242, 262, 700, 880
17. Clermont 382, 448, 508, 679, 1062, 1150
18. Mende 14, 204, 230, 231, 246, 497, 498, 1003
19. Le Puy 144, 221, 363, 641, 648, 667, 916, 920
20. Rodez 100, 194, 214, 364, 533, 896, 944, 1022, 1079
21. S. Flour 95, 562, 947, 1007
22. Tulle 904 (also IX.B.15: English France 1360-1370)
23. Vabres 212, 320, 402, 940, 1057
24. *Embrun* 442, 557, 978 (also VIII.27: Empire until 1349)
25. *Narbonne* 140, 156, 167, 244, 336, 546, 598, 937
26. Agde 65, 341, 881, 1060, 1114
27. Alet 88, 111, 185, 407, 415, 428, 897, 1031, 1043
28. Béziers 39, 198, 277, 462, 586, 618, 858, 995, 1008, 1115, 1175
29. Carcassonne 154, 261, 338, 367, 626, 649, 924, 953, 955, 1044, 1059, 1112
30. Lodève 99, 160, 210, 369, 422, 477, 605, 623, 951, 1025
31. Maguelonne 86, 245, 257, 337, 388, 463, 717, 861, 892, 976, 994, 997, 1000, 1100
32. Nîmes 41, 165, 192, 203, 207, 259, 326, 351, 390, 423, 424, 541, 657, 734, 926, 934, 1026, 1069
33. S. Pons de Thomières 1064
34. Uzés 179, 334, 403, 483, 631
35. *Toulouse* 155, 227, 235, 368, 378, 481, 561, 578, 672, 686, 696, 962, 1018, 1129
36. Lavaur 105, 1024, 1088, 1091
37. Lombez 51, 81, 220, 457, 588, 663, 1090
38. Mirepoix 85, 482, 492, 643, 925, 1027
39. Montauban 213, 452, 889 (also IX.B.16: English France 1360-1370)
40. Pamiers 73, 166, 253, 436, 580, 591, 709, 996, 1002, 1038, 1055
41. Rieux 611, 612, 694, 728, 838
42. S. Papoul 152, 186, 219, 453

INDEX OF TERRITORIAL INCIDENCE 261

43. *Vienne* 862, 928, 1004
44. Grenoble 568, 642
45. Valence-Die 765, 895, 936
46. Viviers 4, 145, 202

B. Northern France

(suffragan of *Bordeaux* in English France:)
1. Maillezais 384, 607, 712
2. Poitiers 209, 290, 425, 512, 669, 697, 927, 1074 (also IX.B.13: English France, 1360-1373)
3. *Bourges* 91, 273, 550, 619, 731, 859, 1092, 1176
4. Limoges 97, 265, 357, 421, 1184
5. *Lyon* 31, 116, 478, 504, 505, 956, 1068
6. Autun 375, 432, 538, 688, 929, 1075
7. Chalon-sur-Saône 344, 502, 539, 628, 718, 727, 888
8. Langres 860, 902, 1144
9. Mâcon 570, 587, 695, 714, 993, 1120
10. *Reims* 124, 646, 685, 739, 1104
11. Arras 177
12. Châlons-sur-Marne 870, 1139
13. Noyon 954
14. Tournai 985
15. *Rouen* 98, 806, 822, 1135
16. Bayeux 863
17. Evreux 150, 701
18. Lisieux 473
19. *Sens* 3, 915, 1076
20. Auxerre 148, 187, 393, 680, 875, 879
21. Chartres 352, 640, 653, 832, 1067
22. Nevers 396, 687
23. Orléans 354
24. Paris 439
25. Troyes 479, 529, 1014
26. *Tours* 15, 63, 340, 451, 491, 556, 910, 945, 986, 1037, 1121, 1128
27. Angers 316, 447, 507, 974
28. Dol 374, 485, 524
29. Le Mans 372, 793, 796
30. Nantes 226, 1085
31. Quimper 12
32. Tréguier 280, 707
33. Vannes 689, 730

II. House of Anjou
A. Provence

1. *Aix* 60, 356, 690, 874, 1056
2. Apt 271, 969, 1034
3. Fréjus 118, 205, 215, 405, 429, 495, 692, 738, 865, 873, 1099, 1102
4. Riez 376, 908
5. Sisteron 343, 1058, 1103
6. *Arles* 193, 208, 217, 330, 335, 446, 603, 636, 766, 1028, 1035, 1131
7. Avignon 5, 890, 1101 (also III.A.1: Papal sovereignty from 9 June 1348)
8. Marseille 1, 22, 506, 627, 632, 656, 1009, 1063, 1084, 1111, 1126, 1127, 1185

9. Toulon 270, 589, 725, 917, 935
(suffragan of *Embrun*:)
10. Digne 272, 499
11. Glandèves 30, 736
12. Grasse 371
13. Sénez 191, 876
14. Vence 314, 493, 1130

B. Kingdom of Naples, "Sicilia citra Farum"
(dioceses grouped by administrative provinces)

Abruzzo:
1. Chieti 450, 574, 575, 710, 909, 1177
2. Marsi 620
3. Penne-Atri 805
4. Valva-Sulmona 312, 747
Terra di Lavoro:
5. Acerra 528, 1072
6. Alife 188, 1154
7. Aversa 56, 500, 856, 883
8. Caiazzo 683
9. Calvi 1123
10. *Capua* 276, 698
11. Caserta 1153
12. Castellamare 788
13. Isernia 982
14. Massalubrense 699, 1125
15. *Naples* 176, 567, 732
16. Nola 760, 804
17. Pozzuoli 840
18. S. Agata dei Goti 837
19. Sarno 723
20. Sessa Aurunca 563
21. Sora 35, 50, 572
22. *Sorrento* 45, 794, 854
23. Teano di Puglia 776, 855, 1189
24. Telese 92, 1147
Molise:
25. Guardialfiera 127
26. Termoli 112, 315
27. Trivento 684, 872
Capitanata:
28. Ascoli Satriano 847
29. Bovino 802
30. *Manfredonia* 300, 775, 791
31. Troia 61, 222, 521
Principato:
32. Amalfi 113, 1171
33. Avellino 983
34. Frigento 750
35. Lacedogna 305, 803
36. Lettere 852
37. Monteverde 757
38. Policastro 297
39. Ravello 1188
40. *Salerno* 129
Terra di Bari:
41. Andria 604
42. *Bari* 1172
43. Bitonto 590

44. Rapolla 143, 610
45. Salpe 324, 613
Terra d'Otranto:
46. Brindisi 189
47. Lecce 540, 1095, 1182
48. Ostuni 299
49. *Otranto* 609
50. *Taranto* 46, 573, 1161
Basilicata:
51. *Conza* 749, 849
52. Gravina 43
53. Muro Lucano 527, 635
Calabria:
54. Bisignano 236, 317, 674
55. Catanzaro 810
56. *Cosenza* 304, 887, 913
57. Cotrone 409
58. Isola Capo Rizzuto 410
59. Mileto 972
60. *Reggio* 987
61. Squillace 743
62. Tropea 1081
63. Umbriatico 414

III. Papal States
A. Comtat-Venaissin

(suffragan of *Arles* in Angevin Provence:)
1. Avignon 234, 350, 401, 433, 434, 487, 509, 559, 650, 681, 864, 923, 1080
   (also II.B.7: Angevin Provence until 1348)
2. Cavaillon 998
3. Orange 347, 706, 922, 1098
4. Vaison 260, 678, 894

B. Patrimonio di S. Pietro in Tuscia

1. *Rome* 175, 426, 1036; Cardinals: Ostia 960 S. Clemente 476 S. Susanna 40
2. Castro 292
3. Civita Castellana 310
4. Narni 93
5. Orvieto 394, 671, 1006, 1036
6. Toscania 47
7. Viterbo 163

C. Campagna e Marittima

1. Anagni 820, 921
2. Tivoli 644
3. Montecassino 48, 406, 1050
4. Aquino 408, 758
5. *Benevento* 68, 238, 342, 416, 417, 418, 474, 617, 799, 844, 857, 943, 1138, 1173, 1174
6. Civitate 784

D. Ducato di Spoleto

1. Assisi 581
2. Città di Castello 950

3. Foligno 386, 576
4. Gubbio 912
5. Perugia 233, 302, 565
6. Spoleto 123, 595, 968
7. Terni 1148

E. Marca di Ancona

1. Ancona 294, 1152
2. Fano 764, 1179
3. Fossombrone 774
4. Recanati-Macerata 819
5. Rimini 130, 355, 383, 566, 808
6. Sinigaglia 1015

F. Emilia e Romagna

1. Bologna 126, 622, 785, 786, 1073
2. *Ravenna* 36, 289

IV. Northern Italy
(grouped by regions)

Piemonte:
1. Acqui 291
2. Albenga 318
3. Asti 82
4. Como 37, 131, 228, 534
5. Luni 323
6. Novara 243
7. Vercelli 761, 773
Liguria and Corsica:
8. Ajaccio 1160
9. *Genoa* 197, 252, 399, 522, 815
10. Mariana 637
Lombardia:
11. Brescia 744
12. Pavia 55, 835
Toscana:
13. Arezzo 32
14. Chiusi 223
15. Fiesole 1143
16. Florence 57, 295, 313, 652, 748, 990, 1105
17. Grosseto 44
18. Lucca 135, 843
19. Massa Marittima 325, 411, 763
20. *Pisa* 110, 250, 705, 720, 842
21. Siena 107, 254, 593
Veneto:
22. *Aquileia* 218, 818
23. Concordia 900
24. *Grado* 38, 289
25. Padua 733, 807, 1186
26. Treviso 771
27. Venice (Castello) 114, 704, 867
28. Verona 790
29. Vicenza 6
Istria:
30. Cittanova d'Istria 682
31. Pola 128

Emilia and Romagna:
  32. Faenza 1178
  33. Forli' 121, 1141

V. Portugal

(suffragan of *Compostela* in Castile:)
1. Lisbon 8, 489, 754, 1145, 1158
2. Evora 18, 348, 624, 659, 778
3. Idanha 7, 782, 1134
4. Lamego 258, 1089
5. Silves 17, 1157
6. *Braga* 519, 677, 886, 1155, 1159
7. Coimbra 237, 311, 339, 640, 1021, 1040
8. Porto 19, 866
9. Viseu 616, 741

VI. Castile and Leon

(suffragan of *Braga* in Portugal:)
1. Astorga 283
2. Orense 20, 518, 777
3. Tuy 638, 651, 1118
4. *Seville* 284, 827, 919
5. Cadiz 517
6. Cartagena 469, 810
7. Córdoba 42
8. *Toledo* 225, 281, 380, 494, 516
9. Burgos 285, 286, 769
10. Cuenca 829, 839, 1124
11. Osma 515
12. Palencia 16
13. Segovia 279, 724, 779, 905, 1156
14. Sigüenza 666, 722
15. *Compostela* 1140
16. Badajoz 1142
17. Leon 249, 971
18. Lugo 606
19. Mondoñedo 608
20. Oviedo 466, 1106

VII. Crown of Aragon
A. Aragon

(suffragan of *Narbonne* in French Languedoc:)
1. Elne 21, 27, 90, 96, 119, 146, 153, 161, 239, 301, 306, 400, 582, 596, 691, 735, 851, 906, 1011, 1023
2. *Tarragona* 70, 174, 899, 1109
3. Barcelona 178, 287, 601, 797
4. Gerona 79, 137, 278, 602, 1167, 1180
5. Lerida 288, 629, 966, 1136, 1183
6. Mallorca 54, 136, 510
7. Tortosa 77, 141, 147, 172, 309, 597, 901, 942, 970, 1137
8. Urgel 76, 488, 545, 931, 939
9. Valencia 133, 552, 1046, 1162
10. Vich 787, 1030
11. *Zaragoza* 599, 716, 932
12. Calahorra 1082

13. Huesca 282, 676, 1181
14. Pamplona 66, 80, 157, 621, 798
15. Segorbe 1108
16. Tarazona 373

B. Sicily "ultra Farum" or Trinacria

1. *Messina* 577, 946, 1096
2. Patti-Lipari 661, 965
(suffragan of *Monreale*:)
3. Catania 670
4. *Palermo* 53, 789, 795, 828
5. Girgenti 989
6. Malta 52, 571
7. Mazzara del Vallo 381

C. Sardinia

1. *Cagliari* 142, 848
2. Suelli 584
3. Sulcis 1049
4. *Oristano* 389
5. Terralba 455
6. *Torres* 117, 248
7. Sorra 625

VIII. Empire

1. *Bremen* 660
2. Schwerin 34
3. Kammin 159
4. Cambrai 170, 869
5. *Cologne* 467
6. Liège 437, 592
7. Münster 767
8. *Trier* 109
9. Metz 846, 1119
10. Toul 664
11. Verdun 633
12. *Mainz* 490
13. Augsburg 721
14. Constance 721
15. Speyer 349, 745
16. Worms 824
17. *Salzburg* 836
18. Passau 379
19. *Besançon* 10, 532, 768
20. Basel 360
21. Belley 484
22. Lausanne 9, 307, 395, 980
23. *Tarentaise* 171, 569, 1016
24. Aosta 104
25. Geneva 11, 464, 816
26. Gap 182, 255 (also I.A.1: French Languedoc after 1349)
27. *Embrun* 89, 256, 1005 (also I.A.24: French Languedoc after 1349)
28. Nice 412, 413, 729, 752, 753, 952, 957, 1097
29. *Turin* 770, 1190, 1191
30. Trento 530

IX. English Sovereignty
A. England

1. *Canterbury* 183
2. Coventry-Lichfield 555
3. Ely 1151
4. Lincoln 535, 711
5. Norwich 435
6. Salisbury 511

B. English Territories in France

1. *Auch* 251 (also I.A.3: French Languedoc before 1360 and after 1370)
2. Aire 240, 332
3. Bayonne 441
4. Bazas 327, 1032
5. Dax 164, 190, 331, 850
6. Lectoure 871, 938 (also I.A.6: French Languedoc before 1360 and after 1370)
7. Tarbes 169, 496, 948
8. *Bordeaux* 23, 25, 151, 206, 263, 267, 385, 419, 420, 430, 558, 891, 930, 988, 1042
9. Agen 247, 1065 (also I.A.9: French Languedoc before 1360 and after 1369)
10. Angoulême 84, 106 (also I.A.10: French Languedoc before 1360 and after 1373)
11. Condom 918, 1165
12. Luçon 345, 634
13. Poitiers 1187 (also I.B.2: French before 1360 and after 1373)
14. Saintes 826 (also I.A.12: French Languedoc before 1360 and after 1370)
15. Tulle 58, 751 (also I.A.22: French Languedoc before 1360 and after 1370)
16. Montauban 67, 201 (also I.A.39: French Languedoc before 1360 and after 1370)

X. Other Sovereignties in Europe

Norway:
 1. Trondheim 833
Denmark:
 2. Ribe 772
Sweden:
 3. Uppsala 274
 4. Åbo 526
 5. Skara 1116
Teutonic Order:
 6. *Riga* 275, 319, 1117
 7. Dorpat 662, 740
 8. Ösell 536
Poland:
 9. Kraków 961
 10. Płock 817
Hungary:
 11. Beograd 33
 12. Vesprém 615
 13. *Split* 614
 14. Knin 241
 15. Sebenico 1013
 16. Skoplje 726

XI. Orient

Venetian:
 1. Kisamos (Crete) 458
 2. Ario (Crete) 814
 3. Korone (Achaia) 293
Armenia:
 4. Tarsus 537
Lusignan:
 5. *Nicosia* 801, 1061
 6. Famagusta 108, 756
 7. Limassol 296, 392
 8. Paphos 831
Nicaea:
 9. *Constantinople* 566, 841
 10. Patrai 49, 229, 813, 841, 903
 11. Thebes 1122
Tituli in partibus Turcorum:
 12. *Alexandria* 67
 13. *Antioch* 899, 1065
 14. Bethlehem 975
 15. *Jerusalem* 122, 301, 429, 894, 941, 984
 16. Jubail (Byblos) 224
 17. *Nazareth* 715

Not indexed by diocese

Died in Curia; no benefice specified: 13, 78, 83, 87, 115, 125, 132, 138, 139, 149, 158, 162, 168, 181, 184, 216, 269, 303, 308, 328, 333, 353, 358, 361, 362, 365, 366, 370, 377, 391, 397, 404, 427, 438, 449, 454, 456, 459, 470, 480, 486, 523, 525, 531, 553, 560, 579, 594, 600, 630, 645, 647, 654, 658, 673, 693, 702, 708, 719, 737, 759, 762, 780, 783, 812, 821, 823, 834, 845, 878, 893, 898, 907, 949, 959, 963, 964, 973, 991, 992, 999, 1001, 1012, 1019, 1029, 1041, 1048, 1052, 1053, 1066, 1070, 1077, 1078, 1083, 1086, 1087, 1093, 1107, 1133, 1146, 1149, 1164, 1170

Regional nuncios and collectors, rectors and treasurers: 21, 29, 65, 69, 89, 91, 102, 142, 150, 163, 187, 211, 244, 252, 263, 322, 346, 352, 359, 394, 406, 416, 433, 444, 461, 465, 468, 471, 472, 477, 489, 496, 497, 513, 520, 585, 639, 640, 648, 653, 655, 668, 688, 703, 705, 709, 745, 746, 755, 781, 800, 809, 826, 868, 914, 916, 922, 923, 933, 981, 1037, 1045, 1049, 1054, 1056, 1110, 1132, 1163, 1166

Others: 120, 423, 440, 549, 564, 665, 825, 911, 1169

Key: Dioceses in the Index of Territorial Incidence

Åbo: X.4.
Acerra: II.B.5.
Acqui: IV.1.
Agde: I.A.26.
Agen: IX.B.9.; I.A.9.
Aire: IX.B.2.
Aix: II.A.1.
Ajaccio: IV.8.
Albenga: IV.2.
Albi: I.A.14.
Alet: I.A.27.
Alexandria: XI.12.
Alife: II.B.6.
Amalfi: II.B.32.
Anagni: III.C.1.
Ancona: III.E.1.
Andria: II.B.41.
Angers: I.B.27.
Angoulême: IX.B.10.; I.A.10.
Antioch: XI.13.
Aosta: VIII.24.
Apt: II.A.2.
Aquileia: IV.22.
Aquino: III.C.4.
Arezzo: IV.13.
Ario: XI.2.
Arles: II.A.6.
Arras: I.B.11.
Ascoli Satriano: II.B.28.
Assisi: III.D.1.
Asti: IV.3.
Astorga: VI.1.
Auch: I.A.3.; IX.B.1.
Augsburg: VIII.13.
Autun: I.B.6.
Auxerre: I.B.20.
Avellino: II.B.33.
Aversa: II.B.7.
Avignon: II.A.7.; III.A.1.
Badajoz: VI.16.
Barcelona: VII.A.3.
Bari: II.B.42.
Basel: VIII.20.
Bayeux: I.B.16.
Bayonne: IX.B.3.
Bazas: IX.B.4.
Belley: VIII.21.
Benevento: III.C.5.
Beograd: X.11.
Besançon: VIII.19.
Bethlehem: XI.14.
Béziers: I.A.28.
Bisignano: II.B.54.
Bitonto: II.B.43.
Bologna: III.F.1.
Bordeaux: IX.B.8.

Bourges: I.B.3.
Bovino: II.B.29.
Braga: V.6.
Bremen: VIII.1.
Brescia: IV.11.
Brindisi: II.B.46.
Burgos: VI.9.
Cadiz: VI.5.
Cagliari: VII.C.1.
Cahors: I.A.15.
Caiazzo: II.B.8.
Calahorra: VII.A.12.
Calvi: II.B.9.
Cambrai: VIII.4.
Canterbury: IX.A.1.
Capua: II.B.10.
Carcassonne: I.A.29.
Cartagena: VI.6.
Caserta: II.B.11.
Castellamare: II.B.12.
Castres: I.A.16.
Castro: III.B.2.
Catania: VII.B.3.
Catanzaro: II.B.55.
Cavaillon: III.A.2.
Chalon-sur-Saône: I.B.7.
Châlons-sur-Marne: I.B.12.
Chartres: I.B.21.
Chieti: II.B.1.
Chiusi: IV.14.
Città di Castello: III.D.2.
Cittanova d'Istria: IV.30.
Civita Castellana: III.B.3.
Civitate: III.C.6.
Clermont: I.A.17.
Coimbra: V.7.
Cologne: VIII.5.
Como: IV.4.
Compostela: VI.15.
Concordia: IV.23.
Condom: IX.B.11.
Constance: VIII.14.
Constantinople: XI.9.
Conza: II.B.51.
Córdoba: VI.7.
Cosenza: II.B.56.
Cotrone: II.B.57.
Couserans: I.A.5.
Coventry-Lichfield: IX.A.2.
Cuenca: VI.10.
Dax: IX.B.5.
Digne: II.A.10.
Dol: I.B.28.
Dorpat: X.7.
Elne: VII.A.1.
Ely: IX.A.3.
Embrun: I.A.24.; VIII.27.
Evora: V.2.
Evreux: I.B.17.
Faenza: IV.32.
Famagusta: XI.6.
Fano: III.E.2.

Fiesole: IV.15.
Florence: IV.16.
Foligno: III.D.3.
Forlì: IV.33.
Fossombrone: III.E.3.
Fréjus: II.A.3.
Frigento: II.B.34.
Gap: I.A.1; VIII.26.
Geneva: VIII.25.
Genoa: IV.9.
Gerona: VII.A.4.
Girgenti: VII.B.5.
Glandèves: II.A.11.
Grado: IV.24.
Grasse: II.A.12.
Gravina: II.B.52.
Grenoble: I.A.44.
Grosseto: IV.17.
Guardialfiera: II.B.25.
Gubbio: III.D.4.
Huesca: VII.A.13.
Idanha: V.3.
Isernia: II.B.13.
Isola Capo Rizzuto: II.B.58.
Jerusalem: XI.15.
Jubail: XI.16.
Kammin: VIII.3.
Kisamos: XI.1.
Knin: X.14.
Korone: XI.3.
Kraków: X.9.
Lacedogna: II.B.35.
Lamego: V.4.
Langres: I.B.8.
Lausanne: VIII.22.
Lavaur: I.A.36.
Lecce: II.B.47.
Lectoure: I.A.6.; IX.B.6.
Leon: VI.17.
Lerida: VII.A.5.
Lescar: I.A.7.
Lettere: II.B.36.
Liège: VIII.6.
Limassol: XI.7.
Limoges: I.B.4.
Lincoln: IX.A.4.
Lisbon: V.1.
Lisieux: I.B.18.
Lodève: I.A.30.
Lombez: I.A.37.
Lucca: IV.18.
Luçon: IX.B.12.
Lugo: VI.18.
Luni: IV.5.
Lyon: I.B.5.
Mâcon: I.B.9.
Maguelonne: I.A.31.
Maillezais: I.B.1.
Mainz: VIII.12.
Mallorca: VII.A.6.
Malta: VII.B.6.
Manfredonia: II.B.30.

Le Mans: I.B.29.
Mariana: IV.10.
Marseille: II.A.8.
Marsi: II.B.2.
Massa Maritima: IV.19.
Massalubrense: II.B.14.
Mazzara del Vallo: VII.B.7.
Mende: I.A.18.
Messina: VII.B.1.
Metz: VIII.9.
Mileto: II.B.59.
Mirepoix: I.A.38.
Mondoñedo: VI.19.
Montauban: I.A.39.; IX.B.16.
Montecassino: III.C.3.
Monteverde: II.B.37.
Münster: VIII.7.
Muro Lucano: II.B.53.
Nantes: I.B.30.
Naples: II.B.15.
Narbonne: I.A.25.
Narni: III.B.4.
Nazareth: XI.17.
Nevers: I.B.22.
Nice: VIII.28.
Nicosia: XI.5.
Nîmes: I.A.32.
Nola: II.B.16.
Norwich: IX.A.5.
Novara: IV.6.
Noyon: I.B.13.
Ösell: X.8.
Oloron: I.A.8.
Orange: III.A.3.
Orense: VI.2.
Oristano: VII.C.4.
Orléans: I.B.23.
Orvieto: III.B.5.
Osma: VI.11.
Ostuni: II.B.48.
Otranto: II.B.49.
Oviedo: VI.20.
Padua: IV.25.
Palencia: VI.12.
Palermo: VII.B.4.
Pamiers: I.A.40.
Pamplona: VII.A.14.
Paphos: XI.8.
Paris: I.B.24.
Passau: VIII.18.
Patrai: XI.10.
Patti-Lipari: VII.B.2.
Pavia: IV.12.
Penne-Atri: II.B.3.
Périgueux: I.A.11.
Perugia: III.D.5.
Pisa: IV.20.
Płock: X.10.
Poitiers: I.B.2.; IX.B.13.
Pola: IV.31.
Policastro: II.B.38.
Porto: V.8.

INDEX OF TERRITORIAL INCIDENCE

Pozzuoli: II.B.17.
Le Puy: I.A.19.
Quimper: I.B.31.
Rapolla: II.B.44.
Ravello: II.B.39.
Ravenna: III.F.2.
Recanati-Macerata: III.E.4.
Reggio: II.B.60.
Reims: I.B.10.
Ribe: X.2.
Rieux: I.A.41.
Riez: II.A.4.
Riga: X.6.
Rimini: III.E.5.
Rodez: I.A.20.
Rome: III.B.1.
Rouen: I.B.15.
S. Bertrand de Comminges: I.A.4.
S. Flour: I.A.21.
S. Papoul: I.A.42.
S. Paul-Trois-Châteaux: I.A.2.
S. Pons de Thomières: I.A.33.
Saintes: I.A.12.; IX.B.14.
Salerno: II.B.40.
Salisbury: IX.A.6.
Salpe: II.B.45.
Salzburg: VIII.17.
S. Agata dei Goti: II.B.18.
Sarlat: I.A.13.
Sarno: II.B.19.
Schwerin: VIII.2.
Sebenico: X.15.
Segorbe: VII.A.15.
Segovia: VI.13.
Sénez: II.A.13.
Sens: I.B.19.
Sessa Aurunca: II.B.20.
Seville: VI.4.
Siena: IV.21.
Sigüenza: VI.14.
Silves: V.5.
Sinigaglia: III.E.6.
Sisteron: II.A.5.
Skara: X.5.
Skoplje: X.16.
Sora: II.B.21.
Sorra: VII.C.7.
Sorrento: II.B.22.
Speyer: VIII.15.
Split: X.13.
Spoleto: III.D.6.
Squillace: II.B.61.
Suelli: VII.C.2.
Sulcis: VII.C.3.
Taranto: II.B.50.
Tarazona: VII.A.16.

Tarbes: IX.B.7.
Tarentaise: VIII.23.
Tarragona: VII.A.2.
Tarsus: XI.4.
Teano di Puglia: II.B.23.
Telese: II.B.24.
Termoli: II.B.26.
Terni: III.D.7.
Terralba: VII.C.5.
Thebes: XI.11.
Tivoli: III.C.2.
Toledo: VI.8.
Torres: VII.C.6.
Tortosa: VII.A.7.
Toscania: III.B.6.
Toul: VIII.10.
Toulon: II.A.9.
Toulouse: I.A.35.
Tournai: I.B.14.
Tours: I.B.26.
Tréguier: I.B.32.
Trento: VIII.30.
Treviso: IV.26.
Trier: VIII.8.
Trivento: II.B.27.
Troia: II.B.31.
Trondheim: X.1.
Tropea: II.B.62.
Troyes: I.B.25.
Tulle: I.A.22.; IX.B.15.
Turin: VIII.29.
Tuy: VI.3.
Umbriatico: II.B.63.
Uppsala: X.3.
Urgel: VII.A.8.
Uzés: I.A.34.
Vabres: I.A.23.
Vaison: III.A.4.
Valence-Die: I.A.45.
Valencia: VII.A.9.
Valva-Sulmona: II.B.4.
Vannes: I.B.33.
Vence: II.A.14.
Venice: IV.27.
Vercelli: IV.7.
Verdun: VIII.11.
Verona: IV.28.
Vesprém: X.12.
Vicenza: IV.29.
Vich: VII.A.10.
Vienne: I.A.43.
Viseu: V.9.
Viterbo: III.B.7.
Viviers: I.A.46.
Worms: VIII.16.
Zaragoza: VII.A.11.

INDICES BY GROUPS

Professional Qualifications

Legum Doctor (LL.D.) 3, 25, 163, 231, 329, 406, 429, 432, 435, 469, 495, 506, 511, 595, 667, 734, 831, 871, 875, 880, 899, 919, 931, 938, 948, 979, 1067, 1068.
Legum Professor (LL.Prof.) 507, 988.
Licentiatus in Legibus (LL.Lic.) 15, 64, 176, 378, 457, 477, 547, 611, 633, 653, 671, 881.
Legum Baccalarius (LL.B.) 151, 583, 713.
Doctor Decretorum (D.Decr.) 85, 100, 116, 161, 228, 250, 298, 343, 364, 496, 590, 593, 663, 676, 687, 724, 810, 812, 843, 884, 960, 1065, 1084.
Licentiatus in Decretis (Lic.Decr.) 8, 171, 214, 242, 282, 339, 375, 508, 569, 811, 974, 1036, 1054.
Baccalarius in Decretis (B.Decr.) 145, 602.
Juris Utriusque Doctor (J.U.D.) 218, 534, 629, 641, 736, 947.
Juris Utriusque Professor (J.U.Prof.) 5, 67, 99, 395, 431.
Notarius apostolicus 179, 254, 262, 330, 341, 406, 442, 450, 543, 725, 838, 865, 938, 947, 991, 1003, 1067, 1071.
Magister Theologiae (M. Theol.) 18, 43, 94, 119, 131, 169, 172, 298, 301, 516, 566, 701, 789, 796, 874, 925, 941, 971, 1015, 1038.
Professor Theologiae (Prof.Theol.) 894.
Magister Medicinae (M.Med.) 654.

Religious Orders

Benedictine (OSB) 22, 27, 39, 59, 63, 68, 71, 90, 95, 105, 114, 116, 152, 154, 167, 186, 192, 196, 208, 213, 219, 227, 243, 245, 261, 273, 294, 320, 321, 326, 344, 345, 354, 364, 371, 374, 381, 382, 383, 385, 388, 390, 401, 407, 415, 417, 421, 422, 423, 424, 425, 428, 446, 452, 453, 462, 473, 478, 491, 496, 499, 501, 502, 508, 514, 541, 542, 545, 550, 576, 603, 605, 618, 619, 621, 634, 641, 649, 691, 697, 730, 735, 752, 766, 806, 822, 833, 842, 856, 860, 861, 862, 864, 892, 897, 902, 906, 918, 926, 929, 940, 945, 951, 960, 974, 976, 983, 1000, 1017, 1025, 1030, 1035, 1043, 1044, 1051, 1057, 1064, 1069, 1101, 1112, 1121, 1126, 1127, 1129, 1137, 1168, 1179, 1185, 1187, 1190, 1191.
Cistercian (OCist) 51, 62, 139, 169, 223, 366, 387, 591, 620, 741, 791, 805, 807, 848, 946, 1048, 1079.
Cluniac (OClun) 31, 145, 212, 242, 334, 347, 393, 448, 475, 533, 704, 877, 879, 980, 1010, 1014, 1050.
Basilian (OSBasil) 47, 1095, 1096, 1169.
Augustinian Canons (OCSA) 2, 21, 29, 30, 66, 73, 74, 80, 85, 161, 166, 198, 203, 205, 215, 278, 311, 384, 405, 419, 561, 562, 599, 636, 665, 676, 686, 870, 884, 927, 932, 937, 996, 1002, 1003, 1027, 1074, 1099, 1102, 1103, 1176, 1184.
Grandmont (OGrand) 343, 675.
Hospital of S. John of Jerusalem 28, 771.
Premonstratensian (OPraem) 251.
Antonian (OSAnt) 727, 928, 1004.
Dominican (OP) 33, 44, 48, 72, 128, 131, 160, 189, 253, 280, 287, 296, 325, 389, 392, 445, 455, 525, 528, 564, 584, 589, 609, 627, 644, 701, 706, 712, 715, 721, 726, 764, 819, 873, 876, 885, 900, 907, 921, 925, 935, 941, 952, 975, 989, 1029, 1097.
Franciscan (OFM) 43, 52, 94, 121, 122, 271, 289, 298, 301, 305, 312, 319, 412, 458, 474, 500, 517, 563, 784, 789, 799, 840, 872, 874, 887, 903, 944, 965, 971, 1109, 1118, 1124, 1160.
Augustinian Hermits (OESA) 6, 93, 96, 123, 172, 300, 310, 566, 614, 682, 684, 699, 917, 1015, 1038.
Carmelite (OCarm) 119, 248, 400, 493, 845, 894, 1123.

Curial Offices
(including offices formerly held by despoiled persons)

Chapel

magister Capellae 878
subdeacons 231, 734, 1152
pope's confessors 72, 525, 845, 907, 959
chaplains (not counting auditors of the Rota) 8, 14, 25, 67, 86, 164, 209, 214,

INDICES BY GROUPS

218, 250, 260, 328, 330, 340, 359, 406, 429, 431, 435, 493, 507, 510, 511, 554, 669, 673, 679, 685, 690, 705, 710, 718, 720, 732, 744, 760, 761, 773, 818, 842, 843, 882, 948, 949, 977, 990, 1029, 1065, 1131
chaplains of honor 133, 146, 387, 487, 596, 825, 906, 1105

Audientia causarum sacri palatii (Rota)

auditors 13, 60, 99, 115, 140, 153, 157, 171, 365, 449, 457, 469, 593, 595, 708, 759, 834, 979, 1107
auditors of contradicted letters 5, 177, 667
notaries 162, 179
advocates and proctors 303, 377, 523, 594, 600, 762, 792, 823, 1078, 1086, 1087

Chancery

papal secretaries and notaries 78, 124, 184, 308, 397, 404, 838, 1071
scribes and grossators 55, 87, 124, 149, 216, 361, 396, 438, 630, 719, 780, 820, 821, 1001, 1036, 1052, 1053, 1130, 1149, 1164
corrector 999
abbreviators 124, 438, 898, 1070
bullators 139, 366, 1048
registrars 181, 511, 737, 915

Camera Apostolica

camerarii 64, 335, 336, 1129

treasurers 1, 337, 353, 586, 976, 1042, 1075
auditors 176, 1138
advocate 812
clerks of the Camera 170, 214, 260, 333, 437, 454, 492, 797
servant 693
emptor coquinae 158
paneterius 551
administrator operum 1008
rectors of provinces 29, 89, 163, 394, 406, 496, 709, 914, 922
treasurers of provinces 89, 220
nuntii and collectors 21, 65, 69, 91, 102, 183, 211, 218, 252, 263, 322, 346, 352, 359, 416, 433, 444, 468, 471, 472, 477, 489, 496, 497, 520, 585, 625, 639, 640, 653, 655, 671, 688, 692, 703, 745, 746, 781, 800, 809, 867, 886, 916, 923, 933, 981, 1037, 1049, 1056, 1110, 1163, 1166
subcollectors 187, 244, 461, 465, 513, 648, 668, 705, 755, 826, 868, 1045, 1054, 1132

Poenitentiaria

poenitentiarii 280, 319, 325, 412, 581, 707, 840
clerks and scribes 83, 132, 456, 459, 835, 992

Pinhota (almonry)

provisors and administrators 358, 645, 893, 911
almoners 138, 553
servants 702, 1133

BX 1490 .W54 1988
Williman, Daniel.
The right of spoil of the popes of Avignon, 1316-1415

GENERAL THEOLOGICAL SEMINARY
NEW YORK

DATE